Developing Variations

Developing Variations

Style and Ideology in Western Music

Rose Rosengard Subotnik

University of Minnesota Press
Minneapolis • Oxford

"The Role of Ideology in the Study of Western Music," *Journal of Musicology*, 2, no. 1 (Winter 1983), by permission of *Journal of Musicology*; "Adorno's Diagnosis of Beethoven's Late Style: Early Symptom of a Fatal Condition," *Journal of the American Musicological Society*, 29 (1976), by permission of the American Musicological Society; "Why Is Adorno's Music Criticism the Way It Is? Some Reflections on Twentieth-Century Criticism of Nineteenth-Century Music," *Musical Newsletter*, 7, no. 4 (Fall 1977), by permission of Musical Newsletter, Inc.; "Kant, Adorno, and the Self-Critique of Reason: Toward a Model for Music Criticism," *Humanities in Society*, 2 (Fall 1979), by permission of the University of Southern California; "Musicology and Criticism," from *Musicology in the 1980s*, edited by D. Kern Holoman and Claude V. Palisca (New York: Da Capo, 1982), by permission; "Evidence of a Critical Worldview in Mozart's Last Three Symphonies," from *Music and Civilization: Essays in Honor of Paul Henry Lang*, edited by Edmond Strainchamps and Maria Rika Maniates (New York: Norton, 1984), reprinted by permission of W.W. Norton & Company, Inc.; "Romantic Music as Post-Kantian Critique: Classicism, Romanticism, and the Concept of the Semiotic Universe," from *On Criticizing Music: Five Philosophical Perspectives*, edited by Kingsley Price (Baltimore and London: Johns Hopkins University Press, 1981), by permission; "On Grounding Chopin," from *Music and Society*, edited by Richard Leppert and Susan McClary (Cambridge: Cambridge University Press, 1987), by permission; "The Cultural Message of Musical Semiology: Some Thoughts on Music, Language, and Criticism since the Enlightenment," *Critical Inquiry*, 4 (Summer 1978), © 1977, 1978 by the University of Chicago, by permission; "Critical Response: Tonality, Autonomy, and Competence in Post-Classical Music," *Critical Inquiry*, 6 (Autumn 1979), © 1979 the University of Chicago, by permission; "The Historical Structure: Adorno's 'French' Model for the Criticism of Nineteenth-Century Music," *19th-Century Music*, 2, no. 1 (July 1978), 1978 the Regents of the University of California, by permission; "The Challenge of Contemporary Music," from *What Is Music? An Introduction to the Philosophy of Music*, edited by Philip Alperson (New York: Haven, 1987), © Haven Publications, by permission.

Published by the University of Minnesota Press
2037 University Avenue Southeast, Minneapolis, MN 55414.
Printed in the United States of America on acid-free paper.

Library of Congress Cataloging-in-Publication Data

Subotnik, Rose Rosengard.
  Developing variations : style and ideology in Western music / Rose Rosengard Subotnik.
      p.   cm.
  Includes bibliographical references and index.
  ISBN 0-8166-1873-9. — ISBN 0-8166-1874-7 (pbk.)
  1. Music—Philosophy and aesthetics.   2. Style, Musical.
3. Musical criticism.   4. Musicology.   I. Title.
ML3800.S9   1990   90-42317
780'.1—dc20   CIP

A CIP catalog record for this book is available from the British Library

The University of Minnesota is an equal-opportunity educator and employer.

Contents

This book is dedicated to my extraordinary mother
Bruna Hazan Rosengard

and to the memory of my beloved father
David Eli Rosengard
(1910–1988)

They were always there,
and they never stopped giving or believing.

"Character isn't taught, it's caught."
—Nathan Krinsky (1899–1984)

Preface

To help the reader make use of this book, I provide here a couple of guidelines. First, those who wish to follow my ideas in the order of their development can consult the following chronology. I have indicated the year in which each chapter was initially written: chapter 2, 1976; chapter 9, 1977; chapter 11, 1978; chapter 3, 1978; chapter 7, 1979; chapter 4, 1979; chapter 10, 1979; chapter 12, 1980; chapter 1, 1980; chapter 5, 1981; chapter 6, 1982; chapter 8, 1985; chapter 13, 1986–87. (The year given for chapter 3, 1978, is not a mistake; because of delays in a publishing schedule, the essay originally appeared in an issue of a journal dated a year earlier.)

For those interested in locating the heart of various bodies of study, my basic position on Adorno is presented in chapter 2; on Lévi-Strauss, in chapter 9; on Kant, in chapter 7. It should be stressed that although all of this work is based on a careful study of works by these men, the readings presented here are my own, and do not necessarily match those that might have been intended, hoped for, or anticipated by the author in question. Though I do not regard an author's preferred reading as either an uninteresting or an insignificant matter—on the contrary, the ideal of such a reading defines a crucial pole of tension in the ongoing processes of interpretation—I do recognize historical limits on the jurisdiction of such a reading as well as epistemological limits on its actual accessibility. However much a figure such as Kant might have wanted to control the terms on which he was understood or to guarantee acceptance of a certain philosophical position through his writings, I have understood my own primary obligation to be the interpretation of such writings from the perspective of a reader (it is hoped an honest and reflective one) in my own time and culture.

In saying this I touch on a principal theme of this volume. Readers who disagree with my position here will undoubtedly find many further occasions in the pages that follow to disagree with me. For some of these, at least, I hope the prospect of a hearty argument is an incentive to read on; they might find (as I myself did, for instance, when reading Allan Bloom's *The Closing of the American Mind*) that a reader may disagree vehemently with an author about an astonishing number of particulars and still share many of that author's deepest concerns.

Though all but one of these essays (chapter 12) has previously been published in some form, each has been revised for the present volume, in part to reflect my own accumulating insights and present perspective, in part to strengthen various connections among the essays and thereby clarify their cohesiveness as an enterprise. Though many new sources have been cited, no systematic effort has been made to update bibliographic information. I have attempted to update as much as possible biographical information about former students and colleagues who are mentioned in notes. I have also tried to eliminate exclusively masculine terminology (he, man, etc.), the use of which I no longer find acceptable. This revision has been both difficult and instructive (nowhere more so in either respect than in chapter 3, where I had to alter an entire paragraph based on the image "God himself"), and I regret any oversights that may be found. Finally, concise information about the forthcoming companion volume to the present one can be found in the Introduction, note 24.

R. R. S.

Acknowledgments

This book owes its existence to Susan McClary, of the University of Minnesota, who proposed it to the University of Minnesota Press, and to David Josephson, of Brown University, who championed it at every stage. To these two *Menschen*, whose intellectual influence on me has been immeasurable and who have backed up their intellectual and moral support with concrete job offers, I owe exceptional thanks. Happily, as this book goes to press, I have become an associate professor of music at Brown University (yes, Virginia, with tenure), thanks to a renewed initiative by the Brown Music Department, above all by its nonpareil chairman, Gerald Shapiro.

Because I wrote half of this book without any institutional affiliation, I have had reason to be especially grateful to a number of scholars who have gone out of their way to support me over the years. In taking this opportunity to express my thanks, I do not mean to imply that anyone listed here necessarily agrees either with all of my views or with any specific view. Among musicologists, I owe a particular debt to Leonard Meyer and Joseph Kerman, each of whom taught me more outside the classroom than most students ever get a chance to learn, and each of whom could fill a book with the letters of recommendation he has written for me. I shall always remember with gratitude the way the late Carl Dahlhaus, whom I met only once, took time out of his prolific schedule to volunteer his support. I also appreciate the support I received at various times from Kurt von Fischer and Edward Cone. Others who have helped or encouraged me in unforgettable ways are Richard Taruskin, Rufus Hallmark, Shulamit Ran, Neal Zaslaw, Ralph Shapey, Murray Lefkowitz, Joel Sheveloff, John Deathridge, Greg Sandow, Marian Green, Ruth Solie, Henry Kingsbury, David B. Greene, Carolyn Abbate, William De Fotis, Jurgen Thym, and Lance Brunner. All of us who studied with Paul Henry Lang owe him thanks for encouraging us to question authority. To Edward Lippman I owe special thanks, for his inspiration as a teacher and intellectual model and for his energetic efforts on my behalf. And to the late Mollie Ehrlich of Boston, an extraordinary pianist, musician, and teacher, I owe a lifelong debt for the selfless dedication she poured into my musical development, from the time that I was four until her death in 1961.

I also want to express my gratitude to various scholars outside of music, some of whom I have never met. I am grateful to the historian Martin Jay, both for his invaluable observations as a reader of this volume, and for his support more generally; and to the sociologist Stanley Aronowitz, whose informed recommendation helped greatly in publishing this book. At the time I was leaving the University of Chicago, the historian Karl Weintraub, then the Dean of the Division of the Humanities, took pains to let me know his high regard for my work. At a later moment, when I felt my world collapsing for a second time, a number of scholars in comparative literature, notably Fredric Jameson, Edward Said, Burton Pike, Fred Nichols, and Gayle Henrotte, went out of their way to register their support for my work, as did Michael Brown, of sociology, and Mary Wiseman, of philosophy. Richard Leppert, an interdisciplinary humanist, worked as hard as Susan McClary to secure me a position at Minnesota. During the earlier part of my career, several philosophers encouraged my work: the late Monroe Beardsley, Ted Cohen, and especially Kingsley Price, who gave me the rare opportunity of delivering one of the Thalheimer lectures at Johns Hopkins University (a lecture that appears, in revised form, as chapter 7 in this book). At a later stage, another philosopher, Philip Alperson, gave me a forum in which to publish (chapter 13 in this book) and, at a critical juncture, some much-appreciated practical help. The extraordinarily articulate support I have received from Katherine Reeve, whom I met only once, when she was a postdoctoral fellow working in both French and music, has helped me through some particularly difficult times. Likewise helpful during those times was the response to my work from Willis Regier of the University of Nebraska Press. I shall always be indebted to Jacques Barzun and the late Lionel Trilling, for the vision and the discipline of their joint seminar at Columbia. The enthusiasm with which the late Sheldon Sacks responded to the essay that appears in the present volume as chapter 9 was a gift that I have valued increasingly over the years. Above all I am indebted to Martha Woodmansee, an extraordinarily original English scholar who, along with the equally exceptional Ruth Ann Crowley (now a lawyer), introduced me to the entire domain of critical theory, including Adorno.

From no one have I learned more in my career than from the many wonderful students who have taken my classes or sought me out independently. Rather than risk omitting some from a long list, I must name only a few. During my years at the University of Chicago, Larry Fuchsberg (now in the U.S. Foreign Service) did so much to help me understand not only Adorno's dialectic but also what it means to think morally that if tuition could pay for such a service, *I* should have paid *him*. David Young, since my first semester at Chicago, when he was my graduate student, has continued to give me tremendous support, both through our ongoing discussions about music and higher education, and through his professional expertise as a career counselor. Edward Rothstein, Jann Pasler, Peter Burkholder, Mark Germer, Steve Bookman, David Brody, Kinerit Jaffe, Ann Feldman, Peter Livingston, and Steve Weinstock kept me in touch with musicology and diverse other worlds long after they left the University of Chicago. To Nancy Newman, who (thanks to the suggestion of the late Jim Moore) sought me out after I left the University of Chicago, I owe a particularly great debt for preventing me from retreating into intellectual isolation. At their social gatherings in Hyde Park, which combined the intellectual exhilaration of a high-powered salon with the uncompromising idealism of youth, Nancy, Pam Barrie, and Matt Malsky, along with Ethan Nasreddin-Longo and Teresa Davidian, kept me in touch with new cultural currents and the concerns of the next generation. Likewise, ongoing conversations with the composer Frank Retzel, a former student, and a correspondence with Andy Jones gave me valuable intellectual sustenance; so did the dialogue, which began in a course I gave on opera at Stony Brook, with Lloyd (Chip) Whitesell, an unusually thoughtful and thought-provoking student, and with the articulate Bill Hayes, who as my student was the very paradigm of the indispensable auditor — as were Mitchell Morris and Greg Salmon, who took time out of their classes at Columbia to participate vigorously in a seminar I gave at the CUNY Graduate Center. And without David Bain, who since his days as my student at the City University of New York Graduate Center, has engaged me in a dialogue of breathtaking range and insight, while also giving me continuous practical and moral support, this book could never have been completed.

I do not find it surprising that some of the colleagues and students from whom I learned the most have moved away from traditional academic environments or left academia altogether. What American universities suffered during the past decade, in my judgment, was not just the loss of many people through a Ph.D. glut but also the decline in an atmosphere that encourages risk, difference — and compassion.

A risk that *was* taken, and for which I am most grateful, was the decision by the University of Minnesota Press to publish my work. In particular I want to thank my copy editor Ann Klefstad, Biodun Iginla, Mary Byers, Craig Carnahan, Diane Lunderborg, Pat Gonzales, and Susan Marsnik for the care and enthusiasm they put into this project. Most of all I want to express my gratitude to Terry Cochran for his unfailing intelligence, sensitivity, and kindness as my editor.

Among the wonderful family and friends on whose unwavering confidence I have relied, I am particularly indebted to my brother, Robert Rosengard, his wife, Carol Rosengard, and Dana Erdevig, Cecelia Shaw Goldfarb, and Bill Levine for helping me shape what I write through the sort of open-ended and intense discussion of ideas that one enjoys with true colleagues. Likewise, within the community of friends that gave me so much intellectual and personal support during my sixteen years of living in Chicago's Hyde Park, several deserve particular thanks: Jeremy Burdett, Ingrid Jackson, Beverly Calhoun, John Courtney, Ann Kieran, Wendy and Mark Evans, Joan and Howard Margolis, Charlotte and David Reiter, Carol Schneider, Carl Schneider, Joan Costello, Lenora Whitehead, and Fredda Horne. So does Kathy Holmes of the University of Chicago Music Department, who has administered my dossier graciously and carefully for so many years now. Since moving to Long Island, I have received great intellectual stimulation from my friendship with Ted Burtness, a scholar and a gentleman, whose marvelous theory concerning James Joyce and Samuel Pepys will someday gain the serious consideration it deserves, and likewise from my friendships with his wife, Else Burtness, a first-rate musician, with Rochelle Siifen, and with Bill Carmel.

Finally, my work owes an incalculable debt to my husband, Dan, now a professor of law at Touro College, who has not only subsidized the larger part of my career but for more than twenty years has also chewed over with me one idea after another (not to mention the same old ideas) and has enabled me, through his own writings, to see how such ideas work in his own fields, especially law and business. For riding the roller coaster all this way with me I thank him as I do my two children, Eva and Joseph (Joey), who have been understanding beyond what any parent could expect.

Introduction

In the army, a superior officer once said to me: "So you are this notorious Schoenberg, then." "Beg to report, sir, yes," I replied. "Nobody wanted to be, someone had to be, so I let it be me."

Arnold Schoenberg[1]

On the night of the seventh game of the 1975 World Series, when my native team, the Boston Red Sox, was taking the field against the Cincinnati Reds (and Carlton Fisk's sixth-game home run was still glorious news), Edward Lowinsky called me down to his home on the South Shore of Chicago. He had just read an essay that I was about to submit for publication and wanted urgently to warn me that if I did not delete one particular reference to Beethoven, I would bitterly regret it in the future. That essay is chapter 2 of this volume. The reference is to the idea that Beethoven's Ninth Symphony might be said to have failed in a crucial respect. Genuinely concerned for my future, Professor Lowinsky wanted to impress upon me that a scholar must be able to stand by his or her work throughout an entire career. My response was to thank him but to explain that since I had arrived at this idea honestly, I saw no reason to believe it would shame me in the future.

Now that that future has arrived, I believe I can fairly say that neither of us was wrong. But perhaps that is not really surprising, for in our assessment of what was most important, we were clearly in agreement. Both of us believed that scholarship must be approached in a spirit of rigorous integrity. If one has done one's best in that respect, I cannot see how the changes of viewpoint that can occur over a career could be a source of embarrassment. As it happens, I have never felt the slightest urge to retract that early speculation about Beethoven. On the other hand, I am conscious that my viewpoint, like my writing style, has undergone a number of changes over the past fifteen years; and I have certainly made many mistakes. Yet reading carefully through the essays in this volume, which were written at different times over that period, I was surprised to find just how consistent and sharply defined the core of my perspective and convictions seems to have been, even from that very beginning. Thus on the point that mattered most to both of us, I believe Professor Lowinsky would have been reassured, even though his misgivings about the future weren't altogether off base.

The Red Sox lost, 4–3.

The work in this volume grew out of a combination of curiosity and dissatisfaction, attitudes I have not outgrown, though over the years their objects have altered and broadened. When I first embarked on postdoctoral scholarship, I wanted to answer one question: what was the relationship between German opera and German society in the first half of the nineteenth century?

The same question had formed the center of my Ph.D. dissertation, which I had completed shortly before (in 1973) at Columbia, and which I had entitled "Art and Popularity in Lortzing's Operas: The Effects of Social Change on a National Operatic Genre." One might suppose that in a dissertation as extensive as mine — it ran to 718 pages and drew on numerous early, unpublished, or otherwise recondite German sources — I had already come up with a satisfactory answer to this question. Yet by the time I had completed my dissertation and moved on to my first teaching position, in the music department at the University of Chicago (also in 1973), I had become convinced that I didn't know how to go about addressing this question, much less how to answer it.

What I had encountered thus far in works dealing with musical relationships were variants for the most part of a scholarly strategy that emphasized particulars. Epitomized by a type of musical biography commonly known as "Life and Works," this strategy consisted primarily in amassing information on either side of the "and." Such a process seemed to promise solid value since, at its best, it could yield empirical information impressive for both the amount and the refinement of its detail. Given this prospect — and the fact that I knew of no other way to investigate relationships — I relied almost exclusively on this strategy to work out my dissertation.

That it was possible even in graduate school to depart from such a strategy did not really occur to me until several years later, when, as an assistant professor at Chicago, I participated in grading qualifying exams for doctoral candidates in music. Asked to define a series of relationships such as the one between musical classicism and the Enlightenment, between Beethoven and the French Revolution, or between music and literature in German romanticism, one of the best candidates deeply disappointed my colleagues by the brevity of her answers.

In keeping with a longstanding academic tradition, the other students acted on the assumption that success in this (as in any other) sort of exam depended on presenting as many facts as possible about X and about Y — not on how well they selected, organized, or analyzed facts in terms of a relationship. By some fluke, however, this one student had interpreted the exam questions literally. She had imagined that what her professors wanted from her was an intelligent attempt to relate two discrete bodies of data. Since, like most of us educated in music,[2] she had had no previous experience with problems of this organizational or analytical kind, she had spent most of the exam hours wrestling in her mind with the difficulties of defining relationships. As a result, she had ended up recording only those facts that she could encompass plausibly in each hard-won framework, and narrowly missed failing the exam.

Witnessing this academic near miss by an unusually qualified student made a strong impression on me, for it helped me become more aware of my own unease with questions about relationships. On what basis can we confidently state that X and Y are related in Z fashion? However much information the "life and works" strategy had opened up for me in my dissertation about German opera and German society, it had not helped bridge the gap represented by the "and" in ways that I found persuasive. It had not helped, for example, in exploring a wide range of ways for defining or establishing a relationship; nor had it helped to develop criteria for evaluating the validity and usefulness of various categories of relationship.

Actually, everything I knew about this empirical approach to scholarship had discouraged me from thinking much about the nature of relationships at all. Many musicologists, after all, had already achieved success dealing with relationships in this intellectually easy-going, disjunct way without showing the slightest interest in the concept of a relationship. Indeed, nearly all of the musicological sources I had encountered in my dissertation research drew their categories of relationships simply from common sense, without consideration of any intellectual problems or limitations that might be associated with such categories.

Occasionally I had come across work that hazarded some suggestion of a more general perspective on relationships. In these instances, however, there always seemed to be a clear assumption that such suggestions, being merely speculative, had only a passing or, in musical terms, "ornamental" scholarly significance. Whereas a musicologist's assertion that some particular relationship had actually existed might evoke heated rebuttal,[3] scholarly works on music did not seem to risk any serious professional penalty — any more than predoctoral exams did — for evincing a simplistic grasp of the intellectual problems that might be involved in defining relationships.

It was within the context of such priorities that I had finished my dissertation curious to understand one particular kind of musical relationship, yet dissatisfied with the extent of my ability to validate any sort of relationship.

Up to that point the musicological literature I knew had not helped or even encouraged me to enlarge my understanding of the ways in which relationships work. It had not singled out the achievement of such understanding as a legitimate scholarly problem; and it had given me no indication that scholars in other humanistic disciplines considered this sort of understanding difficult — let alone important — to achieve.

What I didn't know until well after I had finished my dissertation was that the foundations had already been laid for a domain of humanistic study that would encompass precisely this sort of understanding. I did not know that, by the 1970s, this domain enjoyed a sizable scholarly literature and was steadily gaining in both definition and prominence. This domain was called "theory," and in this name, I suspect, lay a principal source of my prolonged ignorance.

One of the fundamental subdivisions in musicology is called "music theory," an area which in its fully developed technical specifity seems to have no counterpart in any other humanistic discipline. Like most musicologists of my generation, I was conditioned from the start to think of "theory" as an enterprise devoted to the complex technical and formal problems of musical analysis.[4] And because of this conditioning, it was especially difficult for me to grasp the methodological and epistemological sorts of significance that other humanistic disciplines and schools of thought were coming at this very time to attach to the notion of theory.

Fairly early in my graduate education I had come upon the idea that "history" consists not in what "actually" happened in the past but in the accounts of the past that historians constructed. In my youth, eager to appear sophisticated, I had treated this idea (which in truth I found shocking) as if it were self-evident. In fact, I scarcely understood its significance at all. Only as I was struggling in the dissertation to enumerate and exemplify various relationships between German opera and society did I start to sense from the inside out that relationships have no simple, verifiable existence. This allowed me to see that relationships are mental constructs — patterns constructed by an observer — which "exist" only insofar as they can be considered valid by others.

As this sense grew, I developed the idea — though it would be many years more before I grasped it clearly — that my job as scholar wasn't to prove that certain relationships once existed, for that could never be done, but rather to make the best possible case for *saying* that certain relationships once existed. Through this dawning realization I grasped that what I required to give a good account of relationships was not just a knowledge of particulars but a substantial understanding of what constitutes "knowing," in as many of its aspects as possible, including its relation to particulars. In a word, I saw that a fundamental parameter of relationships—the parameter that interested me most though I knew least about it—was epistemological.

To help me focus on this perspective, I needed guidance from a scholar who had already examined the epistemological foundations of musical knowledge, especially of knowledge about the relationship between music and society; and in the musicology I knew, the chances of finding published work on such topics seemed small. So it should not be too surprising that when I stumbled upon the musical writings of Theodor Adorno, at this very moment in my career, I grabbed on to them as if they were a lifeline.

I dwell on the prehistory of this volume because in retrospect it seems clear to me that the crucial decision in my scholarly career was made in the period between the completion of my dissertation and the publication of my first article:[5] the decision to take Adorno's work seriously as itself a legitimate object of scholarship. For it was with this decision that my scholarly attention turned irrevocably away from conventional empirical problems of musicology to far less commonly tackled theoretical ones.

I am aware that from the outside in, my shift from the study of German opera to the study of Adorno was perceived as abrupt and somewhat puzzling. For one thing, whereas the normal progression in a musicological career was to enlarge the body of particular information over which one had mastery, I had elected, as I would eventually come to recognize, to move from acquiring a knowledge of particulars toward acquiring a theory of the knowledge of particulars. In effect, it must have seemed that by directing my efforts toward the criticism of the scholarly process rather than toward the (uncritical) continuation and enlargement of that process, I had passed up, for no compelling reason, a routine chance to complete a forward pass in order to throw sideways. In a culture devoted to relentless progress, the lateral pass is not the tactic of choice. In my case, moreover, the ultimate goal—to achieve some theoretical understanding of how music can be "known"—was one that few in the field at this time were positioned to recognize.

In addition, it should be remembered that when I first started working on Adorno, he was almost entirely unknown in American musicology. In the early 1970s, no more than a handful of articles on Adorno's musical writings had been published in the United States and Britain; and only one of his books, *Philosophie der neuen Musik*, had been translated (less than ideally) into English.[6] Though it appears that American musicologists here and there had already had some personal encounters with Adorno's work, or at least with his reputation—typically while doing graduate study in Germany—none had chosen to publish on Adorno. Even in the late 1970s, when I had received back-to-back fellowships from the American Council of Learned

Societies and the Guggenheim Foundation and was gearing up for two years of uninterrupted research, a senior colleague in my department told me bluntly, "Adorno isn't a tenurable topic."[7]

Adorno's virtual absence from the American musicological scene in those years may be hard to recall these days, when much if not most of his writing on music is available in translation, and when just about everyone I encounter in the discipline (including the senior colleague just mentioned) seems to have given, or to be in the midst of giving, a course involving music and Adorno. Though perhaps the situation is not so different after all today, given the ongoing virtual nonexistence in this country of teaching slots for specialists in texts such as Adorno's musical writings, and the corollary dearth of American graduate music programs offering expert guidance in a wide range of music criticism and critical theory.[8] At any rate, my sudden plunge into the near vacuum of English scholarship on Adorno that existed at the time appears to have struck some others as a bolt out of the blue.

Looking from the inside out, on the other hand, I saw the decision to immerse myself for a while in studying Adorno's musical writings as the direct and logical outgrowth of concerns I had developed while writing my dissertation. Having gone far in investigating aspects of a particular musical relationship, and having been hindered in that investigation by my own theoretical ignorance about relationships, I thought it right to make my next scholarly undertaking an attempt to reduce that ignorance.

In fact, I would go so far as to say that my decision to study Adorno has always seemed to me evidence of a strong ongoing sense of responsibility that I feel toward my past. Like Adorno's close associate Arnold Schoenberg, though without Schoenberg's genius or importance, I have sought to produce logical continuity in my career as in my written texts, stopping repeatedly to try and understand the relationship (!) between my more recent concerns and earlier ones, and to confront newly developed positions with older ones.

This shared concern with continuity accounts for a good part of the affinity I feel with Schoenberg, an affinity I have openly claimed in drawing from him both the title and the subtitle of the present volume.[9] To me, as to Schoenberg, such continuity constitutes important evidence that the essentially aesthetic act of constructing a "text," whether on paper or in one's professional life, has been subjected to rational restraints, in all the Kantian senses of "rationality."[10] From this viewpoint, continuity is valued as a sign that a text has been carefully constructed to meet rigorous standards not only of formal coherence but also of logical precision and, especially crucial, of moral scrupulousness.

This assertion of an intense concern with continuity might surprise those familiar only with the general character of my work, who have not read much of it closely. From the distance of those who know my work only through scattered impressions, it may seem that my writings have taken a tortuous course, interspersed, here and there, by a non sequitur. For once I had gained confidence—and this took a great deal of time to develop—that I had some grasp of Adorno's way of thinking from the inside out, I moved on to consider works by other thinkers, ranging from Kant to Derrida and Mikhail Bakhtin, some of whom had no particular connection with Adorno's work or took positions strikingly different from his.

The diversity of the figures I've studied and written about has exposed me to a charge that is frequently leveled from without at specialists in comparative literature: the charge that I am a dilettante, making disjunct hops from "ism" to "ism," without any effort to develop or connect what I learn at each stop. Perhaps the best rejoinder to this charge would be simply an invitation to read all of my essays, carefully, in the order in which they were written.[11]

No fair-minded reader would emerge from such a process, I believe, without some clear sense of an ongoing evolution in my thought, tempered by a self-conscious grappling with more or less unchanging convictions and recurrent concerns. Among other things, such a reading would dispel two essentially contradictory misconceptions about my attitude toward Adorno: that I have all along made Adorno an object of blind idolatry and slavish imitation; or that, in the dilettante fashion just mentioned, I cynically abandoned Adorno to pursue newer, more stylish gods.

For such a reading would clarify, as perhaps nothing else could, the gradual transformation of my position with respect to Adorno's work itself, from an attempt first of all to understand that work fairly, on Adorno's own terms, to the acquisition of a perspective from which I could set increasingly precise limits on what I valued in that work. By this I mean a perspective from which it was possible to criticize Adorno's work—not necessarily in his own terms but at least knowledgeably, and again, fairly—and also to establish distance between his concerns and mine, without losing sight of concerns we still shared.

Crucial to the development of such a perspective were efforts to understand how the issues that drew me to Adorno were treated by thinkers from other traditions. It was this need for alternative viewpoints that encouraged me, as the opportunity arose, to follow the study of Adorno with some study of semiotics, structuralism, and eventually poststructuralism, movements often dominated by French thinkers. In many respects, the thinkers in these movements approached issues very differently from Adorno, although in their understanding of the issues that face them, they are far closer to Adorno than to representatives of the American empirical traditions.[12]

To an important extent, the distance between my own view today and the one Adorno left as his legacy can be gauged from reservations I have formed about the concept of historical continuity as it was idealized in terms of reason not only by Adorno but also, and especially, by Schoenberg.[13] To put things simply, though I remain bound by what I see as Schoenberg's intellectual and moral code of active historical responsibility to oneself, I no longer share Schoenberg's complete faith in the developmental or historical process as progressive, any more than I share the confidence he expresses through musical imagery in the power of abstract reason *alone* to make sense of experience, or to produce morally good systems.[14]

Like "the Darwinian history of life," as Stephen Jay Gould has described it, Schoenberg's position throughout his career essentially was that "there [is] progress in evolution."[15] By contrast, my own studies, reinforced by personal experience, have led me to attribute (like Gould) a far greater role to contingency in all human structurings of time — even logical structurings — than Schoenberg, in his fierce battle against recognizing nonrational sources of power, was ever willing to concede. What has drawn me toward this conclusion has undoubtedly been, in part, my exposure to a French way of thinking that is far more comfortable with the prospect of contingency than is the German tradition of Schoenberg and Adorno.[16] Most decisive in this respect, however, has been the effect of issues raised through the intricacies of my own analyses and reflection.

Although I hope that my insight into the questions I have asked over the years has deepened, the specific nature of these questions has sharpened my sense that every choice, no matter how logical or even necessary it may seem in its time, reflects to some extent a contingent actualization of one possibility from among many others. And consequently, although I've approached every new piece I've written as the natural outgrowth of previous concerns, I no longer see my enterprise as a linear advance toward some stage of resolution; nor do I any longer expect, as undoubtedly I did when I first set out to extend lines of inquiry from my dissertation, to bring those lines to a definitive conclusion.

Instead, I have come to look more and more on my work as a series of repeated assaults on a handful of artistic, and ultimately human, issues that I find intriguing, elusive, and often troubling. Insofar as each assault has required a new formulation of these issues, and insofar as I have tried hard to exert rational and responsible control over the choices through which these assaults collectively define a shape, I still see a deep-rooted affinity in my undertaking with Schoenberg's concept of the developing variation, in both its aspects.[17] But I have also come to see in my undertaking the basis for a critique of Schoenberg's concept insofar as I now acknowledge limits on the degree to which any enterprise can be characterized as "developing."

To put it another way, over time I have come to view my work not as some inevitable, necessary, or even wholly controlled process of unfolding but as, at most, the rationally plausible outgrowth of a tension between my own fragile capacity to maintain historical continuity and the unavoidability of historical chance. Thus, looking back, I am acutely aware that my work over the years, like an individual article, could at many points have taken a number of different directions—just as today I can easily imagine that, with a change or two in circumstances, I might have had the unbroken secure career I once anticipated instead of the one I have had.

These are, I should point out, much the same terms in which I have come to interpret the musical and literary texts I study. From an initial, almost wholly uncomprehending acquaintance with structuralist and semiotic notions such as "significant difference," I have come to find a powerful source of meaning in the very gap that separates actual structures from imaginable alternatives, or to be more precise, the gap that separates the contingency of what actually occurred in a particular life or piece from visions of what could have happened next—or should have.

The structural parallelism I suggest here, between human life, human work, and the human text, is wholly compatible with Schoenberg's legacy of conscientious consistency; here, too, as in my more general tendency to interpret music as an existential metaphor, I no doubt owe a great deal to the spirit of that legacy.[18] Where I depart from Schoenberg, in this connection, is in the shift of my focus away from compositional structures themselves, as the basis for such a metaphor, to relationships between things that are perceived either as "actually" or (only) as "conceivably" present in a structure— that is, my focus has shifted to the very relationships through which observers define structures in the first place.[19]

Implicit in this shift of focus, of course, is the realization, once again, that relationships themselves exist only as constructs in the mind of the observer. In keeping with that realization, I have come to attach far more substantive importance than Schoenberg did to the reader's role in structuring a text— and thereby also to contingencies that might affect readers' perceptions and produce many different possible readings of the same text.

In one sense, I suppose, this orientation toward the reader can be viewed as a logical extension of my dissertation, which tried to analyze the impact of popular reception on conceptions of structure and art in nineteenth-century German opera. But it is more than just a simple extension. In the sense that this orientation involves a concern to understand the epistemological conditions of interpretation, I have clearly been influenced, as in my attitude more generally toward contingency, not only by themes and directions in French-influenced movements[20] but also by my own experience. Again, there is nothing like living the effects of an adverse reading to discourage discounting the force of the reader's role in shaping a text, beginning with one's own life and works.[21]

If I am to be fair, however, I must acknowledge that my most decisive step toward such an orientation almost certainly came with discovering Adorno's work, especially his notion of self-critical dialectic. Though I have traveled some distance, now, from the territory of Adorno's unremitting severity and despair over the impossibility of a rational humanity based on individual self-determination, his notion of dialectic has guided me so consistently that I could well have entitled the present collection *Dialectical Variations.*

In the first instance, this notion allowed me to begin to understand relationships in the human domain through an analytical dynamic that in my own experience has been confirmed again and again as valid, whether the relationship in question involves music and society, life and work, theory and data, general structure and detail, or text (in the poststructuralist sense) and interpreter.[22] What I mean here is the process of viewing both terms in a relationship as simultaneously prior to each other, in the sense that the thinker's definition of each term is understood to condition the definition of the other in the very act of being conditioned by that other.[23]

And in the last instance, following Adorno's notion of dialectic in some of the directions to which it pointed has enabled me to go beyond merely playing with catchy-but-baffling terms in Continental literary theory (such as "dialectic" itself) to the point of deriving intellectual and even moral insight from those terms. If nothing more, precisely through giving me access to the complex modes and broad domain of Continental thought, this notion has provided useful intellectual tools, and an increased measure of courage, with which to insist on thinking about music in ways that seemed to me important. But in addition, the process of laboring to understand and evaluate Continental ideas has helped discipline my moral sensibility, I believe, as well as my mind. Or at least, this process has sharpened my sense of what one needs to consider in the never-ending struggle to make responsible choices — a self-critical sense that I have tried to share, in turn, with my readers, with the wonderfully idealistic students who have managed over the years to find me, and ultimately with my own children. In short, Adorno's notion of dialectic has turned out to be a rich resource not only in my work but also in my life.

The realization that Adorno's appeal to me involved epistemology came slowly and gradually. Only in working on more recent essays, most of which will be published for the first time in a companion volume to the present one,[24] did I begin to understand clearly that the nature of my interest in music, as in anything else I spent much time thinking about, was and always had been philosophical.

When I began to teach and publish on Adorno, however, what seemed most immediately striking about him was not his treatment of music and philosophy as mutually enlightening. Nor was it the fact that he had thought hard about the relationship between music and society, though this was unusual enough; it was the fact that he had done so from an explicitly political viewpoint.

Nowhere in the ways of thinking handed down by one generation of American musicologists to the next was there room for the admission of any political viewpoint by a scholar. On the contrary, such an admission would have been seen as a violation of Enlightenment ideals that made possible the American spirit, such as scientific objectivity and free speech. Never mind that the relationship between these latter two was not one of simple identity, since the right to free speech was meant specifically to protect the expression of tendentious or partisan viewpoints. American musicology was steeped in the assumption that enlightened scholarship by definition excludes the presence of a political viewpoint.

Since the only school of thought then commonly known to acknowledge a political parameter in scholarship was Marxism, since Adorno's association with Marxist philosophy was more widely known than his cultural elitism,[25] and since in preparation for understanding and writing about Adorno I had once given a course at the University of Chicago entitled "Marxist Approaches to Music Criticism,"[26] perhaps it was to be expected that some people, even in an environment that normally insists on scientific proof, would leap to the conclusion that I myself was a Marxist. In fact, at least as far back as my undergraduate days, when I couldn't bring myself to join in the singing of the Wellesley College alma mater, I've had an aversion to preformed, doctrinaire ideologies of any kind. Yet I'm not really comfortable perpetuating the sort of atmosphere in which, to protect myself from notoriety, I would have to deny an affiliation to which no shame need be attached. On this count I would rather let readers decide for themselves what relations they discern between my work, any political convictions it might manifest, and the value it might have as scholarship.

In any case, to me it seems clear that anything one might have expected to dredge up through red-baiting would have been a red herring in terms of its scholarly importance. What mattered in my work on Adorno was the notion of ideology defined not narrowly, as a specific and explicitly political doctrine, but broadly, as a network of assumptions and values shaped by experience and culture.[27] That is to say, the fundamental issue raised by my work on Adorno wasn't whether either of us espoused Marxism or any other particular political philosophy. The issue was whether it is possible for any form of communication, including scholarship—and ultimately, of course, including music itself—to avoid ideology, that is, to exclude all signs that it expresses an ideological position, or, to put it another way, to render impossible the discernment of itself as the bearer of an ideological imprint.[28]

The American musicological tradition in which I had been educated claimed that what it produced was value-free scholarship. By this it meant scholarship that was utterly free of ideological preference, and thus characterized by the total objectivity required to qualify it as knowledge. By contrast, the Continental tradition, into which Adorno initiated me, perceived this very claim itself as the expression of what I would call an ideological position, that is, as evidence of the inextricability of ideological preferences and value hierarchies from the very process of communication.

From a Continental standpoint, ideological predispositions play an inescapable role in shaping every act and configuration of both expression and interpretation. Thus the criticism of music involves an interaction between the critic's ideologically conditioned framework and the original one(s) in which that music was created. This is, as I have indicated earlier,[29] a slippery business since, although the critic may make every effort to maintain a balance between the claims of the two frameworks on the music, it is only from within the critic's viewpoint or categories that anything "other"—such as an originating ideology or the music "itself"—can be perceived and defined. It is in this sense that dialectical criticism emphatically denies any absolute distinction between the music observed and the musical observer. Adorno himself undercuts the very distinction between criticism and music by presenting both as mediums for social criticism, which is to say, as mediums for the expression of an ideological viewpoint.[30]

By the same token, since the Continental tradition recognizes the mutually determinative (dialectical) impact upon each other of such predispositions, on the one hand, and the shape and selection of "facts," on the other, it recognizes no absolute distinction between the explicitly ideological status of criticism and the supposedly nonideological, pure objectivity of knowledge. From the standpoint of this tradition, *all* discourse on music, measured against a standard of wholly abstract certifiability, amounts epistemologically to a form of criticism.[31]

In a nutshell, it is to versions of this same argument about the role of ideology in human discourse that my own work has returned again and again over the years; and it appears I've been working in the eye of a more general intellectual firestorm. For it is versions of this very argument that have proliferated during the last decade all over the American academic landscape, igniting controversy about topics ranging from the value of studying the Western literary canon to the validity of "critical legal studies," and spreading an atmosphere of acrid disagreement.[32]

An invitation from the Society for Ethnomusicology gave me the chance to confront the issue of ideology head-on, in a lecture that became the essay "The Role of Ideology in the Study of Western Music." Although I knew that ethnomusicology was already conscious of issues such as this, I hoped by publishing this piece to open up discussion in American musicology more broadly about the place and effect of ideology in the definition and execution of scholarly aims.

Similarly, in essays such as "Adorno's Diagnosis of Beethoven's Late Style," and "Why Is Adorno's Music Criticism the Way It Is?" where I tried to introduce Adorno's work to American musicology while simultaneously trying to come to terms myself with that work, my interest was in exploring the effects on scholarship of a self-critical sensitivity to one's own ideological predispositions, not only in Adorno's case but also in my own. (In the latter of these two articles, it will be noted, the attempt to come to grips with Adorno's position has been further complicated by an attempt to square that position with what I was coming to know about structuralism.)

I have the impression that much of the interest students have taken in my work involves its recognition of self-critical ideological awareness as an attitude critically important to the integrity and value of scholarship. By this I don't mean that I alone among the human fellowship have escaped altogether what Paul de Man would call the trap of "blindness" to my own ideological limitations;[33] I do mean that my work is part of a still relatively small body of musicological scholarship where students can at least find mention of this problem, which troubles them. The students I have encountered in the past decade, from a number of colleges and universities, have not only read a far wider and more sophisticated range of humanistic writings than music students did when I was in graduate school. They are also harder to fool (though no less idealistic) about what matters in the life of the mind. For these students it seems to be simply unthinkable that scholars without a reflective and critical self-consciousness should expect to be taken seriously.

Having admitted their own (essentially ideological) susceptibility to bias, these students expect the same sort of admission from their teachers. Such an expectation may well be naive from a practical standpoint; but at least it does not involve the intellectual naïveté of identifying a fundamentally epistemological inquiry into the role of ideology as an attempt to proselytize for a political doctrine. Nor does it involve construing signs of moral self-consciousness — signs that such an inquiry is simultaneously concerned to maintain its moral integrity — as evidence of propagandism. On the contrary, based as it obviously is on moral principle, this expectation of ideological honesty finds the need to meet rigorous standards of morality in scholarship self-evident.[34]

In finding my own way toward such an expectation of scholarship, I was helped enormously by Adorno. In forcing me to consider, again and again, the relationship between expression and ideology, Adorno's writings sharpened my sensitivity to moral questions, not only in the relationship between music and society but also in the processes and goals of scholarship itself. Without doubt, this effect, which I had never before encountered in my studies, accounted for much of the excitement I experienced in getting to know Adorno's musical writings.

At the time, certainly, I was more conscious of Adorno's moral appeal than of his appeal on any epistemological grounds. And yet, in choosing to move my scholarly focus back from Adorno to Kant, I was pursuing a course directly relevant to clarifying epistemological aspects of ideological criticism. In the event, studying Kant brought my concerns with morality and epistemology equally to a head by forcing me to consider both in relation to reason.

Through a close reading, and rather complex formal analysis of Kant's *Critique of Judgment,* I in fact became persuaded of the need to subject the modern Western conception of reason itself to a critique, by reinterpreting reason as a construct informed as much by the cultural concreteness of ideology as by the structural abstractness of theory. This conviction is made clear in my essay "Kant, Adorno, and the Self-Critique of Reason," where I draw some provisional analogies between concepts of reason in the Enlightenment tradition and concepts of structure in classical and romantic musical styles.[35] Through this study I concluded that the only hope for a reconciliation of theoretical and moral reason in scholarship lay in giving precedence to some concrete aesthetic faculty of reason — in a word, judgment — which could admit limits on the certainty of theoretical principles and at the same time make some place for the operation of a rigorous moral sensibility.[36]

To the extent that Kant's account of aesthetic judgment (far differently though he intended it) points toward the possibility of an aesthetic foundation of reason, it seems to me that this third critique is ultimately Kant's most important legacy to modern thought. For myself, at least, a primary consequence of my concentrated exposure to Kant was the development of yet another theme to which I have returned again and again: the proposal of the aesthetic structure — or to be more precise, the aesthetic process, in that the structure by definition includes interpretation — as a model for scholarship.[37] This proposal owes much also, of course, to Adorno's enterprise of deciphering the conditions and values of a society from the structure, broadly construed, of its artworks.

It should not be overlooked, indeed, that within the constrictions of his epistemology, Adorno encouraged disciplined attention to both ends of interpretation; for in a dialectical fashion, his focus of attention moved constantly between his own role as an involved musical observer and the configuration of the music. As a result, it was not only at the level of epistemological theory but also by example, through his efforts to distill into words the character of music, that Adorno advocated the kind of musical "knowing" that is developed through responsible criticism.

My essay "Musicology and Criticism," written at the invitation of the American Musicological Society, was specifically designed to present criticism as a legitimate branch of American musicology. Recognizing that musical scholars unfamiliar with criticism might construe its openly admitted epistemological limitations as evidence that criticism involved neither hard work nor rigorous qualitative standards, I emphasized the demands on responsible scholarly critics, for example, reading widely and intensively in a number of fields, organizing highly diverse variables, and articulating a persuasive rationale with painstaking care.

In this way, I hoped to counteract an impression of criticism, among those musicologists who thought about it at all, as a discipline so "soft" and undemanding that it could easily be mastered as a sideline while one concentrated on the more important business of gathering empirical data. To me it seemed self-evident that mastering criticism entailed sacrificing some degree of expertise elsewhere in the traditional course of musical scholarship. It was my allusion to this necessary trade-off that was taken by Robert Winter, in the *New York Review of Books*, as an exhortation to fragment and narrow musicological specialties even more than they already have been, a process he dubbed "the Subotnik syndrome."[38]

More perspicacious, I hope, was a characterization that the late Jim Moore, once my colleague at the University of Chicago, unexpectedly offered me of my work, as the search for a critical language adequate to music. Though I had never before thought of my work in such terms, this observation had a clarifying force for me. As indicated by the title of my essay, "Why Is Adorno's Music Criticism the Way It Is?" I did have a keen interest, even at an early stage, in trying to fix as precisely as possible in words the distinctive quality of the texts I studied.

In this case, of course, the text in question was verbal; but having now encountered Adorno's theory and examples, I began to believe that musical texts, too, could be subjected to a kind of analysis — criticism — that yielded illuminating characterizations. Gradually, my interest in this possibility dovetailed with my longstanding interest in understanding the relationship between music and society. As I struggled to refine the language with which I thought and spoke about music, the parameter of music toward which these efforts became more and more directed was the one most plausibly defined as articulating the distinctive cultural qualities and values of a society: style.

All three of the remaining chapters in the section here called "Stylistic Criticism" can be understood, at least in part, as efforts to characterize particular musical styles, using the analysis of my own response to those styles as a point of departure. "Evidence of a Critical Worldview in Mozart's Last Three Symphonies" was the outcome of a long and intensive effort to find stylistic analogies between Kant's *Critique of Judgment* and Mozart's last three symphonies — analogies that could be defined and analyzed in terms of recurring structural patterns. "Romantic Music as Post-Kantian Critique" concludes with an attempt to illustrate a complex philosophical and cultural analysis of romantic style, based also on Kant, through the analysis of a Chopin prelude; in "On Grounding Chopin" I tried to demonstrate that the same sort of analysis could be extended to many other pieces by Chopin.[39]

Typically, however, the attempt to characterize style led me to a wide-ranging network of essentially epistemological questions about style. Very quickly I began to see style as part of a more fluid configuration that by definition involves not only subtle sorts of distinctions (on the part of the "reader") between cultural and individual styles but also attention to every aspect of the musical medium, physical and cultural, that is perceived as explicitly related to passing time or historical change.

Above all I became deeply concerned to understand the relationship between what I call "style" and "structure." Of all the issues I have thought about, this is probably the one that has preoccupied me in my writing more than any other. In the sense that "Romantic Music as Post-Kantian Critique" is the essay in which I painstakingly develop my basic position on style and structure, it can be considered the key essay in this collection.[40] And yet, at bottom, this issue is really just a transformation, or perhaps a paradigm (to use structuralist terms), of other issues that have engaged me: for example, the relationship between theory and empirical research, or between scientific objectivity and ideology.

For me, the term "structure" has come to be shorthand for one pole in a dialectical vision of the ways in which we impute meaning to human experience. Within this dialectic, "structure" connotes the pole toward which we refer everything that can be thought of as abstract, timeless, or necessary — just as "style" connotes the other pole, to which we refer everything concrete, transient, or contingent, such as the things we define as physical, cultural, social, historical, or contextual.

Since I do think in terms of a dialectic, I do recognize communication and interpretation as processes that require not just reference but some degree of *deference* to concepts of the unchanging, including scientific concepts of truth, as well as to concepts of the contingency and uncertainty of perception. I am not one to deny the value of abstract ideals, as embodied in Western scientific or legal principles at their best, to recommend dissolving the "otherness" of a studied text into one's own abandoned subjective fantasy, or in other such ways to advocate capitulating to nihilism.

In fact, as I am well aware, for someone with my reputation for radicalism, I maintain surprisingly strong ties with old-fashioned tradition. More venturesome souls than I may well — and rightly — fault my work for sticking to items in the canon of Western "high art" music;[41] for that matter, I've also counseled my children to study Latin. More significant, however, though I don't believe American musicology has allowed access to a genuine diversity of competing viewpoints, my own position has never been to encourage either ending or denying the existence of the traditional musicological enterprise, though I have certainly advocated rethinking the latter.

Here, too, in the relationship between structural abstractness and stylistic concreteness I would stipulate that each term is to be simultaneously construed as prior to the other — "stylistic" data make sense only in terms of "structural" principles, which make sense only in terms of "stylistic" data. At the same time, however, there are limits to the degree of validity I believe can be ascribed to the allegedly timeless pole of structure; that is, I stipulate the equal priority just described with the understanding that structural ideals of pure abstraction and timelessness must simultaneously be recognized as inextricably dependent on the contingent concreteness of the languages or mediums through which they are defined. That is to say, since "structural" ideals and principles cannot be assigned an independent "existence" on the other side of Kant's great metaphysical divide, structure must in my judgment be located, finally, *pace* Kant, in the epistemological domain of a culturally limited and limiting human viewpoint: the same domain that encompasses the writing of the "texts," so to speak, known as "style," "ideology" — and "history."

For Adorno, who worked in the tradition of Hegel and Marx, history was the only arena in which it was either conceivable or moral to understand the dialectic between the subject defined through ideology (in a broad sense) and the object defined through style. From his standpoint, the processes through which the act of observing and the phenomenon observed shape each other's definition were irreducibly historical, to be defined as unfolding themselves through the concrete and changing conditions of experience and its interpretation. In light of both Adorno's value for me as a model and my familiarity with his account of Western music history, it might have seemed inevitable that I would try to develop my own view of the relationship between the critical observer and Western music in terms of a historical process or framework.

Actually, I arrived at such an undertaking by way of an unexpected detour, which was later to develop into a path of much importance for me. Given the chance to review a book on musical semiotics by Jean-Jacques Nattiez,[42] my attention was turned toward the French movements of semiotics and structuralism, particularly as represented by Claude Lévi-Strauss.

"The Cultural Message of Musical Semiology" started out as a review of Nattiez that very soon outgrew itself. The strong encouragement of the late Sheldon Sacks, the founding editor of *Critical Inquiry*, and of Wayne Booth gave me the courage to turn this piece into what it wanted to be: a full-length article proposing a theory of the relationship between Western music and language as they developed in history since the Enlightenment. "Tonality, Autonomy, and Competence in Postclassical Music" was a kind of postscript to this article, prompted by an extended scholarly response.

In both of these essays, the view I took of history was influenced not just by Adorno's dialectical tradition but by the tensions, incongruities, and questions that emerged from confronting that tradition with the essentially ahistorical concerns of structuralist semiotic theory. Those conflicts became a central focus in "The Historical Structure: Adorno's 'French' Model for Criticism of Nineteenth-Century Music," an essay in which, for the first time,[43] I deliberately read Adorno "against the grain," trying to see what would happen if his historical theories were subjected to criticism from the ahistorical viewpoint they opposed.

In a sense, this glancing back and forth between two worldviews, with its suggestion that any attempt to prove the "priority" of either must regress into the indeterminacy of infinity, already suggests an experiment in deconstruction. Looking back, I now see these two whole chapters, "The Cultural Message of Musical Semiology" and "The Historical Structure," as constituting not a simple complementary pair but rather two opposed readings within a process of deconstruction. Similarly, "Evidence of a Critical Worldview in Mozart's Last Three Symphonies," with its strategy of "reading" the symphonies first with, and then against, the grain of traditional interpretation could be characterized as a deconstructionist sort of enterprise. At the time, however, I did not yet know anything about deconstruction or poststructuralism more generally. The viewpoint I opposed to Adorno's in these essays on history was still that of structuralism. Without the work I did on this now underrated movement, I might have remained considerably longer in the study of German critical theories, and the domain of French poststructuralist literary theory would certainly have remained alien to me in a fundamental way.

The last two chapters in this collection return to the spirit and concerns of Adorno, though they are more critical than the opening pieces were of Adorno's legacy. These two essays could be called companion pieces to the extent that "Individualism in Western Art Music and Its Cultural Costs" presents an early version of themes that are more fully developed in "The Challenge of Contemporary Music."[44] The polarity between individual and society presented in the first piece, which has never before been published,[45] is derived directly from Adorno's theory, and the emphasis here on communal values reflects in no small measure the impact upon me of Adorno's insistence on social responsibility. At the same time, the enormous value that Adorno placed on individuality, which to be sure he defined and defended on a level of much greater complexity than my own essay attempts, is subject to criticism here, as is the uncompromising elitism of Adorno's taste.

The same fundamental issues are taken up again in the second essay, though in a more ambitious and intricately designed framework. In this essay, originally written for an audience of philosophers, I singled out for philosophical analysis the main lines of the Schoenberg tradition, which I believe has not only dominated the history of Western art composition for most of this century but has also established decisively the terms of what is widely considered to be the contemporary music aesthetic. That I do not give much attention here to the postcontemporary musical aesthetic that is currently coalescing should not be surprising; my own understanding is that the contemporary aesthetic in music, like the modern aesthetic in literature and art, belongs to an age that we are now in the process of leaving. (See below, n. 46; chapter 12, n. 11; and chapter 13, n. 1.)

In this sense, then, the preoccupation of this essay with a contemporary aesthetic to an extent dates it, as does another element as well. In writing this essay, I was also greatly preoccupied with the relationship between style and structure. In hopes of distilling the concrete essence of "style," I tried, by referring to particulars, to convey the specific quality of the place and time in which I was writing. As a result, in revising this essay for publication here, I have had to update some topical references (e.g., stereos have been supplemented by compact disc players); and some of the references are now irretrievably out of date (e.g., the television program "Miami Vice"). In short, this chapter projects, quite palpably, a quality of datedness in its *style*.[46] Given my reservations concerning the ethos of "progress," I am not especially troubled by this quality. Its irreducible concreteness may actually be useful in an essay that is trying to reassert the claims of social actuality on art, as a counterweight to ideals of theoretical abstraction that have done so much in our century to isolate Western art music, and higher education in music, from society. And at this point I seem to have completed a circle, moving from a fascination with epistemological abstraction back to the concrete social concerns I began with.

I could, perhaps, hope that the *structures* of the arguments presented in this volume hold out somewhat longer against the ravages of age. On the other hand, in keeping with the position I have taken throughout my writings, I certainly do not expect later generations of readers, if they come upon these essays at all, to be able to strip away my arguments from their style as if the latter were some sort of clear and disposable plastic wrap, or to follow my lines of thought precisely as I do, without incorporating elements of my culturally finite style into the very core of what they understand to be the discursive structure of my arguments. I will be happy indeed if, in my own lifetime, this book finds its way to readers who can sense the order and character of my rationale here, and can enter into that rationale sufficiently to take from it something helpful to their own "life and work."

Part I
Ideological Criticism

Chapter 1

The Role of Ideology in the Study of Western Music

Some time ago, an established American musicologist complained to me that I approached the study of music with a philosophical orientation and was therefore bound to falsify music and music history. My immediate reactions to this remark were disbelief that a philosophical orientation should be held grounds for adverse criticism of humanistic scholarship, and shock that my critic saw such an orientation as a flaw in the validity of my work rather than as the symbol of an ideological difference between his conception of scholarship and my own. The remark struck me as patently naive and, on reflection, as an attack upon my intellectual freedom. Yet it is clear that my critic's conviction represents the mainstream of thought in American musicology today, and that very few English-speaking musicologists today would share my evaluation of this criticism as obviously wrongheaded. So the remark has rattled around in my head for several years now, impelling me to reconsider the premises on which the study of Western music is based, and thus to give my colleague's criticism some extended attention.

At the outset, I want to make two observations that I will not have time to develop in this essay. First, it is conceivable that in referring to my "philosophical orientation" my critic really had in mind not any general philosophical bent but rather the adoption of a specific philosophical viewpoint, in my case, of T. W. Adorno's dialectical philosophy. But if this is so, then my critic would open himself directly to a charge that he would be most anxious to refute, and that is precisely the charge of suppressing ideological differences and, thus, of limiting academic freedom. In the long run, though, I don't think it matters much which way the criticism was meant. Both a general philosophical orientation and a specific philosophical viewpoint are aspects of what I intend to call here ideology — by which I mean, generally, a conceptual context that allows the definition of human utterances — and I believe the ultimate force of my critic's objection is directed toward the notion of ideology in all of its possible forms. Second, I cannot take time here to develop a theory of the relationship between compositions — let us call them musical structures — and the structures that are based on compositions, such as historical studies and critical essays. I shall simply assume here that both sorts of artifact belong to a single continuum of semiotic structures, that is, of utterances through which individuals or cultures externalize a conception of reality, and, consequently, that ideology can be considered to play the same sorts of role in both composition and the study of composition. In fact, my critic concedes my point when he charges that my philosophical lenses distort both music and the history of music, since that history itself is a construct superimposed on compositions.

Let me then begin by asking: Are all human utterances based on a philosophical orientation? I think there are today, in academic musical circles, two prevalent schools of thought about this question, which I shall call the Continentalist view and the Anglo-American view. Extending this terminology, which is more often applied to the two dominant schools of philosophical thought, one might also call these attitudes the metaphysicist view and the empiricist view.[1] The Continentalist view, to which I myself subscribe, tends to answer my question in the affirmative. Continentalists tend to approach their studies with the idea that all people, including themselves, operate with a comprehensive, though not necessarily conscious, immutable, or irrefutable view of how things are. Continentalists are thus often prone to treat the study of musical utterance as a kind of metastudy in which various levels of ideological orientation are to be distinguished and taken into account in any work of interpretation or evaluation. These orientations include those of the composer, of the historian or critic, and of any who develop theories about either or both. Moreover, the Continentalist's point of departure is more likely to be an awareness of his or her own ideological framework than the musical artifact, the so-called object of study, itself. But Continentalists are also generally forced into considering the possibility of distinguishing within any artifact between two levels of structure to which meaning and value can be assigned: first, the internal or autonomous structure of the artifact itself; and, second, the structure of cultural, philosophical, and ideological premises underlying or surrounding the artifact and, ultimately, the study of the artifact.

This is not to deny that most Continentalists would sooner or later reject the possibility of making a clean distinction between artifact and ideology, as well as the possibility of assigning true meanings or values to an autonomous artistic structure taken in itself. Continentalists are basically post-

Kantians, who doubt the possibility of stripping away all ideological distortions and penetrating into any object in itself. And one need only consider the Communist disdain for formalistic analysis to understand the lengths to which the Continentalist's preference for ideological context over artistic structure might be taken. In general, Continentalists (up until poststructuralism) have been as concerned with resynthesizing into some sort of enlarged conceptual unity the levels of meaning that they pull out of an artwork as they are with distinguishing those levels. Nevertheless, there are few Continentalists who are not eventually forced, in this very activity of resynthesis, to give some attention to just what an autonomous artistic structure might be. And finally, the Continentalist's attraction to ideological underpinnings or context encourages open distinctions between levels of ideology that are conscious, and constitute political viewpoints or schools of criticism, and levels that are unconsciously formed by a speaker's unreflected assumptions, say, his or her psychological reflexes, economic and social attitudes, or cultural values. What tends, indeed, to madden the empiricist about the Continentalist more than anything else is the latter's penchant for diagnosing some level of unconscious meaning beneath the overt structure of any utterance, thereby reducing empiricists in some Continentalist accounts, to little more than anal-compulsives or bourgeois decadents.

By contrast the Anglo-American scholars, such as my own critic, try to concentrate on an autonomous object of study, focusing on what is physically present in the object or can at least be scientifically validated as implicit in the object. Their wish is to correct ideological distortion by filtering out all ways of thinking that do not lend themselves to scientific proof, including any ideological biases of their own, and thereby getting to something, however narrowly defined, that can be called true. In a sense, then, the empiricist, like the Continentalist, distinguishes between levels of potential meaning. But I would argue that the empiricists' purpose is not to distinguish in order then to construct a more significant interrelationship of meanings, but rather to distinguish to the point of severing an essentially scientific level of meaning from all others. Thus they put themselves in a position where they need not face the scientific uncertainty of relating music to ideological levels of meaning, conscious or unconscious, or of constructing unverifiable patterns of interrelation, such as a theory of history. Typically American musical scholars concern themselves with the physical components of the score, in particular with restoring the musical text to its original form; and the outside information drawn upon—notation systems, watermarks, performance practice, matters of religious custom and provenance—bears directly on this task of restoration. Anglo-American scholars, in fact, tend to regard all scores as autonomous objects, even those that date from cultures that preceded the modern Western conception of the artwork as autonomous, cultures that more or less openly viewed art as part of a more comprehensive ideological whole. In short, whereas Continentalists may theorize about contexts to the point of rejecting the autonomy of the composition, denying its meaningfulness or even distorting its significance to serve unrelated ideological ends, empiricists may remove virtually everything from serious consideration except what they take to be the musical structure. The legendary pinholes once used at Princeton for musicological observation provide a symbol of this tendency at its extreme.[2]

Each approach has strengths and weaknesses to which I shall return. At this point I should like merely to point out that the Continentalist method of approach is likely to require some attention to the problem of musical autonomy, even if only to reject the notion, whereas empiricists may work for a lifetime without giving a single thought to ideological context, which lies beyond their scientifically defined domain of study. Continentalists may consciously suppress what differs from their ideology, whereas Anglo-Americans may never even recognize the possibility of valid differences from their way of looking at things because they are unconscious of having an ideology. And empiricists would vigorously deny the Continentalist assertion that their own anti-ideology is itself simply another ideology, a principle of conceptual selection with no privileged access to the truth. To the empiricist, as to the Newtonian scientist, on whose now-outdated worldview so much empiricist work is still based, anti-ideology is nothing less than the direct road to objective truth.

I am not certain about empiricist ideology, but I do believe that Continentalist ideology need not operate at its most extreme and dangerous poles. Adorno *does* seem to me to represent the Continentalist orientation in an especially flexible and encompassing state. For Adorno insists emphatically upon the need to consider a musical structure in its formal autonomy as well as in its relation to various ideological structures and contexts. Adorno's basic point is that if one takes the trouble to put oneself into the inner workings of a musical argument, or of any human utterance, and to follow it through to its conclusion, one will achieve some understanding of the rationale at work and will avoid rejecting that argument out of hand, *in toto*, as simply the symptom of a foreign ideology, without regard to its inner workings or validity. Thus, to take a crude example, if one understands completely the internal structural argument of *Pierrot Lunaire*—if, that is, one becomes a competent structural listener to the piece—then one will be less apt to reject the work on the grounds that Schoenberg was born a Jew. Up to this point the Anglo-American musicologist would agree, at least on a conscious level, with Adorno. The difference is that Adorno does not, finally, believe that

Schoenberg's Judaism is irrelevant either to the structuring of Schoenberg's music or to the way in which we receive that music. Hence Adorno, in his study of Schoenberg's musical structures, is always openly involved in an effort to relate those structures to Schoenberg's Judaism and to other ideological considerations.

In fact, there is really no denying that precisely because he refuses to rule out ideological considerations, Adorno does openly end by judging works on grounds that are more fundamentally ideological than structural. He can scarcely do otherwise since he is convinced that the internal structure of a composition does not exist in a vacuum but is integrally related to a composer's ideological assumptions, and that an immoral ideology inevitably produces artistic structures that must be considered flawed. This conviction leads him to make judgments that are often controversial, the most notorious, perhaps, being his scathing attack in *The Philosophy of Modern Music* on Stravinsky's work. Stravinsky, it seems clear, openly embraces an anti-ideology very similar to that of the Anglo-American empiricist; that is, he tries to remove all traces of German-Wagnerian metaphysics from his music, and to reduce the composition to a specimen of purely autonomous craft. This position Adorno interprets as a renunciation of the artist's responsibility to fashion a moral vision of reality and, consequently, as a position that is morally reprehensible. But for Adorno, a work based on an immoral ideology is necessarily an artistic failure as well, and, hence, Adorno cannot help but end by condemning Stravinsky's art.

This is a judgment that most of us in America, including myself, would not readily or fully accept. Yet it is important to point out that Adorno does not arrive at this judgment simply by reading up on Stravinsky's philosophy in the *Poetics of Music* and then condemning the music without examining it. On the contrary, Adorno devotes close to half of his book, *The Philosophy of Modern Music*, to Stravinsky's music. Indeed, though he never conceals his ideological starting point, Adorno would argue that he arrives at Stravinsky's ideology principally by way of the musical structures themselves. But of course, despite Adorno's dialectical insistence on having it both ways, this latter is an assertion we may well doubt: Adorno's very definition of Stravinsky's musical structures is quite clearly informed by a strong preexisting ideological bias.

But is Adorno's work on Stravinsky therefore fatally flawed and worthless? I would argue for two points of value in Adorno's method of criticism here. First, Adorno's grounds of rejection *are* based on an ideological predisposition, but at least the ideology involved is not hidden. It is explicit in virtually every sentence that Adorno writes and thus readily available for our own evaluation. However unsettling we may find Adorno's conflation of method and object, we are not left to shadow-box with ideological convictions that Adorno claims aren't there. And second, however much Adorno doubts the absolute existence of autonomous musical structure or dislikes Stravinsky's musical structures in particular, he does not ignore the latter but directs considerable attention to their internal workings. In fact, Adorno devotes to those structures a large-scale and carefully constructed argument that we can judge, to some extent, on its own internal merit, and that, more important, allows us, even if we do finally reject it on ideological grounds, to think about Stravinsky's music on a number of levels, including humanistic levels of meaning and significance. Charles Rosen, definitely no champion of Adorno, has asserted that Adorno gets at important things in Stravinsky's music that have otherwise been missed entirely.[3] To be sure, Adorno himself makes little effort to understand Stravinsky's musical structures in any but a negative way. Nevertheless, by including those structures within the range of his study, Adorno at least provides a possible model for a procedure that the empiricist, I fear, honors considerably less often in practice than in theory: the procedure of trying to understand an ideologically unappealing construct on its own structural terms before condemning it.

Adorno's negative evaluation of Wagner's music is another controversial judgment that helps to clarify the problems involved in making ideological judgments. With respect to Wagner, Adorno argues, in essence, that a fundamentally and even openly immoral ideology produces artistically limited compositions. Now, on the whole, Wagner's position in the Western musical pantheon is even more secure today than Stravinsky's, and yet I would guess that for most of us in musicology there is somewhere a gnawing suspicion that Adorno is onto something in the case of Wagner, something unscientific and yet true, which the empiricist approach cannot quite dare to consider.

Let me elaborate. Suppose Wagner were a young composer coming up for tenure at a major American university today, and that he had, for example, voiced the same sorts of ideas about American blacks as the actual Wagner did about Jews. Wouldn't there at least be some of us who were disposed to feel that no amount of craft could be sufficient to overcome the negative force of such an ideology, and even that the music produced by a mind espousing such an ideology must in some sense be a flawed human vision? Wouldn't some of us be grateful for the development of rigorous critical methods that allowed us to investigate, in a spirit of fairness, the relationship between the ideology and the craft, and to expose for serious examination any instincts we may have about the *human* truth of art?

Still, most of us who have been brought up on American ideals of free speech would be very uncomfortable about rejecting Richard Junior on ideological grounds; so if we could not overcome our gut inability to contemplate his company in our department for the next thirty years, we would probably try to base our rejection exclusively on some incompetence we managed to discern in his musical structures. Like Adorno in the case of Stravinsky, we would focus our criticism on the musical structures themselves; but we would be far less candid than Adorno in calling attention to the role that our *own* ideologies played in our definition of those musical structures.

But how could such a fundamentally dishonest judgment, in the name of academic freedom, serve the pursuit of truth? Wouldn't the notion of truth, even of scientifically objective truth, be far better served by an open admission that one's department could not provide support for an art based on an explicitly antihuman ideology? Are there not ideologies that rationally demand rejection? And are there not ancient precedents for the view that artistic utterance involves not only craft but also ideology and even moral value?

Mind you, I am not arguing for the justice of rejecting all utterances on purely ideological grounds. Far from it. Any argument that serves even plausibly moral ends *should* be judged, as far as possible, on its internal merits. But note the proviso "as far as possible." My assertion is that ideological values contribute inevitably and fundamentally to the structural definition of human utterance, even musical utterance, as well as to the understanding and judgment of utterance, even aesthetic judgment, and thus cannot, finally, be ignored with any honesty. Unfortunately most ideological rejections, Continentalist or empiricist, are directed not at what is morally repugnant to a judge but simply at what the judge finds unfamiliar or different. This latter is not the sort of standard to which most of us would willingly confess, but clearly it poses a danger to which ideological rejections that deny their own ideological character are particularly prone. To protect ourselves from judging unfairly on undiscriminating ideological instinct, we must first recognize the degree to which ideology does inform our judgments. And once we concede this recognition, we must sooner or later be prepared to define rational limits for our ideological judgments, or, if you will, for our ideological intolerance. I submit that such limits should be defined in moral terms—and in moral terms only.

But what is plausibly moral? The Anglo-American principle of free speech works on the modern assumption that moral standards are a matter of variable, subjective discretion, and that allowing discretion to operate in the arena of free speech opens the way to suppression of that freedom by irrationalist and inhumane ideologies. This, as exemplified by the First Amendment, is a general principle that cannot easily take into account individual exceptions;[4] and in the running of any social group that is bigger than a community, it is probably the most moral possible principle in terms of its effect on most individuals. Even in the era of *glasnost*, I would rather live in the United States than in Soviet Russia. But it is not a principle without its rational and moral limits. It is, for example, a principle that is powerless to prevent the moral repugnance of a Nazi march in Skokie, Illinois, where many Holocaust survivors live, because it is a principle that does not admit much discretion by or about individuals.

American musicology, like America generally, for all its ethos of rugged individualism, operates most comfortably through reference to general systems of laws, of which free speech, government by law rather than "men," and majority rule are one sort of example, and Newtonian science is another. (It can scarcely be an accident, by the way, that the free-enterprise system found its premier cultural expression in science; nor should it be doubted that affirmative action on the one hand and the threat of nuclear extinction on the other represent moral limits of the traditional American ideology.) But is American musicology really comparable to a political entity or even to a scientific discipline? Must it resort to such rigidly general, nondiscriminating standards of rationality to protect itself from an inhumane irrationality? Can it not trust itself to have some capacity for moral discretion? Is this discipline not, or should it not be, more like a community, a community with the intellectual and moral capacity to act in good faith, a community in which the risks of rampant irrationalism can be counterbalanced through the development of specifically humanistic standards of rationality that are no less intellectually rigorous than scientific standards but yet permit the humane exercise of discretion?[5] And indeed, is the study of Western music, as it is currently constituted at most American universities, really as conducive as it could be to either the exercise of free speech or the pursuit of truth?

I would argue that in fact Anglo-American musicology today is not a field open to all morally justifiable opinions or even to a wide spectrum of such opinions. It is, rather, a highly exclusionary system that defines its field of study and chooses its practitioners on grounds that are at bottom no less ideological than the grounds of Continentalist scholars; and, again, the empiricist ideology is in one sense more dangerous because it is not acknowledged as an ideology. American musicology today is also a highly normative system in the sense that it excludes from consideration virtually all music that does not fit into the canons of Western art music. I once asked a fellow musicologist if he could think of a single other humanistic discipline at our university that failed utterly to consider non-Western culture. After some thought he replied, "Yes, English." The system of norms that is involved, I might add, is on the whole rigid, and open to little exercise of individual discretion. Adorno may be criticized as a biased judge, but questions of value, being nonscientific and ideological, rarely come up at all in the current empiricist study of Western music. Minor composers are taught alongside major ones as part of a common art tradition, but there are today few rigorous attempts to account for differences in value and still fewer to revise received judgments. A senior colleague once strongly suggested that I delete from an article the suggestion that Beethoven may have failed in the Finale of the Ninth Symphony, a view not without its partisans, even among earlier, less scientific English-speaking critics, such as Vaughan Williams.[6]

Furthermore, American musicology has remarkably little tolerance for divergent schools of thought, least of all for Continentalist schools, even ones that cannot readily be dismissed as morally repugnant. It seldom troubles to master the vocabulary, much less the premises, of unfamiliar schools of thought. (I know a doctoral student who was once advised to delete references to structuralism from her dissertation because the faculty didn't have time to learn the unfamiliar terminology of the movement.) But what good is freedom of thought if it amounts to nothing more than a freedom to refuse to understand? Theoretically, Continentalist approaches are as welcome in the American musicological program as studies of non-Western music are. Doesn't the actual scarcity of both belie an ideological judgment that precludes attempts at understanding the inner workings of an unfamiliar structure?[7] American musicology is excellent at pursuing those kinds of truth that lend themselves to the scientific model of verification, which asks whether something is right or wrong. It is far less good at grappling with those humanistic sorts of truth that do not lend themselves to a single standard but that inevitably evoke large numbers of divergent interpretations, no one of which can consider itself privileged or complete. And within itself the Anglo-American study of music, as it is currently constituted, risks relatively little in intellectual terms and gains relatively little. One is more apt to hear the word "courage" applied to a scholar who challenges the accepted dating of a masterpiece than to one who speculates on new sorts of possible human meanings or evaluations of that work. In short, I would argue that despite its assertions to the contrary, mainstream American musicology today, no less than its Continentalist counterparts, makes its judgments and selections very largely on ideological grounds, but that in contrast to the work of a first-rate Continentalist such as Adorno, empiricist musicology does not make its own ideological biases explicit, that it seldom gives serious attention to constructs which it ultimately rejects, and that it tends to narrow rather than broaden its field of study wherever possible, thereby excluding considerations of meaning and denying itself a specifically humanistic value.

Again, it seems clear that each approach to the study of music has its ideological biases that make for relative strengths and weaknesses. One would think that a healthy academic structure would allow for the cultivation of both approaches, but is this really possible? Doesn't such a possibility in fact depend on which ideology is at bottom the controlling one, and on whether the fundamentally controlling ideology can, without negating itself, accommodate a viewpoint that is diametrically opposed to it? And can either of these particular approaches to study actually accommodate the other?

Obviously both approaches are in some sense exclusionary. The Continentalist tends to reject contrary ideologies, the empiricist not to recognize them. But a case could be made, I think, that the Continentalists incline toward inclusiveness rather than exclusiveness, and that the exclusionary effect of the Continentalist is, or at least can be, mitigated to the extent that Continentalism resembles a traditionally Catholic as opposed to Protestant worldview. By this I mean that the Continentalist, in Catholic fashion, is more likely to allow for some awareness of the ideologies it rejects and to encompass a place, however lowly, depised, or even hellish, for those ideologies in its worldview; whereas the Anglo-American mode of thought, in traditional Protestant fashion, allows for freedom and equality of thought, but only within a very narrow range of the Elect, and simply disregards the human remainder.[8] Of course, the Continentalist can be linked more openly with oppressive political ideologies. Yet there is also a point beyond which excluding all nonscientific ideologies as a protection against irrationalism can itself become irrational. Adorno is not altogether wrong, at least in the academic realm, when he characterizes the opposition of rigid empiricism to Continentalism as terrorism.[9]

And again, I would argue that most judgments of human utterance are made more on contextual grounds that clearly require the exercise of discretion—such as congeniality of style, ambiance, or association, or even confidence of delivery—than they are on grounds of the internal structural logic of an utterance. I believe this is the case whether the utterance in question is a musical work, a musicological study, a movie, an advertisement, a political speech, perhaps even a courtroom statement. Indeed, a well-regarded scientist, who is himself certainly an empiricist, told me recently that because the data in a scientific lecture cannot be verified on the spot, reactions to such lectures, which sometimes determine academic appointments, depend fundamentally on the prior reputation of the speaker. No doubt he is right: How many journal articles, college term papers, or even musical compositions do we humanists really understand, much less assess, on grounds of purely internal logic, in an ideological vacuum, unmindful of the reputation of the writer, the journal, or the performing group that is involved? How many psychotherapists are in business because even between parents and a very young child a good deal more is communicated than the internal structure of the spoken sentence? Why has hermeneutics become such a hot specialty in so many humanistic disciplines (including European musicology)?[10] Why has the phrase "the medium is the message" become accepted as a truism in our culture?

Most utterances, I am saying, are judged, by Continentalist, empiricist, and average citizen alike, more fundamentally on grounds of ideology than on grounds of what is actually said or argued.[11] This may have its unfortunate aspects, though again, I myself feel certain that any assessment of the internal validity of an argument that failed to consider, in the best possible faith, the moral import of that utterance, would be a humanly false judgment. (Hitler's Nuremberg speeches may have had a perfect inner logic, but the listener who failed to use his or her discretion and to assess the morality or sanity of the source and purpose of those speeches would arrive at a very incomplete understanding of them.) Nevertheless, if we do think that an argument should be judged as much as possible on its own internal merits, in John Stuart Mill's impersonal free marketplace of ideas, without regard to any external context, and if, in spite of this conviction, we base our own judgments on grounds that are even partially ideological, then at least we must put ourselves in a position to recognize the tension between our ideals of artistic autonomy and our ideological actions. We should be able to distinguish between immoral and merely unfamiliar ideologies, thereby clearing the way for genuinely structural judgments; to identify all ideological judgments honestly; and, finally, to find ways of handling our own ideological baggage rationally. These things empiricism does not help us to do.

In my judgment, unrestricted empiricism poses a danger to free thought in its refusal to recognize its own anti-ideology—what Adorno calls its "boast of being value-free"[12]—as itself ideological. I would even argue that empiricism would eventually have to negate itself and become Continentalist if it were to allow complete freedom of thought because it would have to acknowledge its own ideological underpinnings and thereby, in effect, become Continentalist. On the other hand, empiricism is, at least nominally, committed in a way that Continentalism, despite its inclusiveness, is not to an ideal of equality of opinion. The problem is for empiricism to extend this ideal far enough to include genuinely divergent ideologies. Empiricism must be willing at least to tolerate attempts by other schools of thought to find rigorous and rational modes of exercising moral discretion, modes that need not threaten the empiricist's own healthy opposition to the authoritarian extremes of Continentalism.

Ultimately, we must probably acknowledge that the relationship between the empiricist and Continentalist approaches cannot be conclusively resolved in favor of either. What exists between the two amounts to an unresolvable tension, comparable to the dialectic that relates the autonomy of an artistic structure on the one hand to the inescapability of ideological values on the other. The best that can be done in any academic community or discipline is to work at maintaining the two approaches in a state of equilibrium, however uneasy. This is a task that requires constant discretion and self-criticism, but these should not be beyond the reach of a humanistic discipline. And in this task the discipline of ethnomusicology could have a particularly good effect on the study of Western art music. For even if their bias were completely empiricist, ethnomusicologists are almost forced by the scope of their study to confront the limitations of their own approach to truth and to acknowledge its status as unprivileged ideology. This is an awareness that needs to be communicated.

Chapter 2

Adorno's Diagnosis of Beethoven's Late Style: Early Symptom of a Fatal Condition

Modern music sees absolute oblivion as its goal. It is the surviving message of despair from the ship-wrecked."

T. W. *Adorno,* Philosophy of Modern Music

I

It is not altogether surprising that as late as 1975, American musicology still lacked a formal introduction, in its own journals, to the social and cultural criticism of the so-called Frankfurt School. Although the Institute for Social Research, around which the Frankfurt School originally centered, was founded in 1923, the first full-length American study of the School appeared only fifty years later, with the publication of *The Dialectical Imagination* (Boston, 1973) by Martin Jay. What is more surprising is that even though Mr. Jay's book has aroused considerable attention in other disciplines, American musicology has continued to show little interest in one particularly celebrated member of the Frankfurt School, Theodor W. Adorno (1903–69), an outstanding musical scholar, philosopher, and critic who developed some provocative theories of art: that Western art has tended toward increasing autonomy from society; that the more autonomous the work of art is, the more deeply it embodies the most profound social tendencies of its time; and that proper analysis can decipher the social meaning of artistic structure so as to criticize art and society simultaneously.

In defense of this discipline it must be admitted that unusual hardships face the American student of Adorno's musical writings. It is discouraging to reflect, for example, that the closest thing to a definitive exegesis of Adorno's music criticism seems to be Thomas Mann's highly complex *Doctor Faustus*, and that the requirements for thoroughly understanding the criticism probably differ little from those for writing the novel.[1]

Penetrating Adorno's written style seems almost to require the close personal collaboration with Adorno enjoyed by Mann during the writing of

Doctor Faustus, or at least Mann's creative gift, with its capacity to construct actively coherent synthesis out of voluminous stylistic and conceptual disarray. The capacity to synthesize is important on several grounds. First, Adorno's texts are really "antitexts":[2] concentrated, cryptic, and—like Beethoven's late style as Adorno conceives it—elliptical. Moreover, believing strongly that "objects" of study can have no meaning for the student apart from the processes of the latter's own consciousness, Adorno deliberately destroys the barrier between the content and the method of his study,[3] so that it becomes extraordinarily difficult to separate Adorno's opinions from what he is writing about. Similarly, rather than isolating objects of study from each other, Adorno insists upon understanding them in a multitude of relationships, so that each of his critical essays leads in many directions, and none exhausts Adorno's ideas on its ostensible topic. To illustrate this last set of problems more concretely, an inquiry into Adorno's conception of Beethoven's late style is complicated for a number of reasons: Adorno left only two essays dealing exclusively with Beethoven, an aphoristic essay on the late style and an essay on the *Missa Solemnis*;[4] the latter is the only detailed study Adorno left behind of any specific work by Beethoven, except for a brief analysis of Op. 111 in *Doctor Faustus*;[5] and it is impossible to understand Adorno's interpretation of the third-period style without examining his discussions of the second-period style, which are scattered in numerous essays and monographs. Such problems, together with Adorno's generally uncommunicative style, have forced the present writer, on a stage far more modest than Mann's, to play an unusually active role in inferring the interconnections and implications of Adorno's ideas. Consequently, this essay, like most about Adorno's writings, is in a nonsentimental sense highly personal, a condition that seems almost the unevadable consequence of the moral urgency attached by Adorno himself to the preservation of individuality.

But something of Mann's novelistic synthesis is not the only demand with which Adorno taxes the American reader. A firm grasp of Adorno's meaning also presupposes the traditional German sort of comprehensive humanistic education that permitted Mann to realize his encyclopedic novel. A degree of familiarity with the principal works of Kant, Hegel, Marx, Kierkegaard, and Husserl constitutes perhaps the barest essential for making sense out of Adorno's musical writings. And, finally, Mann was able to produce a discursive complement to Adorno's fragmentary criticism, at least in part, because the two men, as twentieth-century Germans, were driven by the same tormenting experience: a view from the inside of how an incomparably civilized intellectual heritage could lead with apparent continuity, and even necessity, to total barbarism. Although modern American history is not without disturbing anomalies of its own, probably few Americans can muster out of their own experience the sense of apocalyptic immediacy needed to appreciate fully the moral anguish behind Adorno's music criticism and Mann's novel alike. And yet it must be done, for Adorno's musical essays analyze music not merely as an organization of sounds but as an embodiment of truths perceived by human consciousness; and the purpose of his musical writings is to criticize not merely the technical workings of music but, above all, the human condition of the societies that give music life.

For the American musicologist interested in understanding Adorno's musical thought in spite of such difficulties, the logical place to start is with one of the two composers on whom Adorno's musical writing (like Mann's in *Doctor Faustus*) centers, Beethoven and Schoenberg. The choice between the two is almost immaterial, as each is implicit in Adorno's consideration of the other. Rather than studying one or the other in the traditional isolation of positivism, Adorno's reader must learn to regard both masters as part of a single historical movement, of which their respective music defines critical moments. This movement (which, in a sense, is the true protagonist of *Doctor Faustus*) is Western bourgeois humanism, understood as the dialectical unfolding in history of such essentially bourgeois creations as reason, enlightenment (mastery of nature), progress, dialectic itself, and most important, individual freedom.

From Adorno's perspective, the great achievement of human history took place during the bourgeois era, which in music he dates back approximately to Monteverdi.[6] This was the crystallization of reason and self-consciousness into the concept of the free individual, a self-conscious human being with the freedom to determine his or her own destiny, above all as Kant defined freedom, through the exercise of moral choice. From Adorno's Kantian-Hegelian viewpoint, this highest of all possible conceptions of the human could become a reality only through the coinciding of individual and social interests in a condition of human wholeness or integrity; and the latter, in turn, came close to realization at one unique moment in history, represented in music by Beethoven's second-period style.

Beethoven's late works, with the problematical (and perhaps only partial) exception of the Ninth Symphony,[7] signify for Adorno the irreversible bypassing of individual freedom as a possibility in concrete historical reality (which to a post-Hegelian like Adorno is the only ontological reality). And Schoenberg's music represents merely the inevitable last stages of a process that first became manifest in Beethoven's late style: the severing of subjective freedom from objective reality.[8] Implicit in Beethoven's late style, as Adorno analyzes it, is the eventual dissolution of all the values that made bourgeois humanism the hope of a human civilization.

The dissolution of bourgeois humanism has historical implications for

Adorno that vastly exceed the decline of a particular class to include the end of history and, since history means human history to Adorno, the end of humanity itself in any meaningful sense.[9] For Adorno's vocation to a humanistic discipline, criticism, clearly rests on a preoccupation with the concept "humanity" and a conviction that this concept retains meaning only so long as it can be used to designate a moral species.[10] But as a historical reality, "humanity," in this sense, is inseparable from bourgeois humanism for Adorno; he seems unable to imagine any alternative means to its historical realization. Neither can he imagine any further logical development of bourgeois humanism itself. Consequently, Schoenberg's music marks for Adorno the end of dynamic human development, that is, human history; and the whole history of music from Beethoven's late period to Schoenberg's represents at once the winding down of human history and a prolegomenon to the music of a posthistorical world, which as it continues to exist physically, Adorno considers to have entered into a meaningless ahistorical stasis.[11] Such posthistorical music, the music of our own time, must be considered the art of a posthuman species. There is no other way of interpreting such a remark as, "To write poetry after Auschwitz is barbaric."[12]

Adorno's attitude toward twentieth-century music has been called "the comfortable and aesthetically deliberate posture of the man glancing into the depths from the glass veranda of the Grand Hotel Abyss."[13] Actually, however, in the geography of Adorno's music history, the essential discontinuity is located not in the twentieth century but somewhere between Beethoven's second and third periods. For it is clear that "the landscape, abandoned now and estranged," which forms the concluding metaphor of Adorno's essay on Beethoven's late style,[14] lies not on the near but on the far side of any hope for a human future. It is a landscape that can be filled only with the remains of a fatally wounded humanity.

II

How can such a tragic reversal in human history be explained, and how does it show up in music, particularly in Beethoven's late work? Adorno's most direct answer to these questions, derived directly from Hegelian and Marxist traditions, lies in the character and impact of the "world-historical" events that occurred during Beethoven's lifetime: first the liberating force of the French Revolution was transformed by Napoleon into coercion; in turn, Napoleon's own demonstration of the individual's power to determine world history was terminated by the repression of organized collective opposition.[15] Events of such moment, according to Adorno, necessarily leave indirect traces in great art, which in Adorno's view is fundamentally concerned with what Georg Lukács has called the "defense of human integrity."[16]

Adorno opposes the narrowly formalistic view of art that dominates much Anglo-American music criticism, but he is equally vehement in rejecting the vulgar-Marxist idea that Beethoven, or any first-rank artist, transfers outward events, even world-historical events, into art in any direct manner. On the contrary, Adorno asserts that great art since the maturity of the bourgeois era (the only historical period that interests him) has been created by artists directly concerned not with society, whether the latter was favorable or unfavorable to them, but with the immanent problems of art.[17] Nevertheless, Adorno simultaneously maintains that the more rigorous the exclusiveness with which the artists devote themselves to such immanent problems, the more certain is the resulting art to embody, within its own structure, an artistic counterpart to the structure of external human affairs, or in other words, contemporaneous history and society.

The explanation of this apparent paradox seems to me to lie in an implicit assumption by Adorno of a dialectical relationship between form and freedom. According to such a conception, the two principles are at once fundamentally interdependent and mutually contradictory. Thus form is a principle extrinsic and even antithetical to the subjective freedom or individualistic fantasy characteristic of the imagination — even though form is simultaneously needed to give actual objective existence to the contents of the imagination. In terms of Adorno's philosophy, to put it differently, form is an objective, not a subjective principle.

In more concrete terms, the fundamental elements of artistic form (by which in musical terms Adorno appears to mean both the physical aspects of sound configurations and the principles of organization that govern them) are ultimately derived not from the artist's own imagination but, unconsciously, from the formal categories and models of the historical world outside of the art work.[18] Through a complex process of mediation, which Adorno does not pretend to understand or elucidate adequately, a process involving the artist's early ways of perceiving reality (through childhood assimilation of societal structures) and the contemporaneous state of artistic materials, techniques, and technology (all, like form, stemming from outside the imagination), the essential tendencies of a given historical moment become translated into the formal aspects of great art.[19] Thus form, which appears to be an intrinsically artistic principle, at a deeper level of reality actually constitutes the social parameter of art. Adorno claims that through sensitive analysis, sociohistorical tendencies can be "read off" of the very structure of an art work; and, moreover, that it is precisely the social content thus embedded in artistic form that constitutes the ultimate significance of art.

According to Adorno's formulation of the relationship between art and society, the style of Beethoven's second period corresponds to an external reality that appeared exceptionally favorable to the possibility of dialectical synthesis.[20] In other words, historical conditions provided Beethoven with a basis for thinking of musical structure as a totality that could accommodate a concept (e.g., subject, individual, or freedom) and its opposite (object, society, or form) in a resolution that preserved the essence of each. More particularly, just as Hegel (born the same year as Beethoven) appeared to resolve, through his concept of the State, the contradictions between individual and general will that disturbed Kant's notion of freedom, so, too, Beethoven, in the second-period style, apparently found the musical means to reconcile the contradiction between subjective freedom and objective form, that is, to synthesize subjective and objective principles in the sort of wholeness or totality on which freedom depended for its survival. In the characteristic structures of this style, as Adorno understands it, "the musical individual (. . . being at times identical with the individual tone, at times with the 'theme' or with the part for the concert instrument) is able to develop from within itself and to organize the totality of the musical work from the inner dynamics of the participating elements."[21] What distinguishes such structures or movements, in short, is their apparent ability to derive the principle of formal organization not from any outside source but from within themselves, and thus to establish as a reality the musical analogue of the free individual, the "musical subject," which has mastered external constraint and dissent and determined its own destiny.

The general principle of form through which Beethoven's second-period subject asserts its freedom is what Adorno, borrowing a term from Schoenberg, calls "developing variation."[22] By this is meant a process whereby a musical element subjects itself to logical dynamic change while simultaneously retaining its original identity, thus overcoming the contradiction between identity and nonidentity. The most obvious embodiment of this principle occurs in the development and recapitulation of the sonata allegro, the structure Adorno considers essentially synonymous with the second-period style. Development is the process through which the musical subject demonstrates its self-generated powers as it "goes out," in dialectical terms, from itself into the generalizing world of Other or object—through which it demonstrates, in other words, its freedom in objective reality. The expansion of and focus upon the development section in Beethoven's second period signifies for Adorno the attainment of the musico-historical moment when individual freedom finally overtakes externally given order as the most manifest governing principle of objectively existing structures. The emphatic reassertion of self in Beethoven's recapitulation is equally important in the developing variation theory, for it is through the recapitulation that the subject demonstrates its power to return to itself, no matter how vigorously and far it has traveled into the world of object. In fact, the recapitulation seems to confirm the rational irresistibility of the subject's determination to return to itself, since it nearly always seems to emerge as the logical outcome and resolution of what has preceded. Thus through the recapitulation the subject seems not only to bring together within itself, but actually to derive from within itself, the principles of dynamic development (historical change) and fixed, eternal order (unchangeable identity) and to synthesize the two into a higher level of reality. Moreover, since the principle of developing variation can be extended to all aspects of Beethoven's second-period sonata movements, the latter seem to constitute genuine dialectical totalities, according to Adorno, reconciling force and counterforce, part and whole, self and other, freedom and order.

It is Adorno's claim that the content he extracts from the formal analysis of Beethoven's second-period style, namely, the reconcilability of dialectical opposites, represents an essential sociohistorical tendency of Beethoven's world. Crucial evidence in support of this claim is provided by the fact that the principle of reconcilability extended beyond the stylistic aspects of Beethoven's second-period music to the connection of that music with society. For if dialectical synthesis had any basis in ontological reality at this time, then the individual must have had the potential to establish, and even to embody, norms of general validity. And indeed, by the end of the second period, a large number of Beethoven's highly individualized musical configurations had been appropriated by a large public. This was not, Adorno insists, because Beethoven tried to please such a public, but because for a time his individual artistic interests and the artistic interests of society genuinely coincided.[23] The music of Beethoven's second period effected a momentary reconciliation not only between Beethoven and society but also, on a broader level, between the particular or concrete (the individual human) and the general or abstract (the social human or even humanity as a historical species); and the persona within the music was accorded the status of a collective persona or "universal subject"—the musical equivalent of world-historical individual.

It should be noted that Adorno never asserts that dialectical synthesis was in fact achieved by society in Beethoven's lifetime (or at any other time). What he does contend is that the possibility of such a synthesis was a reality at this time, at least enough of a reality to suggest its own conceptual categories of form to the artist's imagination. To the extent that Beethoven's second-period work attains an actual synthesis, it is utopian, ahead of its time, and more nearly whole than contemporaneous society.[24] This difference between simultaneously existing art and society represents what Adorno considers the critical function of art:[25] by making manifest its own dynamic effect of harmonious totality, Beethoven's second-period style calls attention by contrast to the ongoing lack of wholeness or integrity in the human condition. Again, what Adorno has most in mind here is that division, diagnosed by Kant, between the individual and general or social aspects of humanity which sooner or later turns human freedom into an illusion. Adorno appears to believe that, critical though it was of society, the second-period style could gain social acceptance with relative ease both because it answered a generally felt need for the right to individual self-assertion and because its own universal character seemed to promise that a synthesis of individual and society could actually be achieved.

In reality, however, at least in Adorno's judgment, the synthesis prefigured in Beethoven's second-period style turned out to be an impossibility. The third-period style, according to Adorno, clearly acknowledges this ultimate reality and is, for this reason, the most realistic of Beethoven's styles.[26] By the last period, as Adorno understands it, Beethoven "sees through the classical [i.e., with its promise of synthesis] as the classicistic [i.e., with its illusion that such a promise could ever be kept]."[27] Adorno interprets the third-period style as a critique of the second-period one.

Adorno does not believe that the beginnings of this critique appeared only in the late style. Rather, he holds the dialectical belief that any historical concept contains within itself the foundations of its own negation. He asserts that Beethoven was already questioning the principle of synthesis from within the second-period style, and thereby raising the possibility that this principle was illusory at the very moment when it appeared most real. Adorno tries to establish this conclusion not by singling out chronologically early instances of the third-period style, such as Op. 102, but rather by locating what he calls "negative moments" or "resistances" in the second-period style at precisely its most characteristic.[28] Principal among these are the exaggerated assertiveness of the development and recapitulation procedures, in which Adorno discerns not only the incipient transformation of freedom into force but, even more pertinent, self-doubt on the part of the musical subject with respect to the potency of its own freedom, a suspicion that the limitlessness implicit in freedom is incompatible with form, and that any apparent coincidence of freedom and form represents less of a synthesis than a momentary stalemate.

What Beethoven is beginning to sense in the second-period style, according to Adorno's analysis, is that individual freedom is an illusion, or at least a problem. Even Beethoven's second-period subject cannot completely establish as an objective reality its power to derive the objective principle of formal organization from itself. Up to a point it may appear to do so. But the principle of reprise, for example, arises from no logical necessity within the subject; and overemphasizing the return of the subject to itself only calls attention to the contingency of reconciliation, indeed of destiny itself, and to the ultimate heteronomy of the subject, that is, its dependence on an externally imposed authority.[29]

Adorno seems to argue that Beethoven's second-period style represented the final collapse of the old, predialectical model of structure, a fixed metaphysical order based on an absolute First Principle, in favor of a new principle, the determination of form by the individual self moving in historical time. At the same time, however, according to Adorno's argument, the autonomy of the free individual was already in doubt. But God and self were the only conceivable sources of form as a rational principle. With both eliminated, the individual would find itself subject to an external reality (the source of form) that was characterized by contingency, or in other words was essentially irrational. The musical subject — a creation of bourgeois rationality — naturally recoiled before such a prospect and defended its appearance of self-control with vehemence. But this appearance was no less an illusion, in Adorno's judgment, than Kant's attempt to derive the objective categories, such as moral law, from within human subjectivity.[30]

For Kant could not prove the existence of moral law as a logical necessity; he could only assert it as emphatically as possible on the basis of subjective feelings. In the same way, says Adorno, the exaggerated propulsiveness of Beethoven's development belies the illusion that part and whole can coexist freely in his sonata movements. Ostensibly, the grinding down of materials through the developmental process, together with the friction of materials at different points in the form, suggests that individual elements can be integrated into a totality without losing their own integrity. In fact, however, according to Adorno, just as the work of society ultimately requires the sacrifice of individuality, so too Beethoven's development tends to wear down its engendering material — the musical subject — to the point where the latter negates itself entirely in the service of the larger entity.[31] Unlimited development, in other words, turns freedom into enslavement. Furthermore, the musical subject can only assert the necessity of its own endurance through the recapitulation; and the more uncontrolled developmental freedom becomes, the more arbitrary is the restraining effect of the recapitulation. Thus Beethoven was no more able than Kant to guarantee either individual freedom or the reconcilability of individual and society as necessary objective realities.

And yet, there is no question for Adorno that Beethoven's second-period style is able to go beyond Kant's dualism of individual and general and to postulate a Hegelian synthesis of the two. This involves no contradiction, for Adorno finds precisely the same element of self-negation in Hegel's synthesizing concept of the State as he does in Beethoven's second-period sonata allegro.[32] But the formal model to which both correspond, according to Adorno, is ultimately bourgeois society, which cannot itself decisively overcome Kant's dualism in reality. Hence, neither the Hegelian nor the Beethovenian synthesis of Kant's antinomies is sustainable. Though both temporarily supersede Kant, in each is already discernible the dissolution of synthesis back into its contradictory components.

III

Adorno does not go so far as to call the second-period style negative in effect. The approximation of a synthesis, however precarious, allows art to criticize the imperfections of the world through a fullness of its own means. This process affirms not only the natural tendency of art toward wholeness[33] but also a belief in possible human wholeness; it affirms not only the physicality of art but also the historical and social concreteness of reality. But authentic art could approximate the condition of synthesis only as long as the latter appeared to have any basis in objective reality. By Beethoven's last decade, the predominant characteristic of external reality, at least in Adorno's view, had become precisely the irreconcilability of subject and object, and above all, of individual freedom and social order.

For Beethoven to keep creating powerful illusions of synthesis, as if the latter were a *fait accompli*, in the knowledge that synthesis was after all not possible, would have meant falsifying the nature of existing reality and weakening individual understanding of what is true. At the same time, it would have compromised Beethoven's own understanding of reality and thereby helped to destroy the subjective freedom on which imaginative freedom is predicated. In short, if Beethoven's style had maintained its affirmative character in the third period, giving no sign of the irreconcilable dichotomies now perceptible as fundamental to reality, his music would have become what Adorno calls "ideology": its surface (appearance) would have belied the essential character of reality, and it would have contributed to the preservation of a "false consciousness," which served not human integrity and freedom but an oppressive world. His music would have lost its status as authentic art, which, by Adorno's definition, is always a criticism of society, protesting those conditions of the outside world that dehumanize humanity.[34]

What this meant was that beginning with Beethoven's third period, authentic music had to become in effect a "double negation." In the second-period style, when individual and general needs appeared to coincide, authentic music could maintain an affirmative character and still criticize society. Now to be authentic music must become explicitly negative. Henceforth the artifacts of "affirmative culture" directly affirmed repressive social arrangements; only "negative culture" could defend human freedom. To retain their status as authentic art, the works of Beethoven's late style had to replace synthesis as their formal content with the impossibility of synthesis; their aesthetic content had to become the impossibility of aesthetic wholeness and harmony. By exposing some irreconcilable dichotomy within itself, Beethoven's late music could call attention to the concurrent external disintegration of human integrity, to the enslaving, dehumanizing compartmentalization (for example, into individual and social identities) forced upon humans by society.[35]

The crux of Adorno's aesthetic theory is that the degree of social reality embedded in art is directly proportional to the conceptual autonomy of art; and there does seem to be good reason to suppose that the negative criticism of society can best be carried out entirely within the realm of a given art, without any direct imitation of the external reality being criticized. For in a world where individual and social interests are irreconcilable and where general harmony can be obtained only at the expense of individual freedom, the subject dares not risk any sort of direct confrontation with society, whose powers are superior to its own. Under such conditions, Adorno argues, the only protest left to authentic art is withdrawal from society; for art such as Beethoven's late work to preserve its critical force and protect the musical (i.e., human) subject, the artist must sever, as cleanly as possible, the overt connections between his or her art and society. Artists must actively resist designing (or ultimately even permitting) their art to please existing society or to serve it in any way.[36] Aware of their inability to satisfy both themselves and society, they must fashion their art more singlemindedly than ever before to the specifications of their own imaginations, deriving from the latter both their rules of procedure and their criteria of artistic success. Their art must become consciously and implacably autonomous.

But, as the last sentence may already suggest, this entails a paradox. To begin with, dissociating the individual and social aspects of humanity eventually hollows out any universality from the concept of the individual and reduces the latter to a narrowly personal, isolated, and, in the philosophical sense, "accidental" existence.[37] It splits human wholeness in two, thereby, according to Kant, rendering the individual impotent to protect its own free-dom. Assuming Kant is right, as Adorno does, it follows that the first con-cern of the individual who becomes conscious of his or her own loss of con-nection with society will be to reestablish that connection. Thus, in authentic art, which is dedicated to preserving the free individual, sooner or later the musical subject, however forcefully it appears to develop or determine its own course, will require corroboration of its own free existence from the outside world; it will, that is, try to break through the helplessness of its own isolation by enlisting support from the far more powerful principles of objec-tive reality.[38] Furthermore, for art to become absolutely autonomous, it must be able to expand infinitely the principle of self-determination set forth in Beethoven's second-period style. But even the second-period subject sus-pects limits to its own autonomy. The third-period subject, distinguished by its unqualified realism, has no choice but to reject the notion of its own au-tonomy as an illusion. Hence the paradox: to retain its authenticity, as defined by Adorno, Beethoven's late work must embody simultaneously the principles of autonomy and heteronomy. How could this be done?

Adorno's answer involves a reformulation of the relationship between subject and object that reflects their irreconcilability: to avoid violating its own autonomy, the musical subject had to give up its own place in music by yielding to — or, in effect, taking on — the formal characteristics of objective reality.[39] For subjective freedom and objective form were antithetical, in-deed, contradictory principles; therefore, by increasing the explicitly formal character of music, the subject could acknowledge its own underlying de-pendence on a foreign source of authority, objectivity, without ever going beyond the autonomous processes of musical construction. In other words, in order to satisfy its own craving for objective corroboration, the subject could use purely musical techniques to create structures inimical to the ex-pression of subjective freedom or individuality, for these would most closely approximate the character of the objective reality in which all form ulti-mately originates.

This meant that to protect itself from direct contact with objectivity, the subject had to abandon the place once reserved for the direct expression of subjective fantasy in music to objective forms; in brief, the musical subject had to remove its physical presence from the music. In a sense, the subject still "went out" into the world of object as it did in the second-period style; but now the subject could neither derive the objective, even ostensibly, out of itself nor return to itself in a state of reconciliation with the objective. Whether it tried to banish all evidence of the objective or enter into a genuine synthesis with the latter, the musical subject could no longer assure its own objective survival. The only remaining way for the musical subject to preserve its own integrity was to flee—away from, behind, or even straight through the formal arrangements that now constituted the characteristic physical appearance of music.[40] Thus, in the music of Beethoven's third-period style, according to Adorno, the musical subject seldom showed or expressed itself directly.

Adorno is not suggesting that the subject disappeared without a trace in Beethoven's late style. For history, in the dialectical view, is irreversible, and with Beethoven's second-period style, the consciousness of subject had entered irrevocably into music history. Thereafter, the very absence of a subject from a musical configuration necessarily constituted an integral component of that configuration. If the subject was not present, it would be missed; and it was in this way, through negating itself, that the subject maintained its identity in Beethoven's last style.

Thus, in Adorno's view, Beethoven's late style comprised, in an unreconciled state, the conditions of both artistic autonomy and artistic heteronomy. On the one hand, the musical subject maintained its autonomy by pulling away from objective social reality at all levels of composition. On the other hand, musical autonomy had been created by and for the subject as an instrument of the latter's own individual expression; musical autonomy became an issue only as the artist became conscious of his or her own individuality. But what the musical subject now fashioned, in Beethoven's third-period work, was a kind of structure that by virtue of its explicitly objective character pointed away from the subjective freedom of expression that had made artistic autonomy seem possible to the external origins of artistic form. To put it concisely, the authentic musical subject of Beethoven's third-period style exercised its autonomy to create configurations that acknowledged its inescapable heteronomy.

This highly complex interpretation of Beethoven's late style becomes a bit less formidable when it is illustrated more concretely through music. When Adorno speaks of the subject's taking on the formal characteristics of objective reality, he seems to have two particular characteristics in mind: collectivity and force. For Adorno, the most straightforward musical embodiment of a collective arrangement seems to be, on both historical and physical grounds, counterpoint.[41] Counterpoint is a technique derived from societies that antedated the birth of the subject-object duality and subjective expression, that is, collective societies. Although both Adorno and Mann stress the value of salvaging "primitive" human vitality from the repression of more recent, "civilizing" forms, both are also deeply disturbed by the concomitantly "barbaric" aspect of preindividualistic, pre-Enlightenment cultural phenomena, such as counterpoint.[42] Still, to the extent that counterpoint physically allows the coexistence of genuinely discrete entities—potential subjects—it appears to offer the most promising human possibilities of collective expression and discipline. Indeed, one of the weaknesses Adorno discerns in Beethoven's second-period style (especially in the symphonies) is a neglect of the collective potentiality and responsibilities of counterpoint in favor of the domineering individualism of homophony.[43] For most homophony, in Adorno's opinion, turns out to be merely the extension of one subject: its polyphonic diversity is an illusion as is its very harmony, since the latter is achieved only through the oppression by one subject of all others.[44] (The homophony of Beethoven's third period constitutes something of an exception, as will be seen.)

As a historical phenomenon, of course, counterpoint was only one example of what might be called the collectivity of archaism. The music of older, predialectical societies was a useful source of collective configurations because, at least in Adorno's judgment, it was a general mode of expression, that is, it offered little opportunity for musical individualization. The *Missa Solemnis* took extreme advantage of this characteristic, using archaic devices, according to Adorno, to bar all entrance to musical subjectivity, to negate virtually every characteristic of Beethoven's own earlier style, and to embody the total alienation of Beethoven from his own work.[45] What Adorno finds particularly striking in the *Missa Solemnis* is the replacement of sharply profiled ("specific") sonata-like or fugal subjects and dynamic developmental movement with nonmotivic counterpoint and an additive linking of static segments, more to be expected, Adorno notes rather imprecisely, in mid-fifteenth-century Netherlands polyphony.[46] In Adorno's view, the treatment of archaic materials in this work entails so much stylization that the massive sonority, which might otherwise exclude the *Missa* from Adorno's conception of the late style, loses any semblance of sensuousness;[47] the physical surface becomes abstract arrangement. Adorno emphasizes, however, that the impersonality or collectivity in no way belongs to the fifteenth century, for this quality in Beethoven's work is highly self-conscious, chosen by a subject.[48] Nevertheless, with but rare exceptions, the idea of "subject" in the *Missa Solemnis*—the humanistic aspect of the work, in Adorno's terms—retains its presence and expressiveness only in the poignance of the subject's need to withdraw itself and retreat behind the collective character and significance of an archaistic surface.[49]

Archaic techniques were only one means for representing the generalization characteristic of collective formal arrangements; the same quality was manifest in any sort of stylized configuration, such as the convention. Adorno attaches particular significance to the heightened role of convention (for example, the trill, cadenza, and other ornaments, the accompanimental bass pattern, and the simple V-I cadence) as a distinguishing element in

Beethoven's late style. Convention signifies for Adorno the impervious, unyielding, or, to use Nietzsche's term, the *immergleich* aspect of external reality, that aspect which the subject cannot alter, obscure, or efface, even through the creation of an artistic surface. In the second-period style, according to Adorno, conventions were generally swept away or engulfed by the individualized, subjective flow of development.[50] But the third-period subject, Adorno suggests, sees through its own developmental omnipotence as nothing but an arbitrary, externally derived convention; and the explicit return to prominence in the third-period style of the convention proper constitutes clear evidence for Adorno that the subject has entered into, and therefore abdicated to, the superior force of external reality. The subject has not only failed to assimilate convention, a collective invention, into the individual artistic fantasy, instead allowing "bald," recurring conventions to break apart the smooth harmony of the artistic facade. It has also declared its impotence before all objective reality, nature as well as society, and thus defined itself by acknowledging indirectly its own death.[51]

Paradoxically, the subject is not altogether without power over convention in Adorno's theory. Conventions are a collective or general technique because they have a generally understood formal significance that remains constant from work to work. By focusing particular attention on such a generalized device, the subject necessarily alters that significance. In so doing, the subject does not merely question the existence of any absolute order or meaning, but it actually demands that what appears to be fixed and objective be understood in terms of a particular, subjectively determined purpose.[52] Nevertheless, if convention is now assigned its meaning by the subject, that meaning consists in nothing other than the confirmation of the superior force of objectivity. For the subject can now give expression to its own existence only indirectly, through the rigid, inexpressive face of convention. Even the arbitrariness with which the subject wrenches convention out of its obscurity reflects the subject's deference to the objective, since arbitrariness is not characteristic of a rational subject but is rather a facet of force, the quality that, along with collectivity, Adorno's subject associates with objective reality.

Beethoven's third-period subject, as interpreted by Adorno, acknowledged its subservience to an objective reality that was no longer characterized by rational order but by irrational, indeed meaningless force.[53] Adorno seems to deduce this musically by observing that the formal organization in Beethoven's third-period style took on characteristics of force ranging from the repressive to the willful.[54] At one extreme, the subject, in its great anxiety to shield itself in rationality from irrational force, might bind itself to the logical necessity of strict procedures, such as fugue and canon.

In so doing, however, the subject would move toward denying itself any opportunity for free self-expression and thus voluntarily give up its freedom for what Adorno calls "unfreedom."[55] Ironically, even though the subject's "unfreedom" resulted from rational rules of its own making, the use of such rules could only simulate the objective existence of rationality; what it actually corroborated was the capacity of an irrational external reality to effect extreme coercion. Similarly, according to Adorno, the repressive potentialities of force were acknowledged in Beethoven's third-period style through the replacement of dynamic development with an explicit form of the principle once implicit in recapitulation: static, invariant — contingent and yet inexorable — repetition.[56]

At the other extreme, the willfulness of force was represented, above all, by the arbitrary juxtaposition, or even superimposition, of contrasting extremes.[57] In the latter one might include sonorities built from the outer ranges as well as the instructions for free rendition of the *Hammerklavier* fugue and (originally) the *Grosse Fuge*.[58] In the former, one might include abrupt dynamic contrasts as well as the interpenetration of sections of movements in strict (contrapuntal) and free (homophonic) style.[59] Interestingly, Adorno does not see this last as a contrast between "objective" and "subjective" styles in Beethoven's late work.[60] For what Adorno finds noteworthy about the third-period homophony is its inclination toward techniques that banish the physical presence of the subject; these appear to include unisons, hollow octaves, wide-spaced sonorities (instead of hierarchical, centered triads), static or stylized melodic lines, conventions generally, and nonpropulsive rhythms.[61]

Indeed, in the arbitrary confrontations of Beethoven's late style, Adorno seems to find the flight of the subject from willful force even more remarkable than the presence of willful force itself. Though no longer revealing itself physically in the self-unfolding of logical transitions, the third-period subject is nevertheless sensed acutely in the absence of a mediating center between extremes, in the escape of transitions from between colliding contradictions, and in the spaces, ruptures, and silences that individualize the late style, and above all the late quartets, for Adorno.[62]

From Adorno's viewpoint, at least, the relationship established in such ways between subject and object in the third-period style — to Adorno the most realistic of Beethoven's styles — was the only one congruent with the structure of external reality. Just as the latter no longer permitted synthesis, so, too, the late style could encompass subject and object only by insisting upon the mutual exclusiveness of their respective physical presences, and by presenting them locked in stalemate as irreconcilable antinomies.[63]

IV

Implicit in Adorno's interpretation of Beethoven's third-period style are numerous anomalies, of which only a few can be noted here, that Adorno believes become fully explicit in the work of twentieth-century artists such as Schoenberg. Adorno sees the history of art as the progression of art toward autonomy, that is, independence from society. Beethoven's late style signifies a critical point in that history for Adorno, for it constitutes the first musical acknowledgment that musical integrity cannot coexist in harmony with social usefulness, and that consequently music can retain its authenticity in the modern world only by diverging willfully from contemporary society and turning wholly inward.[64]

And yet, of course, even the late works maintained their existence in physical sound and form, the two concrete properties that essentially by definition for Adorno, connect music to external reality. Hence, the very fact of their physical existence exposed the apparent autonomy of these works as an illusion.[65] Furthermore, the vestiges of second-period totality were still strong enough, in Adorno's judgment, to provide a syntactical context for at least an early third-period work such as Op. 111, and most likely for all of Beethoven's late works.[66] And perhaps most significant, Adorno often implies that, within the framework of dichotomy made necessary by modern society, the best art generally has sufficient internal or conceptual integration to retain something of the utopian reference to synthesis characteristic of Beethoven's second-period style;[67] and there is a strong presumption that Adorno's conception of "the best" modern art includes Beethoven's late work. In short, even the third-period works, as Adorno interprets them, are open to the accusation of embodying illusions, the illusions of autonomy and synthesis. In fact, these works exhibit what Adorno calls the "wound" of all art:[68] the appearance of contributing, by virtue of merely existing, to the perpetuation of false consciousness, that is, to a lasting rupture between critical essence and affirmative or ideological appearance in art.

Now it follows from Adorno's theory that all art can, and virtually all art does, sooner or later become ideology because of its social impotence. Art, like any product of the individual consciousness, can at most change other individual consciousnesses, in Adorno's opinion, but never society itself.[69] Society, on the other hand, has only to assimilate art in order to rob it of its individuality, defuse its criticism, and thereby "neutralize" it into functioning socially, which means serving the dehumanizing purposes of society as ideology. There are many means available to society for wearing down the "resistances" through which art protests against society. Brilliant, glossy, "official" performances, for example, can smooth over any discontinuties that might jolt the listener into detailed concentration on musical structure.[70] Creation of a commercial vogue for esoteric art can turn artistic outrage into high fashion, for even if a work is not genuinely experienced or understood in its critical authenticity, the illusion (or the consistent pretense) of such comprehension is generally sufficient to neutralize the work indefinitely into a "culture good."[71] Music can also, of course, be appropriated to sell aspirin tablets. But even if attentiveness to the particularity of an art work is not numbed through some such abuse, eventually neutralization will usually be achieved simply through the passing of time and the growth of familiarity until once-disturbing novelties become unnoticed clichés.[72]

Nevertheless, Adorno makes a sharp distinction between art conceived as ideology—for example, art like Tchaikovsky's, which ingratiates itself with society by covering over all inner dichotomies with a smoothly sensuous surface—and art that was originally authentic.[73] (Otherwise he would be obliged to reject Beethoven altogether, since it is Adorno's judgment that nearly all of Beethoven's music, including the *Missa Solemnis*, has been neutralized.)[74] And he reserves particular artistic esteem for works that offer unusual resistance to neutralization, which unquestionably include, with the single painful exception of the Ninth Symphony, the works of Beethoven's last period.[75]

For art to have any chance of resisting neutralization, in Adorno's terms, it must alienate society by making itself difficult for society, as a collective entity, to understand. Stated another way, for the musical subject to preserve the essence of its individuality against social distortion, it must express itself through surface means that are not obviously expressive and that can be apprehended only by a few highly individualized listeners.[76] This means sacrificing the surface intelligibility of art (the intelligibility of what Adorno calls its "manifest structure") in order to retain the integrity of what Adorno calls the essence or "latent structure."[77] In a representational art, this can be done most easily by obscuring the correspondence of content, in the traditional sense, to external reality. In music, it requires interfering with the perception of coherence in structural and syntactical elements, something Beethoven's late style found many ways of doing. One might point, for example, to three sorts of perceptual obstacles posed by the prominent use of counterpoint: the physical difficulties of following several different lines simultaneously; the relative unfamiliarity of counterpoint in the early nineteenth century; and the unfamiliar character of Beethoven's counterpoint (e.g., in terms of harmony and sonority). Similarly, obscuring structural correspondences, as in the variation form, omitting transitions, and replacing propulsion toward a goal with static successions of sound all deprived listeners of techniques through which they customarily perceived musical connections over time. Certain familiar devices, such as conventions, lost the significative advantages of familiarity by being put to unconventional uses. Otherwise (and this is of great importance to Adorno's aesthetic theory), Beethoven's late style recognized the need of authentic art to avoid types of musical language already tainted through overexposure.[78] Beethoven was even willing to renounce techniques (say, motivic development) with which he had once defined his own musical identity in favor of unfamiliar devices, ranging from archaic modes to avant-garde dissonances. In all of these ways, Beethoven transformed the self-evidence of his second-period style into the enigma of what Adorno might have called his third-period "code."

The immediate consequence of Beethoven's resistance to neutralization was to start a divergence between structural coherence and intelligibility, which would one day become the abyss between the total organization of serialism and its general incomprehensibility.[79] According to Adorno, such a divergence was required to preserve the great gain of individuality, self-expression, for only through such a divergence could the musical subject give voice to the meaninglessness that became increasingly characteristic of the modern social world.[80] But social content, in Adorno's theory, is immanent in the structure of art. If a society cannot readily make sense of a musical structure, it is not likely to perceive the criticism of itself embodied in that structure. Thus the more general effect of Beethoven's resistance to neutralization was to open up an irreconcilable dichotomy between the ability to perceive and articulate social truth on the one hand, and to communicate it to society on the other.[81]

According to Adorno, then, Beethoven's third-period style marked the beginning of the modern world, that is, a reversal in the prospects for a fully human species, a reversal that made eloquent and effective social protest imperative in art; and yet, it was with this very style that the social impotence of the artist was established irrevocably. By the mid-twentieth century, the social criticism in any remaining authentic music would be as solipsistic in effect as Adorno's own cultural criticism; and artists fully sensitive to the social implications of their own ineffectiveness would, in Adorno's view, have few choices besides embracing insanity, as does Leverkühn in *Doctor Faustus*. Beethoven was not yet so close as Adorno and Mann to the apocalypse of humanity in Germany, but there can be little doubt that he sensed the historical peril of artistic communication. Adorno himself lays great stress on the plea with which Beethoven prefaced the *Missa Solemnis*, using it to characterize the entire work as "imploring." "From the heart—may it again go to the heart!" It is Adorno's suggestion that the very recourse to these words is an admission of their futility.[82]

It is not difficult to extend Adorno's suggestion to the introduction of words into the Ninth Symphony, and in this way, perhaps, readmit the Ninth into the orbit of the late style on terms Adorno could accept.[83] At one point, it is true, Adorno singles out the Ninth as an instance of social criticism that did not have to sacrifice communicability (although he probably overestimates its early popularity).[84] In general, however, Adorno places far more emphasis on the complete distortion of the Ninth by social usage.[85] The latter idea suggests that Beethoven not only failed to communicate the content of his last symphony but actually came very near to violating that content in the attempt to communicate it. According to such an interpretation, which follows the general direction of Adorno's thought, the content embedded in the Ninth Symphony, as in the rest of Beethoven's late work, has less in common with the *Ode to Joy* than with other words of Schiller's: "Wenn die Seele *spricht, / spricht, ach, die Seele* nicht mehr."

This particular discontinuity is by no means the only such anomaly implicit in the need of authentic art to resist neutralization. According to both Adorno and Mann, as more and more musical vocabulary becomes familiar to society, less and less uncorrupted language remains available to authentic music. Consequently, the latter will be characterized by more and more breaks in sound until it eventually falls silent altogether. Only then will authentic music be completely safe from neutralization.

Now, since avoidance of direct communication (resistance to neutralization) and protection of the musical subject from direct exposure are aspects of the same humanizing artistic purpose, the diagnosis of silence as the last refuge from neutralization converges with Adorno's interpretaion of the silences in Beethoven's late work as spaces left by the flight of the musical subject. Viewed as either refuge or flight, the discontinuities of the late style naturally tend to emaciate the physical robustness of Beethoven's music. Adorno believes this process signifies an acknowledgment within Beethoven's late style that for art to retain its authenticity or essence of truth, it must begin to cast off its own appearance, that is, to negate itself.[86] Adorno sees another sign of such an acknowledgment in what he considers the inconclusiveness of the cadences in the *Missa Solemnis*.[87] If art were to negate its own physicality, not only sound but form would have to disappear. Beginnings and endings would become increasingly indistinct until the very possibility of a simple, self-contained work became doubtful. Art would gradually escape from objects into a subjective process, leaving behind a trail of sketches (a term Adorno already applies to the *Missa Solemnis*), fragments, unfinished works, and eventually nothing more than written remnants unintended for, and indeed incapable of, physical realization.[88] Only in this way, again, could art guarantee its integrity absolutely against the deceptions and illusions built into physical existence.

Thus Beethoven's late style, according to Adorno's historical scheme, began to reveal the full implications of the double negation required of authentic music in modern times: to criticize existing objective reality, music had in Mann's words to "do penance" for its excessive "animal warmth" by rejecting its own physical existence. To protect its critical integrity as "negative culture," the music of Beethoven's late style was forced to embody the impossibility of aesthetic wholeness, which meant the impossibility of art itself. Implicit, then, in Beethoven's third-period style was the anomaly that the preservation of authentic art entailed an acceptance of the death-sentence pronounced over all art by Beethoven's contemporary, Hegel.

From these two examples — the loss of artistic intelligibility and the self-negation of art — it is not difficult to imagine still other anomalies that allow Adorno to see in Beethoven's late style the beginning of the end of humanity. Above all should be mentioned the musical subject's flight from or entry into musical collectivity. Both represent the anomalous need of music to destroy the objective existence of the musical subject (i.e., the free individual who alone, according to Adorno, is capable of creating and understanding authentic art) in order to "preserve" that subject.[89] Such paradoxes would seem to be the inescapable heritage of a social system, Hegel's bourgeois state, which in Adorno's judgment does not permit the survival of individual wholeness and freedom. It is important to recognize, however, that by "bourgeois" Adorno means any modern society based on what he sees as the fundamental economic traditions of the Enlightenment: the refinement of technology and the brutalization of nature.[90]

Adorno's musical essays, like all of his works, were written as passionate criticism of a society and world he considered inhuman. Yet, his ultimate understanding of this inhumanity seems to have been based not on political, sociological, or even psychological grounds but on something very like a theory of reality itself. This theory emphasizes the negative tendency of dialectics: that the essence of reality is historical change, that synthesis is a fixed condition that contradicts this essence, and that the governing principle of reality is the endless and irreversible negation of syntheses into the tension of dialectical contradictions.

To be sure, Adorno himself, who emphatically rejected metaphysics, scorned systematic theories in favor of unsystematized methods. And clearly his understanding of reality is inseparable from his own method of studying reality, a method that "has no choice but to affirm the notion and value of an ultimate synthesis, while negating its possibility and reality in every concrete case that comes before it."[91] Nevertheless, precisely his absolute consistency in negating syntheses indicates that Adorno's method, the so-called "negative dialectic," operated as a general theory of reality or ontology.[92]

Still, ontological reality for Adorno was historical reality, and consequently his own ontology has meaning only in terms of its concrete historical implications: that no condition or manifestation whatsoever of human wholeness (authentic art, rationality, freedom, or civilization) is sustainable; and that any such condition is necessarily, at the very moment when it seems to fix itself in objective reality, already giving way to its own dissolution. This means that in the nineteenth century, the identity of subject and object briefly prefigured by Beethoven and Hegel was unsupportable in objective reality;[93] eventually the interests of the two had to diverge.

But this divergence necessarily worked against the subject or individual, who was the far less powerful partner in such dialectical relationships. The individual could neither survive isolated, in opposition to society, nor, having become self-conscious, merge back into a collective structure without destroying his or her individual existence.[94] In terms of Adorno's philosophical outlook, the free individual—the glory of bourgeois humanism—never had a chance to survive, for such a being was an ontological impossibility. By the time the individual recognized the need to protect his or her own freedom through preserving his or her oneness with society, it was already too late, for the consciousness of individual freedom was based precisely on the sense of one's distinctness from the rest of society. Subjective freedom and objective form or existence could not be reconciled. In the very act of becoming conscious of its own freedom and individuality, the subject had already doomed itself to extinction.[95] The consciousness of musical autonomy had scarcely begun to develop (Beethoven's second-period style) when the impossibility of maintaining a society of free individuals, or a corresponding coincidence between artistic freedom and social will, became manifest (Beethoven's third-period style). The realization of self-expression in Beethoven's second-period style thus signified not only the triumphant birth but also the death warrant of the only fully human species conceivable to Adorno. Only in one deeply ironic sense could the identity between individual and general be maintained in the ensuing third-period style, where the indirect acknowledgment of Beethoven's own death as a particular human being converged with the prefiguration of the death of humanity itself.[96]

Adorno does not deny that the remains of human hope are still stronger in Beethoven's late work than they are in, say, Schoenberg's music.[97] Nevertheless, it is an implicitly hopeless ontology that directs Adorno to interpret the style change of Beethoven's third period as the inevitable, Kantian unraveling of a Hegelian synthesis. And yet, of course, Adorno is a post-Hegelian, not a pre-Hegelian; despite the common criticism that he cannot get beyond Kant,[98] it is not really Kant's antinomies Adorno sees in Beethoven's last style but something far more tragic. For although Kant could see no logical way of attaining the synthesis needed for human freedom, he could still assert that "what is necessary is possible." The significance Adorno derives from Beethoven's late work is precisely the opposite: what is humanly necessary is ontologically impossible. The dichotomy to which Adorno points in Beethoven's third-period style is not a Kantian duality, for which no synthesis is conceivable, but the remains of a synthesis, the vestiges of an individual human subject sorely aware of the wholeness, and consequently the survival, that has eluded it forever.

"The historical trace in things, words, colors, and tones," Adorno has written, "is always past sorrow."[99] The sorrow he detects in Beethoven's last style, where "failure [becomes] in a supreme sense the measure of success,"[100] is nothing less than the first historical acknowledgment in music of what is for Adorno the tragic essence of all reality: "The whole is the untrue."[101]

V

Shortly after the bicentennial anniversary of Beethoven's birth, Hans Eggebrecht, in a comprehensive survey of the critical literature about Beethoven's music, suggested that Adorno's interpretation represents the only semblance of a new direction in modern Beethoven criticism.[102] Quite naturally, the distinctiveness and passion of Adorno's music criticism has aroused heated opposition in many quarters. Because the present discussion is designed primarily as an introductory attempt at synthesis of the sort on which a substantial critique of Adorno's work can eventually be based, only a few of the grounds on which Adorno has provoked resistance will be indicated here. (As little attention has yet been given to Adorno's conception of Beethoven, what follows necessarily refers to Adorno's work in a more general sense.) On ideological grounds, for example, it should be noted that Adorno has been criticized for being a Marxist; for being a poor Marxist; for being a bourgeois reactionary and elitist; and for being intolerably fatalistic.[103]

Because of his horror of system (as an authoritarian concept) and his penchant for constant and sharp dialectical reversals, Adorno is particularly vulnerable to attack on the basis of internal inconsistencies in his argument, inconsistencies serious enough to keep most students of Adorno in a perpetual state of disagreement. His frequent references to the utopian function of art sometimes seem to contradict his own thoroughgoing fatalism, a fatalism that "permits up to the very end no consolation, appeasement, transfiguration."[104] Inconsistency can also be discerned in Adorno's attitude toward mimesis in art. His unequivocal denial that art directly imitates reality tends to overshadow the fact that the parallelism Adorno does posit between artistic structure and objective reality might just as well result from direct imitation as from the indirect, complex, unconscious, undocumented, and rather mysterious process of mediation Adorno describes. Indeed, Adorno arrives at very much the same notion of artistic content as Lukács does with a mimetic theory of art, that is, of artistic content as a reproduction of ontological reality.[105]

It is not clear, however, whether Adorno shares Lukács's conception of realism as a measure of quality; for despite its philosophical character, Adorno's music criticism is surprisingly ambiguous about evaluative criteria, and so is open to strong criticism of its aesthetic theory. The fact of Adorno's reverence for Beethoven's music is a good deal clearer than the grounds on which it rests. In the last sentence of the essay on the *Missa Solemnis*, Adorno suddenly refers to this work as Beethoven's greatest.[106] Is this conclusion based on the judgment that the *Missa Solemnis* is the most resistant of Beethoven's works to penetration and dismembering by society, the most alienated from society, and therefore the most authentic? Even if so, Adorno elsewhere makes it clear that authenticity of content in the sense of resistance to society is not sufficient to guarantee the quality of a work.[107] Is it rather the reverse, then, that authenticity will vary directly with the artistic quality of the work? This seems closer to Adorno's general conviction, but it leaves unexplained his original evaluative criteria either for art as a whole or for Beethoven's in particular.

Adorno does, without question, place considerable weight on the utopian approximation of synthesis, that is, a high degree of formal integration, as a measure of artistic quality. But the synthesis must be authentic. How does one decide when art is doing its best to prefigure a utopian totality in the face of despair and when it is trying to conceal inhumanity? Adorno offers no general guide. Conversely, although he differentiates in theory between ruptures of synthesis necessitated by the state of social reality (as in Beethoven's third period) and those caused by the personal inadequacies of the artist, Adorno suggests no means of distinguishing between the two cases.[108] He does associate formal integrity, at least since the eighteenth century, with artistic autonomy, which means, above all, with composition by a free individual,[109] but it is difficult to see how artistic autonomy and individual freedom can be separated out from formal integrity and used as evaluative criteria in the kind of immanent, structural criticism Adorno has in mind. One seems justified in asking whether Adorno ultimately admires the formal aspect of Beethoven's late work for some condition of rigorous aesthetic unity — he scarcely mentions the latter in either of the two essays on the late work except to doubt whether the unity of the *Missa Solemnis* can be understood from what is present in the work[110] — or for its authenticity (its critical realism, its renunciation of direct self-expression, its moral soundness). There is a strong probability that Adorno himself would refuse to separate the aesthetic and moral components of his artistic evaluations: that aesthetic quality is prior to social morality for Adorno, but prior precisely because he discerns in aesthetic quality an ultimate social morality. But this probability, although tremendously significant, cannot really substitute for a full, open discussion by Adorno himself of the bases for his strong, and often undeniably biased, value judgments.

On epistemological grounds, Adorno has frequently been criticized for his avoidance of empirical detail, both musical and historical.[111] Empiricists, and more particularly positivists, might also look askance at Adorno's refusal to make an "overt presentation of content in its own right."[112] Here it could be countered that by acknowledging openly the inseparability of content and method in his criticism, Adorno merely makes explicit the epistemological basis of research established in the natural sciences as far back as the 1920s by Werner Heisenberg. In music itself, Eggebrecht's study of Beethoven's criticism seems to dispel most lingering doubts about the inseparability of critical object and critical intelligence. Actually, Adorno's failure to isolate the content of his criticism probably causes far fewer difficulties than his failure to isolate a critical method that can readily be adapted by others.

Finally, it has been questioned whether Adorno's criticism does not depend on a false theory of history. The central importance Adorno attaches to historical necessity and his particular applications of this concept have both aroused skepticism, as has his hypostatization of historical "Geist" and its various manifestations, especially the "musical subject."[113] The notion of the subject seems the easiest to defend; for if to some it seems that Adorno anthropomorphizes musical notes and phrases, to others his notion of the musical subject may seem the logical result of viewing music as an embodiment of human consciousness.[114] Still, it cannot be denied that acceptance of notions like historical necessity, Geist, and musical subject probably requires an acceptance of the Hegelian dialectic, a principle that to Adorno and many other Europeans commands Beethovenian heights in the history of philosophy but that has as yet gained little recognition in Anglo-American criticism.

Donald Kuspit has recently written that "to truly do justice to Adorno—to object to him—one must completely submit oneself to him, commit oneself completely to his method, live with it and comprehend its effect on life."[115] Although Adorno's critical method resists easy formulation, it is not difficult through sufficient contact with Adorno's work to absorb a general attitude toward music criticism which can be applied in new contexts. Even if one rejects entirely the metaphysical aspects of Adorno's thought, the general notions through which he turns music criticism into social criticism — for example, affirmative and negative culture — are readily available for anyone's use.

Now, obviously this sort of accessibility entails dangers. There is a reason for the traditional insistence of Anglo-American empiricism on distance between the object of study and the student's opinions. Notions such as affirmative and negative culture require moral judgments as to what is repressive and what is humanizing; and since there is no longer any universal acceptance in the West of particular moral absolutes, such notions are clearly vulnerable to limitless perversion.

Furthermore, the more one absorbs the heavy moral atmosphere of Adorno's criticism, the more difficult it may become to maintain a safe distance from what is essentially a lethal interpretation of the modern world. It is striking that critics with the strongest objections to Adorno sometimes end up unwittingly supporting his positions.[116] Still others have seemed able to attack Adorno only through the sheer force of moral fervor (a critical weakness of which Adorno himself has been accused).[117] Indeed, as hard as it may be to prove the prognosis for Western civilization that Adorno reads in Beethoven's late style, no one so far has been able to disprove it. Kuspit links truly doing justice to Adorno with objecting to him, and, no doubt, doing justice to Adorno's agonized humanism requires refuting his fatal diagnosis of humanity. Yet the more one is drawn into Adorno's worldview, the more it may seem that a convincing refutation of that diagnosis would be tantamount to guaranteeing the survival of technological humanity, rather a formidable challenge. Adorno is, to be sure, culturally narrow, and it is at least conceivable that answers to his most anguished existential questions are available in cultures other than those descended, literally or spiritually, from the European Enlightenment.

In any case, despite the considerable risks it involves, Adorno's music criticism does seem to offer something valuable in its reintroduction of moral questions into the study of music. In the first place, there is a clear moral imperative in Adorno's method that the critic remain acutely conscious of the morality implicit in his or her own motivations, choices, and effect. Adorno demands nothing of authentic music that he does not demand of his own work. His music criticism is highly individual; it resists neutralization by requiring painstaking reading; and it protests against the crueltries of existing society. Adorno's attitude toward music criticism is thus in the fullest sense self-critical, reflecting a sort of ongoing self-evaluation that might well be salutary for a discipline that has remained aloof from other disciplines and cultural traditions as long as Anglo-American musicology has.

And in the second place, Adorno's preoccupation with morality is inseparable from a concern to define the human species. The effect of introducing moral questions into his music criticism is to heighten awareness of music as a human undertaking. By criticizing music in relation to other human activities and by bringing knowledge from other disciplines, even those supposed antitheses history and philosophy, Adorno is at least trying to expand the human significance of music. Such an effort is valuable even though many epistemological problems remain to be solved before all of the connections Adorno points to in music can be established with certainty.

Certainly, Adorno does a good deal to establish the most important such connection in his music criticism, the connection between music and his readers, that is, ourselves. In trying to remove music from its technical isolation and reintegrate it into a totality of human relationships, Adorno is trying to do what he claims the best modern art tries to do: to evoke in each of us, without any false reassurances, some sense of human wholeness, if only a longing for it. It is a way of asking us to look for the human in music in the hope of finding the human in ourselves. It is not an unreasonable request of humanistic scholars.[118]

Chapter 3

Why Is Adorno's Music Criticism the Way It Is?

Some Reflections on Twentieth-Century Criticism of Nineteenth-Century Music

Three objections seem to be leveled against the musical writings of the German dialectical philosopher Theodor W. Adorno (1903–69) with particular frequency. Why, it is asked, does Adorno show next to no informed awareness of music before Bach? Why is he so reluctant to engage in purely musical analysis? And why is his language so impossibly contorted?

Perhaps the most informative way of accounting for the apparent limitations to which these questions point involves seeing all of them as responses to discontinuities that are fundamental to modern culture as Adorno envisions it. For, despite his historical rather than systematic orientation, Adorno seems ultimately to characterize modern culture as a system or structure;[1] and this structure seems to include within itself numerous coexisting or synchronic components, which are essentially discrete, though often analogous or homologous. It would appear that out of a need to impose some coherent pattern on the data of modern culture, Adorno focuses much attention on the parallelisms of analogous cultural elements; yet his aggregate image of the cultural structure seems to offer no binding means of connecting such elements. On a larger level, moreover, Adorno seems to conceive of the modern cultural structure itself as something of an analogue to its own components — that is, as one of many such cultural structures, each one discrete though all, very likely, more or less homologous.

Once Adorno's conception of modern culture is viewed from this perspective, one begins to discern a possible explanation for at least the first of his alleged critical weaknesses: his avoidance of early music. For Adorno seems to think of music as part of a single synchronic cultural structure that also includes all of the social, historical, and artistic constructs contemporaneous with music. Therefore, he probably assumes that music appearing at widely different times belongs to cultural systems with relatively little in common, and that it is not valid to treat music throughout Western history as if it constituted a single medium, appropriately addressed by one set of questions. To be sure, the imposition of a distinctly twentieth-century notion, such as "structure," on earlier periods of history is in itself an extension of values from one culture to another. But Adorno, a dialectician, does not evoke the image of structure very explicitly in his music criticism; and unlike certain authentic structuralists, he confines his quasi-structuralist analyses to the most recent cultural system discernible more or less in its entirety. And that system, broadly speaking, is what for Adorno constitutes the modern period in Western civilization, from the aftermath of the Enlightenment to some not fully determinate point in the twentieth century, when something like a postmodern or posthistorical cultural system begins to become discernible, with which Adorno has little sense of identification and which interests him little, even though the notion of structure itself has essentially postmodern origins.

There can be little argument, of course, that the modern or post-Enlightenment cultural system that *does* interest Adorno is widely defined in terms of the historical consciousness that developed within it, or that Adorno's own dialectical method is a product of that historical consciousness. Nevertheless even for Adorno, structure seems in the end to have replaced historical progress as the principal image through which the organization of modern culture, for all its surface historicism, is understood. Thus a wide range of elements in post-Enlightenment culture seem to interest Adorno equally; and the constancy with which his critical method seeks out structural similarities among such elements seems to underscore a tendency to treat modern culture primarily as a multi-faceted structure, open to parallelisms but beset by discontinuities, both inner and outer.

Particularly prominent among the coexistent characteristics of modern culture that preoccupy Adorno are the disappearance of God (and hence of a center or binding force) from our universe, the emergence of "art" as a wholly autonomous concept, and the emergence of "individuality" as a concept of compelling self-interest to the Westerner. These interests are all evident in Adorno's music criticism; it is even possible to discern all three in the principal question that Adorno addresses to post-Enlightenment music, which seems to be this: Why is this music the way it is? For, beyond the obvious revelation in this question of an intense desire to know fully a loved object, the "why is" of this question shows Adorno looking for a force of explanation as binding as that provided by a God. The "music," of course, shows Adorno turning to art as a possible means of finding such a force. And "the way it is" shows Adorno trying to affirm the significance of a precisely articulated individuality. Indeed, as a brief account of his music criticism should demonstrate, Adorno seems unable to characterize post-Enlightenment music without reference to all three of these concerns, as equivalent aspects of a cultural system.

Adorno apparently assumes at some level that in a cultural system where the idea of God is a truly binding force, little need would probably be felt to question the significance (or to define) either art or the individual. God would be understood to constitute a connection among all things, that is, to "explain" them in the sense of guaranteeing their necessity through God's own absolute and encompassing existence and thus embodying within God their significance. But then it would follow that in a culture where the idea of God lost that binding force (and became recognized as nothing more than an idea), all norms that had derived their power from general belief in a supreme authority would be undermined and cease to function as embodied, self-evident explanations. At such a time, the need would probably begin to make itself felt within the given cultural system to reconnect or reunify all aspects of that system with some new encompassing principle (now perceived to function as something external and hence "other") in order to guarantee the significance of each cultural aspect. In other words, the need would become acutely felt in such a culture for explanation—and indeed, one can infer from Adorno's music criticism, such a need began to emerge clearly in Western Europe not long after the French Revolution.

Adorno seems to take the position that no element in post-Enlightenment culture crystallized the need for explanation more clearly than did art, as he argues in essence that the very notion of art came into being in response to just such a need. Without the support of external, generally available, and binding norms, Adorno seems to suggest, aesthetically powerful mediums such as music were forced by default into a condition of autonomy that went far beyond total secularization (already evident in the earliest post-baroque music) to a potentially isolated and highly vulnerable state of self-responsibility in every respect where the need for justification and explanation might make itself felt. This vulnerability was especially intense in a medium that was becoming defined precisely through its nonreferentiality and, hence, self-containment: music. Demands for explanations and quasi-metaphysical justifications by music could be staved off only as long as the composition presented itself in a wholly authoritative manner as a self-sufficient universe, essentially at one with a divinely ordered universe in the totality of its interconnectedness and equally able to justify through its very existence and wholeness the necessity of all its components. Such, Adorno more or less implies, is the case with musical classicism, where composers could create configurations that simultaneously worked as individual expressions of their own humanity—for example, in the sense of temporality and even historical progress palpable in the apparent movement forward of the music—and as the seeming embodiment of universally valid, timeless norms, totally interconnected in a system able to guarantee its own general acceptance as a necessary and objectively significant configuration. As a result, according to Adorno, the microcosm or "universe" created in classical music seems genuinely, and not just by dint of wishing, autonomous. Yet even within the very high degree of musical autonomy that typifies this style, musically posed questions about musical significance come to be asked, Adorno indicates, especially in the works of Beethoven's second and third periods.

In the century that follows classicism, Adorno goes on to suggest, the classical totality disintegrates and music can no longer be perceived as a self-contained universe (even though it is in the musical writings of this period that the notion of the musical microcosm begins to be developed). Rather, nineteenth-century music must be imagined as a cultural fragment, possibly homologous with other such fragments and capable of forming with them a single large, though never really complete structure (say, as the French anthropologist Lévi-Strauss's variants of myth coalesce into an infinitely expandable body or system of myth), but no longer displaying necessary or convincing interconnections, either within itself or between itself and any encompassing universe. For as the semblance of objective norms gives way to individual choice as the premise of composition in the nineteenth century, the objective basis for interconnections and their explanatory force begins to disappear from music.

Hence music, especially German music, feels called upon to provide an explicit, comprehensive, and generally accessible demonstration of its own necessity and significance. And the way in which it goes about this undertaking, Adorno seems to say, is not by trying to restore lost interconnections in any direct fashion, but rather by trying to reconstitute a universe of meaning through the musically individual itself; that is, by trying to make the individual, as this concept is represented in musical art, replace the divine or cosmic as the ground or embodiment of objective necessity.

Thus nineteenth-century music tries through techniques of emphasis or clarification to confirm and justify wherever possible the precise identity of each individual aspect of a work, thereby providing unequivocal evidence for the total rightness—indeed, the necessity—of the entire (or seemingly entire) configuration defined by such aspects.[2] "Rhetorical" exaggeration or extra-musical "signs," for example, are used to insist on the appropriateness of both traditional and individualized forms; attempts are made to fix instrumentation, dynamics, and ornamentation with increasing inflexibility and refinement; attention is called to instrumental and chordal sonorities as distinct ends in themselves; and in general, at both the small-scale level of detail and the large-scale level of work and style, musical individuality does its best to undertake its own defense. In short, one can infer from Adorno's musical writings, nineteenth-century music—which for Adorno means above all nineteenth-century German art music—takes upon itself nothing less than the burden of finding means to guarantee the necessity and hence the objective significance of the individual through the individual, in all the richness and solitude of its particular universe. And it is only in taking up this mission, Adorno seems clearly to conclude, that music becomes fully art—and perhaps the paradigmatic art—at least as the term "art" has generally been used in post-Enlightenment Western society: to connote a highly individualized configuration that makes a plausible effort to guarantee the necessity of being exactly as it is and thereby to embody within itself the objective significance of its own individuality.

Art, then, according to Adorno, crystallizes the need of post-Enlightenment culture for an explanatory force by defining the problem of demonstrating individual necessity without the aid of any preexistent absolute principle. Art constitutes the attempt of the individual to account for itself by means of itself; and yet, Adorno seems to indicate, it is not just the individuality of art itself that is at stake in the artistic enterprise but other, analogous forms of individuality as well. In particular, art provided a concrete means of confronting a question of extreme importance to the human individual. This question might be put thus: How can human individuals substantiate their own inner conviction of the necessity, and hence the objective significance, of their own extraordinarily refined particularity, in the face of their own transience (of which the individual becomes keenly aware in a godless world) and in the face of the monumental difficulty of merely sustaining that individuality within a far more powerful external world, let alone of making any generally perceptible difference to the world through that particularity?

One could argue that this is the central existential question for Western humanity in a world from which God has been removed and in which human beings have been thrown back upon themselves as guarantors of their own necessity and significance. And it seems to be Adorno's contention that the essence of nineteenth- and early twentieth-century music lay precisely in its preoccupation with answering this question for humans through the analogy of its own medium. Indeed, Adorno's fundamental conception of every leading German composer in the nineteenth century, from Beethoven through Mahler, seems to consist precisely in what Adorno deems to be the stance of each composer's music toward this existentially significant relationship between individuality and objective necessity.

Adorno clearly seems to conclude that the best nineteenth-century music did succeed to some extent in evoking, through its own high degree of individualization, the ghost of a lost Classical universe. Yet for Adorno, all of this music, in the end possibly even Beethoven's, failed to transform the individual itself into a convincing replica of the universe; that is, to derive from the musically individual a universal basis for confirming the objective significance of individuality itself. The chief sign of this general failure, from Adorno's position, seems to consist precisely in the fact that in spite of its efforts to constitute itself a universe, individuality in nineteenth-century music so often emerges as something less than whole, something palpably incomplete. Thus, one supposes Adorno might argue, where the individualized entity involved is the work itself, it may be left literally incomplete or in several versions; conclusions often seem curiously inconclusive; elements of the composer's individuality that may be a vital part of his conception (Schumann's fantasy life, Chopin's manner of performance) cannot always be fixed with exactitude on the printed page. Successful establishment of individuality at one level of a piece (say, harmony or sonority) often entails a blurring of individuality at another (say, structure or line). Individual formal decisions frequently seem questionable rather than necessary, whether the form chosen is conventional or not. Works that use conventionalized forms may give the impression of containing individual material at once alienated from its nonindividualized environment, yet incapable of achieving independence from it; Adorno hints at such a condition in connection with the instrumental works of both Brahms and Mahler. And likewise, works using more or less free forms may find it necessary to appropriate a framework that threatens the individuality of music itself; even after Wagner has accepted Schopenhauer's absolute conception of music, he finds it necessary to work with a text.

Again and again, Adorno seems to be saying, individuality in nineteenth-century music seems to present itself as "mere individuality," a condition that cannot be autonomous without also ceasing to be viable. (One could perhaps think of individuality in this sense as permitting identity but not effective choice.) Indeed, in the context of Adorno's philosophy, the principal "message" of nineteenth-century music may be that individual autonomy is a contradiction in terms. If reapplied directly to music itself, such a message would suggest that music after classicism (and perhaps, really, music after Haydn and Mozart) ought not to be thought of as the "absolute" medium that Beethoven seemed to insist upon; Adorno himself might well argue that even in the case of Brahms, nineteenth-century music, rather than projecting itself as a purely (merely?) musical medium, conveyed a substantial philosophical and critical if not a poetic import.[3] The musical implications of such a message may not appeal to the serious modern composer, since by definition lack of autonomy in a medium entails virtually insuperable obstacles to the attainment of autonomy in formal structure (as every generation of composers since Beethoven has probably had to acknowledge in some way). But even less attractive are the implications by analogy of such a message for the fate of the human individual. For the autonomy of the individual is equivalent to the *survival* of the individual as the latter has traditionally been conceived in the West; and a species staring at its own extinction is scarcely in the best position to prove its own necessity.

According to Adorno, Schoenberg made the last mighty effort, in his twelve-tone music, to establish once and for all the necessity of the individual by retaining the signs of individual expressiveness handed down by nineteenth-century music (for example, linear continuity and harmonic freedom), and yet making thorough-going systematic necessity — the elimination of all chance or irrational moments — his controlling principle of construction.[4] Schoenberg succeeded, in Adorno's judgment, to the extent that his "compositions are the first in which nothing actually can be different";[5] in these works, Adorno seems to be saying, the concreteness, the resistance to paraphrase, modified restatement, and generalization that had made music such a compelling analogue to the particularity of the human individual becomes absolute. But in "fixing" the individual so as to stand completely by itself and for itself, Adorno suggests, Schoenberg also essentially killed off the individual; for in embodying a musical definition of the completely individual, Schoenberg's twelve-tone music, as Adorno conceives it, simultaneously projected the totally arbitrary, irrational, and meaningless workings of that objective world in which individuality could so define itself and, hence, the total impotence of the individual to guarantee its own survival or have any impact on that world. Thus, in his effort to preserve elements of linear, thematic, and for that matter, even historical continuity analogous to the human individual's temporal mode of existence, Schoenberg, Adorno argues, produced music striking for its effects of discontinuity and stasis. And likewise, Adorno indicates, in carrying harmonic freedom to the point of systematically emancipating all dissonance, Schoenberg "broke through" (to use a favorite expression of Adorno's) the most sacred taboo of Western music, perhaps the one common element permitting all of Western music to be heard as a single historical continuity, and almost certainly the one element that had above all permitted "autonomous" music to embody meaning: the distinction between consonance and dissonance. But the violation of this taboo, one can infer, meant not only that Schoenberg's music liberated harmonic expression—potentially a good omen for human individuality—but also that it defined conclusively a situation of dreadful import in the analogous world of the human individual. By this I mean the situation that no remnant of an absolute, external authority—in a word, no God—remained to enforce taboos, either in the world of art or in the world of human beings, and hence no authority remained to safeguard the individual from inhuman encroachments on its integrity and survival. In short, Adorno seems to conclude, rather than guaranteeing the necessity and significance of the individual, Schoenberg's music pointed to a world in which no fate was unthinkable, no fate was too horrible for the human individual.

It is on this existential point that most of Adorno's music criticism and philosophy is centered. To fault him for failing to clarify whether his fundamental interest is in the musical or the human aspect of individuality is to overlook the complex system of structural analogues through which Adorno is apparently trying to maintain some semblance of interconnectedness and meaning in modern culture. Rather than simply acquiesce in an image of post-Enlightenment society as a world in which, lacking a center, all components are consigned to total isolation, Adorno prefers to see the crisis of individuality and the crisis of composition as analogous elements in a single cultural system, just as his reader might view Adorno's own passionate desire to explain the individuality of great music as the counterpart of a deeply religious need to account for the modern individual's own perceived existential situation.

Adorno's conception of music as one element in a cultural structure would seem to go far in accounting not only for his avoidance of early music but also for his characteristic avoidance of strictly musical analysis. And yet, without some further elaboration, this account is probably inadequate to dispel suspicions that Adorno's general aversion to the purely technical is rooted not in his philosophy or in the situation to which his philosophy points but is merely a manifestation of analytical incompetence—especially since where Adorno does indulge in long passages of technical musical discussion, such as in his piece-by-piece description of Schumann's *Liederkreis*, op. 39,[6] his criticism tends to be uninspired. In the case of a critic as methodologically sophisticated as Adorno, it is probably worth investigating grounds other than incompetence for the avoidance of technical discussion. Is it not possible, for example—and perhaps a question of this sort might help to clarify a good deal of the current crisis in music theory—that this alleged weakness of Adorno's actually reflects a sound grasp of the music being criticized? In particular, why *should* Adorno be able to find general significance for every technical aspect of nineteenth-century music if this music has already tried to do precisely this in its own terms and has not succeeded? And similarly, why *should* Adorno be able to find autonomous musical significance in nineteenth-century composition if this music itself could not make a convincing presentation of its own autonomy?

Perhaps most of the music with which Adorno deals, say from late Beethoven through middle-period Schoenberg, in fact does not lend itself to and cannot be accounted for adequately through musical analysis. Perhaps this music should be differentiated clearly from those types of music that do seem accessible to purely musical analysis or description. Among the latter, for example, one thinks of what Adorno might call "problem-solving" music, music that has renounced any claim to meaning beyond the correctness or persuasiveness of its solutions to the technical problems it sets for itself, and consequently, music that can be addressed—or more accurately, described or merely restated through verbal homologues—on mechanical grounds alone. Adorno would include much music after Schoenberg (that is, postmodern music) in this category. Classical music too, or at least some classical music, may likewise lend itself to purely musical discussion, though of a more genuinely analytical sort. Thus, if viewed as the microcosmic image, or to use structuralist terms, the "paradigmatic" equivalent[7] of a self-contained universe, still containing a seeming infinity of interconnections that suggest embodied meanings, classical music might conceivably be characterized as a world of sound—or at least the image of such a world—in which sound and meaning are identical. And it might then be the case that this (imagined) stylistic world is large enough to encompass the critic, who has only to find exact parallels in words or symbols to events in the music itself in order to produce an analysis of explanatory force. For if the musical patterns themselves coalesce into self-contained wholes, perhaps, too, the critic's equivalents or signs can be made into cohesive diagrams and essays, at once virtually identical or at least transparently analogous to the meanings wholly embodied in the music and yet sufficiently "other" to seem a plausible explanation as well. (It could, perhaps, even be argued that the identity between sound and meaning in classicism is so complete, and the music so self-contained, so autonomous, that all attempts at verbal exegesis are superfluous and thus tautological rather than explanatory. Such a situation would account for Adorno's avoidance of Haydn and Mozart; and one is tempted to remove Beethoven from the realm of classicism on the very grounds that Adorno has so much to say about him.)[8]

But perhaps, in any event, Adorno is right in his underlying suggestion that nineteenth-century music is not autonomous, either as a sensuous or as a structural medium. Such a lack of autonomy might do much to explain why as far back as the criticism of E. T. A. Hoffmann and of Schumann, attempts at dealing separately with the musical content and with the poetic or philo-

sophical content of post-Enlightenment music have so often been unconvincing; why connections between these two types of critical discussion,
when clearly separated, have so often seemed nonexistent or arbitrary; and
why the purely musical passages in such criticism have so often seemed its
least satisfactory, least explanatory element. For if music itself in the nineteenth century is not autonomous, then presumably any critical account that
restricts itself to being a mere paradigmatic analogue of either the musical or
the extramusical substance of this music, to providing no more than verbal
equivalents (or graphic signs) for one aspect or the other, is going to emerge
not as a universe of embodied meanings but as a fragment, as incomplete as
the musical phenomenon it purports to explain. And purely technical criticism seems even less capable than poetic criticism of capturing the essence
of nineteenth-century music by becoming fully analogous with it, that is,
analogous in the sense of evoking, even negatively through the character of
its own incompleteness, some lost universe of interconnected mediums and
events through which individual necessity might conceivably be guaranteed.

It would seem, in fact, that to have any real chance of distilling a full-
bodied significance from music that is intrinsically incomplete, the critic
would almost certainly have to make some attempt to restore such music to
a binding context of completeness, capable of guaranteeing through the totality of its own embodied connections the necessity of any configuration
under question. Such a critic might do well to admit from the outset the
heteronomy of post-Enlightenment music (that is, its failure to encompass
a universe of discourse) by ceasing to use words merely as transparent signs,
analogues, or paradigms for the incomplete and trying, rather, in complementary or syntagmatic fashion, to fashion a critical configuration in
which musical allusion and verbal interpretation are so tightly intertwined
as to seem fused. If such a configuration proved persuasive on the level of
its detail, it might also establish a large-scale interpenetration of the musical
and critical mediums themselves, on the one hand using words to concretize
the tendency of nineteenth-century music toward union with the nonmusical
and thus to complete the musical experience, and on the other hand, transforming criticism thereby into a vital part of the musical experience. In this
way, the critical enterprise might evoke not so much the "mere" autonomy
or incompleteness of music in the nineteenth century as the perceptible richness of that incompleteness, by conjuring up through words a musical
"otherness" that could complete it. And this means that at its best, such "syntagmatic" criticism could turn out to be an informative analogue or "paradigm" of nineteenth-century music, not merely because of its restriction to
a single medium but also because of its power to convey, in a concrete and
precisely analogous fashion, the manner in which the incompleteness of a

single medium constitutes the essence of nineteenth-century music.[9] But this is not all. Criticism that clearly separates musical and conceptual discussions tends to emphasize the limitations of human temporality, that is, the human inability to elaborate, except successively, elements that may actually belong to a synchronic totality. But a close enough interpenetration of music and concept might overcome that limitation and provide a model, through the manner of its own internal integration, for reconstructing a universe of meaning in which the connections between the musical and extramusical (or individual and nonindividual) values of a postreligious world were all simultaneously and actually present, and not merely evoked by means of their absence. Adorno's musical writings seem to be guided by some such critical model as this.

It should be noted that the attention this critical model draws to its own internal connections and configurations is characteristic of numerous twentieth-century critical enterprises that Adorno would undoubtedly consider postmodern or posthistorical. Like many schools of analytic philosophy (especially ordinary language philosophy), literary metacriticism, and structuralism, Adorno's apparent critical model seems to lend itself particularly well to attempts at extracting some semblance of objective reality from a close investigation of the connections within human sign-systems such as music and language. Many, perhaps most, postmodern critical enterprises (including deconstruction) tend ultimately to transform their diverse inquiries into an examination of the linguistic connections they must make in order to pursue their inquiries and, thereby, into a study of natural-language systems. Adorno's own music criticism is not devoid of the tendency to concentrate interest on the verbal medium of criticism itself; on the contrary, his criticism seems based on an assumption that just as art in the nineteenth century was required to resupply the wholeness and meaning of a lost divine order, so, too, any hope of returning the human world to a condition of wholeness by resestablishing some authoritative source of meaning has now passed from art to the level of commentary upon art, that is to criticism, and hence to natural language. And one could say that the historically grounded belief in the ability of music to solve its own problems through the progress of its own medium has been left behind when the archetypal completion (or perhaps "perfection") of music is imagined as consisting in verbal criticism, which cannot be a literal continuation of music, but at most can constitute an atemporal complement to music.

There can be little doubt that in forcing reflection on the verbal character of criticism itself, Adorno's apparent critical model reveals a widespread postmodern tendency. It may well be that Adorno's music criticism is permeated by the analysis of essentially verbal concepts not only because the music it criticizes may lack autonomy but also because this criticism is formulated, in spite of itself, in a postmodern culture, where criticism has become the principal humanistic medium precisely because natural language has become widely recognized as the fundamental source of human knowledge about the world.

Nevertheless, it is equally clear that Adorno's criticism differs markedly in important respects from most postmodern criticism, which tends—for example, in collapsing knowledge into human sign-systems such as language —to exclude evocation of anything other-worldly or metaphysical from efforts to characterize objective reality or to reconstitute a universe of discourse. Despite its postmodern characteristics, Adorno's music criticism is an enterprise more closely analogous in its concerns to nineteenth-century art, particularly music, than to most postmodern criticism. For even if Adorno does transfer his musical energies, postmodern style, to critcism, nevertheless the underlying purpose of his music criticism, like that of most serious German composition in the nineteenth century but unlike that of most postmodern criticism, remains to provide an objective grounding for individuality and thereby affirm incontrovertibly the latter's objective significance. To this end, Adorno not only defines his principal object of music study as the most deliberately and explicitly individualized repertory in Western music history, German art music between Beethoven and Schoenberg (and Adorno insists on discussing this music in terms of structural autonomy, although "autonomy" in Adorno's criticism, as in Schumann's, clearly means something far richer than "mere" autonomy). Beyond that, he directs attention through his music criticism to natural language in a very individualized sense, that is, to natural language not as any broadly based sign-system (say, natural language itself, or even the German language) but, rather, as Adorno's own highly idiosyncratic critical utterance. In order to achieve his large-scale critical and humanistic objectives, Adorno takes great pains to "complete" nineteenth- and early twentieth-century music through critical configurations as individualized as is that music itself; and like that music, his criticism tries to demonstrate the necessity of individuality by rendering the latter absolute within itself.

Thus it is not mere perverseness that causes Adorno to guard the meaning of his words against easy comprehension, précis, or cheapening, and to offer criticism that reads like Latin. Adorno's esoteric effect is in large measure a by-product of the great care Adorno takes to define and preserve a concept of individual integrity through his use of words, by choosing each word with precision, refusing (like the twelve-tone composer in the musical medium) to augment his words with redundant explanations or appositives, and giving the impression that every decision (the choice of a word, the inclusion

or exclusion of an idea), every detail, and every connection in a highly individualized entity matters in the extreme, so that no element can be adequately duplicated, replaced, or summarized. One can admit that Adorno
does seem to make his point to the extent that most reformulations of his position slip easily into truism, a generalized linguistic configuration signifying
nothing except the possible need for individualization in language to express
the objectively significant.

But does the preservation of individualistic values make Adorno's criticism anything more than what the structuralist might call a "transformation,"
a kind of passive variant of nineteenth-century musical inadequacy, that
merely transfers the problems of one medium to another without making any
progress in resolving them? And does Adorno's insistence on individuality
get his criticism beyond demonstrating, as have many less individualized enterprises in the twentieth century, an intimate association between the structure of a person's expression and that person's perception of reality? Does
Adorno's individualized use of language, in other words, suggest any break-
through to a metaphysical source of meaning *beyond* the individual's view of
reality, yet encompassing it?

To the first of these questions, at least, the answer does not appear promising. In trying to assert some structural sort of identity between the individual
configuration and the totality of a universe, Adorno seems to have perpetu-
ated many of the critical weaknesses that he himself discerns in post-
Enlightenment music. Thus, despite his avoidance of redundance on a small
scale, Adorno's criticism on the large scale (again, like twelve-tone music)
seems highly repetitive, in terms of both its language and its themes, and
consequently static—qualities that may preserve Adorno's individuality
only at the cost of sacrificing important individual differences within the
music that he studies, and qualities that Adorno himself criticizes in post-
Beethovenian music as antithetical to the definition of individuality. And
likewise, far from excelling nineteenth-century music in the projection of a
sense of completeness that embodies its own meaning, Adorno's criticism (as
he himself would say of Schoenberg's music) strikes most perceivers as a
jaggedly compiled aggregate missing a host of internal connections. Like the
composer in nineteenth-century music, Adorno is trying in his criticism to
make a case for the necessity of the individual configuration; yet, as he himself essentially argues of nineteenth-century music, both repetitiveness and
incompleteness tend to vitiate any effect of having to be "just so and not
otherwise." Unless, that is, Adorno's criticism can convince the reader that
its very inability to embody individual necessity persuasively is itself somehow necessary—if only, or perhaps especially, in a metaphysical sense.

In fact, Adorno repeatedly asserts that the flaws of the most individualized post-Enlightenment music are functions not of personal or technical inadequacies on the part of a given composer but rather of the metaphysical vacuum in which this music finds itself. Thus, Adorno indicates, although the flaws of an individualized musical configuration preclude the latter on an immediate, aesthetic level from establishing the necessity of being exactly as it is, precisely this preclusion imparts a sense of necessity on a deeper, metaphysical level because genuine individuality does define a convincingly objective metaphysical reality—a negative reality—that requires such a preclusion. In this sense, at least, the flaws that undermine the appearance of individual necessity in art could themselves conceivably be taken as evidence of a congruence between individualized art and the configuration of metaphysical reality; and Adorno comes close to implying that such flaws are not only necessary elements in great art after the Enlightenment but are also, as points of possible tangency with some genuinely metaphysical source (even a negative source) of necessity, actually the marks of that greatness.

Are Adorno's own flaws of such a magnitude? Most readers would probably be willing to agree that the lack of completeness in Adorno's music criticism—his rejection of linguistic smoothness and omission of numerous conceptual connections—is something of an objective necessity. It is at least a plausible claim that Adorno's criticism could not embody such "finish" or a universe of connections without falsifying both the individual character of the music that concerns it and the nature of the objective reality suggested by that music as well as by most twentieth-century criticism. But Adorno himself might well assert that his repetitiveness, too, is necessary because it corresponds to the metaphysical reality of a godless age: the unchanging and unchangeable inaccessibility of metaphysical meaning, which in its static, endlessly discernible sameness makes a mockery of human pretension to temporal progress, and which the critical enterprise, like the aesthetic, can ultimately do nothing to change. In effect, Adorno makes such an argument on behalf of Wagner even while criticizing him when he says, "The aesthetic weaknesses of Wagner have their origin in the metaphysics of repetition, in the 'it is like that, let it always be like that, one doesn't get out of it, one can't get out of it.' "[10] It is conceivable that Adorno's flaws are necessary in that without them there is no way of delineating the negative metaphysical reality that appears to bind the individual.

But perhaps it is also conceivable that a rigorously individualized criticism might evoke a metaphysical necessity other than the blind necessity that appears to dictate individual impotence, a sense of metaphysical necessity that does not "complete" the individual in such an oppressively and absolutely negative sense. For if there is any vestige of a hope that the individual can someday be proven necessary, that is, reintegrated into a metaphysical totality that imbues it with a positive objective significance, then perhaps it is necessary to keep that hope alive by giving individuality the most rigorous and unyielding protection it has ever had, to keep it from being destroyed altogether before such a synthesis can be completed. Thus, just as it can be said that the various artistic languages in the twentieth century have been withdrawn from general circulation or even yielded up to the medium of criticism in order to forestall the exhaustion of all hopes invested in art, and to preserve at least the hope of one day reestablishing genuinely individual modes of expression — arts — of unquestioned general validity, so, too, it may for the present be necessary to contradict the appearance of individual necessity on the surface of critical language in order to keep alive the concept of individual necessity, if only by unmistakable allusion to its absence, and thus keep alive the hope of establishing individual necessity on a positive metaphysical basis.

Adorno himself returns frequently to the theme of hope superstitiously buried beneath a concrete surface of hopelessness. Perhaps it is possible to interpret Adorno's music criticism, with all its apparent rejection of the divine and classical totalities that once guaranteed meaning merely by existing, as one more necessary configuration in an ongoing attempt to establish metaphysical grounding for the individual. And if Adorno's criticism in fact constitutes nothing more than a "recurrence of the same" limitations already found in nineteenth-century music, it may nevertheless be reasonable to justify the idiosyncratic individuality and inadequacy of that criticism in terms of genuine metaphysical promise — indeed, the same terms that Adorno himself, in one of his more utopian moods, uses to justify the imperfections of Wagner's music:

> Under the constraint of its own metaphysic, his [work] retracted into itself. Because finally it doesn't possess what it has promised, it is given to us . . . fallible, not finished, as being what ought to be continued, unachieved in itself. It awaits that which will continue it until it attains itself.[11]

Chapter 4

Kant, Adorno, and the Self-Critique of Reason: Toward a Model for Music Criticism

The imagination . . . is very powerful in creating another nature, as it were, out of the material that actual nature gives it. . . . [By means of it] we remold experience, always . . . in accordance with analogical laws, but yet also in accordance with principles which occupy a higher place in reason. . . . so that the material supplied to us by nature . . . can be worked up into something quite different which surpasses nature.

Immanuel Kant
Critique of Judgment[1]

The survival that concerns him is moral, not bodily, durability; many who in this sense survived had to die.[2]

Despite one provocative essay on Bach, the period in which Adorno takes a sustained interest as a music critic really only begins at the end of the Enlightenment in "Beethoven's social climate," to use his own words, "with its touch of Rousseau, Kant, Fichte, and Hegel."[3] It is characteristic that in this description of the period, Adorno made reference to music, society, and philosophy. All three figured centrally in his conception of music criticism; and where his music criticism is concerned, at least, it can be argued that it is to this same period that his engagement with each of the three can be traced. It was in this period that he saw emerging the pervasive irrationality of modern society as well as certain specifically musical modes of criticizing modern society. And it was in this period that both music and society began to manifest clearly the impact of certain philosophical attitudes that are fundamental to the moral as well as to the methodological orientation of Adorno's music criticism. Of particular importance among these are attitudes exposed in Kant's critical philosophy, and especially in his third critique, the *Critique of Judgment*. I have found the consideration of relationships between the third critique and Adorno's music criticism useful not only to understanding something of the tradition that shaped Adorno's categories of thought but also to working out a model for further music criticism that draws on Adorno's critical insight in ways and contexts that he himself did not attempt.

In emphasizing a kinship between Adorno and Kant I realize that I may be suggesting a characterization of Adorno's criticism that seems unorthodox to some, perhaps even perverse. So I should say at the outset that it is not my intention to try to "expose" Adorno as an essentially philosophical thinker, uninterested in social praxis, or to deny the Hegelian, dialectical orientation that caused Adorno to shrink from the reification of processes into bounded objects. I do not mean to disparage Adorno's debt to thinkers other than Kant or to dismiss as insignificant connections he suggests between composers and other philosophers, such as Beethoven and Hegel.[4] Nor is it my purpose to associate Adorno with any particular school of thought at all. Rather I intend mainly to apply to Adorno's own work a suggestion that he himself made in connection with the interpretation of Bach's music, a suggestion that is also made by Charles Rosen in his discussion of classical ornamentation and one that I hope to show has its foundation in Kant's critical philosophy; and that suggestion is, as Adorno put it, to be "loyal to him in being disloyal."[5] By redefining elements of Adorno's work in relation to critical categories suggested by Kant's third critique and using them to propose new language for interpreting familiar music, I hope to preserve some humane element in Adorno's work, even if I arrive at conclusions that he did not endorse and even if opposition to such selective usage could in a sense be called the very essence of Adorno's critical position.

Morally, Adorno's music criticism seems motivated above all by the exposure of reason in modern Western history as a construct incapable of governing the universe or of rendering the human species humane. Methodologically, what his criticism offers most generally to other critics, though he never would have put it this way, is the possibility of drawing structural analogies between purely formal aspects of musical art and formal patterns discerned in other cultural or social constructs.

Both these aspects of Adorno's criticism seem to have some clear precedents in various elements, some explicit, some implicit, of Kant's *Critique of Judgment*, a work that can be interpreted as an attempt to secure the ontological primacy of reason in the universe. Kant's general method of sustaining the status of reason was to take what could be called a critical attitude, one which rejects metaphysical levels of being as inaccessible to human knowledge (thereby clarifying human cognitive powers while preserving the possibility of an unknowable metaphysical rationality) and which reduces what one can know to the forms of one's own mind, the forms that one must assume the mind imposes on all data that enter it and on all that it externalizes for semiotic purposes. According to Kant's account these forms, which amount in effect to the forms of reason, must be imagined to exist at a transcendental level of reality that cannot be known although we are pointed toward their existence by a cognitive study of our own mind. Because they are beyond the contingency of all particular experience, they can be posited as universal, and thus reason can be salvaged as a principle that is universal in a subjective, but supraindividual sense, which means, among other things, as a principle that allows universal and perfect communication among people.

By the same token, it is true, these forms, in their state of pure abstraction, cannot be substantively imagined. Nevertheless, the rigorous cognitive method of argument that was followed in the *Critique of Judgment* was intended to convey some close, though concrete, approximation of these forms. And furthermore, the limits that Kant himself imposed on knowledge ultimately make it clear (though Kant would not happily admit this) that the forms of mind cannot be assumed in any cognitively certain sense to have any but a concrete existence. Thus it seems valid to derive from the *Critique of Judgment*, for heuristic purposes, something like a concrete image that conforms roughly to Kant's account of the mind, keeping in view that Kant himself did not think of the mind in all of its aspects as amenable to graphic representation and that the contradictions involved in such a schema preclude the delineation of a neat and simple picture.

Imagined at the level of its wholeness, the human mind, as Kant presented it, seems to constitute an autonomous structure in such a way as to expose the notion of autonomy as contradictory. Thus the mind has outward limits that are the limits of reason.[6] By virtue of those limits, as humanity defines the notion of limits, the human mind can be imagined to enclose or determine the boundaries of a complete subjectively accessible universe or structure that cannot be connected to any extrasubjective levels of being and functions without them, and to encompass a number of systems or faculties capable of imposing form on a rich manifold of data. But by virtue of these same limits the human mind must also be considered incomplete — and thus, though inescapably free, yet also conceivably not free — since the mind has no cognitively certain basis for assuming that it must contain what it thinks of as "the ultimate essence which would explain and produce its own appearance"[7] or that its limits, the limits of rationality, encompass or ever could encompass all possible reality.[8] On the contrary, the notion of limits and even empirical evidence suggest otherwise: for though the formal limits of the mind are, according to Kant, determinate, its empirical bounds are indeterminate in the sense that the mind cannot control the amount of empirical data it encounters or ever know that it has imposed intelligible form on all possible data. In fact, the formal limits involved here appear to be arbitrary, even contingent boundaries that the mind, in its cognitive examination of itself, can see no way out of, save total, arbitrary negation; they are not the logically necessary or cohesive boundaries that would result from a logical internal structure. For as to this latter, the human mind cannot be known as a cohesive whole by any human intelligence since it cannot, finally, be viewed from the outside and since the disjunctions between its internal components render impossible any determinate notion of its internal structure as a unified whole.[9] Indeed, the internal structure of the human mind, as Kant presented it — though again Kant, with his emphasis on the unity of consciousness, would not have characterized his account in this way — must be imagined as a multileveled series of disjunct, unconnectable systems, each, like the mind itself, self-contained and yet incomplete and riven by disjunctions at any number of internal levels.[10]

In brief, this internal mental structure seems to be characterized by a tension between two internal patterns, both of which in effecting relationships preclude connection and hence preserve discreteness. These patterns can be called "anology" and "drive toward an unattainable limit," the limit generally consisting of the realization of some underlying essence or law struggling to become what it is; and the coexistence of these two patterns involves numerous contradictions. Thus, for example, the static nature of the analogical relationship is basically opposed to the dynamism of drive toward a limit.[11] Moreover, the two patterns seem locked into a kind of balanced tension within the mind, and yet because the pattern of drive never reaches its goal, the static and disjunct pattern of analogy must ultimately be seen to govern the internal structure of the mind.

Furthermore, the pattern of drive generally involves two discrete structures, which seem to be disparate in form, that is, formally complementary (and hence capable of connection into a complete unit) or even contradictory (and hence, perhaps, open to dialectical union through synthesis) but which on closer examination turn out to be analogous, that is, different merely in concrete identity (and hence not amenable to either of these formally general sorts of resolution of differences).[12] Consequently, one aspect of the governing position of analogy within the mind is that the distinction between the structural similarity of analogy and the structural dissimilarity of contradiction is undercut by the disjunctive character of both, so that the supremacy of analogy in the mind becomes tantamount or even identical to the supremacy of contradiction. This is one important respect in which the defense of reason undertaken by the *Critique of Judgment* seems ultimately to define grounds for a kind of irrationalism.

Of the three principal mental faculties, as described in the *Critique of Judgment*, the one that comes closest to encompassing analogy and drive in a state of balance is judgment as exemplified by aesthetic judgment. Thus, in the so-called relationship of purposiveness characteristic of aesthetic judgment — and, of course, I am simplifying greatly throughout this discussion — freedom is seen to strive toward a condition of form that it can never attain, while at the same time the freedom of imagination and the form of understanding are conceived as structurally analogous; roughly speaking one could say that the structure of each is the famous Kantian formula of "purposiveness without purpose."[13] In cognition, as it is presented in the third critique, the more evident relationship is analogy, say, between the structure of representation and of concept, or, more generally, between objective and subjective structures. (It is this state of dual reference, that is, of structural conformity between objective constructs and subjective structures of the mind, that gives the cognitive realm its appearance of a general conformity to deterministic laws.)[14] In the moral domain, the more evident pattern is that of drive toward an unattainable limit, as in the drive of free will (or moral causality) toward a final purpose, which is the universal realization of moral law. (And again, it is this emphasis upon drive toward the realization of an underlying law rather than on subordination to law that explains the prominence, within the moral realm, of individual freedom.)

Analogy, drive toward an unattainable limit, and resultant logical disjunctions characterize not only the internal structures of the three principal faculties, as Kant presented them, but the relationships among those faculties as well.[15] Each faculty can be called upon potentially to impose rational form on the same data, even on a universal scale. But each can perform this organization only imperfectly, by the standards of reason as it is invoked in each case. Therefore, each faculty is needed to rectify rational inadequacies of the other two; and yet, there is no rational way of understanding how these three systems could operate simultaneously or converge on each other. Thus the concept of the organism, for example, can be adduced by judgment, in its teleological mode, to remedy certain deficiencies of cognition. For in its clear formal boundaries and apparently total structural autonomy, that is, in its apparent possession of a ground for the necessity of its own structural connections, the concept of the organism suggests a kind of immanent or concretely embodied causality that, unlike the more abstract cognitive principle of cause and effect, can account in some fashion for the particularity of empirical world. But, like the autonomy of the organism, the explanations offered by the concept of the organism are cognitively untenable. The cognitive certainty of mechanistic causality and the explanatory power of the organism metaphor cannot be fused.[16] The two principle remain discrete and unconnectable, though also analogous in various ways. Both, for example, can define structures that seem autonomous in the sense of possessing internally necessary connections; and both can be considered structural analogues of an underlying and universal structure of mind.

Even more significant gaps within the mind are evident between the two faculties that Kant was most eager to connect in some manner, the faculties of theoretical reason (cognition) and of practical reason (the moral faculty or will). The latter was called upon by Kant as an essentially demystified means of salvaging the irrationalities that limit the natural or knowable universe; but despite its grounding in the human mind rather than in a metaphysical realm of being, the moral faculty cannot render the cognitive universe rationally complete, cannot repair its defects on terms acceptable to theoretical reason. In effect, Kant's effort to salvage reason for the human world forced him to divide reason into two irreconcilable though structurally analogous realms, each self-contained and yet each incomplete, the moral no less than the theoretical. For though the human moral faculty was conceived by Kant as in some sense more encompassing than the cognitive faculty, and as located at a deeper level of subjectivity — where it defines a kind of essence as well as goal of the other faculties, where it points toward an unknowable ground for the resolution of all differences among them, and where it presses more forcefully toward an apprehension of metaphysical being — nevertheless, it, too, is limited.[17] It cannot, for example, define being in any but a subjunctive mood, so to speak; and it cannot itself be defined, or contribute to any arguments for God's existence or explanations of the world, except by way of thought and language, as these take shape in the domain accessible to cognition. Hence it always finds its credibility limited by cognitive necessities, especially the law of noncontradiction;[18] and ultimately it can salvage the possibility of a rational ground for the irrationalities of the cognitive domain only by suspending, and hence violating, the laws of cognition, which are for humans the clearest paradigm of rational necessity.

To be sure, Kant presented the theoretical and the moral as analogous rather than as contradictory, but the effect of a logically insuperable disjunction remains the same; for analogies do not admit of logical necessity, or indeed, of any cognitively necessary or certain connections. Kant's strategy was to take a principle, analogy, that is nonexclusionary or formally open in the domain of cognition and try to extend its operation to other levels of thought (or possibly being). In contemplating the resolution of its own contradictions through a shift of levels in the mind, he suggested, cognition can imagine the ontological primacy of reason to be, by cognitive standards, formally possible. But from the standpoint of cognition, a contingent rationality — a rationality that exists only as a formal possibility — is by definition an irrational principle, or rational only in some mystical sense; for theoretical reason cannot reconcile the necessity of its own laws with the freedom of contingency (or of morality). Thus Kant was ultimately forced, in spite of himself, to anchor rationality by the irrationality of moral fiat: Kant established in effect that what is morally necessary, such as the ontological primacy of reason, must on moral grounds be logically possible. And even so, the morally necessary remains necessary in a moral sense only: Kant's "must" cannot reconcile the morally necessary aspects of reason with the logically necessary ones; in effect, then, even if not precisely contradictory, the two remain, as analogues, irreconcilable. Here again, in a context recognized by Kant as crucial to his defense of reason, reason seems to expose itself as in a fundamental sense irrational.

Nor can the faculty of judgment, either in its aesthetic determinations of beauty or in its teleological definition of the organism, be understood, finally, to mediate, as Kant intended it to, between the theoretical and moral in the sense of actually connecting them. This is not to deny that Kant associated the position of judgment in the mind with such notions as "middle term" (*Mittelglied*) and mediation, or that at one point he even asserted, in effect, that aesthetic judgment "makes possible the transition, without any violent leap" from the natural to the moral.[19] The structural analogies among these faculties may well facilitate passage from one to another in the ways that Kant suggested; but judgment cannot bring the two rational faculties any closer together than the patterns of analogy and drive to an unattainable limit permit.

Instead, what Kant designated as the mediating status of pure judgment within the mind is probably best understood to consist in the balance this faculty maintains between discontinuities prominent in one or the other faculties of reason as well as in its crystallization of limitations implicit in both. What makes judgment a middle ground of the mind is not just the nearly even balance between analogy and drive that is characteristic within it but also the disjunctions that cut it off from extrasubjective realms of being and make it openly no more than subjective or formal, since like cognition, judgment claims no direct relation to the metaphysical (say, by way of freedom), and since like the moral faculty, it claims no direct relation to nature (say, by way of law). And yet, though it is subjective and formal, judgment lacks even those advantages of form through which Kant attributed universality to the other two faculties, which are also subjective, in that its form or law is explicitly concrete. Pure or aesthetic judgment is in no position to demonstrate or even to assert persuasively the universal validity of its determinations. And this is because the law of judgment, though amounting to the structure of judgment and in no way binding on sensory data, is yet by definition wholly inseparable from the individuality of each aesthetic determination, that is, from a state of structural analogy within the faculty of judgment that can be defined only in the noncognitive apprehension of configurations in their concrete, and relatively particular, wholeness.[20] In short, judgment is isolated in both the formality of its jurisdiction and the concreteness of its self-definition. Both limitations make it a paradigm of the contradictions involved in the notion of structural autonomy as a condition that manifests itself in subjectively defined or created structures, and both ultimately begin to suggest judgment as the archetypal faculty of the whole mind.

Internally, then, the basic structure of the human mind, which in effect amounts to the structure of reason, is presented generally by the *Critique of Judgment* as a fundamentally contradictory, autonomous structure, or, more accurately, as a bounded field of discrete, analogous structures, all knowable only as forms that define themselves concretely, though all are presumed modeled on some unknown, abstract archetype. This *intra*subjective structure bears a close resemblance to the *inter*subjective pattern of relationships that seem, finally, once the critical viewpoint is adopted fully, to obtain between people in their semiotic activities. Much as the notions of model and analogue seem fundamental *within* the structure of the mind as Kant depicted it, so, too, that mental structure in turn can readily be construed as an analogical model of the field formed by all humans' internal mental images and external semiotic structures. For in this field, too, if one leaves aside for a moment the question of outer boundaries, the post-Kantian must conclude that one is faced with numerous structures, within various minds and externalized. These structures seem to be self-contained and yet are driven toward connections with each other as whole structures, connections that can never be known with certainty to exist; and thus, in the end, one can suppose these structures to be related to each other only in the discrete manner of analogy.

To be sure, Kant worked on the basis of a universal (through internally disjunct) structure of reason that permits a secure communicative connection between minds. But again, despite Kant's efforts to prove otherwise, this transcendental structure is by standards of irrefutable certainty unknowable, not only as to its form but also as to its existence. For in both respects it can be posited only by analogy with known mental structures, which are always empirically defined. And again, analogy is not an implicative relationship: one can imagine but one cannot logically deduce either the independent existence, in any knowable sense of the term "existence," or the precise form of an archetype from any, or even many, of its supposed analogues, any more than one can deduce all possible analogues or variants from an alleged archetype.[21] Nor is there any logical limit to the number of analogues that may coexist in a series; a premise may have only one logical conclusion, but the structure premise-and-conclusion could underlie any number of analogous variants, and none could be understood as more correct (or real) than any other. In short, the relationship between analogues cannot exhibit the necessity of connection, the closure, the completeness, or the verifiable correctness that is associated with logical resolution (or, to an extent, even with mechanistic causality). But since the gaps in identity characteristic of analogues cannot be removed through the formal connection of logic, the process of relating any such structures in terms of formal similarities always involves a fundamental contingency. Therefore, since the archetypal mental structure proposed by Kant can only be posited by the contingent relationship of analogy, one cannot assume with certainty either its existence or its universality. Indeed, once the structure of mind is defined in terms of the inner, subjective mind, which can only be presumed concrete, then one cannot be sure of any connection between two or more such structures either by way of a common underlying archetype or by way of the external structures through which the empirically defined inner mind projects itself. The one universal assumption that the critical attitude seems finally to sanction about mental structures is the negative assumption of their nonuniversality.[22]

Consequently, once Kant's critical position is adopted and rigorous limitations are placed on what can be called certain knowledge, all human semiotic processes must be viewed as contingent. Communication, for example, can be imagined only as the possibility of mediating between discrete subjective minds, which may or may not have a common, abstract archetype, by way of one or more whole (in the sense of autonomous) and external structures—let us call them semiotic structures—which in turn may be recognized or felt by each of the minds in question as, in effect, analogous to one of its own structures and hence as meaningful. But exactly how such a semiotic structure may be analogous to any particular mental structure cannot be known or demonstrated. Being external, all semiotic structures have necessarily been mediated at least once, from an inner mind, and possibly twice, if the originating structure within that mind is after all abstract. And being external, such structures exist in the contingent realm of the empirical or the concrete, that is, their existence has a physical, and one must also add a cultural, component over which the individual mind does not have complete control.

Thus, as Kant himself suggested in the case of genius,[23] a gap exists between a semiotic structure and every subjective mind, even the one that produced the structure, which is to say that every semiotic structure must to some degree constitute a deviation from or even a distortion of the inner structure that projected it. Analogues are not identities. And to demonstrate or explain one's relation to a given semiotic structure, one can only adduce still another mediating and discrete external structure; but no matter how many mediating structures are brought into play in the form of translations, interpretations, or criticism, no knowable connections can be made between any of the minds or semiotic structures in question. In other words, from a post-Kantian standpoint, all semiotic structures must be assumed beyond the reach of any cognitively verifiable connections. One must imagine each such structure, like each inner mind, as totally surrounded by a logically un-bridgeable gap or, in effect, as too particular for total apprehension through the generalizing forms of cognition. Both this surrounding gap (which con-stitutes a boundary) and this particularity mark the semiotic structure as au-tonomous; and in the sense that all semiotic structures possess such auton-omy, they can all be considered analogous.

This is not to say, however, that beyond the condition of autonomy, recognizably analogous and hence meaningful formal features can necessarily be found in all semiotic structures, or any particular ones. On the contrary, from a post-Kantian standpoint virtually no characteristic of semiotic struc-tures can be posited as necessarily present in any recognizable sense since such recognition is entirely a function of the contingently present and partic-ular interpreting mind. As in the case of the mind itself, that is, the autonomy of the semiotic structure is contradictory. Though such structures present themselves as formally discrete and free of any necessary dependence on a particular subject, they can be recognized and interpreted as meaningful only to the extent that they can be identified as structurally analogous to a concrete subjective mind. This means, essentially, that the number of interpretations that can be put on such a structure is as indeterminate as the number of sub-jective minds, and that no meaningful formal characteristics can be imputed *a priori* to any semiotic structures, even though some such structures will clearly seem to some minds (and in some cultures) more amenable to in-terpretation than others, more evidently stamped by traces of semiotic inten-tions, or semiotically less incomplete. Where a single universal interpretation could be guaranteed, a semiotic structure could be considered intrinsically meaningful; where the number of interpretations is unbounded, the structure must be considered intrinsically meaningless.

Still, the cognitive isolation—or, to use a notion more or less suggested by Charles Rosen, the cognitive inexhaustibility[24]—of the semiotic structure does not necessarily preclude those structures from manifesting analogies of structure that are recognizable to some. Though the mental structures—or let us say the forms of reason—which project and apprehend semiotic structures can only be known as concretely defined forms, nevertheless, within this limiting concreteness, one can imagine two poles of form, one tending toward cognitive generality and abstractness, the other toward aesthetic particularity and overt concreteness. Thus, if the form projected by the mind on empirical data is imagined as constituting in a sense a very narrow (or, perhaps, deeply grounded) aspect of the total configuration that is externalized or apprehended, then one can imagine that form as able to impose itself on a great diversity of data and to serve as a recognizable generalizing force among large numbers of semiotic structures. To similarly constituted minds, extensive similarities, and consequently also differences, of internal pattern and outer boundaries could be perceptible and meaningful; and as the narrow form in various similar configurations approached a state of absolute abstraction, the formal differences between those configurations could be imagined as approaching insignificance; and thereby the possibility of highly reliable scientific communication could be maintained. Highly reliable but not infallible: since form cannot be imagined to divest itself altogether of concreteness in the human's empirical world, cognitively insuperable gaps of identity would remain characteristic of human semiotic structures, so that unlike transcendental forms of reason, merely narrow forms of reason, however similar, could not be imagined, in Benjamin's phrase, to "make the similar identical" in any absolute sense.[25]

If, conversely, one imagines the form of reason to be concrete in the broadest possible sense and to constitute a very large proportion of empirical configurations, then both individual similarities and differences among configurations would tend to become subordinate and unnoticeable relative to the collective effect of such similarities and differences, that is, to the collective effect of particularity. And again, though from a Kantian perspective one could not equate such a "broad" or "surface form" with the absolute entirety of an empirical configuration, since the empirical data of the latter must be assumed to originate outside the mind, still, as broad form approached such a condition of totality, the only analogical similarity that one could expect to perceive among semiotic structures would be what amounted to a common physical condition of virtually complete—and meaningless—particularlity, a condition of brute physical discreteness. This could be called an "analogy of difference." As the extreme case of concreteness, this situation could be taken to define the outer boundaries of our semiotic field as a whole.

At either end of its spectrum, however, one must acknowledge that form, as it is connected with the mind, must be construed as concrete; (indeed, although notions of narrow and broad form may help maintain some distinctions between what I have called the formal limits and empirical bounds of the mind, even that distinction is considerably undercut by the common concreteness and contingency of both). And beyond this it must be acknowledged that form in this concrete sense, and, more generally, the kinds of semiotic structures, fields, and relationships that can be associated with it, all bear a strong fundamental resemblance to the character, domain, or operations of the aesthetic faculty as Kant described the latter. Thus the objects of perception in such a field have to be imagined as maintaining a core of cognitively unreachable concrete particularity and as being accessible to the human mind only through the purely formal device of analogy. Likewise, perceptions in such a field are fundamentally isolated in the sense of being undemonstrable. No matter how close an analogy might exist between the forms of a given semiotic structure and a given mind—which is to say, no matter how necessary the internal connections of that structure seemed to a given individual—the individual could not demonstrate that necessity. One could only feel it and try, through the strength of that feeling, to persuade others of it.

But what this means is that if reason is defined as the structure of mind through which we apprehend our world and externalize what we apprehend, then reason itself must be recognized as at bottom aesthetic, which means, at bottom, lacking in capacities essential to reason as man conceives it. Reason, that is, must be recognized as not just a wholly subjective principle but also as an irreducibly concrete and hence a potentially individual and isolated one, unable to demonstrate its own internal necessity and perfectly capable of manifesting itself in structures that are interpreted by others as free of all law, arbitrary, meaningless, or even outright irrational. And thus again, reason must be accounted like aesthetic judgment in its inability to overcome rationally its internal disjunctions between form and freedom. And in this connection it seems significant that the name of aesthetic judgment, that last faculty adduced by Kant in a failed attempt to mediate between the binary symmetry of the two faculties of reason, no longer contains the term "reason."

Despite the old-fashioned Enlightenment rationalism evident in many of Kant's own opinions about art, the *Critique of Judgment* has in fact been associated in many ways by critics with the historical onset of an aestheticized conception of the artwork as an autonomous structure.[26] And the same is essentially true of models like the one I derive from the *Critique of Judgment*. Beginning with Kant's own discussion of artistic pedagogy, for example, models similar to mine have figured, though not necessarily explicitly or graphically, in a number of theories about the character or history of art, including in our own century the rejection of art history proposed by Walter

Benjamin, Harold Rosenberg's notion of "the tradition of the new," and Harold Bloom's suggestion of art as the creative misinterpretation of models—theories all suggestive of "analogy of difference."[27] Such models could also be readily associated with the emergence of criticism itself as a needed, though cognitively uncertain, way of mediating between artwork and society by providing plausible meanings for the artwork. And such a model, with its emphasis on the autonomy of the subjective structure, seems to show up with particular explicitness in the work of a critic like Adorno, who tended to interpret the onset of aestheticism in a political fashion, and to equate the capacity of art to turn inward, toward its own formal resources for order, with its capacity to serve as a force critical of society. Some of the resemblances between Adorno's conception and the Kantian model described here I shall now try to suggest. But before calling attention to such resemblances, it is important to clarify certain elements in Adorno's conception of artistic autonomy as it pertains to music.

In a traditionally referential art, such as literature, an artwork that presents itself as explicitly autonomous can be construed as criticizing society in the sense that it rejects (or at least tries to reject) all principles of order originating in society, and, as Rosen puts it, "substitutes its own order for that of society."[28] In terms of the Kantian model adduced here one could say, as Adorno himself essentially did, that such art cuts itself off from any direct connection with society, renouncing all relationships with it except such analogies with social structures as happen to emerge in the working out of immanent structural possibilities. One could also say that the autonomous artwork exercises its drive to criticize society without ever actually reaching society and being corrupted by its means of organization. In either sense, the artwork becomes less easily comprehended by society, more resistant to interpretation, and more obdurate in its presentation of itself as being a particular, sensuous, opaque, and irreducible semiotic structure. And by refusing to bring about open and direct communication, the autonomous artwork makes evident the contingency of communication and thereby focuses attention on those inhumane conditions of society that foster this contingency and, for example, allow art to define itself as autonomous.[29] In its opaqueness, art calls attention to itself as a failed act of mediation and, hence, as criticism.

In music, however, the notion of autonomy is complicated by the existence of a principle, uniquely proper to music, which by virtue of its capacity to establish premises and imply their resolution over time, seems able to render music meaningful in an entirely self-referential way. The principle is tonality as the classicists, especially Haydn and Mozart in their respective ways, conceived it. Adorno made little explicit reference to tonality—no doubt, too little—but he was unquestionably fascinated with its capacity to define through temporal means a self-referential structure. To be sure, Adorno did not deny the dependence of the apparently autonomous meaning of classical structure on subjective minds; rather, he took advantage of the right I have already noted to call a universally intelligible structure (assuming such a thing is possible) intrinsically meaningful. From Adorno's viewpoint, it is clear, tonality in classicism is used to generate a temporal structure that functions in very much the manner of what I have called "narrow form" and, in fact, suggests itself as a particularly close approximation of a universal form of reason. Adorno often alluded to the temporality of classical music in terms of the semiotic advantages of a pure or universal logic. He argued that this temporality allows the establishment of an apparently cohesive, self-limiting, and more or less intrinsically intelligible argument within the bounds of a musical structure. (One might say that from Adorno's standpoint, classical musical structure fosters the illusion that the outer bounds of reason are not contingent but necessary.) He obviously believed that this temporality permits the perception of functionally significant differences between formally similar, or even virtually identical, structures, such as antecedent and consequent; and he stressed that classical temporality encourages the mind to reason actively in order to follow that argument and perceive those differences (as if connecting itself with cognitive security to "a universal point of reference, with which the representative power of everyone is compelled to harmonize").[30]

All of these capabilities were clearly of great interest to Adorno as metaphors for a condition of humanity that genuinely accommodates individual differences by interpreting them in terms of supraindividual forms of reason, not in terms of contingent and particular identity. Adorno never claimed that classical music signifies such a human condition directly; given the virtually total self-containment of the classical structure or what Adorno approvingly called Mozart's "detachment from empiricism," one can attach such an interpretation to classicism only by the cognitively uncertain device of analogy.[31] Nor did Adorno assert that musical classicism actually achieves the universal intelligibility of a pure or normative logic. But "detachment from empiricism" without question does connote a kind of transcendental reference, and Adorno quite evidently believed that classical music points within itself to an "ideal," beyond its own actuality, of "music as a deductive unity,"[32] an ideal that amounts to a state of complete identity between structural self-government and semiotic self-evidence, a state where, in Rosen's words, "the significance of the form . . . must ultimately be considered inseparable from the form itself."[33] The classical work seems to present such a state of completely rational intelligibility as its own normative condition as a semiotic structure; and because the norm involved here evokes the idea of a fundamentally humane rationality, it seems that it mattered very much to Adorno that classicism is a style that is, to quote Rosen again, "normative in aspiration as well as achievement."[34] Still, the formulation given this norm by Haydn and Mozart, in Adorno's judgment, does not yet call full attention to the total configuration in its full individuality or, therefore, to the relation of such a norm to individual freedom but rather allows "form" — obviously construed here as narrow — "[to] remain an abstract sheath over . . . diversity."[35] (What Adorno seems to have meant by this is, primarily, that various individual elements, and especially thematic elements, are not yet fully integrated into a configuration so tightly organized and comprehensive that they seem to determine its organization completely, and also that these elements, consequently, maintain an explicitly general or exchangeable character not wholly specific to the particular configuration at hand. In some respects, clearly, these opinions are debatable.)[36] At any rate, Adorno seems to have associated this incomplete individualization with something like the absence of a developed analysis, within this music, of the contradictions in the utopianism of its own norm;[37] on the whole he seems to have been inclined to characterize pre-Beethovenian classicism as "pre-critical."[38]

It was Beethoven, in Adorno's opinion, who achieved the first critical state of autonomy in music by fully accommodating the freedom of individuality in his notion of form. This he did, one could say, by changing, and thereby questioning, his fundamental model of autonomy, from the cognitive model of abstract logic and the narrow conception of form associated with it, to the model offered by teleological judgment, the organism, and the closely related broad notion of form as total, particular configuration. The individual piece was given a more overtly concrete character through a drawing of essentially nonimplicative or sensuous musical elements, especially melody but also timbre, into the temporal structure of functional tonality to create what Adorno called a "systematic composition": by drawing all the various parameters of music into the structure as a premise, Adorno argued in effect, Beethoven's sonata movements seem to manifest the internal causality of the organism.[39]

Of course, Beethoven, in Adorno's opinion, did not merely shift from a cognitive model of form to one governed by judgment; in addition, he seems momentarily to have synthesized the two. (Indeed, from Adorno's association of Beethoven's music with individual freedom and his reference to "the Beethovenian must," among other things, one can well conclude that for him, Beethoven approximated a synthesis of all three mental faculties; but this provocative idea requires a lengthy exposition and evaluation of its own.)[40] What Beethoven did in terms of cognition and judgment, one can infer from Adorno, was to synthesize the virtually abstract general logic of narrow form with the openly concrete individuality of broad form in such a way as to make the principle of general order seem to emanate from concrete individuality. Thus Adorno not only asserted of Beethoven that he "seeks to rescue the objective formal canon that has been rendered impotent, as Kant rescued the categories: by once more deducing it from the liberated subjectivity."[41] In addition, he stressed in connection with Beethoven that "the structural element of music . . . is defamed by many listeners as 'intellectual,' though it constitutes the concreteness of the musical phenomenon even more than the sound. . . . "[42] In short, Beethoven seems, in Adorno's judgment, to have saved the general validity of reason for the concretized world of the Marxian tradition,[43] or, to put it another way, Beethoven's music, which in Adorno's words "annihilates . . . the contingencies of the listener's private existence," seems to preserve the necessity of transcendental reason for the newly concretized, contingent, and yet free individual.[44] It is a synthesis that Adorno found at once utopian and critical as well as untenable, and one that he believed Beethoven himself questioned even as he approximated it.[45] Whatever its value as a metaphor for the free individual, Adorno in effect argued, the Beethovenian musical structure cannot, finally, embody a ground that guarantees the universal intelligibility of its meaning, any more than the supposedly autonomous organism can guarantee the necessity of its own existence. It is in Beethoven's music, according to Adorno, that music first reveals the potential isolation of the individual from all the human advantages, including human survival, of a universally binding reason.

It is at this historical juncture, when individual freedom has been both defined musically and exposed as tenuous or even untenable, that music begins to define structural autonomy more in the ways that are available to the other arts, by increasing its emphasis on its own sensuous parameters and thus on sensuousness. This has the effect of calling attention to the particularity of music as a medium, to the particularity of the total, concrete configuration, to particular strata or parameters within the work, and as Adorno stressed, to particular components or units of structure. In other words, the turning inward of music on itself as a closed or "pure" medium can readily be associated with what is clearly seen as a pervasive individuation of music in the nineteenth century by Adorno, who also noted a corollary atomizing of the musical public. In fact, Adorno presented the entire domain of romantic music as very similar to the Kantian archetype of the mind with its disjunct patterns of analogy and blunted drive and its exposure of a contradictory autonomy at each of its levels.

One particular aspect of contradictory autonomy deserves special attention because it led Adorno, on the whole, to judge romantic music harshly; this is the relation of the romantic musical structure to the empirical world. Adorno seems to have reasoned that when a musical composition, like other artworks, presents itself as explicitly autonomous, it becomes more opaque, more explicitly sensuous and particularized, less "exchangeable," both as a whole and in its parts. It focuses attention specifically on its sensuous surface and thereby, though still recognizably semiotic in character exposes itself as lacking any whole, cohesive, or hence, unmistakable intrinsic meaning. But music becomes opaque by giving up an immanent temporal ordering principle that through its quasi-logical character has already brought music as close as it can get not merely to physical independence as structure but also to a meaningful structural independence from socially imposed principles of order. And thus, paradoxically, this rejection of classical tonality, this open revelation of itself as in a strictly intrinsic sense meaningless, brings music *closer* to society, not in the sense of conveying rational meaning—which music can do, according to Adorno, only through a temporally cohesive internal structural argument—but in the sense of taking on the exclusively empirical character of the world in which society exists and operates. Generally speaking, time ceases to be idealized in a synthesis with logic and instead is delineated and experienced in a literal sense. Likewise, the broadly empirical as opposed to the more abstractly formal character of structural boundaries is emphasized. And much as empirical boundaries in the case of the mind are indeterminate, so too what could be called the outer boundaries of the romantic structure—say, perhaps, the clarity of its harmonic pattern and direction, the restrictions it places on its harmonic usage and vocabulary, its opening and closing—are smudged, largely through the substitution of sensuous rhetoric for harmonic logic. (Thus, though a work may be made physically recognizable as an autonomous unit through rhetorical emphasis, it may well not be so recognized in terms of internal logic and, consequently, may be experienced principally in terms of its composer's style.) Because its boundaries are obscured, a sense is fostered that the structure has failed to maintain a clear barrier between itself and the empirical world.[46] In other words, this smudging of external boundaries makes evident the semiotically incomplete character of the internal structure of the romantic work in such a way that the latter seems actively to invite the imposition of meaningful order on itself from without, from the empirical world, in a way that the classical work, with its illusion of self-evident intrinsic meaning, does not.

Thus, first of all, Adorno seems to have argued, the romantic musical structure openly encourages apprehension of itself as a concrete, static block analogous in form to the mind of the fundamentally isolated, merely empirical individual, precisely because of the way in which the music kills off the appearance of an internal temporal argument (accessible, perhaps, to some sort of cognitive connection). The composition breaks up temporally cohesive tonal and thematic argument into discrete self-contained units so that in temporal terms, the piece begins to resemble a field of analogous autonomous fragments. Adorno called attention in romantic music to a repetition (or slight variance) of melodic units that, unlike classical repetition, involves no functional differentiation but just formally static differences in identity between the units repeated. Adorno was especially fascinated by the emergence of the unmistakable theme, or what he called the potential "quotation," which invites the listener to impose meaning in the form of a contingent name on the musical structure.[47] As a result of such devices, both the musical structure and the listener's mind become essentially passive and isolated autonomous structures, according to Adorno: the piece, because it no longer generates its own internal temporally cohesive meaning or argument; listeners, because they no longer need exercise an active and rigorous faculty of reasoning to follow such an argument but can turn inward to make private associations with pieces or themes they can identify by name, or whistle.[48] Adorno did not go so far as to say that the internal argument of a romantic work is as difficult to recognize in Western society or as resistant to interpretation beyond the imposition of labels as, say, a piece of Balinese or Vietnamese music would be; but clearly he views romantic musical structures and the modes of apprehension they draw as a move toward structural unintelligibility.[49] To respond to a work by saying, "It's by Wagner," for example, is not so very different from saying, "It's Balinese." And when people begin to answer the question "What does it mean?" as if the question were "What is it called?"—replacing the perception of significant formal differences within an individual structure with a preoccupation with identity—the force of reason as a principle that binds and protects human individuality seems, at least to Adorno, clearly vitiated.

Similar conclusions could be drawn about what Adorno seems to have seen as the romantic use of essentially nonimplicative, sensuous, or rhetorical devices to simulate a temporal drive that connects its internal moments, a drive that could well be associated with Kant's formula "purposiveness without purpose." Through an accumulation of such devices, Adorno seems to have suggested, romantic music can compensate for the loss of a comprehensive tonal goal by building up a kind of quantitative momentum, a drive that is empirical and imposed, rather than logically self-generated or capable of reaching some rational resolution.[50] Adorno referred, for example, to the "drug tendency" and the "irrational function" of structurally unarticulated sound in Wagner's music, "where the mere magnitude of the sound, into whose wave the listener can dive, is one of the means of catching the listener, quite apart from any specific musical content.[51] Here again, the effect on listeners is to render them passive, turned in on themselves to experience only what Adorno construed as fundamentally private bodily sensations, either physical or sentimental, that can then be projected back onto the piece as its meaning, sensations that clearly lack a ground of rational binding with the minds of other people.[52] What seems to have been involved here for Adorno was a kind of blunted temporal force, a surface temporality paralleling the empirical temporality of human life once the latter is separated from a transcendental ground of reason, where one moves "forward" in the flow of time without any overview of the entire temporal structure or one's place in it, where one begins and ends where one does arbitrarily, and where at most one feels oneself moving toward some revelation of necessity or meaning that can never be reached.[53] It is an impression of empirical time that Rosen, too, seems to evoke in his observation that the romantics tend to "constrict the expressive elements so that they can be cut off at the moment of their greatest intensity."[54]

In defining itself as autonomous, then, the romantic composition moves closer to the empirical world; and yet, so long as one is prepared to accept the notion of a meaningless autonomy, it does not lose its autonomy. It does not yield up a rationally decipherable meaning to society; on the contrary, its intelligibility becomes as contingent as the empirical world itself. Or, to put this differently, if tonal structure is equated with narrowly formal limits in romanticism, as in classicism, then clearly the romantic work does maintain these limits. True, it exposes them as arbitrary and contingent rather than logically necessary and thus, in a sense, seems to draw them toward an identity with the indeterminacy of empirical bounds. But it does not negate the limiting or isolating quality of limits, or effect an actual cognitive connection between itself and that world. In other words, romantic music manages to taint itself with the empiricism of the outside world while simultaneously maintaining an autonomy that retains the limiting character of rational limits without any means of demonstrating them rational.

To Adorno's mind, indeed, the romantic defense of individuality turned out to be a self-indulgent and morally indefensible (though also artistically unavoidable)[55] exercise in individualized expression precisely because the romantic musical structure could not integrate the concreteness and discreteness of its individuality, and individualized elements, with some self-derived, supraindividual, generally binding, or transcendental principle of musical order that guaranteed individual choice as rational. And it must be emphasized that any imposed principle of order, even a purely musical pattern with a generally recognizable character, represented from Adorno's standpoint a patently unacceptable or false source of generality in the sense that it was obtained only through a violation, at the level of internal temporal or narrow structure, of the condition of autonomy or individual freedom that the increased emphasis on music as a sensuously "broad" configuration seems to have proclaimed.[56] (And at that, the form imposed cannot always be construed as fundamentally general. Whereas sonata structure in a Beethoven symphony can still suggest itself as a plausible embodiment of a transcendental and universal rational structure, its counterpart in a Brahms symphony suggests as its archetype nothing more intrinsically necessary, abstract, or general than classical sonata structure or, to be more accurate, Brahms's interpretation of that structure. From a post-Kantian viewpoint it would appear that postclassical sonata-structure, like any configuration defined in pure judgment, can be assumed the projection of a concrete individual mental structure; but it cannot be taken for an underlying source of rigorous order, rationally generated within the individual musical structure itself.) Here again, then, as in the fragmentation of classical temporality, Adorno appears to have perceived a disjunction between semiotic elements of the romantic musical structure, in this instance between the vestiges of a meaningful narrow form and the particularity of broad form. These apparently are two poles of form that no one musical faculty can comprehend in a rational synthesis, any more than a single faculty in the model of the mind bequeathed to us by Kant can make rational sense of both the general or cognitive and the particular or aesthetic (sometimes teleological or even moral) aspects of any empirical configuration, or apprehend any such configuration as a real whole in a securely rational way.

One could make the argument that the various romantic solutions to the construction of an autonomous musical structure actually expose the truth about the limitations of the human mind and its semiotic interactions and in fact expose as illusion the hopes for a transcendental unity of reason lodged in classical structure. Adorno did not openly deny such an association of romanticism with truth, but he seems to have been concerned far more with the antirational consequences of such a critique and in particular, it would appear, with the inability of most romantic music to designate even in a utopian sense any grounds for a synthesis of rational law and freedom or, hence, for a binding force of reason in the universe of humanity.[57] In effect, though perhaps very often in spite of itself, romantic music in its emphasis on its own sensuous autonomy seems from Adorno's point of view not only to have given in to, and to be no better than, empirical reality but even to celebrate the merely empirical aspect of human existence: in failing to point within itself to an ultimate, transcendental rationality, even an unrealizable one, such as Kant's moral reality, Adorno seems to have argued, romantic music renounces even the possibility of intrinsically rational meaning in order to take up merely empirical being—and thereby accepts the inhumane status quo of human existence.

And yet, Adorno admitted in many ways that from his standpoint, the only morally defensible or critical alternative to romantic musical autonomy is a course of action that openly destroys the semblance of art, meaning, and humanity itself in musical structures.[58] This is the solution that crystallizes in Schoenberg's twelve-tone technique of turning individuality itself, or more specifically, the individual identity of the pitch, into a rigorous, indeed, absolute principle of organization. Far from reestablishing a rationally comprehensible continuity, cohesiveness, or drive to resolution, Schoenberg's twelve-tone principle is, in Adorno's words, "capable only of ordering the moments, without revealing their essence in any penetrating way to each other."[59] Here one seems to reach an extreme of the analogy of rationally unbridgeable differences shown possible in the structure of the human mind as Kant presented it.

The dissociation implicit in Kant's image becomes emphasized in another sense as well. As clarified in romantic music, the limits of reason that render the mind autonomous are not the necessary consequence of a logical internal mental structure but ultimately arbitrary and contingent. Adorno seems to have suggested that in the twelve-tone structures of Schoenberg and Webern, the outer boundaries of Kantian reason are virtually denied altogether (or, perhaps, collapsed entirely into indeterminate empirical bounds) in order to reveal human semiotic structures, and the human mind, as nothing more than a random aggregation of identifiable but subsemiotic pitches (or phonemes or atoms), existing in a whole universe of such particles, no longer lending themselves to any semblance of rational connection and no longer definitive of individual structures (or values) within which significant similarities or differences can be generally perceived, much less comprehended.[60] (Serial composers since Schoenberg and Webern, of course—toward whom Adorno was not well disposed—have individualized music well beyond the "atomic" level of pitch, much as scientists have continued to divide the atom into particles. At an extreme, though Adorno did not say this, one could imagine the boundaries of a piece that had undergone pervasive internal disintegration becoming absolutely imperceptible, so that the piece became, for society at large, indistinguishable as an event or structure from the noise surrounding it.) By carrying the principle of individualization far enough, the limits that defined individual structures as humanly meaningful can be negated; and it then becomes possible to define a new universality, consisting in the nonuniversality or unique identity of every particle in the empirical universe. This is not, clearly, a universality suggestive of any universal and humane access among individual people. It is rather a universality of incomprehension and meaninglessness.

Adorno did not suggest that Schoenberg's music goes this far. And yet, despite the fierce intellectual concentration known to have been involved in the works of the Viennese school, its works are probably perceived as little more rationally intelligible inside Western culture than outside of it. In other words, in the twelve-tone technique of atomization, a new universality emerges, a new source of rigor and abstraction, a new "narrow" form, which at last renders the musical structure as absolute in its autonomy as any other sort of artistic structure, that is, as resistant to all efforts within society to impose any plausibly rational meaning on its internal structure. At this point, obviously, the contradictions of subjective autonomy become glaringly apparent.

Of course, Adorno would hasten to assure us that the same effect can be claimed by a great deal of openly antiexpressive, purely formalistic twentieth-century music, stemming from traditions other than German romanticism and Viennese classicism. And the pattern is likewise suggested by the reductive imagery in many twentieth-century disciplines, which tend in some way to fragment values into identifiable or, perhaps, to be more accurate, measurable particles. To all, Adorno might well have argued, despite considerable differences in underlying conception, the message could be attributed that there is no limiting structure of reason to stop one from construing any or all human semiotic structures — or human beings — as mere empirical matter. This universality of the irrational, which seems implicit in the structure of mind that Kant adumbrated to defend reason, seems to have been confirmed for Adorno in the music of Schoenberg, who was to Adorno's mind the last great champion of human rationality in music, but who in failing, unavoidably, to reconcile the broad forms of empirical individual expression with the narrow forms of cognitively rigorous structural organization, exposed the dissociation of both from any rational conception of reason.

In general, Adorno's attitudes toward the musical styles that concerned him seem to have been shaped by an insistence on the necessity for a constant exertion of critical force in defense of a rational individual freedom. He posed this necessity as political; but ultimately, he seems to have shared a sense implicit in the *Critique of Judgment* that the struggle of human reason, represented by critical activity, is up against limits and contradictions of the human mind that, insofar as we can know and define the latter, are rationally insurmountable. In effect, Adorno's seems to have been a stance of metaphysical despair that might well be applied to the criticism of all human societies and their cultures.

At the same time, however, for Adorno as a post-Kantian, metaphysics itself could be seen only as a structure projected by the concrete human mind; and likewise, Adorno was clearly prepared to define reason itself, insofar as it had been institutionalized as a value in Western culture and had defined itself as "bourgeois reason," as a legitimate and, indeed, crucially important object of critical analysis. Therefore, it would seem to be in keeping with Adorno's critical spirit to look at various specific Western musical styles in more detail than Adorno himself did to determine whether, to what extent, and in what ways they conform to the Kantian model adduced here—to see how various music contributes to Western modes of defining reason, to see whether such music, too, like Kant's critical philosophy and Adorno's criticism, suggests certain contradictions in those modes, and to see what ways it adumbrates, if any, of getting around those contradictions. For by means of this sort of criticism one might likewise, perhaps, help keep alive at least an awareness of the need to overcome such contradictions, however unlikely such an overcoming might be. To this end, any music that could be associated with such traditions or movements as rationalism, the Enlightenment, or the growth of technology would merit critical analysis, even music that Adorno himself tended to treat as precontradictory, so to speak, or precritical. And if one considers the prominence of analogy in my Kantian model (and accepts the cognitive uncertainty thereof), a particularly plausible choice would be the mature instrumental works of Haydn and Mozart, produced, like Kant's critical philosophy, at the end of the Enlightenment. For on the one hand, such music could, at least in theory, respond to the same broad cultural and historical forces as Kant's critical philosophy; and on the other hand, it would not yet be subject to the influence of the latter, nor would any relation it bore to Kant's philosophy be complicated by the mediation of post-Kantian intellectual or cultural developments. Adorno himself had relatively little to say about this music, though he did assert that "of all the tasks awaiting us in the social interpretation of music, that of Mozart would be the most difficult and the most urgent," noting that "he who would socially decipher the central content of music cannot use too delicate a touch. It is by force or on occasion only that antagonistic moments will be musically identifiable in Mozart."[61]

No doubt in Mozart's music, and still more in Haydn's, as in Kant's critical philosophy, anything that one might plausibly define as a questioning of reason would be a good deal less explicit than in the critical traditions (musical or philosophical) that followed. Still, without denying the clear emphasis in classicism on quasi-logical connection, functional difference, and the resolution of conflict, one can speculate about certain aspects of pre–Beethovenian classicism that seem to invite further reflection along the lines of the preceding discussion.[62] The characteristic classical work, for example, in some ways resembles the domain of cognition as that domain is described in the *Critique of Judgment*. It has clear formal limits in that it stays within the confines of musical and specifically tonal reference, and these limits are essentially arbitrary. (The beginning and end of a classical sonata movement may be determined by an internal logical tonal structure, but this cannot be said for the classical work as a whole, nor can tonality as a system be characterized a necessary structure by virtue of some internal necessity of structure akin to that in a tonal argument.) Like cognition, the classical structure encompasses all of its apparently complementary dualities within its own formal limits. And until Beethoven began to experiment with linked movements and climactic, synthesizing finales, the classical work conveyed little sense of itself as a counterpart to Kant's moral faculty, which, in terms of the third critique, seems to have incorporated within itself a far more powerful thrust toward the metaphysical than did cognition.[63]

By the same token, of course, the classical work defines a domain that is marked prominently by discontinuities, large and small. Its movements are unconnected though analogous in general tonal sense. And within each movement, the "seamless, almost uniform flow of baroque music" (connected by Edward Lowinsky with Leibniz and the so-called law of continuity) has given way to a pervasive articulation.[64] Within the archetypal classical structure, the sonata, temporal propulsiveness is articulated both at principal junctures and, on the smaller scale, between phrases and within themes.[65] Among general features of classical structure, one would want to give particular thought to the precise moment at which the music, after what Rosen calls "a general drift to the dominant," actually articulates its arrival at the dominant.[66] Can this articulation, which is often marked literally by a pause, be called a gap, and does the gap signify the ultimate absence of any necessity in the movement from I to V? This movement does not, after all, seem intrinsically necessary in the same sense as does a movement from V back to I. (The difference seems akin to that between moral fiat and logical necessity, or between the relation of major and minor premise, on the one hand, and the relation of premise and conclusion, on the other, a difference of great import to all theories of the world as rational.)[67] At any rate, it could be instructive to see to what extent and how the classical composers reinforced or undercut the illusion of necessity at this moment of connection.

On the smaller scale, one would want to look more closely at the relation of antecedent and consequent phrases and the particular ways in which this relationship is defined in various works. Though typically (but not always), the two have complementary harmonic features that distinguish them functionally, their rhythm or shape often make them seem analogous as well; and when the latter parameters seem emphasized, as in the opening of the Mozart A-Minor Piano Sonata (K. 310) (or, later, in the opening of Beethoven's Fifth Symphony), the effect of analogy or variant may momentarily predominate.[68] One would want to examine the context such effects, as well as the instances when particular prominence is placed on stepwise or literal transposition of phrases or when details of diverse movements seem explicitly analogous. And in general, one would want to see in what ways, if any, classical repetition or variance provides a basis for those weakly functional repetitive statements in nineteenth-century music that, as the composer Frank Retzel has pointed out, evoke the notion of a "flat hierarchy."[69]

Of particular interest would be evidences of analogy at the level of large-scale structure, for example, in the relationships between premise and resolution. To what extent and precisely how does the opening material of a classical work serve as a premise? Does it somehow engender what follows? Is its internal structure of antecedent and consequent a kind of archetype of the structure as a whole?[70] Is this material in some particular sense a minature of the entire movement? The C-sharp that Rosen calls the "unexplained dissonance" in the opening theme of Beethoven's Eroica[71] — unexplained, one can suppose, in that the appearance of this note is not accounted for by common harmonic practice — is "explained" later in the movement, presumably, by the appearance of the enharmonic D-flat at the opening of the recapitulation and coda sections. And yet, what sort of explanation is this? Is it a matter of cause and effect? Or is it rather an attempt to explain a relatively individualized harmonic conception in *post hoc, propter hoc* fashion, through the sheer presence of analogous appearances? One could ask the same sorts of questions about certain abrupt changes of key in pre-Beethovenian classical movements. "When this [sort of change] happens," Rosen remarks, "something in the opening section has made it possible."[72] The exact nature of the causality involved here is intriguing. Instances of this sort would bear thoughtful interpretation, especially if juxtaposed against theories of continuity and of archetype (*Urbild*) developed in eighteenth-century philosophy.[73]

Closely related to this critical problem would be the relation of the recapitulation to the rest of the movement, a consideration that brings up the whole pattern of drive toward a limit or goal. Adorno wrote that in "conserving [the recapitulation] Beethoven has grasped [it] as a problem."[74] Typically one thinks of the recapitulation in a classical structure as a synthesis; but it may also be possible to regard it as an attempt to resolve preceding conflicts by a shift in levels of structure in the same sense as Kant attempted to resolve the contradictions of cognition by shifting to a moral level that was at once higher than that of cognition and yet analogous to it rather than complementary. Adorno seems to have had some such idea in mind when he implied, in effect, that Beethoven came to define the return of I as a moral rather than as a logical necessity.[75] At issue here, of course, is not only the necessity but also the very nature and possibility of synthesis. Is a return in I, which negates the particularity of V, actually a synthesis or merely a contingent, analogous return of some sort?[76] Examined from this point of view, the particular ways in which Haydn and Mozart treated both the moment of recapitulation and the relation of the recapitulation section to the preceding structure might contribute substantially to one's notion of the term "reason." Moreover, Adorno's idea that dynamic thematic development carried far enough leads to a technique of static variation might well have relevance to the notions of recapitulation as mere recurrence and of synthesis as an unattainable goal; and in this connection it might be worth investigating Rosen's observation that "it is through the transformation of themes and not their contrast that the classical composer affects us most."[77]

And one further pattern in classicism reminiscent of the Kantian schema proposed here is a pattern to which Rosen has called attention in several contexts: the posing of a direct contrast followed by what appears to be the missing mediation.[78] This is, of course, the pattern suggested in classical sonata structure by the exposition with its two contrasting tonal poles on the one hand and the development and most likely the recapitulation on the other. It also describes the relation of aesthetic judgment, as presented in Kant's third critique, to the polarity of the two faculties of reason that are analyzed in his first two critiques. It would be instructive to determine whether this sort of mediation seems, finally, more complete or convincing in classical music than in the *Critique of Judgment*, and if so, why.

I offer here only a few questions that might be asked of the classical work in a critical enterprise that derives its method from Kant's *Critique of Judgment* and invokes the spirit of Adorno. Clearly, any such enterprise, if carried out in detail, would have to distinguish carefully between what the classical composers seem to have defined as generally necessary (or formally narrow) and what they defined as individually free (or formally broad); and it would then have to see whether the two are somehow rendered identical, or if not, whether and how the composer mediates between them. Here, obviously, stylistic differences between Haydn and Mozart would have to be taken into serious account. And sooner or later, one would have to confront here in systematic fashion the problem of time, which for Kant was a subjective condition of human or sensuous intuition, and which for Adorno was brought into synthesis with formal logic by classical music. In connection with conceptions of the world that began to take clear shape at the beginning of the nineteenth century, Arthur Lovejoy has written, "The world of concrete existence . . . is no translation of pure logic into temporal terms—such terms [are] themselves, indeed, the negation of pure logic."[79] Adorno might well have found value in a critical analysis that could relate classical temporality to that problematical structure of reason that Kant made thinkable, and in which Adorno himself discerned the unthinkable.

Part II
Stylistic Criticism

Chapter 5

Musicology and Criticism

I have been charged with addressing the situation of scholarship in nontraditional areas of musicology.[1] Given the limitations of space and of my experience, I shall focus here on the character and problems of an area in which I myself have worked, that of scholarly music criticism.

Defining this field is itself a problem, especially if one tries to do so through reference to existing American scholarship; for outside of journalistic criticism, which is not my concern here, American music criticism is an elusive and fragmentary phenomenon. For the most part it consists in scattered, highly divergent essays by individual scholars who seldom identify their enterprise as criticism, and who work in relative isolation, since there is rarely more than one such figure in any American music department, since few of their students can afford to remain in criticism, and since few, if any, have generated even a small identifiable school of critical methods or thought. A handful of these scholars are well known and publicly admired, or at least respected, by their more traditional colleagues, although I have observed that even prominent scholars are subject to surprisingly widespread private disapproval in traditionalist circles for the nonfactual nature of their critical works, or else are principally esteemed for those aspects of their work that fall within the domain of traditional empiricist scholarship. Relatively few critical works—and I include here even Charles Rosen's *The Classical Style* and Joseph Kerman's study of the Beethoven quartets, despite the unavoidable use of these books in historical survey courses—have had a major role in defining the activities, goals, or attitudes of American graduate programs in musicology. Instead of being integrated into the very core of musicological study, the methods and viewpoints of critical scholars seem to

87

be subjected to deep analysis mainly in relatively unconventional courses that carry little weight in the student's preparation for doctoral exams.

And just as the critical works of even such leading American musical scholars as Rosen, Kerman, Meyer, Cone, Treitler, and Lippman, not to mention those of such non-Americans as Dahlhaus and Nattiez or such non-musicologists as E. D. Hirsch, Roland Barthes, or Harold Bloom, have individually exerted far less influence than it seems to me they should, so too, collectively they have had relatively little impact on the character and direction of American musicology as an institutional whole. Unlike its counterparts in literature and the visual arts, American musicology has yet to devote any substantial energy or support either to the intellectual issues of criticism or to the definition and study of any extant body of critical investigation or theory. On the whole, in fact, the study of critical literature is openly deprecated by mainstream musicology as a purely derivative and parasitical enterprise, even though for years now it has dominated the curriculum in English literature at most American universities. I myself have encountered strong resistance on just such grounds to the very idea of making Adorno's musical writing an object of serious scholarship, again notwithstanding the fact that Adorno's criticism has affected European musicology profoundly. One established traditionalist actually explained his resistance to my work (which he confessed to not knowing well) and also that of some far better known critical scholars by saying simply "I don't like the category."

Criticism, including the study of criticism, remains an unestablished field of musical scholarship. In part, I would say, this very status, which impedes the definition of criticism, constitutes evidence of intellectual attitudes within the mainstream of American musicology that are restrictive, even to the point of being exclusionary. In fact, I would argue that the tenuous status of criticism reflects in no small measure the stifling effect that such attitudes, operating in positions of power, have on freedom of speech within American musicology as a whole. I shall return to these matters a bit later. In part, however, it must also be admitted that disunity of character and aims is implicit in *all* modern criticism, and that modern criticism by its very nature resists most definitive generalizations. For one general assertion that *does* seem to me valid is that modern criticism is an activity primarily concerned with the interpretation of meaning and, as such, depends heavily on the exercise of individual discretion for both its practice and its interpretation. Interpretation today, I believe, is largely an individualistic activity because it takes place in a world that no longer provides rational support for belief in any single set of principles, values, or conceptions of truth as a basis for universal understanding of one, single, unmistakable meaning. In brief, no particular interpretation of any human statement or artifact can be guaranteed by modern thought as universally valid or, hence, as definitively correct.[2]

Whether or not interpretation has everywhere and always been subject to as much individual variance as is evident today is a matter I cannot take up here. What is more to the point is that the very need for interpretation seems, at least in the Western world, to be a distinctly modern phenomenon, and that in fact criticism in the West has not always been primarily concerned with interpretation. It became so, according to Charles Rosen in the first of two articles on Walter Benjamin, only toward the end of the eighteenth century.[3] Prior to this, criticism was principally concerned with judging value. Neither the nature of this change nor the time in which it occurred should surprise the student of history. Judging the value of an artifact presupposes that the meaning of that artifact has been unmistakably understood. Now in theory, at least, it was possible to assume an intended meaning as self-evident and to pursue judgment in a spirit of confidence so long as Western culture was dominated, as it was during the Enlightenment, by a belief in abstract universal reason as a real and existing standard for the shaping of intelligible languages and for the determination of validity and truth.

But as soon as universalistic conceptions of reason themselves became objects of criticism, as they did not only in the political activism of the French Revolution but also by way of Kant's philosophical critiques and, I would argue, in the more individualized works of Mozart and Beethoven, then confidence in judgments of value was bound to weaken. At the same time, an awareness was bound to grow of those differences in concrete individual experience and cultural values that limit the clarity with which an intended meaning can be communicated, especially as an artifact travels outside the circle of its origin, that is, of differences that turn the interpretation of meaning not into a parasitical diversion but into an urgent human need and also into a problematical process. One could say, into an art. And it was precisely at this historical juncture that great early modern thinkers began to describe the work of criticism as, in the words of Friedrich Schlegel, "itself a work of art," as well as to place the critical act, in Charles Rosen's words, "at the center of the work of art."[4] Even those modern twentieth-century idealists, such as Lévi-Strauss and Chomsky, who still hope to define new bases of universality within the domain of human thought, have been unable to validate the status of their principles or structures with scientific certainty.

Scientific certainty itself is an abstract Newtonian ideal of universality that has been undermined by the passing of the Enlightenment worldview and the growth of the modern critical spirit. The very rise to prominence of empirical research in nineteenth-century Western culture points to a decline of Western belief in abstract scientific certainty in the sense that (as Hume pointed out during the Enlightenment itself) empirical observations cannot claim the same qualities of universality, necessity, and certainty as we impute to abstract mathematical laws. A truly consistent scientific empiricism, that is, as opposed to an empiricism that has merely adopted uncritically the ideals of an earlier rationalism, must eventually take on a skeptical attitude toward universal principles and admit of limits on the scope and certainty of its own observations. Positivism, a nineteenth-century invention, has been a favorite Western response to this pressure, though it is by no means the most humane, resilient, or enlightening one, least of all for twentieth-century problems, largely because beneath its radical reduction of knowledge to the empirical sphere, it has kept intact an inappropriate allegiance to an ideal of essentially absolute scientific certainty.

At any rate, by the early twentieth century, the limits to scientific certainty were marked quite literally by Heisenberg's formulation of the uncertainty principle. And today there is a growing tendency to view modern science, in its totality, much less as a source of universal values than as merely another cultural artifact, an artifact that is no doubt useful and "paradigmatic," to borrow Thomas Kuhn's term,[5] but also restricted in its validity by the limitations of actual experience, especially those amounting to the blind spots of the particular culture that produced it. The uncritical conception of science as a privileged embodiment of universal truth is rejected even by thoughtful scientists, as a potential source of false claims and evil values.

In fact, the limits of scientific validity and certainty must be evident to any thoughtful observer of the modern technological world. And once these limits are acknowledged, one would expect serious attention to be given to new modes of thought, such as criticism, which question a wide range of traditional scientific concepts, from universal reason to scientific objectivity, and which might serve the modern spiritual recognition of relativism, including even its empiricist components, more honestly than do the absolute certainty and the confusion of ethnocentricity with universality that typified the Enlightenment. Yet as Morse Peckham suggested in *Beyond the Tragic Vision*, many Westerners, however modern in style or technology, continue to adhere uncritically to a comforting Enlightenment belief in universal laws and certainty,[6] or at least, one might add, to some newer, thinly disguised, but essentially unchanged version of that belief.

I would argue that mainstream American musicology in its current state constitutes one such backwater. The ruling concept of knowledge within that mainstream seems to me to be shaped by an uncritical and outmoded notion of science, grounded on a dogmatic Enlightenment ideal of general laws and absolute verifiabilty, and overlaid with an accretion of equally dogmatic, though narrower and supposedly value-free or nonideological, positivistic reverence for the so-called hard certainty of empirical fact.[7] And mainstream American musicology has found it easy to dismiss or reject criticism as a significant scholarly activity largely, I believe, because it judges criticism by this notion, even though, as Charles Seeger indicated some thirty years ago, in the *Journal of the American Musicological Society*, criticism is in fundamental ways the polar opposite of traditional science.[8]

Criticism is, in fact, as many noted philosophers since Schlegel have observed, an essentially aesthetic undertaking, a counterpart to the work of art itself. As such, one would suppose it had great value as an instrument for dealing intellectually with music, especially the music of the past two centuries, which, in its own way, has been preoccupied with the same problems of communicating meaning and establishing value in a relativistic world as criticism has been. But there can be no denying that when measured against old-fashioned scientific standards of absolute certainty and universal validity, or even against the alleged hardness of empirical fact, criticism, like composition itself, can be denigrated as a soft or flabby variety of thinking.

Let me dwell a bit on the relations of criticism first to empirical fact-finding and then to more general aspects of the traditional scientific ideal. That the empirical establishment of facts does not bring about any absolute state of knowledge should be clear, if not from Hume's testimony, then at least from the endlessness of the revisions with which we torment our factual textbooks. Even the most authoritative critical score has no absolute way of protecting every one of its crotchets and quavers from future empirical revisions. Still, there is a degree to which empirical studies can be reasonably, though roughly, measured through reference to the current status of fact. Criticism, however, largely eludes even such approximate measures of truthfulness; for expertise in criticism consists not in the mastery of any body of facts but in the refinement of an unquantifiable sensibility. The domain of criticism, moreover, is huge, potentially encompassing all of human experience and thought, for there is scarcely a culture, or discipline, or body of artifacts from which the conscientious critic cannot derive means for refining such a sensibility further. Mastering even a small portion of this domain is quite obviously the work of a lifetime, during which the critic will have far less opportunity than the specialized empiricist to work up facts from scratch or to certify them as up-to-date.

But let us assume that the good critic pays meticulous attention to ongoing empirical research and is thereby able, by current standards of information, to avoid at least significant error. Even in this best possible case, the domain staked out by the critic will still contain, at the close of his or her career, far more messy variables, unknowns, and even unknowables than the severely restricted domain of an empiricist counterpart, and will be far more openly permeated by speculation. This is because criticism is not primarily concerned with elements, conclusions, or kinds of knowledge that can be characterized fairly by the traditional hard scientific choice of right or wrong. Being inherently relativistic, criticism admits its inability to achieve scientifically definitive results or to protect its findings against hazards—hazards shared, I insist, by many facts—arising from differences or changes in scholarly sensibility. In this respect the critic differs sharply from the traditionalist. Whereas the traditionalist may admit that the "facts" of a modern critical edition could someday be challenged, such a scholar can scarcely imagine that the very *idea* of such an edition might be dismissed or rejected by some future culture as an ideal of significant knowledge. The critic, by contrast, must grapple from the outset with the notion of a time or place in which not only one's dates but also one's interpretations of data and the ideals of knowledge underlying one's interpretations may be disregarded or even ridiculed. (By and large the American critic already works in such a time and place.) In effect critics, like the post-Heisenberg scientist but unlike the traditional Newtonian musicologist, have in some sense to acknowledge their own presence in their acts of scholarship and thereby the limitations of pure objectivity and universal validity that are entailed in their results by their particular outlook and decisions. And finally, to complete the portrait of the modern critic as a post-Newtonian, the critic, or at least the fair-minded critic, is likely to distrust the unthinking use of accepted general principles, based on an uncritical belief in a self-evident common sense and to treat the various objects of study as individualized problems of understanding, requiring constant adjustments in discretion and sensibility for fair treatment. For that matter, even the critic who is dogmatically committed to a particular ideological doctrine is forced constantly to clarify his or her relation to that doctrine, thereby giving the reader a fair chance to discern this commitment.

So far I have emphasized the epistemological value of fairness over that of accuracy. This emphasis is of particular importance, I believe, when one goes beyond a mere description of criticism to a consideration of what constitutes good criticism. I do not claim that the good critic can or should be liberated from either a reasonable respect for facts or a healthy repugnance for factual distortion. I do not advocate giving license to self-indulgent fantasies of free association among critics or releasing the critic from the burdens of hard work and discipline. Nor do I think it advisable to try to free the critic from that adherence to rigorous principles of order which, as Stravinsky suggests so memorably in his *Poetics of Music*,[9] seem necessary even to the most imaginative intelligence.

What I do argue is that the kinds of hard work demanded by good criticism are different from those required by empirical research. What I do challenge is the inhuman demand that the critic master, *in their entirety*, not only the skills, literature, and problems of the critic's own craft but also those of empiricist musicology as well as those of any other traditionally defined discipline on whose domain the critic treads, in order to give his or her work a degree of certainty that is neither relevant to criticism nor intellectually attainable. What I do believe is that a diligent effort should be made to understand the critic's principles of order, along with the rationale and discipline based on those principles, on their own terms.

This last request, to be sure, involves problems, for modern critics no longer have available an external set of supposedly true common principles from which to derive their own standards of rigor, but must develop their principles of order from within their own thought. The same is true, of course, of modern composers and even of modern scientists, who in the last analysis must delimit the area, goals, and means of their research through personal convictions of propriety. This need to turn inward may make much of the modern critic's rationale difficult to fathom on first reading, and still more of it impossible to verify as generally valid.

In fact, it is difficult to deny that much of the value of the principles of order through which the good modern critic works out his or her ideas depends on an indefinable, though not imperceptible, quality of honesty that the critic brings to the development of those principles. This is why I emphasize the indispensability of fairness to the acquisition of human knowledge. The ultimate sources of the good modern critic's principles of order, like those of the good modern composer or scientist, are not, I say, fully accessible to scientific demonstration, explanation, or validation precisely because honesty, which forms the foundation of those principles, is an essentially moral rather than scientific attitude. And for the perception of moral rigor, a capacity for fairness not only has power; it has far more power, I submit, than a capacity for accuracy.

Now, however much we may still be tied to an ideal of scientific universality, few in our profession are any longer comfortable with the notion of moral universals. I think most people today, outside the questionably named "moral majority," would admit that even a principle as basic as "thou shalt not kill" admits of diverse sincere interpretations. In other words, we admit that the development of moral principles of order depends more upon the exercise of individualized discretion than upon recourse to what I called earlier "an external set of supposedly true common principles." The closest any of us can come to a universal mode in developing our moral rules as a basis of order is, as Kant suggested in his categorical imperative, by deriving those rules from a strong inner feeling of what ought to be universally binding. But this feeling does not in fact render our own rules universally binding or even acceptable. Remember that it was Kant himself, more perhaps than any other single Western individual, who (in spite of himself) sharpened the modern capacity to appreciate differences in moral imperative among individuals and cultures.

What all this leads to is the following argument. Just as the most authentic modern critic, composer, or scientist derives his or her essential principles of order from an underlying moral sense of what constitutes true and necessary coherence, trying with scrupulous good faith, like Beethoven in his sketchbooks, to work out those principles consistently and intelligibly so as to establish persuasively their general validity, so too authentic *interpreters* of modern criticism, or of any modern expression, ought to approach their material in a spirit of refined moral sensibility. By this I mean that their own acts of interpretation and judgment should be fashioned in accordance with their own highest sense of fairness, even as they admit that sense to have the limitations of individual discretion rather than the absolute status and certainty of universal reason or a God-given decree.

It is my strong conviction that in a world where the rationales of the individuals we encounter are often unfamiliar and obscure, every interpreter of human expression has a moral obligation to go about the work of interpretation in a spirit of scrupulous good faith. And it is likewise my conviction that fulfillment of this *moral* obligation works to the *intellectual* benefit of interpreters because it puts them in an unexcelled position to understand what they interpret. Let me emphasize that I do not define a spirit of scrupulous good faith as synonymous with an attitude of uncritical acceptance, any more than I equate good critical methods with a rejection of intellectual rigor. The good modern interpreter may well have to reject, and quite vigorously, a rationale that, once understood, seems openly evil. Such an interpreter has a right, indeed, an obligation, to point out factual errors as well as inconsistencies of argument, though I believe it is useful to distinguish between significant and insignificant factual errors. And at no time must such an interpreter feel obliged to agree with either the premises or the conclusions of the work under study. Nevertheless, I do believe that modern interpreters are morally bound to withhold judgment, above all negative judgment, until they have fulfilled their *primary* obligation as a good critic, which is to make sure they have come as close as possible to understanding the sources and terms of another person's argument, the precise meaning as well as the main thrust and the spirit of that argument, and by no means least, the positive values of that argument.

I would argue that since all of us, whatever our ideology or specialty, function as critics with respect to each other's work, we ought to go about performing that function in a spirit of good faith and even generosity. We ought to bring to our interpretation of each other's expression at least a provisional assumption that the other has principles of rationality and order that give this person reasons for saying precisely what was said. We ought to ask, wherever possible, for clarification of what we do not understand. We ought to bring enough interest and intellectual curiosity about another's work to refrain from pointing out its weaknesses until we have absorbed at least some of the goodness it offers. We ought to have the courage to rely in our interpretations and judgments on a fair and honest, though always fragile and reflective, faculty of discretion, individualized to the case at hand, instead of on the unexamined authority of general rules that may be inappropriate or unreasonable[10] We ought to bring to our interpretations a genuine conviction that views of knowledge or truth that differ from our own are not necessarily wrong, inferior, or negligible. And we ought to bring an acute awareness of the degree to which our own principles and values, from which are never free, affect our understanding and evaluation of others, together with the flexibility and rigor to reexamine our own standards whenever they run up against the uncongenial. Attitudes like these, which might nurture a magnificent climate of free speech, have not, to my knowledge, been prominent in the response of traditionalist American musicology to most works of criticism, or to any nontraditional essays into methodology, theory, or cross-disciplinary research.

Of course, once the easy certainty of scientifically "hard" and general principles is relinquished, the understanding and evaluation of scholarly work, especially work in an unfamiliar mode, becomes fraught with risk. I would argue, however, that by refusing to risk an exercise of discretion, American musicology faces far more serious risks, such as those of alienating many of its own most gifted students or prospective students, and of removing itself permanently from the mainstream of modern thought. (How many nonmusicologist humanists, even those working on the history or theory of various arts, find it worth their time to attend musicology conventions or to read almost any musicological journals?) Worst of all, musicology faces the risk of perpetuating many of the inhumane practices and values in society at large which stem from an outmoded worship of science and which a true humanistic discipline should be superbly equipped to counteract.

Even now, traditionalist resistance to the unconventional has already had some ill effects so disturbing as to suggest other, less admirable motives for such resistance besides a simple good-faith adherence to old-fashioned scientific ideals. I return here to the current status of free speech within American musicology. Free speech, after all, was an ideal that developed out of the same Enlightenment values as Newtonian scientific ideals. One would suppose that any true believer in the primacy of the latter would be up in arms about the slightest infringement on the former. Yet what musicologist would persuasively argue that American musicology today is characterized by a true state of free speech, that is, by a genuine hospitality to a diversity of ideologies, and by a determination if not to encourage then at least to protect the activities of those who dissent from the traditionalist ideology of nonideology?[11] What counterpart does American musicology in its various institutional forms offer to a civil liberties union that would protect the unconventional scholar from the silencing effects of such attitudes as insecurity with the unfamiliar, prejudice against whole "categories" of study, or just plain intellectual laziness within the traditionalist establishment?[12]

In fact free speech is no more simple and unproblematical an ideal in the relativistic, culturally diversified modern world than scientific or moral absolutism. To foster it in a spirit of genuine fairness has required constant shifts of sensibility, reapplications of discretion, and responsiveness to ever-new questions of individual merit. This is a messy process that holds out no promise of realizing definitive conclusions or even of formulating general laws that can cover every conceivable contingency. It is a process that has forced fundamental reinterpretations of free speech itself as a less than self-evident or absolute value. All in all, this process does not fit well with traditional Western ideals of a clean, efficient scientific thoroughness. And yet there is, at least at present, no alternative to this messy application of a discretion forged in good faith if the spirit of the ideal underlying free speech, the freedom to be individual, is to be maintained in the modern world.

And the situation is similar if the spirit of the ideal underlying traditionalist scientific conceptions, namely respect for truth, is to be maintained. Indeed, it is rarely, if ever, possible to maintain in the spirit of any human value by uncritically maintaining old formulations of that value, even if the technological apparatus for reaffirming those formulations is modernized.[13] If the modernization of means is not itself self-critical, that is, if it does not derive from its own state of change a reformulation of the principles underlying it, then the progress represented by such modernization is merely cosmetic and not humane. With respect to humane values, this sort of modernization is actually injurious, for it fails to confront significant changes in the circumstances and attitudes of the human world, and hence to provide ways of securing humane values in a changed world.

In the case of scholarship, it no longer serves truth to presume the self-evidence and universal validity of one's own laws and values or to restrict the concept of knowledge to a determination of unarguable certainties, even if the abstract notion of absolute certainty is modified into a concrete notion of "hard" certainty, reinforced through ever more sophisticated empirical technologies. What is needed, in my judgment, to preserve the spirit of truth in a modern scholarly discipline such as American musicology, is a recognition of genuinely pluralistic diversity as intrinsic not only to the enterprise of criticism but also to the modern conception of truth. Such recognition can only come about through a reassessment of current philosophies and policies, leading to a radical enlargement of sensibility and spirit, which in turn opens up and expands American musicology to dimensions far more worthy of it. Unless such a self-examination, painful though it be, is undertaken, mainstream American musicologists must expect to be viewed by many of their less conventional colleagues, including critics, as modern-day embodiments of that nineteenth-century anachronism Beckmesser, who would rather chalk up divergences in expression and call them errors than listen for the beauty of an unfamiliar music.

Chapter 6

Evidence of a Critical Worldview in Mozart's Last Three Symphonies

Let it be said at once that this essay is not an attempt to deduce logically or to prove in any scientific way the philosophical import of Mozart's last three symphonies. That is not possible. My attempt here simply is to point out signs of what I have come to understand as an important aspect of meaning in these works.

Nor is there room below for a detailed exposition of the methodological principles out of which this study has grown. Instead it will be taken as more or less axiomatic that formal conceptions and choices can be construed as powerful, though indirect and sometimes metaphorical, evidence of assumptions about the structure of reality. Likewise it will be assumed that from the formal relations perceived in an artwork, a critic can reconstruct plausibly in words some essential aspects of an attitude about what, if anything, is necessary or at least possible in reality as well as about the ways and respects in which humans can impute intelligible meaning to it.

The methodological problems associated with what I call "particularity of identity" will for the most part be left for future studies. For example, I shall not consider the general bearing of stylistic typicality or atypicality on processes of interpretation, except in passing.[1] It must be acknowledged, however, that the significance and value I find in these symphonies—my reasons for choosing them as objects of analysis—inhere less in their presentation of a received cultural style than in their structural particularity. I mean particularity here in the sense not so much of a distinctive individual identity as of a coherence among the diversified components in each work, a coherence much like that of a single complex organism.

Intrinsic to the very worldview discerned in this music (and to the inherited view of our own culture) is the idea that the meaning or rationale of a structure can never be entirely separated from its particularity (the sensuous concreteness) of the form and techniques through which meaning is expressed, and that, consequently, such meaning yields no incontrovertible truth or justification on the basis of abstract universal principles. So in this respect it is important, indeed crucial, to distinguish between generalized and individualized aspects of these symphonies, and to note the relative emphasis given to each. This sort of distinction could be drawn from large-scale statistical surveys of conventional practice, using the methods developed, say, by Jan LaRue, or more recently by David B. Greene.[2] Conversely, it could be drawn also from sketches and revisions if they provide enough evidence to indicate those elements the composer intended to endow with a refined (i.e., individualized) shape. In the present study, however, the notions of "general" and "particular" are defined mainly through analysis of the conceptual character of an element — the question to be decided being whether an element points toward broadly applicable principles, on the one hand, or toward an irreducible individuality of sensuous and expressive identity, on the other.

This study, like all interpretations of particular works, rests on some provisional assumptions about the significance of the original cultural and stylistic contexts of the works in question. My central hypothesis is as follows: the three symphonies give musical articulation to an incipient shift in philosophical outlook; this shift showed itself in a number of late eighteenth-century works of genius,[3] took on concrete implications with the success of the French Revolution, and marked a decisive turn in Western cultural beliefs toward what we, as postmodernists, can call a modern worldview. In brief terms, this shift moved away from the precritical Enlightenment belief in abstract universal laws thought to govern the structure of reality and to give it intrinsically rational, even intelligible meaning insofar as the laws could explain this structure. From a precritical standpoint, it was still possible, among other things, to count on the existence of some supraindividual principle whereby all apparent irrationality (and by extension, all discord, suffering, and evil) could be justified as a rational necessity. The move toward a critical stance involved putting into question the universal status and metaphysical primacy of reason itself, for reason was gradually becoming recognized as a human construct or at least as a structure inextricably embedded in concrete human expression, as human thought in turn became acknowledged explicitly as inseparable from the sensuousness and contingency — in a word, the particularity — of individual and cultural experience. Not only was this shift eventually to engender in the West the spirit of what has been variously called relativism, pluralism, or, to use Arthur Lovejoy's phrase, diversitarianism,[4] a spirit that recognizes the diversity of values and rationales within human expression. It was also to foster the spirit of existentialism which, lacking Kant's confidence in the transcendental (abstract yet knowable) universality of reason, concedes the metaphysical uncertainty of any rational or meaningful foundation in the universe. From such a viewpoint, it becomes difficult to discover either the binding force of any principle transcending experience or any sort of rational or meaningful necessity for suffering. Not unnaturally, as such a worldview develops, more and more attention is given to assessing the quality of actual, sensuous existence as well as to exploring the potential power of individual freedom and choice, at first within the strictures of general laws of reason, but eventually outside them. For whether such laws be those of Newtonian science, religious morality, standard artistic practice, or just plain common sense, both their universal validity and their metaphysical necessity are weakened by ever-deepening doubts as the laws themselves are broken with impunity or proven inapplicable or unpersuasive.

The origins of the shift can be traced, though with unavoidable simplification, to the sources of the enlightened worldview itself, that is, to the emergence of Renaissance humanism, which could be called, plausibly but paradoxically, the beginning of the end of secure Western belief in God as the guarantor of a humane meaning in the universe (i.e., the beginning of the end of the noblest Christian vision). And Bertolt Brecht surely goes to the heart of Galileo's impact on thought in the seventeenth century, the century that, incidentally, created opera—the first secular musical structure in the West conceived on a scale sufficiently grand to rival that of religious music—when he identifies Galileo's vision of a universe as a blow to belief in the necessity of (actual, existential) suffering.[5] The idea of God as the ultimate governing force in the structure of the universe was gradually losing its character of absolute reality and immediacy and thereby much of its irrational terror—hence the eventual concept of "Enlightenment" and its capacity to unify a culture. Still, this idea of God retained considerable ideological power in Europe for several centuries after the emergence of humanism, as Galileo's own tragedy exemplifies. This power can be felt and even demonstrated metaphorically in many artistically significant musical structures as late as those of the last baroque masters, above all Bach but also, for instance, Handel.[6]

Yet as elements of postbaroque style gained prominence alongside eighteenth-century baroque music, and to no small extent in the styles of Bach, Handel, and Vivaldi and, most strikingly, of such French composers as François Couperin and Rameau, European art music as a whole was taking an audible and historically decisive turn toward expressing secular beliefs and affirming their cultural dominance.[7] Though neither scientifically demonstrable nor identifiable without prior historical knowledge, this turn can be associated above all with a shift in aesthetic values that looked to the idealization of musical autonomy. This ideal, which would result eventually in attempts to liberate sound from meaning itself, is already evident in late baroque music, not only in the increasing weight of music without words but also in the sheer physical enlargement of coherent musical structures generally. And the notion of autonomy can be even more readily linked with such aesthetic characteristics in postbaroque styles as the collapse of referential or mimetic ideals (as exemplified in rhetorical affect or symbol) into ideals of expressiveness and purely sensuous pleasure. It seems no exaggeration to assert that one may discern in this new emphasis on musical (and artistic) autonomy a metaphor for the metaphysical autonomy of humans themselves — for their liberation from an older binding conception of God and for their conception of themselves as self-determining beings and even as creators rather than creatures. It is toward the end of this very century, after all, that the concept of creation, once associated exclusively with God, is decisively extended to the artist.

But again, though antirationalism and even elements of irrationalism could be cited in the literary writings of protoromantic figures such as Rousseau, postbaroque Enlightenment culture did not immediately abandon all hope of an ultimate source of intelligible meaning in the world; rather, it developed a more or less posttheistic belief in universal reason. Largely stripped of Leibniz's metaphysics and operating (like Western science today) as a kind of successor to religious belief, this trust in universal reason dominated the more characteristically enlightened thought of Rousseau's French colleagues on the *Encyclopédie* and is equally evident in Rameau's theoretical writings on music. Even in Kant's critical philosophy itself, which exposed the intellectual vulnerability of rationalism by rallying so forcefully to its defense, the analysis of reality was shaped consciously by a vision of the universe as an ultimately rational (at least in the sense of a moral) structure. Indeed, Kant took great pains in the second part of the *Critique of Judgment* to affirm the pervasiveness throughout this structure of *Zweck* or "purpose." This notion not only allows the components of reality to be explained rationally in terms of their large-scale interrelationships of function but also requires a continuing ascription of the laws of reason to a governing mind, that is, to God. At any rate, Kant's universe is fundamentally rational (though not fully comprehensible in a scientific sense) in that all its components are believed to have an underlying moral function or purpose, so that without exception they can be referred to universal laws of moral, or what Kant calls "practical," reason.

It is my conviction that belief in some sort of universal reason retained a governing, though no longer unchallenged, force in the construction of most European art music throughout the eighteenth century.[8] And although it is not possible to provide a systematic justification of method in this essay, I shall single out a few of the many interrelated formal characteristics in Mozart's last three symphonies as metaphorical signs of such a belief. All the characteristics are apparently normal in the sense that they constitute both common and unforced idioms within the style of these works, and all depend, ultimately, on a concept of tonality as a structural principle of general character and applicability. This concept had been clearly developed in European music as early as Corelli, and indeed there is a broad correlation between these intrinsically normative features in Mozart's last three symphonies and the common stylistic language of eighteenth-century European art music, a language that can be taken to signify a widespread cultural viewpoint. What distinguishes the classical formulation of this language, at least up to Beethoven, seems to be the conception of tonality not only as a principle of credibly general force or rationality but also as a means of shaping large-scale complex structures (metaphors for the universe itself?) that are fully and intrinsically intelligible, that is, intelligible in a self-evident as well as in an audible way.[9] That the realization of this conception required great individual powers of choice and purpose seems paradoxical. As will be seen, the essentially general character of this conception was undercut even as it was being realized. Before investigating this paradox, some of the more general traits themselves should be described briefly.

The prevalence of complementary pairings of shape and an attendant effect of necessary connections. In these works, as in classicism in general, formal elements on all levels are organized normally into pairs of complementary structures, such as the antecedent — consequent or periodic phrase, a structure that invariably reasserts itself on the local level after disruption. On a broader level of, say, an entire composition, the I and V (or i and III) areas act as logical counterparts in that the V area normally (though in fact not always) emerges as a kind of necessity through preparation of its own dominant. With some notable exceptions, Mozart is likely to project the connection between I and V as a self-evident and therefore a universally binding necessity. He does not emphasize the actual arbitrariness, the cultural particularity, or the conventionality of this connection by highlighting harmonic patterns so markedly disjunct or individualized (i.e., opposed to the very nature of convention in the intricacy of their inner relations or direction) as to disrupt the forward harmonic momentum and the establishment of a connection.

Indicators of a functional conception of musical identity and difference, and an attendant effect of the general intelligibility of form. In these three symphonies the definition of formal elements as exemplified in periodic structure depends less on the effect of their particular sensuous configuration *per se* than on their functional relationship to other elements. Thus alterations in a melodic configuration, which are routinely effected, for instance, to maintain a key, are less apt to call attention to their own literal construction than to act as transparent indicators of functional significance, much like the distortions of literal size and direction in perspective painting. Similarly, it is still normal for Mozart to ensure that a section of so-called harmonic parentheses is still understood primarily in terms of a larger structural function. The harmonically uncluttered sequential movement, rhythmic energy, and relative brevity of measures 50–64 in the finale of Symphony No. 39 provide an example of such parentheses, acting essentially as the affirmation of V. This procedure contrasts with the style of the romantics, who liked to linger or expand on the atmospheric effects within such sections to the point of undermining the immediate audibility and relevance of their functional connections to a larger structure.

Such handling of formal elements projects an archetypal idea of structure that has great metaphorical power in the analysis and interpretation of human reality, for it suggests that changes over time as well as surface physical differences are to be construed not literally (i.e., not as indicators of the existence or quality of individual identity, which is irreducible to general rational principles of explanation), but rather conceptually (i.e., as evidence of the underlying intelligibility of actual sensuous discrepancies, discords, and conflicts). Thus both of the elements just mentioned can be adequately described with scarcely any reference to specific examples, and both can be ascribed to the general stylistic language of Mozart's culture. This is also true of two other characteristics that will now be noted.

Suggestions of the necessity of rational resolution within form. One of the clearest examples of such a suggestion is provided in the second movement of the *Jupiter* Symphony by a technique common in Haydn's work: the return of material from the exposition (measure 7ff.) toward the end of the movement (measure 95ff.) after the omission of the material in its expected place in the recapitulation. It is as if with this return, the tonic proposition set forth at the opening were capable of being verified as valid in its entirety. Another suggestion of the same sort resides in Mozart's characteristic reduction of tension at the moment of recapitulation; for example, through lowered volume, linear descent, and sequence.[10] Typically absent is the rhetorical rise to a climax in the recapitulation, through which Beethoven seems to assert (in quasi-Kantian fashion?) the moral necessity of or at least moral need for a return to I. Rather, Mozart seems to accept uncritically the necessity of this return as self-evident. It is, of course, also possible, as will be seen below, to interpret some of his moments of recapitulation in other ways, for example, as expressions of resignation at the inability of individualized harmonic elements to break away from generalized tonal laws.

The absence of explicit emphasis on the individual identity of each symphony as a whole. Compared to later composers, Mozart seems content to establish significance in these symphonies within a context of generally binding principles of function rather than through defining their unmistakable identity as individual structures. Thus, there is next to no interest either in explicit thematic links between movements or in a synthesizing close that links together the preceding movements.[11] Presumably, the listener is meant to make sense of these symphonies primarily by following internally intelligible relationships rather than, say, by giving each work a name.

The above four characteristics indicate that a precritical worldview is normal in these three symphonies. Yet an erosion of that worldview is also indicated by elements through which the symphonies, like other mature works by Mozart (consider the *Prague* Symphony), seem emphatically to counter the effect of general stylistic homogeneity characteristic of his culture. This they do by forcing a response to themselves as particular sense objects. In a way, of course, the very success of Mozart relative, say, to J. C. Bach in projecting a vivid ideal of universality lies in the superior refinement and imagination—both qualities of individualization—of the elements projecting this ideal in Mozart's work; it is this sort of situation that critics usually have in mind when they assert the achievement of an identity between the universal and the individual as a hallmark of high classical style. Mozart's last three symphonies, however, seem to move away somewhat from the ideal of universality itself by means of an emphasis on elements with intrinsic individuality, that is, elements that impair the primacy of functional significance by calling attention to sensuous values.

One could say that in works such as these, Mozart the classicist crystallized the general stylistic language of eighteenth-century music into a conception of an encompassing, yet particular, universal structure, only to dissolve that structure simultaneously into an expression of (merely?) individual style. And just as a broad correlation seems possible between the intrinsically more general characteristics of these symphonies and the outlook of Mozart's culture, so too one is tempted to associate the intrinsically more individualized features of these works with Mozart's personal vision, and to argue, moreover, that the erosion of a cultural viewpoint inheres precisely in one person's well-defined deviation from the norms of that culture. Whether or not all changes in cultural outlook are effected in the first instance through individual deviation is a question of great complexity, given the great differences of values and concerns among various cultures, and one that cannot be answered here. Still, when the main content of a cultural viewpoint is that of confidence in general principles *per se*, and, likewise, when deviation from this viewpoint consists in the very opposition of individualistic principles to general ones, then the individual's impact on the state of cultural beliefs, if not unlimited in power, can be construed as having some special significance. Again, this is a question for consideration in some other place. In the present context, it is possible only to set forth some of the more intriguing individualistic aspects of these three symphonies.

Wholeness of Identity

Unquestionably, Mozart's last three symphonies stop short of the self-conscious romantic stress on the single identity of a whole structure; yet all three, and especially the last two, contain numerous elements that give them a cohesiveness more explicitly defined than would be possible through the agency of nothing more than a cultural homogeneity of style. Whereas the second movement of Symphony No. 39, in its broadest formal outlines (though not in all of its particulars) and the third movement, in its fairly conventional simplicity and relative lack of propulsion, differ clearly from the norms of sonata structure set forth in the outer movements, the inner movements of Symphonies No. 40 and 41 seem fully integrated within the sonata conception that frames them if judged by their degree of structural, textural, and harmonic complexity or drive. Both the later symphonies are pervaded by the use of chromatic intervals or lines, often in a contrapuntal context; and it should be recalled that the senuous value traditionally attributed by Western culture to chromaticism not only undermined tonality during the nineteenth century but also allowed chromaticism to signify some aspect of irrationality throughout Western musical history.[12] These symphonies also display small motivic resemblances among movements as well as larger patterns of similarity to be discussed shortly. But even Symphony No. 39 exhibits one striking element of wholeness in its pervasive and emphatic pitting of string color against wind in either antiphonal or contrapuntal contrasts. On one level, to be sure, this use of color reinforces a functional conception of identity and difference in that the technique in every movement is used either to clarify thematic significance, demarcate structural relations, or resolve preceding conflict.[13] Nonetheless, the very reliance on the sensuous element of color to reinforce and, in no small degree, to effect intelligibility tends to heighten the individual character of Symphony No. 39 as well as to weaken the primacy of functional (i.e., tonal) norms of rationality. From such a conception, it is not difficult to project an increasing emphasis on autonomy of pure sound such as has led to the divorce of sound from meaning in much twentieth-century music.

Disjunction

Relative to norms of linear and rhythmic continuity found in later baroque music, all must in subsequent styles, from the earliest postbaroque styles through Beethoven's middle period is to some extent music of discontinuity. In the initial stages of these newer styles, breaks between phrases and between sections create breaks in tension that Charles Rosen associates with a lack of "inner necessity."[14] Much of the interest of high classical music arises indisputably from its ability to integrate such breaks into new conceptions of connectedness, mediation, and the temporal unity of concept and effect. And yet, certain aspects of the treatment of conventional discontinuities in Mozart's last three symphonies seem to call attention as much to the intractability of disjunction as to the notion of transcending it. Why, for example, must music that has just affirmed a cadence in the dominant or relative major go on to dissolve harmonic certainty, as in the so-called development section? At the beginning of the development section in the first movement of Symphony No. 39 (which features a melodic augmented fourth at measures 144–45) and even more strikingly at some point in the outer movements of No. 40, norms of logical harmonic movement are markedly abrogated. Hermann Abert concludes that, although the transition at this moment in the first movement of Symphony No. 40 "seems sudden," it is "inwardly entirely justified by what has gone before."[15] But Abert never explains this inward justification; and it may well be that in his introduction to Abert's analysis, Nathan Broder is nearer the mark when he asserts that "the development sections of the first and last movements have baffled [all the theorists]."[16] Broder goes on to say, "There are many *descriptions* of what happens in these sections, but no analyst . . . has given a satisfactory explanation of the *function* of each occurrence there in terms of the whole organism." Furthermore, perhaps only some sense of the ultimate arbitrariness of structural discontinuities can explain Mozart's conspicuous use in Symphony No. 40, especially in its first movement, of chromatic lines as a kind of literal seal not only bridging anticonventional harmonic gaps but at times appearing even within apparently normal transitions — between V and I, or between principal structural subdivisions.[17] Conversely, scarcely any effort is made to conceal the tonal shifts occurring near the opening of the development sections in the outer movements of the *Jupiter* Symphony; they move with a conciseness that borders on the abrupt.

In the slow movement of each of the three symphonies—and to a greater degree the later the symphony—the transition out of the opening tonic section is marked by an increasing degree of ambiguity of structural significance. Rosen claims that when the change of key in the exposition is "startling and abrupt, and the new tonality is introduced without modulation . . . something in the opening section has made it possible."[18] Conceivably, the shift from tonic major to relative minor in Symphony No. 39 (measures 27–30) is prepared by an earlier momentary allusion to the tonic minor (measures 22–25). In the G-Minor Symphony, however, the ostensibly slight disjunction between I and V that occurs at measures 19–20 has virtually no prior justification, and its effect seems to be actually heightened by the harmonic instability that follows it (measures 28–35) as well as by its clear reformulation in the recapitulation (measures 82–98, especially measures 86–93), both of which passages cast doubt on the precise structural function of the B♭ gesture. The clear break at this point in the *Jupiter* Symphony will be discussed presently.

Analogy

Analogy, a technique that became common in Romantic music, refers to the presentation of elements (ranging from motifs to large-scale patterns) as parallel entities. By definition, then, analogy suggests the impossibility of bridging discontinuity through such rational principles of connection as function. And in contrast to complementary pairing, analogy admits of no completion, much less of necessary resolution, but instead can be extended indefinitely to encompass any number of members. Though large-scale patterns of coherence may emerge through analogy, they will be arbitrary, in the sense of freely chosen or individualistic patterns. Their tendency is to establish the particular identity of a work rather than the self-determining pattern of an implicitly logical structure. The effect of surface similarities and differences among elements likewise tends to be less the transparent indication of functional significance and more the purely sensuous experience of literal physical identities. The components of analogy frequently draw attention to their own self-contained coloristic qualities; in any case, where such components are not identical, the differences between them suggest arbitrary variance of surface rather than functionally rational development. Shift between parallel major and minor modes are a good example of analogy. It is significant that this technique achieves some structural prominence in Mozart's last three symphonies: on a local level, for example, in the development section of the finale of No. 39 (measures 112–45); on a more extended structural level, again in No. 39, in the use of alternate triadic forms at the opening of the development sections in the outer movements (G minor in the first, measure 143; V of C in the last, measures 104–6); and in the *Jupiter* Symphony through the interpenetration of E major and minor triads or tonalities in the finale (compare measures 166–69, 207–19, and 241–44).[19] Abrupt, unmediated, and often stepwise transposition, commonly associated with Beethoven, is another analogical technique worthy of note in these works, especially in the *Jupiter* Symphony.[20]

In fact, the *Jupiter* Symphony could well be characterized as a study in analogy, beginning with the almost immediate shift of the opening C-major motif not to an altered, complementary consequent on V but rather to a literal transposition in G, complete with F# (measure 5). Mozart makes striking use, for instance, of a locally analogical pattern of stepwise shift, from C to D to E, in the development of the first movement (measures 165–70) and in the "recapitulations" of the minuet[21] and the finale (measures 233–41) to create larger-scale analogical correspondences among all three C-major movements. At each of these moments, periodic complementarity unravels explicitly into parallel recurrence; furthermore, functional progression between unmistakable tonalities is momentarily threatened by elements of cross relation, even of polytonality, in the first and third movements, and by conflicts between harmonic and melodic "logic" in all three. Indeed, the effects are such as to suggest a conception of C not as the center of a functional tonality but as a mere pitch-identity that can be placed in any number of individually and perhaps arbitrarily chosen relationships. If the opening of the development in the finale of the G-Minor Symphony may be likened plausibly to Schoenberg's row, then it does not seem altogether farfetched to compare the pervasive relationship between C and E in the *Jupiter* Symphony to Stravinsky's nonfunctional juxtaposition of polar pitch-centers or even to his fondness for the C–E relationship in particular.[22]

Moreover, in all the analogical instances just mentioned, the parallelism is actually extended by the ensuing stepwise return from E to C (though this is not effected in the third movement until the "recapitulation" of the trio at measures 76–81, itself a moment of marked internal analogical character).[23] Thus, the full large-scale pattern in each case is that of the palindrome, a pattern found elsewhere in the *Jupiter* as well, notably in the development section of the first movement, where it operates as the apparent means of closing the gap between G and E♭ that is opened up at the start of this section.[24] It seems worth mentioning here that similar patterns—that is, gap followed by closure—are cited by Charles Rosen in connection with various aspects of the classical style, including the dynamics at the opening of the *Jupiter* Symphony itself; Rosen indeed seems to consider this pattern archetypal of the classical power to mediate.[25] Is it not also conceivable, however, that in its order and its emphasis such a pattern signifies at least incipient recognition of real dichotomies or disjunctions that cannot be fully bridged by any general laws of reason? The palindrome, after all, is not a pattern of logical complementarity, and one cannot discount the significance of its association in structural terms with the music of still another twentieth-century composer, namely, Bartók.

The Drive to an Unattainable Limit
and Its Relation to Analogy

Alongside the undeniably connective force of functional principles, there are moments in these symphonies that suggest the unattainability of rational connections between disparate elements, elements that often involve a dissolution of momentum into the static condition of analogy. At the approach to the recapitulation, for example, the rhetorical diminution of force alluded to earlier could be construed as a resigned return to a pitch-center that cannot connect itself by logical necessity to something "other." For in all the sonata movements of these symphonies, except for the first movement of Symphony No. 41, the development section works its way toward an *unresolved* dominant in some key other than the tonic.[26] This pattern is most pronounced in the outer movements of Symphony No. 40: in the unresolved climax on V of D minor in the first movement (measures 138–39), and in the emphatically unresolved drive in the finale (measures 175–93) toward the tonal antipode C#, a drive that stretches the unifying functional power of the tonic to the point of raising doubts as to the logical necessity (and inevitable potency) of a resolution into I. This question may also be raised by Mozart's tendency (associated by Rosen to some extent with release of tension)[27] to reserve much of the harmonic instability for the recapitulation, not least because these very passages so often deviate sharply from unthinkingly (uncritical) conventional syntax (or transposition of the exposition) and thereby call sensuous attention to themselves.

Likewise, even the security of the arrival at V (or III) in the exposition, though normally eased by a dominant preparation, can be undermined in a striking way, and not just in the slow movements as already noted — for instance, in the sudden stalling on IV of III near the start of the third section in the first movement of the G-Minor Symphony (measures 58–62). Such undermining is especially prominent in the first, second, and fourth movements of the *Jupiter* Symphony, in episodes within or near the dominant area that are centered on the pitches and sensuous quality of the C-minor triad.[28] In the second movement, this episode, ostensibly functioning as a bridge, undermines the very notion of "bridge" by rocking back and forth in a momentary stalemate between i and v (that is, the tonic and dominant degrees, now stripped down to, or dissolved into, the minor modes of F and C), as if to question whether and why V should ever be reached.[29] The effect of a momentary, self-contained, sensuous digression—unconducive to logical tonal movement, much less required by it—is similar in all three movements. On the level of the entire symphony, the localized checking of forward drive establishes a remarkable pattern of analogy.[30]

In fact, virtually all the so-called critical techniques adduced here are prominent in these three episodes. Together they help give the *Jupiter* Symphony a distinct, sensuous identity as a whole. Individually they help create a marked disjunction in conventional sorts of tonal patterns as well as in mood. All three play on the sensuous effect of analogical shifts between parallel major and minor. All three suggest the dissolution of C from a functional premise and goal into a conception of C as a pitch and an occasion for color. This last suggestion gains particular vividness from the fact that C defines the center of the episode even in the F-major slow movement. By the same token, and thus more or less analogously, the F-minor triad laced with D-flat, which alternates with C minor and C major in the first episode of the F-major movement [measures 23–25], defines the color of the recapitulatory episodes in the two outer movements, both in C. In the recapitulations of the outer movements,[31] moreover, the episodes are not transposed in a merely literal fashion, as they could be, but rather stretched physically in length and range, as if to force renewed active attention on their irreducibly sensuous reality and to suggest that an absolutely conclusive resolution, relying on the rational imperative of the tonic, is unattainable.

Rhetorical exaggeration of length and range is also evident in the second version of the slow-movement episode, which occurs in the development section (measures 47–55). Arguably, the absence of the episode in the recapitulation signifies the overcoming of the disturbance created by its presence in the earlier sections, where, though never exactly incomprehensible in structural terms, it nonetheless conjures up the powerfully contingent and irrational sides of actual sensuous existence, an existence such as cannot be totally reduced to prediction, explanation, or control by general laws. On the other hand, the episode's absence in the recapitulation may also be taken to mean that the recapitulation cannot provide anything closer to the degree of resolved tension than the one already presented in the earlier episodes themselves; the episodes can then be viewed as self-contained blocks lending themselves only to analogical variance, not to conclusive resolution even by means so powerful as the tonic (here F). Furthermore, the vestiges of the episodes that do show up in the recapitulation, centered on the notes C and D♭ (measures 73–75), can be read as signs of an unresolved drive that dissolves into an analogical statement and of the continuing possibility of conflict that cannot be wholly resolved by a generally rational conception of tonality; for these same two notes are prominent, not only in the original statement of the episode in this movement (measure 23) but also in the recapitulation episodes of the outer movements, notwithstanding the different key of the slow movement. And whereas the episode in the exposition of the slow movement *broke away* from the hold of C by way of D♭ (measures 23–24), the D♭ in the recapitulation (like the one in the corresponding section of the first movement, measures 271–75) cannot escape the pull of the pitch C and turns downward immediately toward an eventual, though not completely unchallenged, resolution in the tonic F. The resolution here does not dissipate totally the unsettling sensuous effect of the stalemate between D♭ and C.[32]

To be sure, the last episode in the recapitulation of the finale does break through D♭ in a triumphant rise to the tonic (see the violin line, measures 328–32.[33] Mozart has not, after all, relinquished his optimistic belief in Enlightenment rationality. But neither has he presented this belief in an untroubled or uncritical manner. Quite the contrary, in such music a path seems to be opened to a new worldview, which challenges the ultimate rationality of reality, or at least alters radically the interpretation of rationality itself. What has been a conception of rationality as a universally unified and grounded structure seems to be changing in these works to the far more problematical notion of rationality as an individually or culturally particular vision.[34]

Chapter 7

Romantic Music as Post-Kantian Critique: Classicism, Romanticism, and the Concept of the Semiotic Universe

In the attempt to develop a critical language capable of characterizing musical classicism adequately, a useful starting point is provided by the notion that in certain respects this style suggests as its structural model a cognitive system: logic, assuming logic is defined broadly. For both the characteristic classical structure (which could be referred to loosely as a sonata structure) and the logical demonstration seem to propose the same ideal of the semiotic structure as a semiotic universe, a universe that can be described succinctly as an autonomous intelligible whole.[1] Just as a logical argument contains its own premises and conclusions, which define themselves in temporal succession, so too the characteristic classical structure seems to include a temporally unifying tonal premise out of which it is possible to imagine that the entire structure, in all its parameters, is rationally derived. As a result, the classical musical structure seems capable, at least in its normative state, of embodying all of its meaning within its own, internally determined structural boundaries. Thus its structure suggests itself as a semiotic whole.

The characteristic classical movement, moreover, seems to manifest a structure of tonally based premise and conclusion at each of many hierarchical levels, from its encompassing plan down to the pairings of antecedent-consequent phrases that constitute its typical structural unit. And in classical music, as in logic, the temporally defined connections between premise and conclusion appear to be necessary. There is, indeed, a degree to which, like the language used in a logical demonstration, the music in a mature symphony by Haydn in particular suggests itself as a kind of window onto a syntactically true structure, an underlying structure that is necessary, and hence true, in itself. And since classical music, unlike baroque, lacks all semblance of the external object or *signifié* characteristic in cognitive discourse, it would appear to be even more self-contained, more purely syntactic than logic, and thus closer to truth, by standards of logic, than is logic itself.[2]

It could be said, of course, that all explicitly cognitive structures, even logic, by virtue of their cognitive character seem ultimately to make some sort of direct claim about the reality of the world outside of their own language, if only the claim that the relationships they describe actually exist.[3] By comparison, classical music, in the seeming totality of its truth of coherence, appears to forfeit all claim to any direct truth of correspondence. Still, within the bounds of its own structure, classical music seems to affirm as valid that pattern of cognitively necessary connections between the complementary sorts of structures—structures such as antecedent and consequent, cause and effect, and even subject and object—through which cognitive thought ordinarily seems to promise a verifiable connection between human conceptual structures and the external world. Just as, in Kantian terms, the unity of logic can encompass a manifold of sensory data, so, too, by implying within the particularity of its structure the entire hierarchy of systematic tonal relationships, the classical structure seems able to encompass within its own rational framework the diversity of a whole universe.

Classical music, moreover, seems to project itself, at some level, as Everyman's art, an art that each of us can imagine ourselves creating as we hear it unfolding in time, paradoxically, because this music, in exposing its own premises, suggests that it can be generally verified as meeting exacting and exclusionary standards, the standards of rightness and wrongness. In other words, the style that has been taken for the very norm of musical art seems to have accepted as its own normative standard of judgment a criterion ordinarily associated with the objectivity or apparent autonomy of cognitive structures, the capacity to embody truth. But of course, the classical structure can convey the impression of embodying universally verifiable truth only because its own structure is somehow imaginable as universally comprehensible, as a universe of discourse encompassing all human beings as competent interpreters. Beyond an innate human capacity to understand the self-evident necessity of its internal structural connections as they are unfolded over time, it seems to promise that nothing is needed to understand it—no outside information, no specialized cultural knowledge, training, or ideally, even identity. Its seemingly pure intrastructural meaning projects itself as open to all who have the musical equivalent of a faculty of reason.

If, however, one points to logic as a structural archetype for the classical style, then it is important to note the qualifications that are necessitated in ordinary conceptions of logic by Kant's critical philosophy, a philosophy precisely contemporary with the maturity of Haydn and Mozart.[4] Thus, though a logical structure is indeed a syntactic structure, it cannot, Kant makes clear, be considered an *absolutely* autonomous intelligible structure, a structure necessary or true in itself, for to be so it would have to exist in some metaphysical realm of being beyond intelligibility as that term is humanly understood. Instead, the structure of a logical demonstration must be viewed simply as the analogical projection of an entire structure existing somewhere within a human mind. In other words, inasmuch as a logical demonstration is a semiotic structure rather than a structure beyond the possibility of meaning, its "autonomy" must be defined as a paradoxical state of physical discreteness and fixity which is yet formally dependent on a subjective mind that designates its internal connections as necessary or true, and imbues it with meaning.

Furthermore, Kant's work clarifies that no cognitive structure, including logic, can make a cognitively certain connection between the internal mental structure on which it depends and any realm wholly external to the mind. For insofar as they can be known, all of the complementary pairs encompassed within cognition, including subject and object, amount to structures that take their form from some internal subjective structure and thus are not, in that form, to be taken as elements of two distinct realms of being. Indeed, from the account given in Kant's *Critique of Judgment*, one can conclude that what seem to be complementary constructs bound in pairs through cognition are actually more like analogues themselves, related to each other only in the parallel or disjunct sense in which analogues can be related. (One thinks here of an image common in deconstruction, a chain of signifiers.) At any rate, though cognitive semiotic structures, through a discreteness of *signifiant* and *signifié*, point explicitly toward two discrete levels of being, even they can be construed, finally, as no more than one-dimensional or entirely syntactic systems; the most nearly certain knowledge they can be assumed to convey is a knowledge by analogy of the mental structures that project them.

Thus logical knowledge has no absolute objectivity, but is bound by the limits of a subjective structure. However, even within the limits of its subjective realm, cognition, no matter how far extended, cannot, solely through its own rules of theoretical reason, define a rationally whole system or universe.[5] For sooner or later, cognition encounters contradictions or irrationalities that it cannot resolve. True, the mind can, according to Kant, imagine such a resolution to occur at a level of mental being inaccessible to knowledge, and the *Critique of Judgment* suggests how the other two mental faculties, judgment and practical reason, can account for what seems irrationality to cognition. But the structures of these other faculties, as Kant's own treatment of them makes clear, cannot ultimately be synthesized in any wholly rational way with that of cognition; they can only draw the same data into their own domains. Hence, the realm of cognition itself, which includes logic, can never be counted as a knowable rational whole.

This inability to know the realm of cognition as a rational whole, moreover, has a corollary, which assumes prominence with Kant, in our inability to know any particular, empirically defined cognitive structure in its entirety. For though human cognitive structures — for example, our logical demonstrations — are to be understood as analogues of whole inner mental structures, we do not know with certainty the ultimate basis of either our outer or our inner cognitive structures, which we do not, after all, form consciously. Indeed, despite Kant's derivation of apparently pure (that is, nonempirical or formal) and, therefore, ultimate cognitive structures — the famous categories of the *Critique of Pure Reason* — from empirically used linguistic constructions, his account actually invites the conclusion that one can neither know with certainty the composition (which would, of course, include the intrinsic rationality) of any ultimate mental structure nor certify the ultimacy of any mental structure that is projected as ultimate. This is precisely because such structures are conceded by Kant to exist not simply within the mind of the individual, at a level accessible to complete rational verification, but rather behind or beneath the mind, at a so-called transcendental level of abstraction, beyond the reach of either logical or empirical proof, a level where they can only be imagined as plausible, or at most posited, in axiomatic fashion, as ultimate archetypes of empirically known cognitive structures. In other words, Kant's desire to preserve a universal basis for cognition forces him to locate that basis at a level of nonempirical formality, where it becomes inaccessible to human cognition, which, as he stresses throughout the *Critique of Judgment*, operates exclusively in conjunction with the senses, that is, by way of either sense-data or empirically defined symbols (such as words or geometric shapes).

To be sure, by locating the fundamental structures of the mind at a level beyond the reach of all conscious control, experience, and subjective or cultural variance — and it is extremely significant that Kant does not recognize concrete cultural limits on the "purely formal" cognitive categories he derives from culturally particular (Western) linguistic structures — Kant not only finds a workable way of designating such structures as universal, and as such rational, but also locates them at a level that is as resistant to conclusive disproof as it is to conclusive proof. It is in this sense that although he can no longer ground the universality of cognitive truth, including logical truth, with cognitive certainty in any absolute objective or metaphysical level of being, Kant can claim to have preserved at least the formal possibility of such truth on purely subjective grounds, the grounds of human mental structure.

Nevertheless, it must be emphasized that grounding subjective universality at a transcendental level of thought or being by definition precludes establishing that universality as a cognitive certainty and exposes the fact, in a sense recognized but never fully analyzed by Kant, that ultimately it is no more possible to prove connections between structures existing within two separate minds than it is to prove connections between subjective and extrasubjective levels of being. At most, within the terms of Kant's critical philosophy, if one leaves out the moral desirability of such connections, one can posit only the formal possibility of analogies between subjective structures.

To put it more simply, once we have accepted the terms of the critical philosophy and reduced the field of human knowledge to the structure of the forms through which our own minds work, then no device, not even the device of transcendental subjectivity, can spare us from admitting that the only mental structures we ourselves know anything about and can deal with cognitively, at a level beyond merely naming them as formal possibilities, are concrete, particularized, or mediated structures. Even within one's own mind, any abstract structure for which one may look (if it exists at all) has already been mediated, at least through the concreteness of sensory images and generally through some physically and culturally particular system of language as well. One can posit the blind fact, so to speak, of an abstract analogue to these concrete structures: one can posit an archetypal structure that is at once similar to known structures and yet not identical. But one cannot know for certain the existence, rationality, or exact form of such an archetype.

Is it then possible to have such knowledge with respect to other people's minds or to deduce with certainty a universal archetype from the external semiotic structures through which humans signify and communicate? Since no mental structure can know or control entirely its appearance from the outside, it must undergo substantial mediation to externalize itself, and the resultant externalized structure must be still further mediated for interpretation by others. Hence, although it is often useful to posit such a universal structure, and even though, if Kant is right, one seems more or less forced by the rules of (Western) reason to do so, at least in certain contexts, nevertheless one has no cognitively certain basis for describing such a structure, for assigning its existence anything more than a heuristic status, or for defining its presence in any semiotic structure, or process, as more than a formal possibility.[6]

In fact, the adoption of Kant's critical attitude leads to a consciousness of the irreducible differences between all known and conceivable semiotic structures. It brings about awareness that, precisely by virtue of the physical and cultural definition that allows even the semblance of communication, all externalized semiotic structures must be assumed to distort any internal structure, whether abstract or concrete, that may have projected them. And to the extent that the physical (and even cultural) domains of being are beyond conscious, subjective, or rational control, external semiotic structures must also be assumed to incorporate elements of arbitrariness (such as Saussure's signs), which elude demonstrable rules for usage, which open up these semiotic structures to misunderstanding, and which invariably place an empirical restriction on the number of those competent in each system. Thus, just as the only individual mind to which one can claim access is an empirically particular mind—broader in the sense of being more concrete, yet narrower in range than any transcendental mental structure—so, too, the broadest subjective structure to which one can claim access must be imagined to have an empirically real or mediated existence and therefore to be cultural rather than universal. And the cultural structure has no clear status of cognitive certainty.[7]

Consequently, a full acceptance of Kant's epistemological position requires renunciation of any cognitively certain basis for regarding communication as a direct and accurate connection between subjective structures. At most, the post-Kantian is justified in thinking of semiotic processes as indirect, consisting in the establishment of a series of structures, both internal mental ones and external or autonomous ones, as analogous. In terms of such a process, an autonomous semiotic structure can be characterized as whole only in the sense of having a more or less discrete and fixed physical existence, accessible as such to perception by one or more subjective minds. It cannot be assumed to be a whole in the sense that it is rationally knowable in all of its potential meaning by any individual (poststructuralists would add, "including the author," and in fact this whole account calls to mind the deconstructionist definition of a text). For without an established universality of mental structure among its potential interpreters, the autonomous semiotic structure cannot be construed as having any intrinsic meaning at all. One can imagine it to have only that meaning that is imposed upon it by subjective minds, no two of which need perceive it in the same way even if each mind perceives it as its own structural analogue.[8] For a post-Kantian, the communication of any particular meaning must be accepted as a contingent process.

From what has been said already about the classical style in music, it should be clear that here, too, one could characterize certain structural elements as pointing toward a universalized and quasi-objective conception of subjectivity similar to Kant's transcendental subjective structure. Most suggestive in this respect, no doubt, is the tonal principle that today is generally associated with the term "sonata." On the one hand, it seems to underlie the temporal structure of most movements by Haydn, Mozart, and Beethoven (at least up until his later works, and possibly even then). On the other hand, theorists reiterate that the sonata-allegro, or whatever they choose to call it, exists as an abstraction only; it is, to use Charles Rosen's words, a "unifying principle" rather than a "preexistent shape."[9] Again, the quasi-logical way in which the classical composer draws upon the structural implications of tonality allows him by and large to suggest an avoidance of that arbitrariness that is apparently inseparable from the concrete mediation of abstract structures. In Beethoven's music, where the binding force of tonality is first explicitly exposed to question, the presence of stylistic particularity, and hence of potential grounds for a general effect of arbitrariness, can no longer be overlooked, even in an idealized characterization. With Mozart and especially Haydn, however, it is often possible to entertain the illusion that the empirical particularity and arbitrariness of style have been integrated seamlessly with the universal necessity of an abstract musical structure, so that one could momentarily believe that the style *is* the structure and that for this music, stylistic understanding (the stylistic perception or, in a sense, the apprehension of structure as a surface) and structural understanding (the understanding of structural meaning or the apprehension of internal structural connections) are identical.

With classical music, however, as with logical discourse, the semiotic process can be established only as a contingent delineation of analogies, not as that effecting of necessary connections which would follow from the demonstrable existence of a universal subjective structure. Thus none of the syntactic connections affected within classical music, or the meanings that can be attached to those connections, can be considered necessary in itself at either the most narrowly technical or the most broadly philosophical levels of interpretation. The movement from the tonic to the dominant key in a major-mode classical movement is "inevitable" only in the sense that, as Rosen points out, "it was a necessary condition of intelligibility" for the audience of its time and place.[10] Furthermore, even if it were generally agreed, say among Westerners, that by basing its entire structure on normative principles, such as the need to resolve implications properly, classical music designated implicit universal intelligibility as the normative ideal of art, it would not follow that such intelligibility necessarily *is* the proper goal of art. Instead, one would be able to posit this norm of classical music as the mediated analogue or variant of some underlying structure that could at best be identified, and from the outside only, as a particular structure.

We would most likely call that particular structure in this case a value of Enlightenment culture. Other sorts of syntactic connections, such as reference to the opening thematic material at some point in the second part of a sonata exposition or an infusion of chromatic harmony into the diatonic context of a sonata movement, we would attribute, rather, to some archetypal structure within the mind of a particular individual, here Haydn and Mozart respectively.[11] Mozart's music, indeed, presents such a palpably sensuous surface that in any account less generalized than this, one would want to investigate the ways in which the particularity of his style diverges from the logic of his structure, and thus the extent to which his music deviates from its own classical norms. In fact, we would eventually have to conclude from a genuinely critical analysis of any classical music that to make sense of the pattern of syntactic connections within a semiotic structure, no matter how forcefully that structure suggested itself as meaningful and thereby evoked the idea of an autonomous or implicit meaning, it is necessary to assume some analogical conformity between that pattern and some particular subjective conception, underlying but different from that pattern, of the needs of structure. Such a conception we associate, by and large, with the notion of style, either individual or cultural; it is a conception that we can "know" only through the mediation of our own particular mental structures.

As one final sort of evidence for the notion that classical music as a semiotic structure actually works by way of contingent analogy rather than necessary connections, it could be noted that classical music in fact falls considerably short of achieving implicit universal intelligibility. True, the style succeeds for many educated listeners in projecting the norm of a semiotic autonomy in which a more or less logical universality of structure wholly absorbs particularity of style. In actuality, however, classical music probably comes closer to defining something like that Enlightenment ideal of Everyman described by Jacques Barzun as "a clothed creature, whose proper, because logical, language is French, and whose destiny is to live according to the Christian religion under an hereditary king."[12] Like most manifestations of the universalistic ideals of the Enlightenment, which turn out to be normative in an exclusionary sense, classical musical structure has in fact been found understandable by only a relatively small number of people, even within Western society, people for whom, we can suppose, that musical structure constitutes some recognizable variant of an internal conception of meaningful structure. For the rest of society it would appear that the particularity of style in the classical work, be it cultural or individual particularity, obscures the clarity of structure.

Enlightenment rationalists, including Kant himself looked down on music for the weakness of its capacity to signify cognitively.[13] In fact, "pure" music seems to expose the epistemological limits of all human semiotic structures in a somewhat paradigmatic fashion. This exposure becomes more dramatically clear in romantic music, as will be seen, but even classical music, with all its quasi-logical clarity, suggests finally that the meaning of all semiotic structures, even that of logic, can be verified only through an explicitly intrasubjective or one-dimensional establishment of a state of analogy, a state that is indemonstrable, contingent, and internally disjunct. This is a state that Kant himself associates specifically with aesthetic judgment, wherein sensory perception or imagination and abstract or conceptual understanding are defined in essence as disjunct, equally subjective faculties that are at most related through the contingent state of analogy, and wherein a proper object, typically a beautiful structure,[14] establishes such a state of analogy, thereby defining itself in essence as structurally analogous to judgment.[15] Indeed, in suggesting logic as its own structural model, classical music, which has been taken for the norm of musical art, seems to do precisely what Kant's critical philosophy appears to do in spite of itself: reveal the necessity of logic as nothing more than an aesthetic necessity.

As logic, with its self-embodied truth and necessary connections, loses status as a model of universal truth in the wake of the critical philosophy, one might expect to find an increasing emphasis in music on properties of the analogy, the pattern that Kant in effect links with his reduced concept of the truth accessible to the human mind. In fact, such properties do become evident at many levels of nineteenth-century music. Indeed, romantic music seems to take up Kant's critical principle in some analogous fashion of its own and use it explicitly to undermine the classical ideal of the semiotic universe. In the nineteenth century, the classical norm of an autonomous universe encompassing all of its own meaning seems to have been shattered into a new cultural paradigm of many semiotic universes, universes that are separated by irreducible differences of total identity and are yet analogous in their emphasis on particularity. And just as the notion of a particular universe (like that of subjective "autonomy") is paradoxical, so, too, the paradigmatic nineteenth-century semiotic structure, at least in music, seems, by virtue of its particularity, to be markedly autonomous as pure, externally defined, physical structure, and yet explicitly incomplete in meaning. As a result, whereas the classical musical structure projects the illusion of involving a logical sort of competence, one that permits the establishment of necessary connections between disparate minds or their externalized structures, the romantic musical structure seems openly to acknowledge that it can count only on modes of competence that involve the contingency of analogy; rather than assuming or evoking "universal" normative notions of right and wrong, romantic music seems simply to want and to seek an understanding of what it is saying, and thereby to acknowledge the very act of understanding as problematical.[16]

Thus, for example, music of the nineteenth century tends to renounce a normative conception of structure in the sense that tonality stops patterning itself on the logical model of premise-and-conclusion and ceases to resemble a universal norm. The functional use of harmonies for purposes audibly explainable in terms of large-scale temporal structure gives way increasingly to structurally arbitrary coloristic uses of harmony, highly varied for individualized purposes; established rules for the choice of scale degrees and chord progressions are at times broken so as to admit effects of modality, which are not merely subversive in effect, like chromaticism, but openly irreconcilable with tonal relationships; and tonality in general loses its effect of determining whole structures and governing the other musical parameters.

Once tonality ceases to function as a universal norm, however, music clearly loses its capacity to project itself as a semiotically autonomous structure, a structure embodying all of its meaning in its internal connections. Indeed, centrally involved in this loss is an apparent disintegration of those connections or, more generally, of the structural cohesiveness out of which the classical musical component seems to have derived its meaning. For, characteristically in romantic music, the temporally unified wholeness of tonal argument gives way to a pervasive individuation, which tends at every level of the musical structure to define semiotic units that cannot be rejoined in any immanent structural sense because, though incomplete as a source of meaning they are also, in a physical sense, self-contained or autonomous.

Only a few examples of this tendency can be suggested here. Typically, in romantic music, the purely implicative propulsiveness of tonality tends to work in audible fashion on the more localized levels of the passage or segment (which, to be sure, can be sizeable in literal terms), rather than at the overarching level of the whole piece. Similarly, there is a tendency to strip the antecedent-consequent phrase of its implicitly large-scale structural significance by dissociating it from the function of a tonal premise and reducing it to one of many harmonic (or even primarily melodic) components too self-contained to imply, so that even when an entire structure is dominated by the recurrence of the antecedent-consequent pattern, the pattern has only a localized effect. Corollary temporal signs of this disintegration, all with clear precedents in Beethoven's music, include an increase in the static repetition or variance of self-contained units (which are defined as discrete in identity rather than joined through development); the building up of thematic patterns or rhythmic momentum through a cumulative repetition or variance of discrete units;[17] abrupt and harmonically unprepared shifts of tonal plane; and close juxtaposition of major and minor modes, especially of major and minor forms of the same chord (a technique that not only produces harmonic ambiguity, but also emphasizes harmonic identity as an individual element over the long-range constructive powers of functional harmonic implication).[18] All of these devices tend to vitiate the effect of an intelligible, temporally defined wholeness in romantic music by undercutting both overall cohesiveness and also the internally effected determinacy of the outer boundaries of a structure. And all, it should be noted, constitute striking evidence for the notion that romantic music, here at the level of temporal structure, takes on manifest characteristics of a field of individual analogues, not only in terms of the physical appearance it offers to perception but also in terms of the possibilities it allows for interpretation. For in order to derive a cohesive meaning from such elements of temporal structure, a meaning in relation to a whole, one is openly forced to impose from without connections between them of one's own making, that is, to construct a kind of individualized interpretative or critical structure that is in some sense an analogue to the structure externalized by the composer (see note 16, this chapter).

If structure in romantic music, as in classical music, is defined narrowly, as an abstract internal relationality or as the quasi-logical temporal unfolding (which could be called the tonal unfolding) of events, then most romantic works lack a complete internal structural intelligibility and present themselves, regardless of size, as semiotic fragments rather than universes. (Paradoxically, therefore, those that seem the least incomplete are often literally very small.) This means that the meaning and even the rationality of most actual romantic structures, when set against this narrow, temporal definition of structure, become clearly open to question, even when use is made of traditional or easily stereotyped structures, since such forms tend to seem imposed, like preexistent blocks, upon the harmonic material of the romantic piece rather than to project themselves as evolving temporally out of some internally defined necessity. One loses the sense in romantic music that a piece employing such a form can be analyzed logically from within as its temporal connections unfold. Instead, it becomes necessary to wait until the piece is complete and one is outside of it, able consciously to perceive or construe it as a fixed object, in order to analyze it, and then only on the empirical basis of what actually happened in it—a process that is clearly arbitrary since no general rules for structural analysis can be deduced from the mere existence of successive events that are governed by no implicit connective principle.

Consequently, whereas classical structure seems to promise its own explanation, the intrinsic character of romantic temporal structure is such that in order to understand its rationale one must acquire techniques of retrospective analysis. And since the harmonic elements of romantic structure no longer seem to carry out a self-evident logical argument (and are often highly complex), specialized training in romantic practice is manifestly required before one can attempt to explain the significance of those elements on both the large scale and the small, thereby gaining some idea of the kinds of significance that might be involved. Thus, in shifting from a normative ideal of competence, such as the ability to judge correctness, to a process of trying to make itself understood, romantic music actually increases the difficulty of understanding its individual temporal structure. Unlike competence in logic (or in natural language, as it is ordinarily used), structural competence in romantic music seems to require a self-conscious perception of an entire structure; unlike its counterpart in classical music, structural competence in romantic music openly demands specialized empirical knowledge and training.[19] Of course, although this training can be acquired, it need not be. Given the difficulties involved in obtaining it, romantic expertise is apt to be limited to a small number of specialists who may, in fact, have trouble communicating any understanding of structural connections that goes beyond an ability merely to perceive or describe individual elements. Even these specialists generally have no clear basis for knowing that the semiotic connections they impose on the romantic musical structure are "right," since the individuality of romantic harmonic practice and temporal conceptions tends explicitly to preclude general norms of correctness with respect to the internal connections of a musical structure. On the whole, it would seem that musical specialists can at most claim authority to pronounce romantic works not "right," but "elegant" or "good," since, as Kant makes clear in the *Critique of Judgment*, grounds for the latter sort of judgment are without question indemonstrable.

In brief, the patent lack of semiotic wholeness and the individualized, empirical character of the romantic temporal or harmonic structure tend to emphasize the contingent and specialized status of structural competence in this music. This emphasis precludes any identification of the structurally competent with the general listener, so that if competence in romantic music, as in classical music, is defined as structural competence, that is, as competence with respect to temporal connectedness, then the probability is strong that no listener is totally competent and that most listeners are incompetent.[20] Unlike classical music, romantic music cannot sustain the illusion of a universe of competent listeners.

On the other hand, the same characteristics that suggest a restriction of structural competence can also be interpreted in an obverse manner. Precisely because the romantic structure, if defined narrowly in temporal and, especially, tonal terms, does not seem to embody a whole self-evident meaning within itself, one can suppose that the romantic work points to other sorts of meaning that do not inhere in its temporal structure. In fact, romantic music does seem to make explicit the possibility of another sort of musical competence, one that has a much greater resemblance to its counterpart in natural language than structural competence.

This second sort of competence, which I call stylistic competence, involves replacing the quasi-logic semiotic autonomy idealized in classicism with the literal breadth of a more concretely physical but semiotically incomplete sort of autonomy. In this connection it is useful to recall (see note 8, this chapter) that in aesthetic judgment, as Kant presents it, cognitive weight is shifted from an insufficient faculty of understanding, which cannot sustain its own ostensible claim of a cognitively privileged status, to an openly contingent and concrete faculty of empirical perception, which neither contains nor leads to any one comprehensive or cognitively necessary interpretation. Unlike the classical structure, which evokes so powerfully the Kantian vision of a secure cognitive universality, the romantic musical structure seems explicitly designed as an object for the aesthetic judgment, with its far more manifest epistemological uncertainties. The romantic musical structure, that is, seems to present itself to the concrete subjective faculty of empirical perception (operating within concrete cultural limits) as an object that can be taken for autonomous only in the sense of having a physically fixed or static existence. Beyond asserting its condition as a physical (and humanly produced) structure, it makes no claim to an implicit meaning that must, out of objective necessity, be understood completely or deduced unmistakably over time. On the contrary, it gives concrete shape to a strong doubt that such unmistakable understanding is even possible. Accepting the irreducible contingency of perception as itself universal (and as a limiting condition of all apprehension), and conceding the contingency of the connections that may be made between perceptual meanings and a given semiotic structure, the romantic musical work seems to shift from an abstractly logical to an empirical, and in many ways linguistic, ideal of meaning, and to define itself through more or less broadly external features that, within arbitrary cultural limits, seem least likely to be missed.[21]

Thus romantic music gives the impression of trying to compensate for the loss of the classical semiotic universe by reconstituting a semiotic universe of another sort. Unable any longer to simulate the *temporal* generation of a logically unified meaning out of a single tonal premise, the romantic piece seems to go about defining a universe of meaning in a *spatial* manner, by broadening the concept of musical structure. This it does by superimposing on its tonal structure, in a fashion that suggests the establishment of a series of analogous structures, what seem to be various other, autonomous layers of potential meaning. These may include nonmusical layers (titles, texts, programs). What is primarily involved, however, is a phenomenon of a sort already noted within the harmonic structure: an individuation of essentially nonimplicational musical parameters and their internal components, especially parameters other than harmony, such as melody, dynamics, and timbre—although one could also include purely coloristic aspects of harmony as examples of sonority in itself. The increased emphasis on these parameters could, admittedly, be interpreted as an attempt to clarify for the understanding, through the imposition of rhetoric (a term that I do not use pejoratively),[22] the rationality of the underlying tonal argument. The effect, however, is exactly the opposite, for this emphasis on the broad structure or total, concrete configuration and its self-contained, concrete details helps to obscure the temporal connections of tonal argument and to limit the role of the latter as a source of meaning. Thus it happens, precisely as in the case of purely structural analysis, that the listener becomes pointed away from the temporal structure, in its evident semiotic inadequacy, to the possibility of a semiotic universe defined outside that structure and, ultimately, outside the music altogether.

To enter into such a universe or draw upon it as a source of meaning, the listener must be able to refer to what can be imagined as analogous, essentially stylistic structures, both cultural and individual, coexisting outside and yet somehow underneath the music. In making such reference, listeners can develop a type of competence whereby they are able, on the basis of static associations or isolated details, to recognize the musical structure as a whole in the sense that they can identify it: assign it a provenance and date, for example, or a composer, a particular history, even a name.[23] What this means, in essence, is that by renouncing the classical veneer of cognitive abstraction and reveling in the autonomy of music *as a concrete sensuous medium*, the romantic musical structure exposes far more clearly than the classical one a fundamental limitation that post-Kantian thought can begin to associate with all semiotic structures. It exposes the ultimate cognitive direction of human semiotic structures as being not outward, toward something wholly other, with which subjectivity could establish a verifiable connection, but backward or inward toward the particular archetypal structure or structures that project them in acts of expression, and for that matter, of interpretation as well.

This limitation is clear in the extent to which romantic music defines its own styles by evoking other musical styles.[24] It is, perhaps, especially obvious in the massive efforts at structural autonomy that became so common during the nineteenth century, by which I mean those romantic works that seem to aspire quite literally to the grand size or systematic status of the physical universe, through a large-scale accumulation of nonimplicational devices that, again, often have some sort of important precedent in Beethoven. I think here of works that link their movements through cyclical returns or even through actual physical transitions (for example, Liszt's *Les Préludes*); of works with thematically retrospective perorations that seem more like rhetorical climaxes than logical syntheses (Mendelssohn's *Scottish* Symphony, for example, or even Wagner's overture to *Die Meistersinger*); of works that employ gargantuan orchestras (such as Strauss's *Also sprach Zarathustra*); and of works that incorporate or evoke a rich diversity of preexistent musical sources (for example, Mahler's First Symphony). The more the nineteenth-century work tries to encompass—and there may be some parallel here with the dialectical system through which Hegel overcomes Kant's disjunctions (see also note 16, this chapter)—the more evident it becomes that its boundaries remain limited by a determining subjectivity. To find anything close to a whole meaning in such works one is virtually thrust outside them into a kind of hermeneutical excavation for highly particular underlying sources; to interpret such works adequately, one is forced to regard them as texts for some painstaking sort of deconstruction rather than as self-explanatory worlds. Mahler used the very term "world" in connection with his symphonies; these works are indeed much larger and more ambitious with respect to diversity of content than any Mozart symphony. Yet for all its scope, Mahler's symphonic world has such an extraordinarily explicit personal and cultural particularity that it simply cannot project, even as a norm, the ideal of universal intelligibility and communication, except, perhaps, by way of the obvious absence of their possibility. Instead, through its extreme emphasis on style, it virtually spells out its fear of incomprehension of itself as an internally distinct structure, as well as the high degree of specific cultural information it requires for any sort of comprehension at all.

This is the sort of information that is involved in the notion of stylistic competence projected by romantic music; there is no doubt that with respect to the scope of communication, this sort of competence has certain advantages over the purely structural competence suggested by classicism, in large measure the advantages of linguistic competence. Thus, much of the knowledge needed for stylistic competence can be acquired passively (for example, by living within a culture or by hearing certain music constantly). Much of the rest of this knowledge, having a particular or empirical identity, can be learned (say, as discrete facts). Moreover, once gained, stylistic competence involves no active processes of reasoning; hence, competent stylistic descriptions can be made by many who are unable to produce the types of analysis, above all harmonic analysis, traditionally demanded of the structurally competent.

Stylistic meaning, however, clearly involves substantial semiotic disadvantages as well. First, the semiotic relations involved in stylistic meaning are openly contingent. This means that although a musical configuration, insofar as it has stylistic meaning, is without doubt formally governed by some configuration of particular subjective structures, the relationship between these two kinds of configuration is at most the disjunct relation of analogy and cannot be conclusively demonstrated.[25] Nor is there any certain way of knowing how close one has come to identifying all the layers in the configuration of governing subjective structures, let alone to "learning" that configuration itself. Consequently, stylistic meaning cannot be considered a meaning ever present in a musical structure, open to complete or secure reconstitution through an exercise of reason; rather, it is a meaning that must be assumed to be incompletely known at best, a meaning that is readily severed or lost through historical time or distance, leaving the structure essentially meaningless to most. (Indeed, to use a notion of Jacques Derrida's cited below in note 29, it may well be that a good deal of stylistic meaning is "always already" lost at the very moment a configuration takes physical shape.) It is because of this semiotic volatility that romantic music, once it has emphasized stylistic elements of structure—elements that appeal primarily to sensory perception rather than to any quasi-conceptual sort of understanding—seems to be explicitly conceding the contingent relation of all meanings to structure, and even the possible imminent loss of its own meanings.

Furthermore, the competence associated with stylistic meaning is by definition a limited and partial mode of comprehension; for recognizing the physical identity of a whole structure, or that of its details, is not the same as following the formal connections within that whole. Indeed, stylistic competence may, in a peculiar sense, even preclude structural competence. For much as those who are fully competent to follow the course of an argument from within, as if its style were transparent, are less likely than the falteringly competent to perceive that argument consciously *as* an autonomous meaningful structure, so, too, conversely, the more compelled the listener is to experience a musical structure in terms of its stylistic or physical identity, or of elements that give it a particular identity, the less one seems compelled, or even permitted, to have the illusion of perceiving that structure from within, as a temporally unfolding argument. And without question, it is a far greater misunderstanding of musical meaning to confuse the identities of two symphonies by a romantic stylist such as Brahms than two by the archclassicist Haydn. In fact, a good deal of romantic music seems to suggest, on the one hand, that neither structural nor stylistic competence is adequate by itself to understand a musical structure in its entirety, and on the other hand, that once the two are distinctly defined, it is virtually impossible to reintegrate them.[26] It is as if romantic music revealed a disjunction between these two autonomous yet incomplete modes of comprehension to be inherent in semiotic processes, as these are construed in the West, precisely as the *Critique of Judgment* reveals such disjunctions as are inherent in the relationships between the inner faculties and capacities of the (Western) human mind, such as perception and understanding.

In the end, indeed, romantic music seems strongly to support the post-Kantian thesis that stylistic and structural understanding simply cannot be reconciled because of contradictions between the norm of physical autonomy, which precludes (as heteronomous) an intrinsic dependence on interpretation or on meaning, and the norm of semiotic autonomy, which promises objectively independent, or intrinsic, meaning. Although from the same post-Kantian standpoint it seems clear that the two norms have an analogous element in that each is defined by a concrete subjective faculty — the former, primarily, through perception, the latter, primarily, through understanding — nevertheless, it is an element that undercuts the distinctiveness of understanding, with its abstract norm of semiotic autonomy, leaving only perception, which makes no claim to universal validity, and its norm of physical autonomy, which, strictly speaking, rejects every vestige of intrinsic meaning. Thus again, though it would appear that stylistic concreteness of structure cannot, despite the promise of classical music, be fused in any knowable way into an identity with logical abstractness of structure, romantic music indicates that the latter can be subsumed under the former in a self-negating way or as an analogical variant of the former, which means, in either case, subsumed in a way that exposes the common reference of both perception and understanding, not to a purely abstract universal structure of reason, but to an absence of universal or intrinsic meaning in any semiotic structure.[27] In its exposure of a disjunction between stylistic and structural kinds of competence, romantic music then seems openly to criticize the idealized classical universe, with its identity of stylistic perception and structural understanding, in much the same way as Kant's *Critique of Judgment* tacitly exposes as an illusion the possibility of an autonomous, in the sense of an implicitly intelligible, semiotic structure. What Kant inadvertently suggests, romantic music, with some self-consciousness, exemplifies: the contingency — and almost certain empirical impossibility — of a semiotic universe.

Before closing I should like to illustrate briefly some ways in which the general conception of musical romanticism developed here might be used in a specific critical interpretation. Let us take a small work that is instructive in that it crystallizes the characteristic elements of the romantic conception of autonomous musical structure with great vividness. I have in mind Chopin's second Prelude for the piano, in A minor (example 1).

Example 1. Second Prelude. Copyright Fryderyk Chopin Society, Warsaw.

The work has no title, and few would deny that tonality figures in it in an important structural sense. By starting on the dominant minor, E, instead of on the tonic, A, and wending its way through a series of analogous or partly analogous harmonic patterns to a relatively brief cadence on the tonic, this piece raises fascinating questions about aspects of classical tonality that can, in a postclassical perspective, be grasped as problematical, for example, the logical necessity of assigning hierarchical precedence to (and, hence, cadencing in) one particular key. Moreover, every pitch in this piece has harmonic aspects that can, in retrospect, be related in some fashion to the tonal identity of the final cadence.

Nevertheless, this piece is hardly to be understood as the realization of any implication within an embodied premise concerning A minor. Thus there is no way in which one can hear the movement from the opening of the piece to the closing as an essentially abstract, logical relationship that binds the piece in a self-evident fashion. In the first place, the opening triad of E minor defines a key that is tonally quite distant from the closing key, A, and which in fact bears a modal rather than tonally logical relationship to A minor if it is put into a direct relationship with it or considered to be in the key of A. In actuality, however, the opening triad is never even heard in direct relationship to A minor. It is heard first as i in E minor, than as vi of G major, the first cadential key; but it can be identified as v (if, indeed, that is its function) only when the identity of the closing key is known, at the end of the piece. And by then, several harmonic disjunctions have separated v from i, disjunctions that likewise keep the opening harmonic phrase from functioning as a premise. It is true that the first five measures after the opening two of introduction have roughly the shape of the antecedent-consequent structure so suggestive of a premise in classical music. Once the first full cadence is reached, however, on G, the unit is closed and implies nothing further.[28] To continue, the composer is forced to heighten the tension rhetorically by moving to a literally higher pitch, making a harmonically unprepared leap to a fairly distant triad, iii of G—significantly, the only link is one of pitch identity between the two Bs in the melody (measures 7–8)—and by compressing the rhythm in the opening of the next phrase (measure 8). He then repeats, through the analogical device of transposition, the antecedent-consequent phrase up to its cadence.

Up to the deviation at that second cadence (measure 11), a repetitive pattern has been established, which one might expect to continue; if it did, the key reached in the *next* repetition would be A, the parallel major of the final key of the piece. But any such expectation is a response to the rhetorically induced momentum of repetition; it is not at all the same as the logical expectation of a structure that is sufficiently different in form (for instance, a complementary structure) to function as a resolution. On the contrary, there is no general form that could be conceived in advance as offering a proper close to the series initiated. Technically speaking, it is true, the bass notes that begin the three segments at measures 1 (E), 8 (B), and 13 (F#) bear the relation of successive fifths, as would their harmonic destinations if these were kept strictly parallel (actual G major, hypothetical D major, hypothetical A major). What one actually hears here, however, is nothing like the so-called cycle of fifths used so commonly as a device for tonal propulsion in earlier music, especially in the baroque style. For even if the second and third goals hypothesized here were actually reached, the effect of the disjunctions between the segments, coupled with the absence until measure 5 (in the archetypal first pattern) of any inner tonal propulsiveness (and with the emphasis on the physical immediacy of harsh color), is to hollow out from this vestige of constructive tonality the force to imply its own end. In fact, no propulsion is felt toward the key of A major (which in any case is tonally quite different from the A minor on which the piece actually ends); nor is there any reason to think that the next repetition of the pattern would be the last. Indeed, there is no reason to think of the empirically actual first phrase in this piece as the logically necessary first phrase of such a series. Leonard Meyer has characterized this opening phrase as "already part of a process."[29] Both in this sense and in terms of the divergence between the opening and the closing harmonies, one could well describe this piece as essentially beginning somewhere in its own harmonic middle. It certainly lacks not only the clear bounding framework of a single, unmistakable tonic key but also the clear outer boundaries of function and the corollary effect of intrinsic wholeness associated with the quasi-logical structure of premise-and-resolution.

Because no logical sort of implication is set up at the start of this piece, the breaking of the harmonic pattern at the end of the second phrase (measures 11–12) is not experienced as the kind of deviation from implied progress that increases propulsiveness toward a goal. Nor does the passage between the second and third phrases (measures 12–14), though it falls within the longest segment of nonresolutionary harmony in the piece (measures 11 to the last half of 14), constitute a propulsive drive toward resolution in the same sense as a classical development section moves toward resolution. Instead, the effect of a physical disjunction is heightened and prolonged by the sudden physical exposure of especially harsh and largely unresolved dissonances in the bass pattern; by the arbitrary drop of the left-hand pattern to a different and lower version of the same chord (measures 12–13); and by the suspension of harmonic movement over a diminished-seventh chord, the most unsettled but also the most ambiguous of harmonies and, hence, the least logically implicative harmony in terms of any specific goal. In terms of physical effect, the length, dissonance, and low (dark) color of this passage are so striking that they undercut the propulsiveness logically associated with instability and call attention to the concrete existence of this passage in itself, almost as if instability were now the norm of sound. Admittedly, this passage is at the same time rhetorically smoothed over by the conjunction of the downward movement of the bass, the fading of volume after a preceding rise, and the early entrance (analyzed in note 34 in this chapter) of the next melodic phrase on a single clear sustained pitch in the right hand (measure 14). (The opening note of this last phrase, which is, of course, A, the ultimate tonic, has the traditional characteristics of an anticipation: it appears over an unstable harmony, before the appearance of a stable one; and relative to its two earlier counterparts, it is itself prolonged, and appears on a weaker beat.) Thus on grounds other than those of harmonic implication or of any sort of temporal self-generation, the passage between measures 11 and 15 can be interpreted as signifying the rise and fall of uncertainty as a kind of imposed effect (with the fall continuing through most of the remainder of the piece). But neither these techniques nor the last-minute introduction of a harmonically resolving gesture (that is, of an augmented-sixth chord resolving to a six-four chord in measures 14–15) can overcome entirely the effect of a harmonic disjunction between the second and third phrases. One still has the sense that a diminished harmony, physically important in itself, breaks off to be replaced by the resumption of an arbitrary repetitive pattern at a harmonically arbitrary (though rhetorically plausible) point. Leonard Meyer sums up the impression of a lack of harmonic necessity at this supposed juncture when he notes, "It seems perfectly clear that any technical explanation of measures 12 to 16 purely in terms of harmonic goals and modulations must be inadequate."[30]

Finally, the last cadence, in A minor, does not serve as a logically inevitable or even implied goal of harmonic motion in the same sense that a tonic chord relieves the tension of a dominant pedal. Again, given the absence of a preceding clear implication of A minor, the final triad cannot have such a function; it can only be heard retrospectively as constituting the actual, empirically definable closing point of the piece, something quite different. Moreover, even within itself, the last segment of the piece (measures 14–23) does not define unmistakable movement toward a harmonic destination. For one thing, the dominant triad on E, which is needed to secure A minor as a harmonic goal, does not appear until two measures before the end (measure 21). To be sure, the six-four position of the first A-minor triad in this segment (measure 15), reinforced by the presence of A in the top line, does differentiate that triad from its earlier counterparts (E minor, measure 1, B minor, measure 8), and thereby suggests a potentially significant change of direction. Initially, however, the change defines simply a relation of identity or difference to earlier elements, not the approach to an inevitable harmonic conclusion. The anticipatory harmonic function of the six-four triad of A minor becomes clear only in retrospect.

It is true that a six-four triad in an unambiguous harmonic context — for example, immediately preceding the cadenza in a classical concerto movement — can strongly imply a closing tonic; and one might, on the basis of this external historical information, predict the resolution of Chopin's six-four triad to one in root position. Even then, as already suggested elsewhere, one could not be certain in advance, on purely internal or harmonic grounds, that such a root-position triad would define an ultimate goal, or true tonic, rather than another intermediate one. Moreover, despite the familiarity of the harmonic device from classical practice, the effect of the six-four chord in the prelude is different, for the harmonic context here is not unambiguous. On the contrary, the melodic line tends from the start to pull away from A minor, at first toward a C-major triad, which an analogy with the two preceding melodic phrases suggests as the final sonority of a melodic phrase beginning on the note A, and then toward B-flat major. For though in retrospect the melodic F in measure 7, which breaks the exact parallelism of opening melodic gestures, can be construed as a kind of tonal foreshortening that negates the importance of its literal identity, the sudden unprecedented silence in the left hand calls rhetorically emphatic attention to this F in itself, as if it were the literal continuation of a melodic phrase that began on the note G. In other words, this F, left in a striking manner unharmonized, suggests itself, by analogy with its counterparts in measures 5 and 10, as the dominant of B-flat. And even in measure 20, the grace note F, which contrasts strikingly with the F-sharp in measure 5, does not portend a tonic with the same propulsiveness as does a Beethovenian lowered-sixth degree; and here, too, as in measure 17, the melodic line literally resists harmonization. (It is by no means inconceivable that this latter F-natural, the sole note distinguishing the melodic pattern and pitch level of measure 20 from those of measure 5, could be denied tonal significance and exposed emphatically as a mere variance in pitch through a resumption of the earlier harmonic goal, G major.)

For that matter, even the extended repetition of E in the bassline (from measures 15–22), which in another situation might readily be taken for a conventional dominant pedal preparation of the final tonic, does not assume that function unequivocally until the very last appearance of that E, in the rhetorically deepened dominant-seventh chord at the end of the penultimate measure (22). Up until measure 21, the dominant triad is avoided altogether, and the bass E seems at most the foundation of a relatively consonant sonority. The fact that the E taken up by the bass at measure 15 is the same note on which the bass began the piece seems to signify a coincidence of pitch identities rather than a logical necessity of tonal construction. And at measures 18–20 in particular, the divergence between the tonal identity of the droning bass and the tonal implications of the moving treble is so wide that for a moment all semblance of tonal mooring seems absent from a pattern defined by pitch and sonority.

At any rate, the harmonic identity of measures 15–20 is sufficiently uncertain as to deprive the pedal points on E and A in measures 15–16 of a classically definitive V–I cadential function. Here the two notes seem part of a nonpropulsive, nondirectional, or, at most, ambivalent harmonic pattern, an impression strengthened by the dissolution of the octave on A in measures 15–16 into a sixth on A and F in measures 18–19, by the unresolved alternation of the A-minor triad, at this latter point, with the dissonant notes B and F, and by the blurring effect of the single sustaining-pedal indication.

Without doubt, the final cadence on A minor does put an actual end to all preceding harmonic uncertainty; but rather than constituting the only conceivable and thus logically necessary end to the piece, it is a forcible and contingent end, more rhetorical than harmonically logical in its persuasiveness. In terms of rationality, it can at most be heard as one of many plausible endings, susceptible to an ex post facto, empirical explanation of what actually (or historically) happened, but not to analysis as the necessary realization of a logical premise. Even the clear link between the melodic D and F in the last segment (measures 18–20) and the D and F-sharp in the first segment (measures 4–5) involves identity and difference, or arbitrary repetition and variance, rather than implication and resolution. Moreover, the momentum of the bass pattern is definitively broken not by harmonic resolution but by literal silence (measure 19), which confirms the structural importance of the silence just preceding, measures 17–18). And finally, the prolonged dynamic diminuendo as well as the *slentando* and *sostenuto* markings (measures 18 and 21), the prolongation of the final V and I chords indicated by the arpeggiation signs, and the closing fermata — all clearly imposed rhetorical markings — are essential as physical or empirical calming effects to render the final cadence fully coherent as a functional close to the piece.

In fact, this is a piece in which the conception of harmony as a force for constructing a continuous whole has given way to a preoccupation with problems of harmonic identity. Harmonic meaning in the sense of recognizable harmonic function is not absent in this piece, but by and large, harmonic structure has disintegrated into localized and roughly (though not in every respect audibly) analogous harmonic units.[31] These can be designated roughly as measures 1 to 7, 8 to 12, and 13 to the end. Each unit presents comparable progressions; each is seemingly involved in the attempt to wrest a harmonic identity out of harmonic ambiguity; and thus, each can be characterized as calling attention to the question of what it is, rather than as pointing temporally forward in a kind of semiotic metaphor to what it might mean. To be sure, there are harmonic differences among these units in terms of both their large-scale inner patterns and their chromatic and other detail; in particular, the last segment is distinctive in that it moves into its eventual key from an unstable harmony, stays in its key longer than the earlier phrases do, and is threatened by independent harmonic implications in the melody. Still, because of certain clear overall similarities of shape provided by harmony and even more by nonharmonic parameters, and because of the perceptible gaps between these units, these differences are experienced far less as differences of harmonic function in relation to a temporal whole than as differences in the actuality and the quality of particular identity.

Again, this is not to say that the total configuration is harmonically incoherent and to be dismissed as irrational. Clearly, tonality is still being used to an extent in this piece to convey the sense that something happens in time. And without question it is possible to provide one's own semiotic connections between the segments of this piece, and therefore to render a plausible account of the piece in terms of its temporal structure. Nevertheless, the interpretation that results is very likely to involve an undercutting of the temporal dimension of this piece, at least insofar as temporal and logical unfolding can be defined as identical; to the extent that this piece persists in evoking the logical constructive force of the tonic, it has become more a mention than a use of functional tonality.[32] One could well characterize it as a piece that is *about* classical tonality; for the emphasis on the individual identity of its component phrases seems to encourage, and certainly allows, one to construe this piece, in a kind of temporally frozen quasi-spatial sense, as an inventory of a few highly individualized aspects of a physically actual as well as conceptually definable entity called "A minor," an effect that is emphasized by the four distinctly different harmonizations (or nonharmonizations) of the cadential repeated-note patterns in measures 6–7, 11–12, 18–19, and 21–22. As a harmonic sort of meaning, of course, this is considerably more restricted than the impression of a self-embodied totality of generally valid meanings that a classical structure might seem to develop out of an A-minor proposition. Again, the piece projects the sense of being a harmonic fragment, a sense that is in one way confirmed by its extreme brevity, which seems to acknowledge renunciation of any large-scale constructive force inherent in tonality.

In short, Chopin's A-minor prelude is not without harmonic meaning, but the meaning does not present itself as a complete meaning. By the same token, not all of the meaning in this piece seems to inhere in its temporal harmonic structure. Melody, for example, makes a relatively independent contribution to the coherence of this piece by projecting its own disjunct pattern of analogues, one that differs from the harmonic pattern in overall shape (the melodic pattern is resumed at measure 14 with much smaller differences than those in the final harmonic pattern) and in harmonic identity (from measure 14 to the end). (On the whole, the pattern of analogues is more consistently audible in the melodic than in the harmonic structure of this piece; much of the structural clarity of the prelude depends on the ease with which similarities and differences in the melodic analogues can be retained over its relatively brief duration.) Though the relation of melody and harmony has significance in this piece, it is a relation that consists largely in coexisting differences of particular identity; in no sense can the harmony be said to imply the melody. Instead, one can begin to form an idea of the piece similar to the deconstructionist image of a text: a total musical configuration consisting in an indeterminate number of relatively discrete, though potentially analogous, layers of structural significance that are not grounded in an implicit and unifying tonal premise. Such a configuration can be "explained" only in the sense that it can be imagined as originating in some individualized archetype of a rational configuration existing outside of the piece itself in the mind of the composer.

Likewise, pitch level (the rise to the first transposition of the opening pattern, measure 8, and the gradual fall after the highest pitch in the piece is struck on a grace-note in measure 10), the prolonged harshness of dissonance mid-piece (measures 10–14), dynamics (the implied rise to measure 12[33] and subsequent fall), tempo and touch markings, and literal silence (the rest over the falling bass in measure 13, the sudden cessation of the accompaniment in measures 17 and 20, and the complete break before the final melodic phrase in measure 19) — all define a pattern of rise and fall that becomes very common in romantic music as the constructive power of pure harmony weakens. This pattern of rhetorical emphasis, clearly a fundamental source of coherence in this piece, is used to reinforce harmonic uncertainty and closing, but it is no mere function of tonality. On the contrary, unlike the tonally generated dynamic of the classical structure, this essentially static pattern of internal rise and fall is imposed on the harmony, so to speak, precisely because it offers in physical terms a continuity that no longer has a quasi-logical counterpart in the disjunct harmonic pattern. In some ways this temporally imposed rhetoric is more integral to the structure of the piece than is the harmony. This seems especially so in the last segment, at measures 13–15, where the almost isolated falling bass patterns seem not to need the older harmonic and melodic patterns. Despite being grounded on what turns out to be the dominant of the final tonic, the last return of these patterns (with the harmony altered) seems thrust upon the rhetorically flagging energies of the piece, pushed in arbitrarily as if in passing—an effect heightened by the rhythmic and harmonic anticipation in the precipitate melodic entrance (measure 14) that follows a prolonged melodic pause,[34] and an effect that, while literally narrowing the gap between the second and third phrases, adds also to the sense of a physically disruptive disjunction between phrases, already noted with respect to the harmony. Here again one is faced with the coexistence of discrete, though in some respects analogous, musical parameters that intensify consciousness of the presence of an outside source from which they must emanate.

Within such a context, even the melodic A at the beginning of the last phrase, in measure 14, seems less the beginning of a tonally logical resolution on the tonic, a process that can be perceived fully only in retrospect, than the gathering of techniques derived from rhythm and register into a gesture of rhetorical emphasis. Or to put it another way, the physical emphasis on this A suggests that its functional identification as the tonic requires rhetorical reinforcement—as if the coincidence of physical strength and logical meaning at this moment were a matter of chance, for which there were other less logical but equally plausible alternatives.

Still another element that seems to give this piece a kind of sense independent of a tonal argument is its high degree of coloristic particularity, evidenced in the first instance by the striking restriction of a potentially wide pianistic range to a narrow, relatively low sonority. This particularity is provided even at the level of harmonic detail, for example, through the complexity and pervasive dissonance of the chromatic sonorities (which no amateur could comfortably analyze), and through the constant small changes in sonority and symmetry, as well as through the pervasive ambiguity of major and minor sonorities, both of which can be effected by differences of one or two notes.[35] The breaking of common rules, such as the resolution of dissonance[36] and even the avoidance of parallel octaves,[37] also adds to the effect of coloristic particularity, as does the close, thick spacing of the individual pitches. Along with the relentlessness of ostinato rhythm and the percussiveness of the constant pianistic attack on pairs of low-pitched notes, which is softened for only one moment by the sustaining pedal, the chromatic and pianistic sonorities of this piece give it the meaning that is almost surely the one most often attached to it—its character of harshness as a total configuration.

This is a kind of meaning, however, that must be called stylistic, in my sense, in that it points attention forcibly away from the internal structural connections of the piece to other sources of meaning, such as the entire set of preludes and beyond that, Chopin's style; for it is only in terms of its somewhat exceptional character relative to these latter that this harshness of identity can be said to make full sense. And indeed, the contrast of sonorities and textures among the various preludes is a principal source of intelligibility for them all. But it should be noted that the entire set of preludes does not bear the same relationship of implication or reciprocity to the individual preludes that seems at every level of structure to connect part and whole in a classical work. Unlike a classical work, which seems to project its total structure as the realization of tonal relationships implicit in its component units, the whole set of Chopin's preludes cannot be said to inhere in any of the individual preludes (except, perhaps, in the odd sense that the key arrangement of the entire set might be needed to secure positive identification of the tonic in the second Prelude). Instead, the set must be acknowledged as external to the individual prelude and as related to it only in a contingent fashion. One could say that the set seems something like a contingent analogue of a piece such as the second Prelude, since the set, too, consists in a nontemporal, quasi-spatial inventory of discrete, analogous components.

In its presentation of preludes in each of the twenty-four keys, the set is actually a romantic attempt at a systematic structure. But just as the configuration of each prelude cannot in any way be taken as a set of abstractly logical, generalizable, or intrinsically "true" relationships, so, too, the "system" here is far more openly particular than classical tonality and hence far less easily interpreted as the embodiment of a universally accessible, abstractly meaningful structure. In classical tonality (or any natural language), it is possible to imagine maintaining constancy of meaning in a structure even if its particular components were to be replaced by others (say, through the use of transposition, instrumental transcription, synonyms, and so on). This is because utterances in these systems are understood to refer to more encompassing, cohesive structures of meaning that are separate from those of any particular structure; in linguistic terminology, these systems have a dual structure.[38] It is this assumed fungibility of physically defined components that, paradoxical as it may seem, allows Westerners to construe the individuality of a high classical symphony as exhibiting a universally significant and even necessary form. Precisely because its particular components can be referred to a general system within which they are assumed exchangeable with an open-ended number of equivalents, the classical structure as a whole can comfortably be interpreted as possessing a highly general, in fact abstract, validity. By defining the individual as a choice made through reference to a seemingly binding system of universal, rational principles, classicism makes it possible to imagine that each individual element has been freely chosen, from among many others, to serve some purpose that is rationally not just plausible but necessary.[39]

This is not the case with Chopin's preludes. Whereas the classical style persuades us to interpret its individualities as fungible aspects of an abstractly unquestionable meaning, Chopin's individualities seem explicitly contingent. His cycle of preludes is completely and empirically fixed in its actual physical structure, and its expressive possibilities (though not the interpretations that can be applied to it) seem inalterably finite. In other words, no further manipulation of this system is possible, because as a *langue*, so to speak, the cycle is nothing more general than the sum of its *paroles*, or individual preludes; like the second Prelude and its component phrases, the cycle, too, seems more concerned with autonomous identity than with implicit meaning of structure. To be sure, the empirical contingency of its particular character may well send the listener to a more general source of identification or meaning, such as Chopin's style, or, in the case of a scholar, a still broader configuration of romantic style. But again, neither individual nor cultural style constitutes the sort of system that one could imagine deducing from either the individual prelude or the cycle. In terms of the second Prelude, then, all of these broader structures — set, style, cultural movement — can be construed as providing legitimate sources of meaning for those who already know them or know how to look for them; but they cannot be designated a single, cohesive meaning that is completely embodied in the second Prelude.

It seems fair to say that through a work as seemingly autonomous as the second Prelude, Chopin makes what is in effect a post-Kantian critique of the norm of the autonomous semiotic universe idealized in classicism. It even seems symptomatic of the limitations that such a critique sets upon human semiotic structures that this apparently pure musical structure has been cited for its qualities of "doubt and uncertainty,"[40] not only in the essentially formal terms of Leonard Meyer's criticism, but also in that mixture of poetic and technical terms (itself indicative of romantic attitudes toward musical autonomy) that typifies so many nineteenth-century interpretations, such as this one, called "Presentiment of Death":

> This is as uncertain in character as in key. It begins in E-minor, goes into G-major, then to B-minor, only to lose itself slowly in A-minor. The mood is constantly changing, yet it always comes back to one and the same thought, the melancholy tolling of a funeral knell. The two-voiced accompaniment in the left-hand is difficult to play legato. The right hand bears the inexorable voice of death, though toward the end it falters and loses the measure in uncertain tones, as if saying, "He comes not, the deliverer! It was a delusion." This is what the questioning end seems to say.[41]

From the accounts of both Meyer and von Bülow, one could guess that Chopin has captured in this piece something of the contingency surrounding all semiotic objects. And just as this piece seems to involve the relationship of analogy in its temporal segmentation, its layering of semiotic parameters, and its reference to its parent work and stylistic origins, so, too, it would seem that the construction of vastly different interpretations by Meyer and von Bülow around the common notion of uncertainty provides good evidence of the analogical relationships at work in acts of criticism.[42]

Chapter 8

On Grounding Chopin

Autonomy versus Contingency

The notion that society lies at the heart of music—at the heart not only of its significance but also of its very identity—is a notion, I have come to realize, that is for me not a hypothesis, not a thesis the scientific proof of which is the goal of my study. In fact I would say that this notion does not lend itself to any popularly conceived model whereby an inductive investigation of a hypothesis leads to scientific conclusion, whether one thinks of it as a general notion (the notion that music and society in general are intimately related) or as any particular version of that notion (say, the Marxist version, that music takes shape out of some set of underlying economic conditions). That is to say, not even the existence of such an intimacy, much less any particular account of it, is susceptible of scientific proof through a presentation of facts.

This is why studies based on the notion I describe are so suspect in mainstream American musicology. The latter remains dominated by positivism, defined in Webster's second edition as "A system of philosophy . . . which excludes everything but the natural phenomena or properties of knowable things, together with their relations of coexistence and succession." It is a discipline commited in its materials and methods to a rather old-fashioned, vulgarized notion of scientific models.

For me, the notion of an intimate relationship between music and society functions not as a distant goal but as a starting point of great immediacy, and not as a hypothesis but as an assumption. It functions as an idea about a relationship which in turn allows the examination of that relationship from many points of view and its exploration in many directions. It is an idea that generates studies the goal of which (or at least one important goal of which) is to articulate something essential about why any particular music is the way it is in particular, that is, to achieve insight into the character of its identity. This process involves decisions (which can never be definitive) as to what constitutes the significant ways in which this music differs from other forms, even related forms, of human expression.

Critics sometimes complain that authors of studies based on this assumption of social intimacy are not really interested in music but rather in philosophy or anthropology or some other "extrinsic" discipline. This criticism is actually two-pronged in that it reveals an insistence on the autonomy not only of music but also of musicology, which positivists tend to see as an extension of the autonomous domain of music itself. As to this latter notion, I would say it is deceptive, for positivist musicologists do not derive their methods of study from the music they study any more often than serious contextualists do; on the contrary, as I hope to show, they do it less. The real objection here, I believe, is not that contextualists violate the autonomy of musicology as a strictly musical undertaking but that they look to the wrong outside disciplines for help—to philosophy and anthropology rather than to a positivistically conceived model of science.

As to the charge of a lack of interest in music, it seems to me patently wrong. No doubt massive collections of facts about a body of music can indicate a love, at least of some antiquarian sort, of that music. But is love not evident also in studies that, based on the assumption that society lies at the heart of the very identity of music, aim at understanding why music is the way it is? Good contextualist studies start from the music and lead back to it. In this respect contextualists often resemble Adorno, whose repeated assaults on the problem of social mediation remained inseparable from a concomitant, if seemingly contradictory, insistence on autonomy as the ideal condition of musical structure.

But along the way, of course, in the dialectic that occurs between the departure from the music and the return to it, serious contextualists grapple with problems that cannot be solved through the mere establishment of facts or simple models of cause and effect. Typically, contextualists alternate between following the music into its relations with its social context and reassessing their own method of studying those relationships. Serious contextualists want to go beyond questions that can be answered through "His Life and Works" or "The Music and Its Times," studies that, like other more clearly positivistic studies, may produce information that is useful to others but need not go beyond the connections implied by "and" in the framing of questions or methods.

Serious contextualists try to deal with the relation between music and society in a way that recognizes the complex questions raised by human forms of expression and, consequently, the need for methodological honesty, refinement, and self-critical capacity in the study of those forms. For example, recognizing, as post-Marxian or post-Freudian scholars do, that no single principle is likely to find scientific acceptance as the universal explanation of human forms of expression, serious contextualists do not thereby renounce, as do positivists, the problem of social mediation as one worthy of serious study or even, necessarily, the theories of Marx or Freud as helpful sources of insight into forms of human expression. Rather they acknowledge that they have hold of an assumption, and of theories and problems concerning that assumption, that can never be definitively proved but only asserted, manipulated, stroked, and viewed repetitively through a series of altered angles, or returned to periodically as patterns of identity strung through a medium of shifting contexts or perceptions until, it is hoped, some persuasive pattern of intelligibility emerges.

   To be persuasive, of course, an account requires internal rigor; but though simple scientific models do not supply a basis of rigor for such contextualist studies, it does not follow that no such rigor is possible. Scientific structures are not the only sort that the human mind has fashioned persuasively; the rigor of religious systems, for example, has probably exercised sway over far more human minds than that of scientific models. Nor is science the only model of study available to serious contextualists. There are other forms of human expression which suggest that, while it may be difficult to convey the presence of mental rigor in connections forming patterns other than those of mechanistic causal explanation or empirical induction, it is not impossible. I think particularly of aesthetic forms of expression. The persuasive demonstration of such rigor has in fact been a central agenda of the high arts themselves in the past two centuries of Western history—certainly of music since Beethoven—and the difficulty has not yet entirely vanquished those arts (though it threatens to) or eliminated them as credible instruments of human understanding. Criticism, too, tends to model itself on artistic rather than scientific patterns of connections and has had an enormous impact on a good deal of twentieth-century thought, though not on mainstream American musicology. Indeed, I would argue that the problem of trying to relate music to society *is*, fundamentally, a problem of criticism, requiring very much the same sorts of means that one would take to the interpretation of a literary text.

   In choosing science over art as a paradigm for seeking truth, positivist musicology seems to believe it is safeguarding its double ideal of autonomy—in the domains of both music and musicology. But is it really safeguarding either? In actuality, the structural autonomy posited as an ideal for music by Adorno is extended by the positivist to include a number of things besides the superficially most plausible autonomous entity, the composition itself. The positivist definition of musical autonomy includes music that preceded a composition, the instruments and other material conditions of performance that figured in composition, and above all the composer's mind, the iconic status of which is shown by the massive attention given to sketch studies and especially to the making of so-called authentic editions.

Such considerations define the autonomy of music for positivist musicologists. Yet even they seem uneasily aware that this extended definition itself already involves music in a kind of heteronomy, to use that dreadful and misleading word, and that in order to work, this extended definition requires certain kinds of connections that cannot be supplied through the positivist principles of coexistence and succession.

Consider this passage from the conclusion to a recent highly regarded essay on Chopin: "Perceptive analysis and comprehension of the sources and intetpretation and evaluation of the music form, or ought to form, inseparable parts of one line of inquiry. . . . If this article has addressed a fundamental aspect of source studies in Chopin, work must now take up the associated issue: the critical reassessment of his music."[1] "Work." But whose work? And how "associated"? Time and again we are exhorted at the end of such an article to go out and synthesize the preceding collection of facts into some account of the music itself, but we are given no clue how to approach such a synthesis, much less any reference to nonpositivist work on such a problem.

Or again, consider the material and stylistic sources of music. Positivist methods can gather genuinely useful facts about instruments, orchestras, and opera houses; they can quantify certain kinds of similarities and differences between works; they can prove (though not always disprove) contact between two composers. But can they—do they—offer us any theory or account, for example, of how musical influence actually works? Judging even from my own experience as a composition student, of cribbing the opening to Mendelssohn's *Reformation* Symphony in total ignorance of my theft, I would suspect that influence is an extremely complicated mechanism.

Or again, consider sketch studies. One frequently encounters a defensive tonic in such articles as authors seek to justify the validity of the enterprise, assuring us of their familiarity with the intentional fallacy and respect for it.[2] The reason for this defensiveness seems to be that here, too, as in the case of source and style studies, authors sense the inconsistencies within their received definition of musical autonomy. Likewise they probably sense the need for modes of connection that might be found in models they do not know how to construct or to justify.

Even sketch studies, it seems, which try to do no more than connect a work with earlier versions of itself—surely the narrowest extension of the concept of musical autonomy one can imagine — even these studies, to maintain their own validity, require ultimately a kind of connection-making that the positivist dares not risk. Outside the characteristically expansive last paragraph, in which they simultaneously admit and shrink back from the need to establish connections, positivists avoid asking seriously about such connections. If these scholars took up the challenge of their own concluding speculations with methodological honesty, they would soon run up against precisely the same kinds of epistemological and methodological uncertainties for which they castigate the serious contextualist. Is it any wonder that the positivist, who cannot close the conceptual gap between the sketch and the work, experiences acute discomfort in the presence of efforts to close the much larger gap between music and society? Musical autonomy as the positivist conceives it, I fear, consists less in the persuasive demonstration of musical autonomy than in the shaping of scholarly work so as to evade hard thought about autonomy.

The autonomy positivists impute to musicology, as I have already suggested in another context,[3] is no less problematical than that they impute to music. Even if we suppose, as positivists do, that musicology, though a legitimate part of the autonomous musical domain, nevertheless cannot draw its structure from music, and if we accept scientific method as an appropriate model of autonomy for work in any discipline, it does not follow that all positivist studies conform to such a model. On the contrary, many a positivist musicological study dispenses with even the simple conceptual framework of hypothesis and conclusion and presents a mere chronicle or at times even a scarcely disguised list of archival findings, in which not even verbs, much less connective theories, seem really necessary. Such studies can hardly be said to present a scientifically autonomous argument.[4]

Ironically, although positivists reject everything outside of music in order to keep the study of music pure, they fail to look to music itself for the incomparable insight it could give into a problem central to their own work. I mean by this the rigorous and painstaking job of trying to fashion a persuasively whole structure exactly suited to the character of their materials themselves. Because everything included in a positivist study must be "accounted for," everything tends to be treated as equally important. No structure is generated to serve the particular needs of materials because such needs are not seriously considered or defined.

Such conceptual limitations may in some ways actually counteract scholarly efforts to preserve for us the original spirit of earlier music. In positivist studies, for example, questions typically do not arise (because they cannot) about the inherent purposes and the results of reconstructing textual accuracy. Achieving textual accuracy is more often than not simply accepted as an *end* of musical scholarship, rather than envisioned as one part of a larger project. But even if we assume that reconstruction of a composer's exact intent is the highest duty of musical study—an assumption questioned by all the great composers who reworked the compositions of their predecessors—does it follow that textual accuracy is necessarily the best means to such a reconstruction?

In preparing this essay, I used my own old edition of Chopin's etudes, edited in 1916 by Arthur Friedheim.[5] At one point I was struck by a *rallentando* marking and wondered if it was authentic. This question led me to Friedheim's preface, which astonished me. Friedheim openly acknowledged altering, omitting, and adding to various received markings in the music, but not thoughtlessly, or because he thought he could improve on Chopin's original markings. Rather, he had actually heard some of these works performed by Liszt (and by Anton Rubinstein, who was audibly influenced by Liszt); and he assumed, reasonably, that these performances preserved as well as possible Chopin's own spirit. Attempting to preserve the "tradition at second-hand" that he had in his mind's ear, he had used the markings that were most likely to get that rendition from the modern performer.[6] This is in keeping with Adorno's idea, in "Bach Defended Against his Devotees," or more recently, with Richard Taruskin's idea, that to preserve the essential quality of old music, which requires maintaining its vitality in our own context, it is sometimes necessary to change the material conditions of its performance.[7] Is it not possible that the faithful rendering of Chopin's expressive markings, some of which may now have altered significance, and which to some extent reflect values different from ours, could actually bring about performances unfaithful to Chopin's intent? Positivists do give such matters some consideration at the level of the immediate editorial decision, but unlike the less scientific Friedheim, they do not ordinarily address the broader conceptual implications of such problems, let alone make room for persuasive reinterpretations.

I have no quarrel with the notion that the quality of a work of art is related in some central, though not necessarily exclusive, way to its persuasiveness in projecting its own structural wholeness. I have no thought that enlarging the domain of musicology to include the methodological concerns of contextualists would invalidate the value of formal analysis. Nor do I have any quarrel with the notion that composers, at least in modern Western history, experience the working out of a creative problem as a self-contained exercise, even when their structural solutions or materials seem actually to be drawn, at least in part, from outside the traditional musical medium.

I see no fatal contradiction between the acceptance of autonomy, in the sense of wholeness, as one sort of paradigm for interpreting structure and the rejection of autonomy as an epistemological ideology. Nor do I view various composers' experience of their own autonomy as an epistemological barrier to my view of their work as something inseparable from its environment. Rather I see such conflicting concepts as part of a dialectic that exists not only in art but also in life. In life, too, we tend to experience the working out of a problem or relationship as a self-contained activity; our preoccupation with internal relationships tends to distract us from observing any connections our works and problems may have to the world beyond them.

And yet upon reflection, such experiences often make more sense to us viewed as elements of patterns that are presented, repeated, varied, or returned to in the course of our lifetimes, precisely as patterns are treated in art and in aesthetically modeled studies. In fact, I would argue that the structure of art and the experience of life support each other in ways that affirm the value of serious contextual studies. On the one hand, the patterns of problem-solving provided by art seem well designed as models for trying to impose coherence on—to make sense of—our experience.[8] And on the other hand, though our reflection on experience cannot pretend to a specifically scientific sort of rigor, we are certainly in a strong position to judge the adequacy of our reflections to the undeniable hardness of our experienced reality itself.

And our reflected experience, I believe, gives us ample support for the notion that even as we define problems and relationships in apparent autonomy, we are reflecting complex interactions with society of which we are largely unconscious, and for which the most useful metaphor of explanation is not the simple one of cause and effect but the more complicated assertions and intertwinings of art. In terms of my own life, I think of the shock I experienced in coming to realize that the decisions I had made about bringing up my own children (involving patterns I had imposed on them and relationships I had developed with them), decisions that I had experienced as being drawn from an instinctive, very personal set of values, were highly characteristic of parents in my generation. Why? Was it because we were all reacting against the "defects" of an identical inherited set of child-rearing values (how did *those* become identical?)? Because we were all working parents? Because we were all living through the same technological revolution?

Not even the most sophisticated statistical methods could sort out these elements into their "correct" causal proportions, let alone establish conclusively their connection to my problem-solving as a parent. And yet clearly there were patterns out there in society that exactly paralleled not only the materials—the values—I brought to my activities as a parent but also the shapes of the decisions and relationships I defined. Here was a personal example of the mysteries of mediation, unscientific, and yet not necessarily less real, or less worthy in an epistemological sense of further exploration than were Piaget's observations of his own children. If I could look into the future and hear the account given by some contextualist historian of this phenomenon, I could judge out of the hardness of my own experience whether his or her account made any sense of reality. This does not mean I would, or in fairness could, limit future explanation to my own perspective; but surely this ability to judge would validate the historian's very attempt to connect my actions to a context of which I may have been unconscious. Should not our own attempts have the same legitimacy in our studies of composers past?

Contingency in Chopin

Chopin at first blush seems to most of us an unlikely candidate to propose for any study aimed at countering the notion that music is purely autonomous. Certainly his music seems to satisfy criteria for autonomy on a number of levels. Most obviously it is mainly instrumental music, meaning it does without both voice and word, those two obtrusions of the human presence which drag music down so heavily into our own mundane world and out of the ethereal realm where early German romantics imagined it existing as a kind of disembodied significant form. This absence is felt not as a renunciation, such as that implied by Mendelssohn's title *Songs without Words*, but as a simple and rather persuasive fact of independence. Indeed, the instrumental source is largely confined to a single intrument, the piano, which is likely to exist in the performer's home, so we can say that even in the most external sense, Chopin's music requires relatively few social resources, though of course it does require some.

Chopin's music, furthermore, is basically nonfunctional. True, certain works, notably the etudes and preludes, are often, though certainly not always, used as a means of improving the performer's skill. This is a time-honored function of music, and yet it does not seriously threaten the characterization of Chopin's music as autonomous at the level of which I am speaking. At most, in Chopin's case, this function seems merely a minor variant of the ideal of autonomy; the principal effect of these works is no more pedagogical than that of the other music that the instrumentalist's enhanced skill may serve. On the contrary, even the preludes and etudes can readily be taken as designed to pass through time, or perhaps to define it, in an aesthetically pleasing way. (One is never surprised to find a Chopin study piece in a recital of music designed for just this seemingly autonomous purpose of self-presentation, whereas a Clementi etude or even a Bach invention may seem a bit out of place on such an occasion.) Despite its well-known evocations of patriotic, military, and elegiac sentiments, and with some allowance made, perhaps, for the widely used Funeral March from the B♭ Minor Sonata (Opus 35), Chopin's music does not strike us as dedicated in the same way as baroque music was to state occasion or the glory of God. True, we happen to know the absence of such function from outside sources, but it is also the case that Chopin's piano pieces help define or at least conform to the shape and sound of a genre that can readily by interpreted, even without external knowledge, as essentially aesthetic, as opposed to functional, in character. Moreover, though it would not be true to say that listeners, either in Chopin's time or since, never associate Chopin's works with places, events, or other things outside of them — a point to which I shall return later — in our own time, at least, such associations are not thought necessary to make sense of those works.

Finally, Chopin's music seems autonomous to us in the sense that each piece seems to have a sensuous identity, a personality, so to speak, of its own. This sensuous distinctiveness does not seem to motivate the form of eighteenth-century music in quite the same way. One could argue plausibly, I believe, that with perhaps some noteworthy exceptions, typically tending toward a postbaroque expressiveness (such as the Prelude in B♭ Minor in the *Well-tempered Clavier*, book I), Bach's preludes and fugues carve out a sensuous identity to some extent in spite of themselves. In other words, the achievement of such an identity does not seem to be what these works are principally after. Or again, even within the keyboard works of François Couperin or Rameau, works of a palpably aesthetic rather than functional character, it is not difficult to imagine mistaking one piece for another. Neither of these situations characterizes Chopin's music.

And yet the very nature of this last sort of autonomy — sensuous distinctiveness — must give us pause, for in Chopin's case, at least, it is almost inseparable from another characteristic. Some time ago I published an analysis of Chopin's second Prelude, the notorious A Minor, arguing that it represented a turn away from a belief in the possibility of truly autonomous intelligible structures, structures able to present wholly in themselves a self-evident (and hence universally intelligible) meaning.[9] I argued not only that this work failed to achieve such genuine internal structural autonomy — in my view all works ultimately fail in this respect — but more significantly, that the piece did not even project such autonomy as an aesthetic ideal. At the time one critic accused me of setting up a straw man by choosing a piece that was atypical of nineteenth-century music. This criticism surprised me, for although it is clear that there is something especially distinctive about this piece (all Chopin's pieces are distinctive but some are more distinctive than others?) I would have said it was not atypical but merely extreme. I thought this piece pushed to the outer limits characteristics that were very typical of romantic music, and that for precisely this reason, as Walter Benjamin suggested more generally about extreme examples,[10] it made a good locus of style study. At any rate, I would like now to continue that line of analysis with reference to other, less controversially characteristic pieces by Chopin.

What is unusual about the second Prelude is this: its harsh and somber sensuous identity is so powerful that it threatens to overwhelm another sort of identity that we typically associate with Chopin's music, and that ordinarily defines a more fundamental, even ultimate ground or context for making sense of a Chopin piece. I mean, of course, Chopin's compositional identity itself. The second Prelude seems unusual and puzzling very largely because (at least up to measure 17) we are unsure, or can imagine being unsure, that the piece is by Chopin at all. On the whole this is not the case with Chopin's music. We hear a work by Chopin, and our first impression, which remains throughout the piece as a kind of grounding principle, is that we are hearing a piece by Chopin.

This is no tautology. I do not deny that other composers achieved styles in the centuries before Chopin: I am told that Renaissance scholars can easily identify Josquin, and I myself have forced undergraduates to identify Dufay on listening exams. Still this is a rather specialized sort of experience. Likewise, it is possible to follow the structure of a work by Bach without having the listening experience overshadowed by the awareness of Bach's identity. And no matter how distinctive the most characteristic gestures of each may be, we can at least imagine confusing moments of Handel and Bach, or of Haydn and Mozart. Even Beethoven's personality, it could be argued, is grasped only secondarily to a sense of his energy, propulsiveness, and scale; that is, it is possible to imagine the experience of even a characteristic middle-period work preceding our recognition of Beethoven's authorship—if only there were a few such movements left that we did not already recognize! By contrast, it seems to me, the first sense we make of Chopin's music is almost always, to use the words of Robert Schumann who pointed this out repeatedly: "This is by Frédéric Chopin."[11]

I have sometimes been thought to look down on romantic music,[12] and certainly there is a school of thought that sees the establishment of this sort of personal identity in music as a sign of structural weakness. Again I am speaking of Adorno, who considered the definition of individuality on a personal level evidence of an open failure to define individuality on a level of universal validity. For Adorno the highest achievement of music would be to define and resolve a structural problem, on a purely structural plane, uncorrupted by society. Adorno would have agreed with me that this is in practice an impossible achievement, but he associated the notion, rightly I believe, with classicism in the sense that the projection of such an achievement as an ideal formed a constituent principle of the classical style.

But I have never shared Adorno's negative judgment toward the music that followed Beethoven. On the contrary it seems to me that if one must make value judgments, then there is something very positive to be said about the romantic style in general — the very thing, incidentally, that makes me see in the romantic musical structure a more useful model for modern humanistic scholarship than those provided by Enlightenment paradigms of scientific universality. It can be argued that classicism aimed at a high ideal of human universality, in which all rational structures would be self-evident without recourse to a supplementary knowledge of particular individuals, circumstances, or cultures. But I believe it is also true that romanticism gave honest voice to the dawning recognition by modern Western society that such universality did not characterize human reality. Increasingly since romanticism, the human universe of discourse has been understood as an aggregate of relationships among discrete, particular individual consciousnesses, cultures, and values in which humans need always to decipher each other's meanings, whether in the case of the Rosetta Stone, a musical composition, or a television ad, using whatever external knowledge and coherent patterns of fragments they can find. In composing music that seems to require of the listener prior knowledge of Chopin's authorship, Chopin seems to me, like the very different Mahler decades later, to affirm that we draw meaning from another's expression not only from its inner structure but also from its sensuous qualities and from our knowledge of (and reaction to) the particular context in which it originated.

Furthermore I would add that within such a context of sensed fragmentation, it took great courage for Chopin to persist in efforts to create generally comprehensible structures of sound. It also took great ability to create a personal style that succeeded in functioning as a ground of meaning for large portions of society far removed from Chopin and his culture.

In the entire history of Western music, even allowing for the fact that at least in modern times it has generally been easier for composers outside the center of Italo-German norms to project distinctiveness of style as a central value, I think it fair to say that no composer has ever exceeded the extent to which Chopin infused the listening experience with his own identity, and that very few have matched it. And where I would agree with Adorno is in his implicit suggestion that music dependent in any fundamental way on the identity of its composer for its general intelligibility is not to be characterized as autonomous music.

For this sort of dependence is something rather different from that identity of the composer's mind and his works that positivist scholars define as autonomy in their studies of autographs and sketches. The dependence I speak of shifts attention to the composer not as an ultimate arbiter of textual accuracy but as a particular individual in a particular cultural situation existing outside of the music; and it shifts the center of meaning away from the enterprise of self-generating structure, that is, from autonomy in a meaningful sense as opposed to a condition of mere physical wholeness. Those who take my denial of Chopin's autonomy as a criticism ought perhaps to rethink their own criteria for compositional excellence. My observation casts no aspersions on Chopin as a craftsman but is, simply, a characterization of his style, of the means he used to create the style, and of the kinds of meaning and value I think can be imputed to that style. I simply do not think that Chopin's music solves, or intends to solve, the problem of creating autonomously intelligible structures, though it may well refer to the difficulty of doing so. Certainly Chopin took the trouble to give his works a generally intelligible shape, but I do not believe his pieces are to be understood as efforts to create a whole out of self-contained means.

What I do think Chopin's music does—and I think this is true not only of the second Prelude but also of his music more generally—is something quite different. I think what this music does primarily is to recognize the reality of the contingent. I think it accords hard reality to the concrete, to the physical, to the particular, to the discrete, to the here-and-now, no matter how arbitrary, ephemeral, or fragmentary. And I think the problem posed in Chopin's music is how to achieve intelligibility with materials so defined—how to make persuasively intelligible structures that acknowledge the reality of the contingent at a multiplicity of levels. Saying Chopin used tonality to insure intelligibility does not do justice to his solution to this problem. Certainly he still depended on tonality; but to avoid irreparable contradiction within his own stylistic context, Chopin had to use tonality in a way that did not allow its promise of self-evident intelligibility, as defined in classicism, to overshadow his assertion of the contingent. This meant working against or in spite of the communicative virtues of tonality to a certain extent, emphasizing its cultural and sensuous particularity over its capacity for abstract structural logic. The center of Chopin's intelligibility, I believe, lies not in his tonal architecture but in his successfully projected and explicitly sensuous interweaving of the fragmentary and particular against a lingering background of tonal tension, which is now perceived only secondarily as a source of connection or "explanation." This sort of interweaving is extraordinarily difficult; it requires the composer to persuade his audience that the connections and relationships between contingent elements are rigorous, even necessary. The compulsiveness with which Chopin continuously polished his works, in some cases even after publication, lends credence to this vision of this style.[13] Chopin seems, like Beethoven before him, to have had a compulsive need to "get it right," a need that is bound to be paramount in a society that no longer endorses general standards of intelligibility, and in which successful communication seems to depend on the eloquence of the individual.

Within such an enterprise, it seems to me, the achievement of an internally generated wholeness is an irrelevant criterion of musical value, for this sort of achievement has been abandoned as a possible or even desired goal of the composition. Rather, the shape of an independently existing physical entity is recognized as ultimately particular, not universal, and therefore contingent, not eternal, precisely the way in which its component details are recognized. Therefore it is perfectly consistent with the character of the undertaking for the composer to impose recognizable limits, signs of wholeness, from without. He need do no more than create generally plausible outer shapes and conclusions in order to avoid the really brute, arbitrary physical independence that emerges, say, when a symphony orchestra presents snippets of the classics to an audience of underestimated children. As long as the sensuous experience of the piece remains absorbing—and it does in no small measure because this sensuous quality can be identified as the product of a real, known person—it will be accepted as a plausible whole even if this wholeness is not projected as internally generated. What Chopin demonstrates rather explicitly is that structure need not be autonomous in the sense of internally generated in order to be perceptibly coherent (that is, perceptibly coherent not in a universal and necessary sense but to listeners within the framework of a concrete, contingently existing culture).

Stated another way, it is aesthetically acceptable if a piece by Chopin is internally fragmentary. That is a part of its particular kind of wholeness. And precisely because this is music in which style is of greater importance to intelligibility than is form, much of the same value can be obtained from the fragments or details of Chopin's pieces as from the whole. Thus the opening of the well-known Etude in E Major (Op. 10, No. 3) is not a statement of a harmonic premise that will unfold itself but a self-contained section that leads nowhere and could well stand, with just a few rhetorical changes, as an independent piece, plausible in structure and intelligible as an experience of sense or color. The fact that it goes on to something else is, and is experienced as, arbitrary. Were the piece to end at measure 21, that decision, too, would be arbitrary. What we have here is a sensuous fragment. The decision to continue the piece increases the values it offers us quantitatively but does not really change them qualitatively. It would not ravage the sense of the piece to end it here as it would to end at the corresponding point in a Mozart structure.

Example 1. Etude in E Major, measures 1-21. Copyright Fryderyk Chopin Society, Warsaw.

For the balanced tension Mozart maintains between physical immediacy and structural implication, even in the most sensuous slow movement, is in this passage of Chopin's, not atypically, undercut by the overwhelming presence of the here-and-now.

Much the same quality of arbitrary self-containment is heard in the following fragment from Chopin's Ballade in G Minor (Example 2), which has even less of a conventional tonal function than the E major opening just described. Is it a "second theme?" Its key is Eb, not the relative major Bb, which the modulatory "bridge" (and classical convention) leads us to expect; and it is not experienced as a polar magnet to the opening. Rather, it makes sense as a coloristic contrast to the passage immediately preceding and as the bearer of certain motivic fragments of melody that recur throughout the work. Later, after numerous fireworks and a scale descending the length of the keyboard, it returns *fortissimo*, in the same key, Eb, with a syncopated rhythm and rapid accompaniment. The contrast to its opening delicate character is thrilling, especially for the player, and cannot be fully appreciated out of context. Yet in structural terms, this return is purely arbitrary; nothing requires it. For a moment tempting us to hear, through almost purely coloristic means, the connection he so forcefully asserts between these two passages as not only intelligible but inevitable, indeed logically inevitable, Chopin simultaneously exposes that auditory vision as a poignant illusion. For in what does this connection consist except the rhetorically emphasized return, coloristically varied and in a changing context, of a self-contained fragment?

Not all the details conveying intelligibility in Chopin's works have the degree of plausible self-containment of the passages just cited; many are more openly fragmentary. Yet they are intelligible, and more to the point, in contrast to Mozart's fragments, they are *as fragments* perceptibly all that they can be. Take, for example, the passage that leads back to the opening of the Etude in E Major (Example 3), the so-called retransition. In a classical work, such a passage is defined above all functionally (though again, Mozart, as I have argued elsewhere,[14] unquestionably begins to undermine this functional priority in his marked attention to the sensuous surface of his music at precisely such points). It has been said that such a passage in a characteristic classical structure can instantly be located by the listener because of its clear functional definition.

This is not true of the passage at hand. When I first thought of writing this essay, it was this particular passage that came to mind, and not its function within the piece but its internal character. Here, if ever, it seemed to me, was music about the here-and-now. One could listen to it and suspend caring about where it is coming from, where it is going, whether it ever ends.

True, it has the main harmonic feature of a functioning retransition, an ex-

Example 2. Ballade in G Minor, measures 67-82. Copyright Fryderyk Chopin Society, Warsaw.

tended dominant pedal point (on B). Further, one can point to many features in this passage that by convention signify the impending return of the tonic.[15] And certainly one could not deny that the eventual return of the tonic in the reprise (measure 62) is experienced, on the level of harmonic logic, as providing closure.

And yet I would argue that the return to an all-powerful, all-clarifying, all-resolving tonic is not the primary focus of attention in this passage. However necessary harmonic coherence may be to achieving the primary focus, that focus itself is on the dense, leisurely, undulating, and iridescent quality of the so-called musical surface. It is on the manipulation, the stroking, the luxuriant ornamentation, and the repetitive examining of something concrete, particular, and unchanging in a succession of slightly altered contexts.

It is on the simultaneous experience of sameness and constant change, and on the imputation of reality to both the concreteness and the ephemerality of the particular.[16]

To me, this focus is so strong as to be prior to any formal musical analysis.[17] In part this impression derives from a feature of Chopin's style that I have elsewhere analyzed in detail: his replacement of implicative or causal classical structures (such as antecedent—consequent) with a reliance on discrete "analogy"—on parallel segments and layers—that turns attention away from propulsive relationships to the immediacy of the moment.[18] On a local level, for example, one could point to the numerous adjacent, mosaiclike particles consisting of strong-beat dissonance and momentary resolution, or to the immediate presentation, in measures 55 and 57, of varied repetitions, which throw substantive weight, sustained throughout the passage, on the ornamental triplet figure in the bass.

Especially characteristic of Chopin in this respect is the way in which measures 56–7 present themselves as an analogue (rather than a consequent or resolution) to measures 54–5. True, the two pairs of measures have the melodic alteration characteristic of tonal "correction"; and true, the bass line in the later pair contains no transposed parallel to the dominant B on the first beat of measure 55, and also 56 (except in measures 54 and 60, this first beat is on the dominant pedal B throughout). Nevertheless, these measures have other features that suggest the later pair primarily as a rough transposition (or, in structuralist terms, "transformation") of the earlier one. Not only are the two segments equal in length and more or less parallel in melodic shape, both of which would also be the case with an antecedent and consequent. In addition, the tenor line in the later pair offers the same lowered-VI to V movement (but this time on G♮–F#, with the new goal, B, now simultaneously anticipated in the bass), and the same melodic movement downward, essentially by step, toward a goal (but again, here B rather than the E of the previous two measures). And, of course, the second pair of phrases is not brought to a harmonic resolution. Rather, it is left as open-ended harmonically as the first pair, so that the effect of the later two measures is not one of closure but of indeterminate continuation.

In fact, it seems fair to say that the very system of tonal implication is used against itself here to produce an effect of analogy that counteracts the force of harmonic resolution. That is, even the harmonic structure of these measures has analogical aspects that work against the conventional function of drive toward the tonic. One might suppose, looking at the bass line of the score, that the presence on "strong" beats first of B (measures 55–6, first beats) and then of E (measures 56–7, second beats) defines the pattern of closure (V to I) common in antecedent-consequent construction. On a (rela-

Example 3. Etude in E Major, measures 54-62. Copyright Fryderyk Chopin Society, Warsaw.

tively) broad harmonic level, moreover, the pairs of measures 54–5 and 56–7 do seem to shift in their circling from a moderately unstable polar center of IV and V (A and B) to a more stable one of V and I (B and E), a shift wholly consistent with the antecedent-consequent structure. But just as the physical weight of an antecedent gesture comes often to overshadow the logical force of consequence in Chopin's music, so too, here, the richness of the surface blunts the harmonic thrust of the larger-scale underlying pattern. In actuality, both melody and bass are harmonically ambiguous in measures 56–7, pointing simultaneously to E and B in ways that may contradict each other (such ambiguity, as well as conflict between layers, is typical Chopin).

Of particular importance in this respect are ruptures in symmetry made precisely to maintain the presence of the dominant pedal B on the first beat of the bass line in these measures. Had Chopin followed the large-scale progression of IV (on the relatively weak second beat, or anacrusis, in the bass of measure 54) to V (on the strong first beat in the bass of measure 55) with a corresponding one of V-to-I in the next two measures, he would have fulfilled our logical expectations of an antecedent-consequent pattern. He would have preserved the effect of symmetry, proceeding *within* each phrase from a less to a more stable harmony, while also effecting a complementary connection *between* the two, moving from a half-cadence on V to a qualitatively different, conclusive full cadence on I.

Instead, to avoid removing the first-beat presence of B in the bass, Chopin reverses the literal rhythmic ordering of stable and unstable in the second polarity, presenting the V–I polarity not in the logically progressive form of V-to-I, but in the form of I-to-V. In actuality, he moves not from B to E but from E (on the relatively weak second beat in the bass of measure 56) to B (on the strong first beat in the bass of measure 57, emphasized and lengthened by being struck in anticipation). As a result, the nominal tonic E is rhythmically presented in the latter pair of measures as the analogue not of B, the dominant (V), but of A, the mere subdominant (IV), in the preceding pair.

Adding insult to injury, moreover, Chopin in effect "neuters" the tonic E major into the tonally unrelated minor form of E (by adducing, in the last parts of measures 56 and 57, adjacent to an E-major triad, the G-natural that suggests itself as the lowered form of VI in B) — as if this tonic were no more privileged, harmonically, than the subdominant A major, which underwent the same indignity when *its* third was lowered (in measures 54 and 55) to C-natural, the supposedly propulsive lowered sixth degree in the tonic of record, E. In this way, too, the tonic E is suggested as an analogue to its own subdominant.

But tonally as well as literally speaking (and one has a strong sense of the deconstructive internesting of these terms here), E itself *is* the subdominant IV in contexts where B can be taken for a tonic. And clearly there is much to suggest B as the tonic in measures 56 and 57 (including two details already mentioned, the appearance of G-natural, a plausible lowered VI in B, and the direction of the right-hand melody). The very fact that B is maintained as a surface goal of harmonic motion in both pairs of phrases contributes strongly to this effect. For though it would be going too far to say that B becomes the unambiguous tonic in the latter pair, the conventional expectation of tonal progress toward resolution in an antecedent-consequent pair encourages us, *mutatis mutandis*, when reaching the second pair here, to reinterpret the constantly maintained pitch of B as having more functional stability than it did when it appeared in the first pair. It encourages us to associate B with the intensified stability of a final resolution in the tonic — or at least with the idea of such a resolution, even if that idea cannot be fully insulated from the let-down of finding ourselves no further ahead, in actuality, than the same old V sonority already reached.

By drawing both on the potential ambiguities of tonality and on the smallness of the physical changes needed to alter functional significance, Chopin at this moment undercuts the illusion that the order of these two pairs of phrases is a logical necessity. Instead, he characterizes the order here as a contingent condition of location (be it the disjunct repetitiveness of parallelism or even, as poststructuralism would have it, of mere contiguity). And what is at stake here, in this questioning of the force of logic, is something more than just our ability to explain the order of four particular measures.

At this crucial point in the retransition, the harmony supports a hearing of the phrase in measures 56–7 as an analogue in B to the earlier phrase in E. Within such a hearing, the bass note E in measures 56–7, though technically part of a dominant-tonic cadential formula, is experienced as a passing subdominant on its way to B. Though retrospectively E can be explained in these measures as a tonic that will resolve the dominant (B), on an immediate sensuous level, helped (in just the manner that deconstruction finds typical of verbal language) by the very tonal logic that it undermines, E is heard as a pitch that cannot distinguish its own supposedly tonic function decisively from that of a subdominant. Treated as a physical analogue to its own subdominant, E simultaneously suggests itself as a functional subdominant to its own dominant. In other words, playing upon the conventional ambiguity of the plagal relationship, Chopin presents the pitches of the conventionally definitive V–I cadence in the bass as devoid of the force needed to effect persuasive resolution, and hollowed of any certainty except the identity of these pitches themselves (B and E).

This effect is reinforced by the extended alternation of B and E in the bass of measures 56–60. Placing E as a way-station between octaves on B that are now ascending (measure 56), now descending (measure 58), mixing up E and B into three different permutations of rhythm and range in the second, third, and fourth bass triplet figures (measures 57–9), and omitting all forms of A from measures 58–60 — thereby refusing to decide between the claims represented by A-natural (IV of E) and A# (the leading-tone of B), Chopin makes a rhetorically persuasive case that the order of E and B here is immaterial. Neither can claim the unchallenged precedence over the other that is due a tonic. If anything, given the clear evocations of V–I in B in the right-hand harmonies (measures 58–60) — and in the final left-hand triplet figure (measures 60–1) — B seems (until the A-natural is finally struck again, in measure 61) to have a clear edge in this functional respect.

The cumulative effect of all these details is to suggest not only that the status of E as the tonic in this specific piece is open to question but that, beyond this specific instance, the very authority of a tonic — or of any logical formulation — depends to some degree on merely contingent or arbitrary, rather than logically irrefutable, claims to power. No necessary connection is demonstrated at this point in Chopin's Etude between the timelessness of logical force and the temporality, even the temporariness, of actual force. Perhaps that is why one's reaction to the premature return of the tonic here, in sharp distinction to the effect of corresponding moments in Beethoven's middle-period work, is one of indifference.[19] "So what?" one might say, or "Plus ça change, plus c'est la même chose."

One might even refer the entire retransition to the disjunct image of analogy on a larger structural level: to the extent that its boundaries are emphasized, the passage as a whole suggests itself as a discrete and equal counterpart to other sections of the etude. And the argument can be made that this passage is jagged at both its ends.

The break at the opening is clear. After a pause following the extreme pitch of unresolved hysteria reached by this piece, the retransition simply takes up as if to answer a cry for help with the words, "Now another thing." Although the retransition may well be meant to soothe the preceding outburst, it does not really resolve it, least of all on any commensurate level of rhetorical passion. Far more, the import of the retransition seems to be, "Are you through? Now as I was saying . . . ." In effect the retransition seems to argue that here, in contrast to our image of the classical development section, even a passage that attains extreme tension has no privileged claims on structure. Such a passage cannot count with certainty on altering irrevocably the ensuing action or on reaching resolution; rather than moving toward a self-determined destiny, it is just another section. The join at the end of the retransition may appear seamless. Yet here too, especially in conjunction with the melodic phrasing in Friedheim's edition, one experiences between the D# of measure 61 and the E of measure 62 a palpable moment of discreteness. One has the sense that something of importance is being left behind, as the music leaves to take up a different, but no more privileged activity. In short, given the clarity of its boundaries as well as the intense focus on its internal content, it does not seem far-fetched to construe the retransition as a sensuous fragment.

What I am arguing, finally, is that in this passage, techniques and ambiguities that were formerly used unequivocally as means to a harmonic end are well on their way to becoming a sensuous end in themselves. The harmonic function of this retransition is so challenged by considerations of color and identity that harmonic function itself has given way, in no small degree, to harmonic identity and thus, ultimately, to sensuous color. Even the early return of the tonic (measure 56) is experienced here as just another coloristic element, a change rung on the basic recurring melodic pattern. We have here something very much of the physical world, inertia (defined by Webster, in part, as "the property of matter by which it will remain . . . in . . . motion . . . unless acted upon by some external force").

Indeed, it is the rhetorical, harmonically extrinsic devices of melodic *stretto* and literal deceleration through tempo markings that ultimately serve to wind down this recalcitrant passage, forcing it finally to give way to tonal authority. Nevertheless, the sensuousness of the repetition in the last half of the passage is so mesmerizing that the anticipatory interest in the "actual" return of the tonic very nearly disappears. One could almost imagine being happier without it, especially if one had the choice of lingering forever on the leading-tone D#, which "hangs" far more than it "leads" here. Nor is it difficult to extrapolate from this passage the possibility of musical movement so insistent on particularity, or even so narcissistic or effete, as to turn the very category of resolution into an irrelevancy.

Of course, the tension is not altogether gone. We are not yet in the wholly atemporal, post-tonal, even existential realm of Debussy (or Satie), where we are given the here-and-now with hardly the memory of a hope of anything beyond. As the preceding analysis should clarify, much of the poignance we feel so keenly in passages by Chopin such as this one comes from the remaining ability of tonality, now a ghost of its former self—unable to produce or even promise the encompassing wholeness and progress of functionality—to let us know that the thickness of the present physical moment will not last; the awareness of the impermanence is as real as the physical immediacy. Indeed, this awareness is a part of the physical immediacy, a function of it, an intrinsic element in its definition. It is in part this very use of tonal function, largely fragmented into tonal physicality or localized down to a condition of identity, that tells us that the balance between the optimism of functional structure and the uncertainty of physical immediacy has shifted toward the latter.[20]

This same technique of repetition is used often by Chopin at various points in his composition. It appears characteristically, for example, in the coda of the Berceuse[21] (Example 4). And the entire fourth Prelude, in E minor, seems to be built in the same way, as a study of means by which to make sense of the fragmentary. Here also the experience of repetition in an endlessly shifting harmonic (or, more accurately, coloristic) context, the arbitrary decision to repeat the first section in order to get beyond its fragmentary condition, and the externally imposed, rhetorical, or dramatically expanded means with which the second part varies the first all point to a conception of the compositional problem not as the task of achieving the self-generation of form but as that of wresting sense from the intrinsically fragmentary. They point to a sensibility that recognized the ultimate reality as well as the contingency of the here-and-now, along with the tragic implications for humanity of a world vision in which the real is not the eternal but the transient.

Conclusion

These remarks, I know, open up more questions than they answer. For example, what, more particularly, was the relationship of Chopin's music to the rest of his culture? And how can we go about trying to determine the significant ways in which Chopin's music resembled, as well as differed from, the other art of its culture in its principles and values?

It could be argued that what Chopin's second Prelude was to his own oeuvre, Chopin's oeuvre itself was to European art of the time, that is, the achievement of an extreme in which the cultural values at work can be most clearly deciphered. And this was not just an extreme in any old sense. It was an extreme in the sense of creating a personal style; and herein lies an important clue, I believe, to Chopin's historical significance, at least from our current vantage point. In successfully projecting his individuality, Chopin embodied in his music something paradigmatic of romantic culture: the existential and in a sense even the essential priority it gave to the contingent, the concrete, the individual. But Chopin's particular achievement, his style, signifies even more than this for us. For style is the very medium through which modern Western culture decodes meaning in structure, as epitomized in the cliché of our times, "The medium is the message." It could be said that Chopin's achievement helped mark a shift in Western thought away from metaphysical beliefs, and even away from complete confidence in the innate rationality of any structure; or ultimately, I would say, from confidence in the universal rationality of science. It helped to mark a shift away from all these things toward a fragmented, essentially aesthetic view of human reality. We take it for granted today in many areas of our lives that the achievement of a personal style signifies competence, fluency, and eloquence — that is, a mastery of what is sometimes, rather inelegantly, called communication skills;[22] but this was not always an assumption in Western culture, which previously associated such skills far more closely with metaphysical vision or powers, with the mastery of conventional rhetoric or craftsmanship, or with logical clarity.

To obtain a more integrated view of Chopin's stylistic relationship to his culture, one would want to establish, I would argue, some dialectical sort of movement between Chopin's music and various other selected structures in his society, seeing the extent to which patterns discerned in his work seemed relevant to those in other structures and bringing back from the latter still

Example 4. Berceuse, measures 47–63

other patterns to test against Chopin's compositional strategies. One would want to give further attention to critical methods being developed in other disciplines. For such work to go forward beyond the level of suggestion I have offered here, American musicology would have to develop a respect, comparable to that it gives the unearthing of empirical data, for the kind of scholarship that demands from its outset an ongoing interpenetration of theory and fact. This could result, finally, in the establishment of a serious musicological discipline of criticism, which I think is what the scrutiny of forms in any medium really amounts to, and which I think holds the most promise for confronting the nature of the relationship between music and society with a kind of rigor that meets the genuine needs of this task.

I would like, though, in closing, to remark on the well-known fact that many listeners, even apart from their ability to identify Chopin's style, have never really listened to his pieces as autonomous music but have made associations with them. Listeners in Chopin's time, as Edward Lippman has shown us, listened concretely rather than abstractly.[23] They attached all sorts of poetic and visual associations to instrumental music, even Chopin's. And in our own time, I believe, many listeners perceive Chopin's music as the articulation of a fairly specific mood or emotion. Earlier I suggested that the kinds of patterns I discern in Chopin's music, and which I believe have value for the criticism of music, were also patterns that seem to characterize the modern Western experience of life. If this last is so, then perhaps the reason that Chopin's music succeeded so brilliantly in its own society and continues to have meaning for ours is that it was able to project something about the human condition in a civilization that was his and is to some extent, despite many differences, still ours. So though I would not advocate going back to the "stupid titles" which so enraged Chopin,[24] or substituting newer ones of our own, I would suggest that such titles constitute not negative judgments on Chopin's lack of structural autonomy but a complement that pays a compliment.[25] They may, indeed, be evidence that Chopin's music functions as an archetype of the patterns out of which Western society makes sense of its experience.

Part III
Perspectives on Western Musical History

Chapter 9

The Cultural Message of Musical Semiology: Some Thoughts on Music, Language, and Criticism since the Enlightenment

The rate at which new critical methods reach the various arts often seems dictated by something like a Marxian law of unequal development; for better or worse, music is almost invariably the last art to be affected. Thus, whereas structuralism is already a bit outmoded in certain literary circles, it is only now beginning to have a noticeable impact on the study of music, thanks mostly to the efforts of French musicologists, who for some time have manifested a particularly strong attraction to systematic, as opposed to historical, forms of music criticism. The publication of Jean-Jacques Nattiez's *Fondements d'une sémiologie de la musique*,[1] the first full-scale semiology of music to have appeared, provides an appropriate occasion for reflecting upon certain cultural trends that have led in recent decades to an increased interest, within Western musicology generally, in semiotic aspects of music[2] as well as upon the benefits that musicology can anticipate from an essentially structuralist critical method like Nattiez's.

Perhaps one should hesitate to identify Nattiez with the structuralists. After all, structuralism hardly constitutes a monolithic movement, and Nattiez himself dissociates his method of analysis from structuralism on the somewhat odd grounds that his method goes beyond the limits of the single art work. Nevertheless, the affinity of Nattiez's musical semiology with work by such figures as Roland Barthes, Roman Jakobson, and especially Claude Lévi-Strauss seems clear enough to warrant some generalization from Nattiez's work to French structuralism on a larger scale. Nattiez's starting point, for example, like that of so many French structuralists, is Saussure's linguistic theory, specifically, its distinctions between sign systems, which are socially based, and utterances within such systems, which are individual, as well as distinctions between synchronic or systematic aspects of language, and diachronic or temporal ones. Out of the latter distinction Nattiez derives a model for the analysis of art, the biaxial inventory or taxonomy of component or corresponding units. (Nattiez's taxonomies include not only tables of paradigmatic equivalence or transformation, such as Lévi-Strauss uses in his analysis of homologous myths, but also tree-diagrams of the sort favored by Noam Chomsky, which permit a limited hierarchical ordering of selected units.) Such inventories in effect grant a priority to the identification of discrete units over the characterization of relationships, much as Barthes gives temporal precedence in "the structuralist activity" to what he calls "dissection" as opposed to "articulation."[3] Thus although such tables are concerned with "a certain relation of affinity and dissimilarity,"[4] their graphic format lends itself to the presentation of "relations" in the sense of static orderings rather than to the investigation of any inner dynamic. What emerges from such tables is a vision of structure that is characterized above all by discontinuity.

Discontinuity is evident in many French structuralist studies, not only in the tabular analyses of particular art works but also in more general conceptions of the structures accessible to analysis, including large bodies of works (Lévi-Strauss's myths) or even whole systems of cultural expression (Michel Foucault's epistemes). The lack of integral connection between most formulations of structuralist method and any concept of history is often remarked (Jean Piaget's works are one notable exception). Not unrelated is the dissociation that tends to occur between what Jakobson calls the "message" on the one hand and the "addresser" and addressee" on the other, that is, between human artifact and human subject.[5] For example, Lévi-Strauss, who characterizes myth as a "message that, properly speaking, is coming from nowhere," proposes by "disregarding the thinking subject completely [to] proceed as if the thinking process were taking place in the myths" themselves.[6] In Nattiez's semiology, this particular discontinuity takes the form of a denial that communication is a primary function of music. Nattiez dismisses as "myth" Leonard Meyer's normative assumption that "certainly the listener must respond to the work of art as the artist intended"[7] and argues instead that such a coincidence of meaning is at most a happy accident. The basis of this argument is not, as some have contended, that music cannot signify;[8] quite the contrary, Nattiez justifies the application of semiology to music on the very grounds that music is a symbolic phenomenon, that is, it is possessed of a "referential" capacity that enables it to function in some sense as a sign.[9] The basis for Nattiez's argument lies in his assumption that a discontinuity between sender, message, and receiver, and hence between the expression and the communication of meaning, is inherent in the structure of musical symbolism, regardless of its cultural context. In essence he understands music in much the same way as Lévi-Strauss understands myth: as "objectified thought" that "takes on the character of an autonomous object, independent of any subject."[10] For both scholars, the underlying structures of human artifacts (in this case language and music) are imagined as embodying completely within themselves the rationality of the human mind.

The extension of this depersonalized notion of cultural phenomena to the Western art work seems clearly to depend on a confusion, by no means rare in French structuralism, between structures that are essentially social in origin, such as Ferdinand de Saussure's sign systems, and those that originate through the conscious enterprise of identifiable individuals. Now, whether or not mythological thought can be expanded into a concept of universal mental structures, there are plausible reasons for Lévi-Strauss to ignore individual creativity in stressing the character of myth as a collective heritage that, as Saussure said of language, "no individual, even if he willed it, could modify in any way at all" and that is "fixed, not free with respect to the linguistic community."[11] The reasons are far less compelling to assume that in the creation of art works, as in the use of language, "the categories which are formed always remain unconscious" or even, as Lévi-Strauss claims about individual speakers and myths, that "although the possibility cannot be excluded that the [artists] who created and transmit [works of art] may become aware of their structure and mode of operation, this cannot occur as a normal thing."[12] The justification for analyzing Baudelaire's "Les Chats" or Ravel's *Boléro* as if art "operate[d] in men's minds without their being aware of the fact" is by no means self-evident.[13] Nevertheless, Lévi-Strauss asserts without hesitation that "the difference between individual creations and myths recognized as such [i.e., presumably as myths] by a community is not one of nature but of degree."[14] Nattiez goes still further: he refuses to differentiate between the music of collective non-Western societies and even the most self-conscious and esoteric music of the Western avant-garde. Since Nattiez defines "symbol" in terms of a referentiality that exists for no one, he sees no need to distinguish between the impersonality of social signs and the depersonalization that may occur in private symbols. Rather, he deems it irrelevant that certain Western art music has tended to remain accessible to only a small number of individuals—for example, the "experts" in Adorno's typology of listeners[15]—who can be considered extensions of the composer rather than genuine "others" drawn from society at large. Nattiez cannot afford to recognize that works that are not socially (as opposed to privately) based cannot strictly, in Saussure's terms, be considered semiological objects at all; such a recognition would amount to admitting what appears to be a total discontinuity between the application of his method and its supposed epistemological justification.

The absence of a clear distinction between notions of the individual and the social or general must, in fact, raise particularly strong reservations about any critical method as preoccupied as French structuralism is with comparisons between art and natural language. To be sure, this preoccupation has led to the isolation of many suggestive likenesses and differences between music and language. Among the likenesses, for example, is the assertion that both language and music constitute semiotic media within which the same techniques for verifying competence (in Chomsky's sense) and correctness of usage (related to Chomsky's "performance") can be applied. Lévi-Strauss is insistent that musical as well as linguistic usage must be subject to verification through reference to some sort of "double articulation," or what will more generally be called here "dual structure," that is, through some method whereby, in effect, speakers and listeners can test each other's competence by altering the relationship between a more general and a more particularized level of a system (such as the levels of sound and of meaning, or the underlying level of a code as opposed to the surface level of a message) and observing each other's responses.[16] Nattiez essentially rejects this method of verifying competence, but he proposes two others that have analogues in the linguistic theory, respectively, of Zellig Harris and of Noam Chomsky;[17] interestingly, these methods, which appear to be more "modern" than Lévi-Strauss's, rely far more heavily on faith in fundamentally unexplainable judgments by single individuals, especially by individual "experts."

The differences adduced by structuralists between music and language can be equally provocative. To be expected, of course, are allusions to the absence, or at least the gross imprecision, of musical "signifiés"; that absence is seen to entail the apparent nonreference or at most self-reference of much Western music. Less obvious, perhaps, is Lévi-Strauss's contention that "only a tiny minority of people are capable of formulating a meaning" in music, especially when contrasted with Chomsky's insistence that, in Lyons's words, "the vast majority of the sentences in any representative corpus of recorded utterances would be 'new' sentences, in the sense that they would occur once, and once only."[18] Unquestionably ingenious, however, are the ways Lévi-Strauss has found of opposing music to more than one type of linguistic structure: to natural language itself (as two corresponding metalanguages); to myth (as two opposed subcategories of language); and to literature (as two subcategories of myth).[19]

Structuralist inventories of likenesses and differences can suggest discontinuities not only between objects under comparison, such as music and language, but also between elements within those objects, between the likenesses and differences themselves, and at times (not always intentionally) between aspects of the structuralist method itself. It is when structuralism is pushed beyond the mere presentation of discontinuities to the definition of relationships that might explain those discontinuities that its limitations as a method become evident. For when called upon to explain, structuralist method must reach outside of itself for some external principle that, rather than illuminating directly any connection between elements already isolated, seems merely to enlarge the field of discontinuities by adding a new one. In Nattiez's case, the principle is semiology, which ultimately proves irrelevant to the method of analysis it is supposed to justify. For Lévi-Strauss the principle is history. Putting forth a theory of historical disjunctions not fundamentally different from Foucault's antihistorical theory of epistemes, Lévi-Strauss argues not only that myth as a mode of expression gives way to music in the course of history but also that his entire system of polarities (which includes mathematics as well as language, myth, and music) is valid only in one particular historical context, Western civilization from "the sixteenth-seventeenth centuries" until sometime in the twentieth.[20] But history remains extrinsic to Lévi-Strauss's undertaking; his recourse to it enables him neither to explain why music should have supplanted myth nor to characterize the relationship between music and language with any of the particularity implicit in the notion of history.

I do not mean to imply that discontinuities between music and language cannot be explained in terms of history. Quite the contrary is suggested by dialectical criticism, which uses as its point of departure the one discontinuity denied by structuralism, that between individual and general, and defines that discontinuity as historical rather than structural in nature. When limiting itself to recent Western history, dialectical criticism appears able to explain not only the origins of the discontinuities observed by structuralism between music and language but also the impact of those discontinuities on modern critical methods of dealing with the two mediums, including structuralism itself. This assertion cannot be fully tested here, but it seems worthwhile to sketch, even provisionally, the outlines of such a dialectical explanation.

It has often been noted that in the early nineteenth century, following Kant's failure to demonstrate a necessary coincidence between individual and general interests, a dissociation of the two, together with a breach in various senses of community, began to emerge clearly in European society. It is less frequently noted that in the same period the separation of Western music from natural language, which had been taking shape for some time, finally became an overt rupture; or, more precisely, the break that had already occurred between music and language in practice was finally recognized in theory. As far back as the later Middle Ages (when "sounding music" had begun to detach itself from cosmology), and especially after 1600, close connections had begun to develop in musical theory between music and language, and above all between music and rhetoric; not until the decline of baroque aesthetics in the eighteenth century did the bond between music and rhetoric finally weaken, and then only to be supplanted by new analogies between structure and usage in music and in language, especially prose.[21] True, instrumental music began to receive more serious theoretical attention during the eighteenth century, but on the whole the explosion of great instrumental writing that occurred in this period had little impact on contemporary aesthetic theory. Vocal music still enjoyed superior status; and indeed, music itself, on account of its inadequate ability to represent the outside world, was generally considered the lowest of the arts. Only in the early nineteenth century, when the classicism of Haydn and Mozart — that is, the style that had produced the first great paradigms of a wholly autonomous music — was already part of the past, did cultural interpreters begin to exalt "absolute" music as the highest aesthetic, or even human, expression.

This decisive break between music and language appears to be inseparable from the dissociation of individual and general already mentioned. As long as the European worldview was dominated by the idea of external authority — if not God, then at least the logical necessity of reason or, in arts other than music, classical models — existing independently of any particular individual and available to all as a common point of reference, natural language was assumed to provide everyone with direct access to what could be generally verified as objective truth. But once the vividness of subjective experience was grasped in a way that undermined belief in external authority — that is, once a certain incommensurability was sensed between individual and general formulations of the true — a need was felt to supplement the generally serviceable epistemological *means* of natural language with a different sort of *medium*. The need was for a medium solid enough to embody physically the fragile particularity of images of truth that were clearly envisioned in individual fantasy, especially in the fantasy of the artist. And to protect that particularity. For as the modern association of (mere!) fantasy with irrationality suggests, establishing the rationality of a highly individual imagined vision is so difficult that even if the mental image could be perfectly translated into physical terms, the slightest public exposure of that vision creates overwhelming pressures to tamper with the specifics of the vision. Unwilling to characterize the contents of fantasy, however problematical their rationality, as simply and intrinsically irrational (especially when working in the wake of a philosophy, Kant's, that made it thinkable that rationality itself rested on an irrational base), the romantics instead looked at the concrete sensuous images of individual fantasy as a source of truth to which they could impute a universal status, if only in the sense of some mystically transcendent significance.[22]

The concreteness of the aesthetic was evoked, then, and in a sense called into being, to shore up failing confidence in the indisputability of human access to general truth or knowledge; and of all the arts, music, with its lack of clear links to the outside world, seemed least susceptible to widespread debasement, and hence most able to embody individual formulations of truth with precision. Music, in other words, separated itself from natural language in response to a division, now felt with unprecedented sharpness in European society, within the Western conception of humanity in its relation to the world.

To an extent, after this separation of music from language occurred, the two mediums followed roughly parallel courses in their respective pursuits of truth: music, the aesthetic medium, became recognized as the paradigmatic configuration of subjectively acquired knowledge; language, once Kant's *Critique of Pure Reason* had revealed the epistemological indispensability of natural language, became recognized as the paradigmatic medium for the configuration of objectively acquired knowledge. From the start, however, neither medium could be confined within the single category of individual or general. Despite all the new status the romantics gave to the truth of individual fantasy, for example, the eighteenth-century identification of "real" with "objective" retained a great deal of force. In fact, however much composers turned inward for truth to the imagination (a faculty vulnerable to the charge of irrationality) and took refuge in private circles, they were not happy to relinquish that general recognition of validity associated in the eighteenth century with the products of reason, or to accept the difficulty of establishing the rationality of a subjective vision. Quite early in the nineteenth century, therefore, composers began to crave external means for verifying the validity of their musical ideas and, concomitantly, for guaranteeing the precise communication of those ideas.

In language the problem was somewhat more complicated, even apart from the existence of an aesthetic domain within natural language, that is, poetry — a domain where, as in music, it became vital to find ways of individualizing a social sign system.[23] Even within the realm of epistemology, no simple identity could be made between natural language and objectively valid knowledge, that is, in eighteenth-century terms, knowledge verifiable on a general scale by reference to external authority. For not only had belief in the very existence of external authority been weakened by many political, social, and cultural circumstances. In addition, Kant's critical philosophy had opened up grounds for suspicion that language (and hence reason) originated and even operated on the same subjective side of experience as music, yet

Kant himself could not establish any necessary connections between the subjective and objective realms of truth.[24] Thus, in calling attention to the dependence of objective knowledge on language, Kant had provided a basis for questioning the objectivity of the knowledge obtained through language, that is, for doubting the power of language to reach any such objective truth as did exist.[25] Hence, the impression given by language, with its dual structure of *signifiant-signifié*, that it could mediate reliably between the individual and the world—the very impression that had allowed language to be taken so for granted as a binding force within eighteenth-century society—began to seem in the nineteenth century a liability for a medium concerned with truth. So language in the nineteenth century, not unlike music, found itself in the position of needing to reestablish its own objective validity as an epistemological medium; otherwise it faced the risk that its availability for general use would disintegrate into the formation of numerous private codes not grounded in a common objectivity.

In order, then, to embody any satisfactory conception of truth, language and music were each faced with the need to integrate individual discourse with general verifiability, which meant that each had to establish (or reestablish) within itself a "duality of structure." But since the inadequacies of both language and music were a function of the very qualities that had linked one with the principle of generality and the other with individuality, there was a current in each medium that tended to strip it of its own identifying characteristics and to lead it toward a convergence with the other, a convergence that has not yet, however, resulted in any resynthesis of the individual and the general.

Only some rough suggestions can be given here of how this tendency might be traced in the history of natural language. Using Foucault's extremely interesting account as a point of departure, one can imagine language in the eighteenth century as a hierarchy of interconnected, indeed inseparable, binary mediations; these mediations come to an apex in the *signifiant-signifié* relationship, which sums up the neoclassical belief in a necessary correspondence between cultural and natural structures (itself a good example of dual structure).[26] The basic form of language is the proposition; belief in the connective powers of the verb "to be" is unrecognized but nevertheless—or perhaps therefore—universal. As a "transparent" medium of representation, language mediates without distortion between human and nature and between one human being and others; objective knowledge is assumed to be inherently communicable on a social scale through language; and the truths conveyed by language can in theory be evaluated by any member of society in terms of their correctness.

In the nineteenth century, as faith in the mediating power of language is undermined, all of the various binary relationships once characteristic of natural language begin to collapse; to use Foucault's terms, the binary representative function of language gives way to an essentially severed signifying function, an idea of obvious importance within poetry. In the realm of epistemology, the loss of connective powers shows up in the tendency of language to become opaque, to define itself as a concrete entity detached from the subjectivity of any particular speaker and to limit its field of knowledge by turning back on itself as its own object of study. The discipline of philology emerges, calling attention to sounds and internal structural elements within language itself. Thus language as an epistemological medium in the nineteenth century begins to emphasize characteristics that come to be associated in the same century with the aesthetic medium of music: opacity (nonreferentiality), autonomy (be it physical, social, or semiotic self-sufficiency), sound, and internal structural coherence—along with a tendency toward self-destruction.

Over the nineteenth century into the twentieth, the same similarities to music are evident in a number of programs to reestablish the objective validity of knowledge obtained through language. The effort, for example, to make language more objectively believable by increasing its scientific character entails emphasizing still further its autonomy and internal coherence, both "musical" qualities. Accordingly, epistemological language is guided ever closer to a purified state of "objective existence outside the consciousness of transmitters and receivers."[27] At the same time, an attempt is made to replace the truth of correspondence gradually ravaged in language with an increasingly rigorous truth of coherence; in a word, language is to be formalized. Both tendencies are evident in the specialized metalanguages of the twentieth-century academic disciplines into which epistemological language is fragmented. Likewise, the attempts of scholars to locate universal bases of language below the level of individual consciousness (Jakobson's "distinctive features," Chomsky's universal mental structures, even Lévi-Strauss's abstract "binary oppositions") reveal a continuing tendency on the part of language to turn inward on its own sounds or structure.

In its turns both toward metalanguages and toward structural linguistics, epistemological language has, of course, given way to structures that in eighteenth-century terms could hardly be called recognizably linguistic in any respect. This tendency of language to shed its own traditional identity is even more apparent in such projects as Russell and Whitehead's symbolic logic, Bloomfield's nonsemantic linguistics, Barthes's and Nattiez's semiologies, and Lacan's efforts to systematize prelinguistic features of private symbols. All of these enterprises, which are outgrowths of the scientific or substructural orientations of language just mentioned, and which have common similarities to music, would seem, taken together, to constitute a total collapse of the epistemological hopes once invested in natural language.

Certainly, the twentieth-century epistemological languages have not been able to establish their own objective validity by means of any general verifiability. On the contrary, the increased precision of the metalanguages, for example, has assured their incomprehensibility on a social scale precisely because their precision is not referential but merely (imperfectly) self-consistent. In sharp contrast to eighteenth-century language with its interlocked mediations, epistemological language in the twentieth century has more or less dissociated itself from the communicative functions of language. Despite attempts by Wittgenstein and his followers to demonstrate the logical impossibility of private language, fears of a complete reduction of epistemological language to solipsistic absurdity have not been laid to rest.[28]

Yet the potentiality for solipsism does not lead to the conclusion that language has given way to aesthetic mediums in which individuality of expression is preserved. Again, quite the contrary; the self-sacrifice of natural language has come about precisely through attempts to rid language of epistemological uncertainty, and thereby prove its general validity, by purging it of susceptibility to individual variation. The only individuals for whom contemporary epistemological languages still work are the experts who have virtually relinquished individuality of utterance in mastering the rigors of specialized, yet impersonal, usages. Thus, despite the tendency of currents within epistemological language to converge with music, no reintegration of subjective and objective has taken place in language. Instead, the discontinuity that remains between the two principles has severely weakened the capacity of language to embody the sort of truth associated with either. Natural language has undermined its own strengths without acquiring those of music.

Nowhere does Lévi-Strauss's attribution of a dual structure of particular and general levels to tonal music seem more appropriate than in the classical style. True, with the loss of the baroque "affects," music was no longer expected to refer to any external realm of *signifié*; even in Mozart's opera ensembles, where analogies of extraordinary brilliance were drawn between musical and dramatic relationships, the music made "complete sense" in musical terms. Nevertheless, if the *signifiant-signifié* correspondence of natural language can be replaced by a system of what Leonard Meyer calls "embodied meanings," defined by wholly musical relationships, then the model of neoclassical language derived from Foucault, a hierarchy of binary mediations which permits the establishment of general sorts of validity, works surprisingly well for classical music as well. Charles Rosen's diagram of the tonal hierarchy at work in classicism, for example, suggests exactly such a model;[29] even the Roman numeral I that stands at the apex is not, of course, an isolated entity but the quintessence of an embodied relationship because it implies a complete hierarchy of numerals other than I. The very use of Roman numerals is possible because the tonal system is defined by relationships rather than by particular ("absolute") pitches; of all the musical systems developed in Europe, eighteenth-century tonality is almost certainly constituted of the most readily generalized relationships.

Furthermore, as Rosen has well demonstrated, classicism was the only tonal style characterized by binary relationships at every level of construction. In contrast to the baroque style, for example, its normative unit was the antecedent-consequent relationship, in a sense the musical analogue of a verbal proposition. In contrast to the romantic style (as will be seen), the normative structure was one of premise-resolution. And as Rosen himself has more than once implied, it was in the classical style above all that the relationship between unit and structure was essentially one of antecedent-consequent.

Yet, although all of these relationships were embodied, or immanent, in classical music, their implications were never confined to a particular piece. Rather, as has already been suggested, the classical hierarchy of binary relationships continued beyond the limits of the individual work, linking it and the elements within it to more generalized principles or norms of classical style. Thus, in a way, this music was able to use to its advantage the eighteenth-century notion of external authority without suffering the disadvantages of rigid authoritarianism.[30] For on the one hand, the choice and treatment of premises in a classical work could always be referred—indeed, *audibly* referred[31]—to more general classical principles and procedures; similarly, the one hundred-odd symphonies of Haydn, to take but one example, could be related to some normative conception of genre not literally embodied by any one of them. On the other hand, the norms underlying classical music were never derived from nonmusical sources (unless the apparent rationality itself of these norms be considered alien to music); nor were such norms, except perhaps in the sense of defining outer limits, imposed as restraints upon classical music. On the contrary, far from preexisting and even predetermining composition in the manner of ancient generic models, classical models, such as Haydn's symphonic norm, were very largely created by the classicists themselves.

In short, the classical style of Haydn and Mozart seemed to be in possession of something very like an identity (or, at least, an embodied relationship) between the general principles assumed in eighteenth-century natural language and the more particular or embodied principles subsequently associated with music. And scholars appear generally to agree that classicism has come closer than any other Western style to providing the basis for a coincidence between purely musical meanings intended by the individual composer and those understood by society at large. Embodying its own meaning yet retaining in that meaning a basis for generalization (that is, a second structure), classical music became a paradigm for later composers hoping to avoid public lack of understanding, or misunderstanding. Certainly the style has lent itself more readily than any other to a mode of criticism that presupposes the eighteenth-century norm of generally verifiable correctness, as when Rosen writes of a Haydn string quartet, "All we need, as here, is one moment *when we are not sure what the meaning of a note is.* . . . It is not until the next chord that *we understand why* the little motif was left without harmonies. . . . Playing the three notes softly each time . . . *hides their true significance.*"[32] The assumption in such writing of a single, generally ascertainable musical meaning is clear.

The music of Haydn and Mozart, then, established a firm basis for recognizing an identity between individuality and generality as artistic, social, and even philosophical principles. Yet not until Beethoven was a composer widely and unmistakably acclaimed during his own lifetime for embodying such an identity in his music. By then, to be sure, it was less a question of an identity than of a reconstructed synthesis since by the time of Beethoven's maturity, the notion of the individual could be clearly distinguished from the general. In important romantic circles, moreover, there was now open distrust of the generality at work in both society and natural language as a source of truth.[33] Beethoven's music was revered in many such circles because it appeared to shift the traditional balance between individual and general values. Whereas once the general was considered logically and even morally prior to the individual, the impression made by Beethoven's music, especially the second-period music, helped sustain, indeed even create, the romantic dream that the individual could become the new locus of the universal.[34] Furthermore, because most of Beethoven's music was purely instrumental, it awakened hopes among romantics like E. T. A. Hoffmann that autonomous music, in its wholly aesthetic being, could embody a level of ultimate truth inaccessible to natural language.[35]

And yet, when one looks for the musical sources of this Beethoven mystique, one comes upon the curious probability that his music impressed the romantics as being individual and autonomous precisely because it gave the sense that these qualities were in peril. An awareness of some such peril seems to have been deeply rooted in Beethoven himself; one can surmise, for example, from the extraordinarily self-critical manner in which he composed and the uncharacteristic care with which he held on to old ideas and sketches, that he attached tremendous importance to the individuality of his work and, moreover, to the clear definition of that individuality. At any rate, what gives the second-period style, in particular, so distinctive a character is its strong suggestion that the very precision with which Beethoven was able to articulate an individualized musical utterance constituted a threat to the precision with which that utterance would be understood by others. This suggestion is raised by the very strenuousness of Beethoven's efforts to avoid just such a dissociation of individual and general in his music, primarily through two techniques, rhetorical emphasis and the concretization of content. Both are fundamental to the second-period style; and ironically, both undermined the autonomy of Beethoven's music by bringing it closer to natural language at the very moment when it gave birth to the concept of absolute music.

By "rhetorical emphasis" I mean an intensification in the manner of utterance. This term would include increased reliance on techniques that direct more attention to their own force of expression than to implicitly intelligible relations (such as antecedent-consequent).[36] Among such techniques in that quintessentially second-period work, the Fifth Symphony, are fermatas, numerous dynamic indications, accelerations of tempo (the Presto closing of the last movement, measure 362), and special instrumental effects such as solos. Requiring as they so often do some written indication beyond what could be inferred from the notes themselves, such techniques suggest even in their notation a certain loss of musical autonomy. Extended reiteration of one or two elements, such as the V-I cadences at the close of the work — prefiguring what Rosen calls the "cumulative rather than syntactical" effects of the romantics[37] — likewise constitutes rhetorical emphasis. Still another sort of rhetorical emphasis is provided by a deviation from expectation so forceful that it calls attention to its singularity as a gesture and may even evoke a sense, however unwarranted, of the arbitrary; an example might be the solo oboe passage that surfaces at the beginning of the recapitulation of the first movement in the Fifth Symphony (measure 268) although it has no counterpart in the exposition. (Interestingly, this particular passage anticipates the opening of the third movement [measures 6–8] with such explicitness that one might almost say, as Tovey does of an analogous passage in the opus 131 quartet, that here Beethoven "goes out of his way to accentuate his point."[38] Yet the very distinctness of this gesture draws attention away from the relationship it embodies, though, to be sure, it could be argued that the relationship therein embodied is no longer one of implied necessity but rather only an arbitrarily imposed likeness.) Manner of delivery likewise becomes the primary focus in the instrumental recitative so characteristic of the late style; the recitative is interesting more because it seems to be straining toward natural language than for anything it might be trying to say.

Wagner once characterized Beethoven as the artist who "places [the] transparency [of his predecessors] in the silence of night . . . out from which he throws the light of the clairvoyant against the back of the picture."[39] This image suggests that Beethoven's music, in comparison with that of eighteenth-century classicism, had become opaque, a suggestion to which Wagner further contributed with his somewhat bizarre observation that Beethoven's was "a skull of unusual thickness and firmness" which "guard[ed] in him a brain of extreme tenderness, in order that it might look towards the interior only."[40] In a sense, this opacity marked an increase in the purely musical or aesthetic character of music, just as it did in contemporary natural language. But musical opacity was not the same as musical autonomy, a quality at least as essential as opacity to the definition of pure music. For if Beethoven worked almost entirely within the medium of music, he nevertheless used it in a way that turned it back toward the outside world; in seeming to apply heavy rhetorical emphasis on his music "from without," Beethoven gave the impression of a messenger behind a barrier, who, no longer able to rely on the self-evident clarity of his message, found it necessary to shout.[41] Indeed, what his rhetorical emphasis primarily projected was a sense that he was manipulating his own music, that he had moved into his music in order to make sure that it conveyed his meaning unmistakably. Such an intrusion of Beethoven's personal presence, of course, undermined the autonomy of his music.

Somewhat paradoxically, perhaps, this very emphasis on manner of delivery was largely indistinguishable from the other device that undercut the autonomy of Beethoven's music, the concretization of content. In general, this technique seems to have arisen in the nineteenth century out of a sensed need to replace the lost eighteenth-century principles of external authority with a new point of reference from which all people could derive a common meaning. In Beethoven's music the concretization of content at times manifested itself quite explicitly: his occasional titles and superscriptions and particularly his use of a text in the Ninth Symphony all contributed to the notion of a rather literal reunification of music with natural language. Even more threatening to the autonomy of Beethoven's music, however, was the degree to which his very presentation of self became palpable as the essential content of his music. As a valuable study by Hans Eggebrecht has demonstrated, criticism of Beethoven's music from the very beginning was unable to dispense with verbal characterization of musical qualities that were almost invariably associated with Beethoven himself.[42] By managing in this way to embody discrete, even nonmusical, content in the very sounds of instrumental music, Beethoven probably did more than any composer has since to destroy autonomous music as a socially viable concept, that is, to destroy the possibility that a precise coincidence between individually intended and generally perceived meanings would ever be established through the medium of music alone.

Yet the heteronomy toward which Beethoven's music tended so forcefully was not that of music before 1750. Rather than reestablishing any straightforward and widely acknowledged identity in society between musical sound and philosophical value or rhetorical convention, Beethoven instead began the process that would eventually collapse the dual structure of classicism into an essentially private code or organization of symbols, thereby depriving music not only of the autonomy through which it had come to epitomize the uniqueness of art but also of the social viability it had once shared with eighteenth-century language. For in making the content of his work indistinguishable from the individuality of his style, Beethoven began to remove from pure instrumental music that discrete general level of socially defined norms which had made the correctness of classical usage, at least in theory, generally verifiable. And this loss of generality was further reinforced by Beethoven's rhetorical emphasis which, by calling attention to gestures in themselves and to their identifying particulars, such as timbre or range, also limited opportunities for generalization, for example through reinstrumentation or transposition. In short, Beethoven's heteronomy began to suggest that art might not provide a way after all for individuality to subsume and articulate the generally valid and, as a corollary, that impotence on a social scale might render the exercise of free will meaningless.

Still, the actual collapse of dual structure did not occur in Beethoven's own music; throughout the second-period works, at least, Beethoven was able to preserve intact a genuinely viable dual structure by retaining the total relationality of classicism, thereby permitting a momentary synthesis of individual and general (which isn't to say universal) principles within one style. True, the synthesis was uneasy because it manifested the manner of its own decomposition in the very act of constituting itself. And true, the romantics' sharp sense of Beethoven's work as autonomous music almost surely arose from the very threat to such autonomy posed by the thrust of the second-period style toward heteronomy. Nevertheless, however powerful Beethoven's rhetoric and self-evocation, the continued binding force of classical relationships still allowed his music to embody all of its own meaning in a socially decipherable way, that is, to maintain a meaningful autonomy.

It was Beethoven's successors who first experienced the complete loss of musical autonomy as the manifold connections implicit in classical dual structure began to collapse and a clear dissociation emerged between increasingly individualized musical expression, on the one hand, and general apprehension of pure musical meaning on the other. Since the mediations of classicism were all interconnected, the collapse of classical duality was, of course, evident not only in the social situation of nineteenth-century music but also within the structure of the music itself. Once the eighteenth-century ideal of external models began to collapse into what Adorno has called "the genre of the masterpiece," in which each individual work was to constitute its own universe, the classical derivation of compositional premises from conventional tonal relationships began to give way to compositional premises so highly individualized that they tended to call attention to themselves rather than implying relationships to other musical constructs.[43] Whereas the premises of a high classical composition were inseparable from a generally accessible sense of the infinitely variable sign system underlying them, the premises of a work by Schubert in his later years or by Berlioz might shrink to a combination of intervals and progressions implicitly evoking little more generalizable than a sense of the peculiarity, or indeed, the arbitrariness of free choice.[44]

In effect, this weakening of dual structure in romantic music undercut not only the quasi-referential "correspondences" between classical levels of articulation but also the coherence of relationships within a composition between premise and resolution. Where, for example, it was at least conceivable that large-scale tonal relationships of tension and release could be generally inferred from the opening definition of E-flat in Beethoven's *Eroica*, the vast quasi-spatial E-flat pedal that began Wagner's *Rheingold*, and indeed the whole *Ring*, no longer functioned in any sense as a proposition. The fact that this implicitly nonrelational, self-contained passage, going well beyond the wholly immanent implications of classicism, drew upon extreme rhetorical exaggeration as well as upon a detailed plot to establish connections between itself and anything beyond itself only emphasized the contingency of such connections as Wagner embodied them in his music.[45] The weakening of the relationship between premise and conclusion in nineteenth-century works was equally evident in the difficulties that were often attendant upon ending those works, as if the composers themselves were no longer certain at times just what the implications of their own premises were or when they had been successfully realized. Even in a piece as seemingly well defined as the *Symphonie fantastique*, every movement gave evidence of the uncertainty or self-conscious manipulation that became characteristic of musical conclusions very early in the nineteenth century.[46]

But in failing for the most part to establish palpably necessary connections between the premises and conclusions of their works, Beethoven's successors obscured the precision with which any musical meanings immanent in those works could be perceived and verified by society at large. Therefore they undermined the autonomy within society of the one structure through which it was possible to realize highly individualized premises with integrity, the individual composition itself. For the more self-contained and singular a work appeared to be, the more explanations of it were sought in principles essentially extrinsic to it; and because such principles of explanation, unlike the embodied norms of classicism, *were* extrinsic, they helped stimulate a redefinition of musical meaning in a way that excluded the semiotic autonomy of musical structure. Indeed, even among the most educated listeners, attention was frequently diverted away from the particularity of the work at hand, if not to atmospheric, nonmusical associations (for illustration one need only consult the first section in Schumann's criticism of the *Symphonie fantastique* or Hans von Bülow's exegesis of the Chopin *Preludes*), then at least to the identity of the personal style exemplified in the work (a situation normally adverse for unknown composers). Schumann's criticism of Chopin's music, for example, came to center on a fascination with the unmistakability of Chopin's style, just as more than a century later Edward Cone's exceptionally thoughtful analysis of the *Symphonie fantastique* was to arrive at the conclusion "that the symphony is really by Berlioz."[47] But paradoxically, although the identity of the nineteenth-century composer's style generally defined a realm extrinsic to the particularity of a single musical structure, that style was not sufficiently more general than the structure of a particular work to serve as a socially decipherable basis for defining the individuality of a work. Hence, whereas Beethoven had seemed able to render autonomy of style identical with meaningful autonomy of structure in his music, the stylistic autonomy of his successors tended to vitiate the meaningful structural autonomy of their individual works, and acceptance of a particular romantic work often became essentially a means of validating the composer's stylistic personality.

The result was that more and more over the course of the nineteenth century, music, especially pure instrumental and nonfunctional music, began to depend for its acceptance outside the composer's own circles on an irrational and uninformed faith in the importance (and, conceivably, also the sincerity) of the composer's manner of utterance. Not surprisingly, as force of stylistic personality became essential to the public survival of individualized music, nineteenth-century art music manifested an increasing capacity for rhetorical emphasis, a category of technique that had already threatened the autonomy of Beethoven's music and brought it closer to natural language.

Moreover, just as the collapse of dual structure made correctness of usage increasingly irrelevant to artistic creation (despite Wagner's faculty for egregious violation of self-proclaimed "rules") so, too, this collapse tended to destroy purely musical methods for verifying whether a particular interpretation of a given piece was the correct one. Even rhetorical emphasis, no matter how exaggerated, was seldom able to guarantee uniform understanding of a work in wholly musical terms; faced with loss of control over reactions to their music outside their own circles (and after their own lifetimes), many nineteenth-century composers also followed Beethoven's second lead and supplied their works with explanatory titles, texts, programs, or critical commentary, often hoping thereby to crystallize the intrinsically musical essence of their works but in fact replacing the internal coherence once definitive of music with the correspondences more characteristic of language. In this way too, then, music after Beethoven was brought ever closer to natural language, and the chances were further reduced that autonomous musical utterance could ever be assured general yet precise comprehension; indeed, however much the romantics themselves idealized autonomous music, their own compositions as well as their criticism gave numerous indications that such a medium had virtually ceased to exist by mid-century.[48]

During the second half of the nineteenth century, awareness grew among composers and critics that individual utterance had not established itself as a new universal and that the discontinuity between individual intention and general apprehension was threatening complete destruction of the very autonomy that had made music so promising a medium for the embodiment of individually perceived truth. As early as 1854, for example, in *The Beautiful in Music*, Eduard Hanslick criticized the inability of music, as then constituted by romantic individualism, to mediate between either human and nature or one human being and others and thus provide a basis for objective certainty in the understanding and judging of music. In fact, music was failing in much the same ways as natural language to certify the objectivity of its own truth content; and Hanslick, acutely sensitive to the ongoing convergence of music and language, stressed the natural enmity of these two mediums as the cause of contemporary musical insufficiency.[49] Significantly, however, in this, his most famous work, Hanslick himself found it impossible to discuss music outside the framework of natural language; in retrospect his differences with Wagner seem far less striking than the degree to which both men were obsessed with the relationship between music and language.[50]

Sooner or later in their critical writings, Hanslick and Wagner, like Brahms in his composition, both tried to establish a new universal basis for absolute music which would in effect replace the lost embodied relationships of classicism: Wagner, by trying to identify music with (among other things) a universal psychological substructure (e.g., in the late monograph on Beethoven, where the influence of Schopenhauer is particularly evident);[51] Hanslick, along with Brahms, by emphasizing the need to increase the rigor with which internal musical relationships cohered. Brahms probably came closer than any composer after Beethoven to restoring the semiotic autonomy of music by approximating a resynthesis of individual and general values in his works, but even Brahms could not ultimately assure an objective mode of musical perception. Those of his instrumental works that achieved popularity allowed the majority of listeners to perceive in them simply the individuality of Brahms's themes, gestures, and instrumental colors; within his works the classical identity of subjectively designed gesture and objectively rigorous structure could no longer be characterized as generally audible. Even Brahms could not remove from his abstract music the concreteness of his own contingent presence as an extrinsic content.

The strategies suggested respectively by Brahms and Wagner bore a strong resemblance to the quasi-scientific formalization and the investigation of underlying structures characteristic of epistemological language in the latter nineteenth and twentieth centuries; and neither that formalization nor that investigation encouraged the hope that music in the twentieth century would prove any more successful than natural language in eluding solipsism by reintegrating subjective and objective values. On the contrary, both approaches provided a strong basis for denying that the individual subject had any means of establishing a common link between himself or herself and others that would be either comprehensible or verifiable in general terms. For in the twentieth century, each of these techniques (like total serialism and chance music somewhat later) essentially removed the subject from ostensibly objective methods of construction: formalism by rejecting individuality of expression more or less outright; investigations of underlying structures, such as expressionism and primitivism—and there are obvious analogues here with the influential analytical methods of Heinrich Schenker—by moving toward a level of psychological reality below any level of individual consciousness or of any recognizably individual mode of expression—toward a level, that is, which may well be deemed irrational.[52]

With respect to irrationality, it might be added, the substructural approach to composition went considerably beyond the romantic position. In trying to impute transcendent significance to individual subjective fantasy, the romantics had made the suggestion that that which eludes indisputably rational apprehension—and which is, conceivably, the intractably irrational —constitutes the one remaining possible basis for human universality. By the turn of the century, the specter evoked by Kant's critical philosophy of an unverifiable (and thus conceivably absent) rationality as the universal ground of the human mind—as indeed of all reality—had engendered visions of such a ground as explicitly irrational.

And the substructural approach to composition provided strong evidence that even a universality of the irrational could not be proven objectively valid in a generally verifiable way. Thus Schoenberg and Stravinsky both turned to relatively extreme kinds of formalism to give their music at least a semblance of verifiable "objective" validity; and in Schoenberg's case, at least, the formal principle (the twelve-tone system) was even derived quite logically from expressionistic materials. Nevertheless, Schoenberg and Stravinsky were unable, respectively, to synthesize the style of expressionism or primitivism with audibly persuasive formal logic. In the end, only traces of individual expression and of a generally comprehensible principle of structure managed merely to coexist at any perceptible level in the music of these composers, and at least as often the same traces appeared to be completely polarized. Far more conspicuously than in Brahms's music, the principles of individuality and generality failed to coalesce into an identity in the music of Schoenberg and Stravinsky, and consequently, each principle remained unmistakably less than complete, even within itself.

Without such a synthesis, nor much prospect of one, progressive twentieth-century art music headed toward a condition of solipsism that was no longer mitigated by that generally recognizable individuality of style that had come to lie at the very heart of the definition and perception of autonomous music during the preceding century. Whereas musical judgments in the nineteenth century could still be based on direct personal intuitions about a composer, judgments about the value of twentieth-century music had to rely for the most part on faith in the expertise of one or another critic. And thus, the dream of general verifiability in music faded away as the understanding of music became an academic specialty. During the course of the twentieth century, music gradually abandoned the aesthetic realm, which it had once virtually defined, for another realm that had once been the preserve of natural language — epistemology. As a bearer of truth, the aesthetic, at least in music, no longer seemed capable of the autonomy needed to function as an alternative to the epistemological, much less to subsume it. Moreover, just as epistemological language had severed itself from general communicability, so too the aesthetic was now explicitly distinguished from the communicative.[53] Music and language were both yielding to a conception of truth that was discontinuous with communication.

To be sure, efforts to avoid solipsism in music continued, but the most important of these merely hastened the process by which music divested itself of its own distinctive features to take on the characteristics of natural language. Most pervasive, perhaps, was the tendency to make verbal criticism so "internal to the experience" of art music that "often one [did] not know whether interest [was] elicited and sustained primarily by the object or by what [could] be said about the object."[54] Many such critical explanations, moreover, themselves required mastery of a complex metalanguage, especially those that consisted in nothing more than the further elaboration of some closed (autonomous) system of musical construction.[55] Far more explicitly than in the nineteenth century, music in the twentieth century seemed to concede that the more autonomous its principle of construction, the more it stood in need of an explanation — even though the explanation offered was likely to be that much more irrelevant to the musical experience than its nineteenth-century counterpart had been.

At the same time, the loss of generally audible connections within music itself reinforced another means, pointed out by Adorno, whereby music shed its own identity: a certain renunciation of sound, that is, of the very physicality that had rendered music an aesthetic medium as distinct from the epistemological medium of language.[56] The pointillism of Webern, for example, represents not only the end of Schoenberg's efforts to retain the propositional relationships of classicism but also the marked incursion of silence into precisely the musical style that is most often said to initiate modernism. Here too, as George Steiner's work in particular suggests, one can find analogies with natural language — in the extent, for instance, to which musical silence constitutes a sealing off of the means to communication — and especially, analogies with modern linguistics. Certainly there is a striking resemblance between Webern's systematization of musical discontinuities and structuralist analyses of language. Even more than Stravinsky's neoclassicism, which by making music its own subject suggests the transformation of music into a metalanguage, Webern's music evokes a sense that music and language, once defined as truth-bearers through their capacity to embody connections, are finally converging on some common metalanguage that reveals both as obsolete. It is not impossible to conceive of that metalanguage as the semiology of music.

The parallel yet convergent courses of music and natural language since the Enlightenment have not only failed to synthesize the truth-bearing capacities characteristic of each at the time of their separation but have also left each medium largely bereft of its own capacities to convey truth: both objective knowledge and self-expression appear to be dwindling as sources of truth in the twentieth century. In the largest terms this situation seems to be the outgrowth of historical changes of focus in Western conceptions of truth. Over time a shift has occurred, from a predialectical belief in God as the transcendent locus of all meaning; to a belief in reason, still capable of existing as an absolute value beyond the limits of the individual, as the higher faculty in a divided conception of the human; then finally to a collapse of firm belief in the objective status of reason and a growing sense that irrationality may be the basis of truth. Within this progress the Western person has moved, again in very general terms, from a sense of existence in an undifferentiated state of cosmic unity; to a state of perceived duality between subjective consciousness and anything outside of it (together with the invocation of, or at least the search for, various kinds of mediations between the two); and finally to a state of isolation in which the discovery of means to reconnect self and other is no longer seriously expected. From the beginning of Western humanity's assumption of its own duality, principles of universality have been sought as a means for verifying the truth of the individual's experience of the world and thereby for establishing the right of the human as a conscious being to survive. Irrationality, however, has not proven itself in history to be a workable principle of universality, at least not in any way that benefits the survival of humanity in the world. Despite the great hopes for the synthesizing power of the imagination in the early nineteenth century, when optimism about the nature and potency of subjective perception was still apparently possible, irrationality has not supplied connections between human and nature or between one human being and others. Rather, it has been confined to suggesting analogies between one state of being and another.

The historical inhumanity of irrationally based notions of truth has, of course, been recognized for some time, as have the epistemological inadequacies of such notions. An awareness of such inadequacies has, indeed, propelled the structuralists' search for rational structures as a basis for epistemology and, in some cases, as in that of Lévi-Strauss, as a basis for ontology as well. What a project such as the semiology of music essentially proposes to do is to find a rational structure "deeper" than language, which by virtue of its greater generality allows the acquisition of precise, objectively verifiable knowledge from nonlinguistic mediums, which once seemed even less capable than language of yielding such knowledge. The semiology of music thus offers not merely through one but through both of its constituents to circumvent the discredited objectivity of knowledge obtained through natural language. Hence its apparently exceptional epistemological promise.

But hence, also, the unlikelihood of realizing that promise. For on the one hand, Western music has never seemed less likely to convey generally accessible knowledge without some dependence on natural language; the apparent increase of objectivity in the character of so much contemporary music signifies not a return of generally verifiable truth or meaningful autonomy to music but rather the continuing reduction of musical expression to a socially nonviable state of nonindividual solipsism. And on the other hand, no less a semiologist than Barthes himself has emphasized the continuing dependence of objective knowledge on language by suggesting the methodological priority of linguistics to semiology.[57] Lévi-Strauss has turned from music back to language as the paradigm of an epistemological medium, with only a passing reference to semiology.[58] Certainly, Nattiez has yet to dispense with either linguistic models or the explanatory capacities of natural language. His most ambitious quasi-wordless taxonomy is not more explanatory in nature or effect than is the undifferentiated work, Debussy's *Syrinx*, which it purports to analyze;[59] arguably, the taxonomy is less explanatory.

Without question, notions such as identity and difference, taxonomy, paradigm, model, and structure have a value for musical analysis, even for a dialectician like Adorno, whose historical explanations invoke social and artistic structures that are never adequately described. The foregoing discussion, which is based on Adorno's dialectical method, has found such notions particularly useful in summarizing essential aspects of musical classicism.

Yet, of all Western musical styles, classicism may well be the most resistant to understanding by means of structuralist methods. For it is not so much the identity of its related elements in themselves that distinguishes classicism, nor is it the discontinuities that are implicit in any hierarchical sort of organization; rather, it is the persuasive resolution of those discontinuities that constitutes the uniqueness of classicism, the very quality of classical relatedness itself. This is a quality to which no amount of taxonomic inventory gives access, just as the inventory has no means of preserving within itself the essence of that individuality that above all characterizes nineteenth-century European art music. In fact, a theory of symbols that is capable of removing the concept of relationship from the term "signification" and enclosing the words "understand" and "communication" in quotation marks seems at most an appropriate model for the study of the marked discontinuities of avant-garde Western music. True, the redundancy that structuralist analysis requires to construct tables of paradigmatic equivalences tends to be, in Leonard Meyer's words, "unnecessary and irrelevant" in much avant-garde music.[60] Still, even the epistemological limits of such a model are suggestive in a culture where the static structure has replaced the synthetic proposition as the paradigm of explanation.

But suggestive only, for removed from its historical context, such a model offers no more demonstration than does any irrational principle of a connection between its own and analogous discontinuities, or hence of its right to be considered paradigmatic of its own culture. If it is indeed a true model, the very nature of the truth it embodies precludes precisely the verifiability of that truth; and a model that can do no more than parallel the discontinuities of contemporary language and music offers no epistemological advantage over the enervated mediums it proposes to replace.

It might, perhaps, be argued that by putting the discontinuities of language and music in a structural rather than a historical perspective, structuralists have simply assigned the principle of discontinuity an ontological status that justifies the discontinuities of all their epistemological models.

And, indeed, Lévi-Strauss does explicitly define the first principle of reality as a discontinuity, and at times even as a dialectical contradiction.[61] But Lévi-Strauss also explicitly denies that discontinuity characterizes art in all societies, while at the same time he admits the historical limitations of such a condition in the West, thereby casting strong doubt on the structural status of discontinuity;[62] and he is unwilling to give dialectical relationships any priority in his epistemology. No matter how close an identity he posits between cultural and natural structures, then, Lévi-Strauss remains no more able than Nattiez to establish connections between his general ontology and his particular cultural homologues.

And yet, it appears that no model for obtaining truth developed in Western history since the Enlightenment—not music, not language, indeed, not even natural science—has come close to maintaining credibility without offering some mediating principle between levels of particularity and generality, including, ultimately, between self and other. Reason itself lost its universal status in the West because it could not protect both individual and society, two coeval constructs of history.[63] Thus historical evidence suggests that by ignoring the historical nature of the discontinuity between individual and general in the West and trying simply to exclude the notion of the individual subject from its pursuit of truth, French structuralism perpetuates the inaccessibility of objective knowledge which it is trying to overcome.

Seen in this light, it is not really surprising that structuralism has proven no more successful than irrationally based philosophies in restoring the lost universality of absolute reason. Indeed, it is difficult to understand why any undertaking that is indifferent to the historical fate of individual consciousness and free will should be considered a fundamentally rational undertaking; nor is it by any means clear why structures located far beneath the surface of human consciousness, for example, in the molecular structure of the brain, should be considered rational structures. No matter how serious the problems entailed in the historical reduction of reason to a component of the individual mind, rationality cannot be reinstituted as a universal principle through mere fiat, through some arbitrary declaration that rationality need have no connection to the individual subject or that individual subjectivity and the historical mode of consciousness out of which it derives are nothing more than insubstantial accretions to be removed from rational structures by philosophy.

To be sure, all contemporary Western critics, dialectical or structuralist, must at some point consider discontinuities as well as relationships; nevertheless, differences in the order of their priorities will produce substantial differences in the power of their criticism. Thus Adorno, no less than Lévi-Strauss, bases his work on what is, in effect, an ontology of discontinuity. Likewise, Adorno is also preoccupied with the relationship between music and language; and both men consider Western avant-garde music to be essentially a dead language.[64] But Adorno *begins* by defining discontinuity as part of a historical process — the dialectical process — through which he can define, connect, and explain historical phenomena; whereas for structuralists such as Lévi-Strauss and Nattiez, dialectics (like relationships in general) are somehow to be grafted onto predefined autonomous things, as a kind of "bridge," to use Lévi-Strauss's own words, "which analytical reason throws out over an abyss."[65] A method constructed in the latter manner will not ordinarily achieve the binding force of an explanation. Certainly it leaves a structuralist semiology of music unable to explain how two logically opposed approaches to critical inquiry, the systematic and the historical, converge on a single image: Western avant-garde music as an extinct language. And this inability points to a grave structural weakness in the methodological foundation of musical semiology, since the social extinction of modern music is almost certainly the principal burden of contemporary music theory. For as the dialectical exegesis of musical semiology itself appears to demonstrate, the same historical conditions that have made autonomous music — music fully capable of sustaining itself in every sense in society — obsolete also account for the limitations of most music theory today. In failing to provide any means for understanding those limitations, a structuralist semiology of music has renounced the possibility of overcoming them.

It is true that Adorno's dialectics, too, lead eventually to an abyss: to contemplation of the historical end of the individual and of humanity. It is a vision with analogues in the work of Foucault and Lévi-Strauss,[66] though it appears to be a source of anguish only for Adorno. But since Adorno's destination is reached only as the result of a long historical process through which it can be explained, he need not confront an abyss every time he wishes to establish a relationship. As a result, by preserving at least the possibility of a synthesizing principle, Adorno, despite his overwhelming pessimism, offers far more hope than the French structuralists that the objective values of an older rational order may one day be attainable in a form not incompatible with the integrity of subjective experience.

But no doubt some structuralists will continue to argue that the dialectic itself, along with history, relationships, and comprehension, is only a detail of one particular and obsolete episteme, enclosed in an infinite taxonomy of unconnected (and essentially nonrational) categories. Clearly this viewpoint has the advantage of putting the end of both musical and linguistic mediations "into perspective," whereas the dialectician may have only the melancholy satisfaction of wielding a synthesizing tool that, once consciously grasped, renders one impotent to change the history it defines. And probably only some radically antihistorical history such as Foucault's can provide even the semblance of an epistemological justification for a musical semiology that forces us to abandon the "anachronistic illusion of community or intersubjective accessibility"[67] once embodied in Western language and music, only to seal us off in a new musical metalanguage that lacks even the imperfect connective powers of those two mediums. If, on the other hand, structuralism considers itself a more honest appraisal than dialectics of the modern Western capacity for truth because it recognizes the Western discontinuity of individual and general as absolute and unbridgeable, the same honesty should require an admission that structuralism bases its entire critical enterprise on an assumption of its own futility.

Chapter 10

Tonality, Autonomy, and Competence in Postclassical Music

(In its original form, the historical framework offered in the preceding chapter elicited an extended response from Lawrence Kramer. This allowed me the opportunity for the following rejoinder.)[1]

Lawrence Kramer's objections to my sketch of postclassical music history center principally on my treatment of tonality as a historically evolving construct. Kramer would have it that tonality is a constant entity undergoing "constant metamorphosis" but unchanged in its essentials since the latter part of the Enlightenment (or, perhaps, even earlier?). This conception of tonality as an ahistorical complex, admitting only of change in surface detail and precluding any associated sense of historical direction or significant qualitative differences between styles, reveals so clear a structuralist orientation that one wonders less why Kramer attacks my critique of structuralism than why he seems to share my reservations about this movement so wholeheartedly.

  Constant as tonality seems to Kramer, however, his own account of its contribution to musical intelligibility since the latter eighteenth century suggests, curiously, inconsistencies. His closing assertion, for example, that "as long as music from the Enlightenment to the present has maintained some relationship to the tonal system, it has been widely intelligible *as* music"[2] can only be interpreted as agreeing with my contention that tonality has thus far proven the only workable basis [in the West] for purely musical intelligibility on a socially general scale — assuming that by "intelligib[ility] *as* music," Kramer means an engagement of the mind that goes beyond either the mere recognition of a medium as music or a physical response to sound. The attainment, or at least the approximation, of such a tonally based general intelligibility is, almost surely, a feat most readily associated with the classical style. Yet

195

it is precisely in connection with the classical style that Kramer seems most anxious to adduce sources of intelligibility other than tonality. No one could dispute his contention that an adequate analysis of Haydn's or Mozart's music would have to involve a consideration of musical elements besides tonality. The question I try to raise, however, is whether other elements are able to engender musical intelligibility in the same autonomous—that is, intrastructural—and general sense as classical tonality seems able to do.

I try to indicate this special quality of classical intelligibility by linking it with the notion of "dual structure," a notion that should not be flattened to mean any sort of intelligibility to those listeners deemed competent, especially if the term "competence" is used without qualification. Dual structure in music, as I construe it, is an intrastructural system of reference between pairs of discrete semiotic constructs both members of which are in some sense wholly embodied in a given musical structure. These constructs include a general ground of meaning and more particularized semiotic configurations derived from that ground; and because both are present in the musical structure, the relationship between them—the meaning of the music—can be retrieved directly, wholly, and on a general scale. No extrastructural mediating explanation or specialized information or training is needed; the interpreter need merely use the musical equivalent of reason. The archetype of such a system in music seems to be the relation of implication or self-generation that obtains between premise and conclusion within a pure system of logic, which, as described by Kant in his account of theoretical reason, would be universally intelligible.

The meaning of any music that realized fully this notion of dual structure would be universally intelligible because such meaning would be constituted not through its relation to any particular mind that imposed it on the music but through an intrinsically necessary, cohesive structural connection, existing outside of any particular mind and equally accessible to all minds, much like the "universal point of reference" associated by Kant with cognitive reason.[3] Because this meaning *was* universally intelligible, that is, since every interpreter through the use of reason would necessarily find this same unmistakable meaning in the music, it could be considered intrinsic to the given musical structure. In a sense, one could say that such meaning would achieve simultaneously the condition of being necessary in itself and for its interpreters. Only music that embodied such meaning could be said to possess autonomy in what seems to me the single rational sense of the term: a meaningful autonomy. Clearly, competence in the case of any music possessing such meaning would be identical with structural competence; and the structurally competent would be identical with the generally competent, with the musical Everyman.

Obviously, this sort of meaning, and consequently this autonomy, is in actuality unattainable by any semiotic structure, including music. As Kant's critical philosophy makes clear, no structure can totally embody its own meaning and still be accessible to any human intelligence. No matter how intrinsically necessary they may seem, all structures are dependent for meaning on subjective minds existing outside of those structures; meaning is not intrinsic in humanity's semiotic structures but imposed on them. Furthermore, the meanings that humans impose on such structures, like the structures themselves, always present themselves by way of some concrete, particular medium, involving a contingency not wholly within the control of a transcendental and universal mental structure of reason, if such a structure exists; even logic is always mediated through some empirical sign system. Because of this contingency, no such system can be guaranteed universally intelligible or, therefore, be designated intrinsically meaningful. All semiotic structures must finally be assumed to depend for meaning on particular minds extrinsic to them.

It may be helpful to put this slightly differently. It has been pointed out in the case of Kant's *Ding-an-sich* that to define the thing-in-itself, one must contrast it to the thing as it exists for us; but to bring the former into such a relationship undercuts its purely intrinsic necessity and brings it into the domain of the latter, as something relative and limited by human subjectivity.[4] In a roughly similar sense, even what might appear in music to delineate something like an intrinsically necessary and universally intelligible logic must ultimately be seen as the product of particular subjective minds; and logical necessity, or intrastructural autonomy as it is defined in music, can at most be accounted the ideal of one or more particular styles. It is my contention that this sort of necessity or autonomy is in fact a characteristic ideal of only one Western musical style, the classical, where, as an ideal, it constitutes a norm that is definitive of style.[5] To make such an association is not at all necessarily to denigrate other styles; indeed, Kramer himself in a way suggests precisely such a limited association when he contrasts the classical effects of "autonomy and intelligibility" with baroque values of diversity and fullness.[6] I would argue that although other parameters of music may have varying degrees of implicative power, and although even in classicism tonality does not work alone or determine every aspect of musical structure, it is nevertheless principally by using the power of tonality to generate a quasi-logical musical structure over time that classical music projects the ideal I describe.

In his efforts to emphasize nonharmonic aspects of classical intelligibility, Kramer suggests that Beethoven was even more concerned than Haydn and Mozart to utilize "dynamics, timbre, rhythm, texture, and speed" as sources of intelligibility.[7] I do not disagree; it is, indeed, precisely such an emphasis that leads me to associate the onset of rhetoric and other extrastructural semiotic devices in music essentially with Beethoven. Presumably, Kramer would have us believe that these parameters of music can and do generate large-scale systems of intelligible meaning; but locating connected elements of such a parameter in a given work is by no means the same thing as proving the generational force of that parameter. Nor can Kramer demonstrate such a force, say, in the Fifth Symphony, merely by invoking "recurrence of forms" (which no one would deny as a fundamental organizing principle of the Fifth). At the very least, he will first have to ask himself whether recurrence itself can embody meaning in the same more or less implicit, and hence implicitly general way as can be claimed for the antecedent-consequent structure that seems inherent in classical tonality.

Kramer, for example, characterizes the return of Scherzo material on the oboe in the last movement of the Fifth Symphony (measures 172ff.), as a climax or culminating resolution that is in some sense logically required by premises inherent in the Fifth.[8] But what is logically necessary about this decision to repeat? Isn't this recurrence more an element in an individual, and ultimately arbitrary, scheme of repetition than a logically required resolution? To me, at least, this very gesture suggests far less the equanimity of a peroration based on indisputable logic than the tenuousness of doubt, an impression that is heightened by the break this recurrence causes in the forward thrust of the Finale as well as by the exaggeratedly protracted repetition of simple, conclusive cadence formulas at the very end of the movement. In both these sections, it seems to me that repetition is notable for its introduction of a certain arbitrariness and its suggestion of an individually voiced doubt in the universal necessity projected by classical structural procedures, whether repetition is used to substitute for these procedures or to emphasize them.

I would argue that repetition in itself is not a quasi-logical technique but an intrinsically arbitrary and contingent technique that lends itself readily to individualized, emphatic, and essentially rhetorical efforts to impose on musical structure a meaning that is in some quantitative sense plausibly general. To call attention to this character of repetition is not to deny that Beethoven projects, along with doubt, something like a force of necessity in such a device as the return of the Scherzo material. But it does Beethoven's individuality a disservice to try to demonstrate the implicit *logical* necessity of such a return when its power stems precisely from the fact that it is *not* intrinsically implicative, or general in meaning, but rather a fundamentally arbitrary pattern (or part of one), shaped according to highly individual criteria of necessity and significance.[9] It is likewise a disservice to characterize such a pattern as "perfectly compatible" with classical tonality as if the synthesis of an individualized and nonimplicative technique with a generalized and implicative one were a routine accomplishment. It was indeed Beethoven's genius that he seemed able momentarily to fuse the logical necessity of tonality with the individual necessity of rhetoric. But this was an unmistakably individual feat and, as such, offered no implicitly generalizable means through which subsequent composers could count on rendering individual meaning universally intelligible. On the contrary, by leaving the example of his own individuality as his principal artistic legacy, Beethoven made room in music for all the elements that threaten the general intelligibility of an individually based sign system, including the apparent arbitrariness of private symbolism and the effects of the individual's contingent relation to his or her own culture.

One might suppose that having tried to show a significant break with tonality as the governing basis of general intelligibility, Kramer would go on to develop this line of argument in connection with the earlier romantics, especially since the first half of the nineteenth century is the one period in which he acknowledges an evolutionary change, and a dissolution at that, in tonality. Strangely, however, it is with Chopin and Schumann that Kramer seems to *begin* alleging what he denies in the case of the classical composers: that the intelligibility of the musical structure inheres wholly in the realization of tonal premises.[10] But is the unarguable presence of tonality in nineteenth-century music identical with a "propositional" conception of tonality? Can "a shifting or elusive norm," "the organized instability" of an ultimate but unstable point of reference, or simultaneity and ambiguity (which are, indeed, characteristics of nineteenth-century tonality) engender a virtually complete system of embodied meanings in the same way as classical tonality seems able to? And can "tonality as such," a phrase that suggests tonality as but one of many structurally fixed and self-contained (as well as physically specific) elements of nineteenth-century music, really constitute a dynamic governing principle from which whole structures can be evolved?

The answer almost assuredly is no. Tonality after Beethoven can rarely be construed, least of all in any audible sense, as engendering out of itself large-scale, temporally cohesive, and generally intelligible structures.[11] On the contrary (as I have tried elsewhere to demonstrate),[12] as romantic harmony becomes increasingly governed by individualized conceptions of structure and color, it ceases to suggest structural relationships of a general character. Instead, the harmonic patterns of romantic works (for example, with respect to their beginnings and endings) present themselves as quite openly contingent and arbitrary in rationale. This does not make these patterns hopelessly unintelligible, but it does tend to restrict the number of those competent in romantic harmony, as does, of course, the harmonic complexity.[13] Thus, if structural competence in romantic music is equated with harmonic competence, the structurally competent listener can no longer be identified, even ideally, with the general listener. Furthermore, the structural supremacy of tonality is clearly challenged in romantic music, which strongly emphasizes other, far less implicative but more concretely sensuous musical parameters (including, to be sure, coloristic aspects of tonality). Such emphasis does suggest an autonomy of *medium* for music. But liberating the sensuous elements of music from the rule of extramusical goals or conceptions is not the same as generating a unified and semiotically comprehensive structure out of immanent musical materials or rendering meaning precisely coextensive with structure. Nor does the recognition or acceptance of sensuous musical elements amount to the understanding of a composition as an internally cohesive and particular structure. In fact, emphasis on the sensuous autonomy of music tends to call attention to the semiotic incompleteness or lack of semiotic autonomy in music at the level of internal structure because elements that are essentially sensuous (which means self-contained) rather than implicative must clearly be referred to sources outside a given structure (including the composer's style and cultural identity) for interpretation. This lack of wholly intrastructural intelligibility is likewise made evident by the opportunity romantic music offers for a second sort of competence quite distinct from (and only partially reconcilable with) tonal competence, a mode of comprehension that could be called stylistic, cultural, or general competence. Though it requires less rigorous concentration than tonal competence, and thus in a sense is less demanding and more accessible, stylistic competence is by definition contingent and thus limited, rather than potentially universal on the basis of a common rationality, because it explicitly involves empirical elements outside the particular musical structure, elements that will be connected with the structure only by the specially trained or the culturally initiated.

I emphasize the erosion of an intrastructurally meaningful autonomy because I suspect it is really this idea, which Kramer interprets as antiromantic, rather than my evolutionary conception of tonality that is bothering him. For all his objections to my "rigid and limiting" conception of classical intelligibility,[14] Kramer seems actually to share my conviction (though largely with respect to music *after* Beethoven!) that tonality has so far proven the only workable basis for general musical intelligibility. For me this conviction does not exclude others sorts of intelligibility or, for that matter, other sorts of musical greatness. For Kramer, however, it is apparently imperative to link all intelligibility in music to tonality, even at the cost of leveling significant stylistic differences. This is so, I suspect, because of a twentieth-century formalistic prejudice that all great music must present itself as a purely musical and formally discrete structure. This prejudice is coupled with the somewhat naive or precritical assumption that physical autonomy can in fact be reconciled with an implicitly general, intrastructural intelligibility, an assumption that ignores the historical dissociation of such autonomy and such intelligibility not only in romantic music but in the music that has followed it.[15]

But why must "the most widely played of all Western art music"[16] manifest a purely intrastructural intelligibility or be accessible wholly by way of tonal norms? Kramer seems to assume that allowing nineteenth-century music "to define its own context" requires interpreting that music as wholly autonomous, preferably in tonal terms, and rejecting any additional ("semiotic") kinds of meaning as something that "was always secondary and *now no longer exists*" (emphasis added).[17] In fact, however, both the critical writings of the period and subsequent scholarly studies of that criticism point decisively away from what we would now call an "autonomous" conception of music in the first half of the nineteenth century.[18] The absolute quality of Beethoven's music venerated by German romantics was actually treated in romantic music criticism as a susceptibility to poetic interpretation; and likewise, the power of musical purity for the romantics lay not in musical form per se but rather, as Kramer himself suggests, in the evocation by pure music of a metaphysical reality.[19] The subsequent disappearance of poetic or metaphysical meaning from romantic music is actually evidence that we twentieth-century listeners, with our formalistic orientation, lack complete stylistic competence in romantic music; and this disappearance reinforces my contention that intelligibility in music after classicism becomes openly contingent.

Without question, Brahms wanted to retrieve something like the autonomous quality evident in intrastructural classical logic and for this reason relied heavily on a sonata structure descended from classicism. The result, however, was far from the simple transformation of Beethovenian dual structure that Kramer seems to have in mind. (Is Kramer's Brahms, the unproblematical neoclassicist, the same composer in whose music Charles Rosen discerns an "[omnipresent] sense of the irrecoverable past . . . [an] openly expressed regret that he was born too late"?[20] This disparity in interpretation alone belies the presence of a single, unmistakable musical meaning in Brahms.) As is suggested by Kramer's own characterization of certain Brahmsian sonata elements as "too intelligible,"[21] the sonata structure can no longer be taken in Brahms's works fundamentally as a principle in the process of working itself out over time. Tovey's claim that "given a page of an unknown [classical] work . . . one could tell whether it was from the beginning, middle, or end of a movement"[22] is not germane to the particularity of Brahms's music; and for the general listener to the Second Symphony in D

Major, the "lyric theme" of the first movement (a theme that appears first in F-sharp minor, at measure 82, and only subsequently in the dominant, A major, at measure 156) is almost certainly experienced more readily as "Brahms's lullaby" than as a moment of structurally significant harmonic change. For Brahms, as for most nineteenth-century composers, the sonata structure functions as a preexistent, static structure, a point of reference external to the musical structures in which it is used. From constituting a source of autonomy, the sonata has become a kind of explicitly concretized historical content.

It is significant, moreover, that of the three pieces adduced by Kramer as paradigmatic of Brahms's "transparently 'classical' structures,"[23] no fewer than two make explicit reference to a style, the baroque, external not only to romanticism but to classicism as well. And in all three the most prominent organizing device is not the tonal principle of sonata but melodic repetition. In Brahms's late works, it may well be the case that it is through a de-rhetoricized, so to speak, and often imperceptible, but still clearly nonimplicative or formally static, technique of repetition rather than through traditional form that he finally came closest to achieving an autonomous objective rigor. But at this point Brahms's music must be interpreted less as a synthesis of Beethoven's objective autonomy and Wagner's subjective expressiveness than as a moment of historical suspension between the expressiveness of the entire German tradition and the essentially nontemporal and antiexpressive structural autonomy of postromantic formalism. Within this historical suspension a dissociation of structural pattern and intelligible meaning becomes increasingly overt. (In this connection, it is worth considering, for example, Rosen's description of the symbolist movement in poetry, with which Debussy had close links, as one that "renounces communication for presentation," "asserts the independence of language and its emancipation from communication," and "renounc[es] directed argument."[24] Such an autonomy can well exist in a nontonal musical structure, but it is not an autonomy that Kramer seems prepared to accept.) Something of the nature of this historical suspension in Brahms's music between two essentially irreconcilable aesthetics can perhaps be discerned in a late structure such as the first movement of the Clarinet Quintet—a "textbook" sonata heavily reliant on motivic transformation—in which all the expressivity of line, color, chromatic inflection, and tonal ambiguity cannot overcome a profound impression of nonimplicative, atemporal immobility.

No doubt the antihistorical tendencies of postromantic formalism require a more complex critical approach than my dialectical schema offers, and I have subsequently attempted elsewhere to refine the relationship between historical and ahistorical conceptions of music and time.[25] The character of

modern formalism is not likely, however, to be elucidated by any straightforward equation, such as Kramer suggests, between this movement and a
return to tonality as the basis of intelligibility—least of all where the music
of Mahler is used to date the beginning of such a movement in the twentieth
century.[26] For it is difficult to think of a composer whose symphonies contributed more to tendencies, already noted in romantic music, toward moving away from tonal or any other sort of intrastructural intelligibility, tendencies that involve individualization of expression and, especially,
concretization of content. Few, I suspect, would agree with Kramer's casual
suggestion that the individual expressiveness of rhetoric is subordinate to internal structural relationship in Mahler's music in the same way as it is in
Haydn's or Mozart's music;[27] and few could deny that an understanding of
Mahler's music explicitly requires the listener to be saturated with knowledge of a particular culture. To characterize Mahler's music as "perfectly intelligible in terms of a dual structure based on tonal practice," as if tonality
defined Mahler's symphonic world even figuratively in the same comprehensive and more or less abstractly universal way as it defined Haydn's, is to
miss, it seems to me, the very essence of Mahler's style.[28]

I also find somewhat puzzling Kramer's reliance on Stravinsky's own testimony to document the self-evident intelligibility of the Symphony in C.[29]
Kramer would have us believe that any number of twentieth-century composers have successfully reestablished tonality as the basis of genuinely autonomous, in the sense of internally self-generating and self-explanatory,
musical structures. Are we to assume that the Symphony in C is a case in
point? Surely no one could argue that any implicit dynamism of the tonal system generates the structure of this work or that the tonal system continues
to function within it in any sense as a living language.[30] In this work (written
close in time to Stravinsky's repeated assertion in his *Poetics of Music* that the
tonal system had already lived out its life cycle),[31] tonality has petrified completely into a historical relic, useful as a source of intelligibility only to the
extent that its vocabulary and conventions, now isolated from the context
of a general system, can still provide a veneer of familiarity.

But, again, recognizing discrete musical elements is not at all the same as
understanding why, in terms of a given musical structure, the music takes the
course it does, why it begins and ends where it does, or what relation each
element has to the structure as a whole. And whereas one can at least imagine
deciphering a symphonic movement of Haydn's as a coherent structure on
the basis of a general competence in the tonal system and arriving at a more
or less comprehensive understanding of the movement, tonal competence
alone is clearly not sufficient for an internally cohesive or comprehensive understanding of, say, the "sonata-like" first movement of Stravinsky's Sym-

phony in C. Even to grasp fully the rationale of the internal structure one would need some knowledge of Stravinsky's own structural idiosyncrasies, such as his attraction to the interval of the third. And though the purpose of importing past conventions into this movement (as into the Symphony generally) is to strip them of their traditional meanings and incorporate them into a very nontraditional semiotic structure, still, this removal of historical meaning and value is fundamental to Stravinsky's conception of the musical structure; one cannot claim to understand this movement, or the work, as a total conception without some knowledge of this purpose together with a knowledge of the external traditions from which the musical materials are drawn and the ways in which the functions of those materials are altered. Despite an apparent effort to free pure formality in this work from the burden of signification, the work seems almost to ask for external imposition of meaning on its intrinsically meaningless materials and structure, or at least for recognition of such an imposition by its composer. To understand this work in purely formal terms, one seems to need an extrastructural familiarity with cultural tradition and individual style in order to understand that the original composer in a sense tried to impose on the formal character of this work an absence of immanent meaning as a kind of immanent meaning.

But where Stravinsky's, as opposed to Brahms's, music is concerned, such particularized cultural information is unlikely to enter into the general listening experience, both because of the highly specialized manner in which Stravinsky historicizes—or dehistoricizes—his cultural heritage and because of the antiexpressive (antirhetorical and abstractly patterned) way in which he defines a personal style. Indeed, in the case of a work such as the Symphony in C which presents itself as autonomous in a modern formalistic sense,[32] even knowledge of substantial cultural information no longer provides much access to an alternative general competence that can dispense with a more specialized structural competence. Instead, such knowledge seems needed here simply to achieve structural competence; or in other words, structural competence seems to be redefined here as a newly enlarged sort of prerequisite cultural knowledge, which is in effect the only sort of competence this antiexpressive, formalistic, and formally sophisticated music permits. This prerequisite knowledge is so extensive that it is almost guaranteed to render structural competence a far more socially restricted phenomenon than it has been even with respect to nineteenth-century music, where it is not the only sort of competence available. Kramer's demand for musical autonomy apparently requires that tonality as an immanent, governing, vital, unified, and self-referential system be equated with an imported, unprivileged, petrified, and deconstructed source of materials, a source from which all traces of intrinsic meaning have deliberately been removed. Far from protecting postclassical music from disadvantageous comparisons with classical music, this sort of equation actually prevents the critic from defining even approximately the particular character of any postclassical style or its own modes of greatness.

Chapter 11

The Historical Structure: Adorno's "French" Model for the Criticism of Nineteenth-Century Music

If Adorno asserts through his criticism that Beethoven's third-period style prefigures the end of humanity and that Schoenberg's twelve-tone conception signals the arrival of that end,[1] what does he think happened to the music in between? Typically, Adorno himself left no cohesive answer to this question. Nevertheless, an analysis of his principal essays on nineteenth-century music does suggest a comprehensive view of that music which might surprise Adorno himself—especially if one declines to examine Adorno through his own dialectical apparatus, and tries instead to develop fresh means of criticizing both Adorno and nineteenth-century music by reading his writings, as it were, against the grain. Once his work is subjected to criticism outside of its own methodological framework, evidence begins to appear that Adorno actually understands the history of nineteenth-century music in something like the way that the antihistorical French scholar Foucault understands other aspects of nineteenth-century history.[2] Indeed, although Adorno's interest in nineteenth-century music is almost entirely limited to the work of German composers—principally Schubert, Wagner, Brahms, and Mahler—the traits to which he calls attention in this music, and ultimately, too, the traits to which he calls attention in his own criticism, turn out to have a great deal in common with salient features of French music and criticism since the Enlightenment, and especially with modern French structuralism. It does not seem an undue exaggeration to say that Adorno, to some extent in spite of himself, views the nineteenth century as a period in which German composers demonstrated the validity of a French worldview more modern than their own.[3]

Thus in spite of his attachment to Marxist-Hegelian dialectic, Adorno does not present nineteenth-century music primarily as a progressive development or, in a sense, as a phenomenon that is in the last analysis historical at all. This is not to deny that his basic approach is that of a historian. Without question he understands Schoenberg's music, for example, as the realization of certain historical elements present as far back, stylistically, as Beethoven's last works; and in general, the specter of historical disintegration can never be far from a philosophy like Adorno's so-called negative dialectics, which is concerned with the coming apart of whatever appear to be historically attained syntheses.[4] But it is precisely this negativism that informs Adorno's conception of history in nineteenth-century music, and that determines the image of that music which finally emerges from his criticism. For history, as Adorno presents it in connection with music after Beethoven, seems to be no more than a vestigial surface that has already been cut off from any blood supply and is now stiffening into rigor mortis. It is possible to argue that Adorno's principal composite image of nineteenth-century music is not that of a historical process but rather one of a static structure.

Substantial support for this argument can be derived from the fact that for the most part Adorno treats nineteenth-century music less as a gradual decline from Beethovenian achievement than as a single unit or system, the essentials of which are established early in the century and remain more or less constant thereafter. The initial boundary for this system is particularly clear because of the sharp distinction Adorno makes between Beethoven's second-period style and other early nineteenth-century music. That is, like Foucault's epistemes — Foucault's last relatively well-defined episteme also begins around 1800 — nineteenth-century music as Adorno conceives it is separated by a discontinuity from the music immediately preceding it.

Beginning with the works of Beethoven's last period (which will not be discussed here), nineteenth-century music is consistently characterized by Adorno as exhibiting what might be called a condition of "post-totality," an inability to recover the quality of wholeness achieved briefly in classicism, especially in Beethoven's second period. This in spite of the fact that it was in this very century that the notion of the musical masterpiece, containing an entire universe within itself, emerged as an ideal. Even Schubert's music, as interpreted by Adorno, is able to suggest the quality of wholeness only at isolated moments (Adorno thinks, perhaps, of a tendency to proceed and develop in self-contained units);[5] and in a pointed contrast to the total unity of Mozart's *Zauberflöte*, he likens the episodic organization of Weber's *Freischütz* to the fragmentation of imagery in a contemporaneous invention, the kaleidoscope.[6] Similarly certain Wagnerian works — Adorno specifies *Meistersinger* — manifest a need for an unusually powerful kind of unifying principle, capable of holding together material that has been fragmented into a multitude of self-contained and specialized particles.[7] This is much the same kind of principle needed by the modern French structuralists to bring their highly refined, discontinuous binary oppositions or distinctive features into a system. Failing to find such a principle in music, Adorno contends, Wagner must continue to rely on texts for his fundamental organization.[8] And at the far end of the century, Mahler, clearly the nineteenth-century composer to whose work Adorno is most sympathetic, can do no more than confirm the greatness of the Beethovenian moment of synthesis by evoking its negative image, so to speak — an image of totality lost, of the negated or impossible masterpiece — by constructing enormous symphonic patterns out of elements too discontinuous to effect any large-scale unity.[9]

Adorno also seems quite often to suggest possible end points to the nineteenth-century episteme, among them *Parsifal* and *Das Lied von der Erde*. But as in Foucault's historical "archaeology," these latter boundaries do not yet emerge as wholly distinct, despite Adorno's open disdain for most music after Schoenberg. Indeed, the continuity of Adorno's dialectical methods with certain historical traces in nineteenth-century German music tends to undercut distinctions between the musical cultures of the nineteenth and twentieth centuries. This tendency permits a view of his own work as a part (really a variant or transformation) of an older, outmoded system of musical thought.[10] But even more, it encourages an understanding of the entire quasi-historical tradition of post-Beethovenian music and musical thought, which sooner or later reveals the outmodedness of its own historical content, as an element subsumed in a still larger, more modern, ahistorical cultural system or structure.

Thus the terminus that Adorno most frequently indicates for nineteenth-century music is Schoenberg's twelve-tone music, the culmination of a historical process whereby Schoenberg, to follow Adorno's account, derives from Brahms precisely the unifying principle Wagner needed — though only to show that the one basis of integrity left in the modern world is lack of wholeness. But it can also be argued that the principal historical characteristic for Adorno of Schoenberg's twelve-tone system — the final disappearance of all vital traces in the historical content of music — is merely a superficial occurrence that does not affect the fundamentally ahistorical structure of music defined in the early nineteenth century when classical wholeness splintered into self-contained yet incomplete "masterpieces." Viewed in this way, Schoenberg's twelve-tone music constitutes the fulfillment of a historical implication only if history implies the absence of history and of historical implication. Do the initial forms of life imply the condition itself of death? Can nonimplication be implied? Although Adorno himself tends to focus on such questions principally in connection with the music of Schoenberg and Webern,[11] they are brought to mind frequently by his criticism of nineteenth-century music.

As Adorno sees it, wholeness eludes the nineteenth-century masterpiece because wholeness is a property of *processes*, whereas nineteenth-century music, at the compositional as well as the historical level, is essentially a *structure*. In general this structure seems to consist of a hierarchy characterized at every level by the same pattern, a pattern readily associated with Adorno's own self-negating dialectic: the fixing or congealing of dismantled classical processes (such as history itself) into self-contained fragments, that is, into structures. The classical processes that seem to interest Adorno most are those through which music might be said to identify "the human" as "the real," in the sense that they embody clear and compelling analogues to the human as Adorno conceives it. And though what Adorno characterizes as human in the classical style are precisely such things as its encouragement of the listener to follow its unfolding actively and its strong metaphorical suggestion of individual self-consciousness, he would probably agree that these classical processes, together with their humanistic import, gain full and explicit recognition only in the nineteenth century—much as Foucault's episteme becomes fully recognizable only when completed. (Certainly no one was more sensitive than Adorno to the kind of paradox noted on p. 127 of chapter 7, above, whereby the perception of structural autonomy becomes apparent only with the loss of structural competence.) At any rate nineteenth-century music, which is in fundamental ways a reading or criticism of classicism, invites more urgently than any music before it a comparison between its own constituents and the human condition. But Adorno would further add that as musical processes are fragmented into separate, self-contained constituents, the latter—however anthropomorphically suggestive they may be—are transformed into something essentially nonhuman.

On its most general level this structural pattern of congealing processes seems to involve a shift in music from living or quasi-organic modes of existence to inanimate (sometimes formal) ones. Adorno lays stress, for example, on a shift from the temporal modes that characterize organisms to spatial modes: while classical musical elements exist only in processes of change or development over time, like organisms, nineteenth-century musical elements exist more in the manner of objects fixed in a spatial dimension. Nineteenth-century music, he notes on occasion, tends to converge on painting.[12] Adorno also seems to think of a shift from relational modes of being (associated with time) to nonrelational modes (associated with space) as illustrative of the move away from the organic. Organic life depends on common bonds between genuinely different things, that is, on relationships: relationships among the organism's own constituents, which are differentiated by function, and relationships with an environment that is outside or "other" than the organism itself. The apparent functioning of such relationships in musical classicism evidently prompts Adorno to associate this style with notions such as "wholeness" and "vital center."

By contrast, inanimate objects as Adorno implicitly presents them seem to be characterized by discontinuity, rather than by common bonds, and by what Adorno would probably consent to call "insignificant" as opposed to functional differences. As far as bonds are concerned, what makes inanimate objects "inanimate" is the lack of vital connection among their components, and what makes them "objects" is the discontinuity between them and their environment. And as regards differences, such objects can readily be imagined as cut off altogether from any external environment, that is, capable of existing in a vacuum from which all otherness has been removed. Likewise the elements within an inanimate object need differ only in some formal and static (rather than functional and interrelated) manner, for example in details of surface organization. The structure of such an object might even consist of identically constituted components that differ only in actual identity. This could probably be said of the hierarchical patterns that Adorno sees in nineteenth-century musical structures. In this context, the principal metaphor that he applies to Schubert's music, that of crystalline structure, seems particularly striking. It is Adorno's claim that the music of the first great successor to Beethoven can be taken apart and reworked into potpourris because, like a sheet of crystal, it no longer forms a vital, organic whole.[13]

Of course, a structure of identically constituted components (for instance, cells) could also belong to an organism that has been stripped of its former functional differentiation. In fact, it is exactly through a reduction to this level of formal (as opposed to functional) likenesses and differences that a French structuralist such as Lévi-Strauss claims to bridge the gap between animate and inanimate forms of being.[14] And Adorno, too, in effect undercuts the difference between the animate and the inanimate by treating nineteenth-century music as a sort of organic residue that in its essentials is already inanimate. In terms of the positions they ultimately take toward this distinction, there may well be no significant differences between these two scholars. Still, one can hardly help noticing that they arrive at their common depreciation of the difference between animate and inanimate in markedly dissimilar states of mind. In contrast to Lévi-Strauss, Adorno is deeply troubled by this depreciation because he comes to it not from an interest in structural isomorphisms (as, for example, between the animate and inanimate) *per se*, but rather from a concern for what he considers classical humanizing processes in nineteenth-century music. For Adorno, the removal of the line between the animate and the inanimate signifies the congealing at a second important level in nineteenth-century music of processes vital to the definitions of a *human* organism in particular. And the processes in question are those connected with the transmission of *meaning*.

For it seems clear enough that Adorno's discussions of nineteenth-century music are predicated on the post-Kantian notion that anything that can be said to exist in the same realm of reality with the human organism must be a construct of the mind, and more particularly, of reason. Something becomes real, in humanly understandable terms, only when the mediating action of reason imbues it with meaning. But Adorno also clearly believes that meaning in music requires (or, more properly, inheres in) some sort of interaction, some process of correspondence, some discharge of tension, between functionally different elements.[15] And in nineteenth-century music such interaction ceases, for functional differentiation and its resultant force of tension give way to static differences of appearance that produce no grounds for interaction and hence remain "insignificant." Or, to state Adorno's view another way, nineteenth-century music enters into a condition that he terms "nominalism," essentially the elevation of the musically unique or individual to a status of absolute reality.[16] Such a condition is obviously antithetical to interaction and consequently to meaning.

This is why Adorno, in apparent contrast to Lévi-Strauss, could never think of a musical structure that consisted of identically constituted components as merely some fundamental pattern of organization, common to organisms and objects alike. Like any human construct that lacks a basis for interaction, such a structure would necessarily also represent for Adorno the remains of an organic being that had lost the capacity for meaning. A structure that cannot go beyond mere being to meaning cannot "be" in any human (or humanly understandable) sense of the term. Consequently Adorno ends up by seeing nineteenth-century music as a structure that does not permit the delineation of any distinctively human mode of reality. And once the human center of reality has been removed from a human construct such as music, it reverts to a lifeless configuration that, again, is indistinguishable from the inanimate.

Thus despite his humanistic orientation, and despite the differences of attitude that separate him from Lévi-Strauss, Adorno in effect is forced to admit nineteenth-century music as evidence for a lack of distinction between the animate and the inanimate, evidence that supports Lévi-Strauss's way of viewing the world far more than it does Adorno's own. And of course this blurring of distinction is no synthesis of the animate and the inanimate, but rather a subsumption of the former by the latter which underscores the negation of the human. Adorno's criticism suggests, then, that any reality manifested in the structure of nineteenth-century music excludes human reality as a possibility. And this suggestion in turn argues further, by analogy, for a total divergence of human from objective reality—precisely the condition that above all seems to define Foucault's modern episteme. Here again, Adorno's interpretation of nineteenth-century music brings him in spite of himself to the point of affirming the unconcerned posthumanistic ontology of much French structuralism.

How can Adorno purport to derive such tremendous significance, or indeed any meaning at all, from the notion of a structure that he characterizes in essence by its very loss of a capacity to mean? The meaning of nonmeaning, like the implication of nonimplication, is an issue to which Adorno's criticism of nineteenth-century music frequently leads; and raising it in connection with Adorno's own work shows the critic himself caught in a paradox not unlike those he points to in connection with nineteenth-century music. By applying dialectical methods of analysis to post-Enlightenment cultural objects, such as nineteenth-century music, Adorno forms a conception of what can be called modern reality as an irreparably fragmented totality. Atop this fragmentation he is able to impose some semblance of coherence by viewing the entire phenomenon as, in essence, a single hierarchical structure, in which analogues and analogous patterns can be found at every level. These patterns are clarified, sometimes brilliantly, by analogues within Adorno's own criticism, which by virtue of its extensive reliance on such analogues, seems clearly to form part of the same structure. But like the components of any hierarchical structure, Adorno's critical analogues remain discontinuous. Though they emerge out of a potentially connective principle, dialectics, they cannot by themselves guarantee the ontological or epistemological validity of dialectical connections.

As a result, Adorno's criticism is often considered successful in its ability to stimulate momentary insights, complete in themselves and isolated from the dense processes of dialectical historical reflection that produced them. But the large-scale analogies that stem from Adorno's dialectics, including the fundamental analogies dialectical philosophy requires between itself and reality and between various manifestations of subject and object, as well as his analogies between reality and art considered as a form of cognition, and especially between the musical and the human—all these have been rejected by many musicologists as arbitrary, unproven, unwarranted, and even fictitious. Adorno seems able to evoke his most convincing analogues of music and ontological reality only at the cost of cutting off his work from a belief in the dialectical connections through which he might demonstrate that one or another likeness actually exists. And similarly, Adorno's critical pieces often seem to work less well as explanations of particular musical effects than as verbal equivalents, homologues, or even models of those effects.[17]

Whatever Adorno's motivations may be, then, his musical criticism as it actually stands seems to exemplify the same pervasive structural discontinuities that he discerns in nineteenth-century music. And since even in his own terms a system of discontinuities is more characteristic of structure than of process, it can be argued that through the very persuasiveness of its analogues, Adorno's criticism demonstrates the superiority of structuralist models of objective reality over dialectical explanations thereof—except, of course, that without recourse to *some* connective principle, the accuracy of these analogies must remain unverifiable.

As the leading exponent of negative dialectics, Adorno can hardly fail to understand that his own critical method, as applied to music since the Enlightenment, comes dangerously close to self-negation. In a sense, the cryptic aspect of his entire enterprise—his "deconstruction" of critical language, if one must—constitutes what Adorno himself might call a "utopian" resistance to such self-negation. For in choosing and ordering his words with great care, Adorno, like many a twentieth-century artist, is trying to do more than produce in his own medium a rigorously precise structural analogue to ontological reality (an analogue, not an embodiment, of reality in Adorno's case, since the content of his words still tries to define a reality outside of those words). He is attempting to keep process alive as a means of reaching truth, by forcing his readers to participate actively in the deciphering of his thought. He tries, in other words, to prevent having his ideas tied up into a neat bundle that—like his notion of the self-contained (and sometimes cosmically proportioned) nineteenth-century masterpiece—will seem to assert a structural likeness between human and all other reality. For this is a structural likeness that the post-total condition of such a structure decisively belies.

In the end, however, the resistance of Adorno's criticism to transformation into the rigidity and discontinuity of structure probably fails—just as nineteenth-century music, in Adorno's opinion, fails to preserve a convincing sense of the continuity and development of classical process. For the most part, either his ideas are received as disconnected fragments that can at best be reassembled, structuralist fashion, into disconnected homologous groups; or, in the manner of latter twentieth-century metacriticism, new structures in the form of new critical essays are piled on top of Adorno's own to "explain" the latter. Where the subject is Adorno's attitude toward Beethoven, the metacriticism may approximate the winding up and down of a dialectical synthesis. Where the subject is Adorno's conception of nineteenth-century music, it may be more appropriate to look at a single element in that conception, such as the notion of individuality, from a number of different viewpoints, in order to convey a cumulative sense, by analogy, of its transformation from a force within a process to a component at numerous levels of a large-scale, inanimate, and ultimately meaningless structure.

Individual Necessity

Individuality seems the obvious element on which to build such a multileveled investigation. On the one hand, the individual constitutes the supreme organism for Adorno, the form of life that alone (through a capacity for rational self-determination) allows the species to become distinctively human. On the other hand, the notion of individuality is central to the shift from process to structure that he discerns in nineteenth-century music, since the entities into which the classical process fragments and congeals are self-contained—that is, individual. Thus individuality provides a direct means of "reading off" the fate of human reality from nineteenth-century music—assuming that human individuality is to be associated with musical individuality. That Adorno does in fact make such an association is clear from his ready use of a term such as "the musical subject" in a way that refers equally and generally without distinction, to a composer's (or some other human) persona within a work and to technical and other aspects of the music itself. Indeed, he seems to attach an overriding importance to precisely this analogy between human individuality and musical individuality; the latter has for him a bearing on the survival of humanity that is little less direct than that of the former. For Adorno clearly considers the individualization of music in the nineteenth century inseparable from the elevation of the medium to the normative category of "art." And high art, Adorno's music criticism suggests strongly, constitutes the chief means through which nineteenth-century civilization attempts to preserve the distinctiveness, and hence foster the survival, of humanity as a morally superior species—a species attaching an absolute importance to the integrity of each individual.

It is not difficult to show that from Adorno's standpoint the notion of musical individuality, like the notions of music in a more general sense and of music history, seems to undergo a transformation from process to structure in the transition from classicism to romanticism. In Beethoven's second-period style musical individuality does not manifest itself as any discretely identifiable object (such as a theme)[18] but only as "moments" of an ongoing interaction that defines individuality and general validity simultaneously. It is in this style, where the individual cannot be separated from the general, that Adorno finds the notion of musical individuality most viable; thus not only the French Revolution but also Beethoven's own personality seems to him ineradicably imprinted in the second-period style.[19] In later nineteenth-century music, by contrast, Adorno seems to understand individuality as emerging at any number of levels as a distinct entity. This is not to say that the *same* elements embody individuality in every nineteenth-century work; on the contrary, he seems to consider individual any aspect of music that demonstrates certain attributes of individuality, such as deviation from tradition, resistance to conformity, and above all, freedom of rational choice and action. These aspects vary from work to work. Thus the developmental process in a middle-period Beethoven sonata is conceived of by Adorno as analogous to a challenge by a free individual of predetermined fate (manifested, say, in the use of an inherited form or in the necessity of recapitulating elements of the exposition), whereas individuality in a Mahler symphony is more likely to be found in self-contained moments that resist the traditional push to develop.[20]

Yet again and again Adorno stresses the essential irrelevance of the composer's actual identity to nineteenth-century music after Beethoven. Schubert's personality, even Wagner's personality, he asserts, are trivial considerations that leave no permanent traces in the music of these composers.[21] This incapacity of music to give a lasting and concrete embodiment to the human individuality of even its own creator may today seem an aesthetic truism, but from an older point of view it marks the overt failure of music to accommodate individuality, the failure to establish any connection between the human and the musical that goes beyond the mere probability of an analogy. Despite the crystallization of individuality in nineteenth-century music, Adorno seems to argue, composers were unable to confirm the objective reality of this concept through either of the means that Beethoven was able to use so successfully: the convincing demonstration of individual necessity, that is, of the objective necessity for an individual force to take precisely the form that it does; and the convincing demonstration of the individual's ability to act with real freedom.

In order to establish the reality of the individual, according to Adorno, it is vital to have proof of individual particularity as an objective *necessity*. For Adorno also believes that individuality must be grounded in rationality,[22] and a fundamentally rational principle must be able to demonstrate the objective necessity of its own workings. Hence failure to establish the necessity of connections or events in any individualized configuration is tantamount to admitting that the status of that configuration — and, by analogy, of the individual in general — is essentially accidental or random. This in turn means negating the very concept of individuality as a possibility. Of course, brute force, too, can make a good showing of its own objective necessity, just as that necessity can be demonstrated by empirical as well as by logical means. Adorno would almost certainly contend that Wagner undertook an empirical, as opposed to logical, defense of individual necessity — tried, as it were, to give his own style an even greater aura of inevitability than Beethoven's — on grounds of brute force, that is, by a direct and powerful assault on the listener's emotions.[23] But brute force can never quite dispel the suspicion that its own ultimate basis is arbitrary; and Adorno evidently agrees with Hume that necessity cannot be proven by empirical means. At any rate, Adorno condemns Wagner's defense of individuality as actually inimical to individuality in its very conception.[24]

More complicated is Adorno's apparent negative judgment upon even quasi-logical methods of individual necessity in nineteenth-century music. Brahms's efforts to secure the integrity of the individual composition by organizing it with rigor and consistency likewise failed to provide musical grounds for belief in the objective necessity of any individual configuration. The line of argument here seems circular, at least in part. Starting with the assertion that in Brahms's music "subjectification and objectification are intertwined," Adorno concludes that the very approximation of such a synthesis between subjective and objective principles — one might say of compositional integrity — destroys the claim of Brahms's individualized expression to objective necessity or even to objective validity, because no such synthesis could objectively exist in the world in which Brahms lived.[25] Adorno clearly admires Brahms for taking on the most difficult and scrupulously honest defense of individuality that his times allowed. Nevertheless he asserts that since in Brahms's lifetime any suggestion of wholeness was an illusion, any successful maintenance of individual integrity, no matter how rigorous the means or honest the motivation, was objectively a lie.

As will be seen, this line of argument is introduced by Adorno in part as a commentary on Brahms's freedom of action. But apart from such elements of circular reasoning, Adorno does suggest some evidence to support his judgment of Brahms's failure by pointing to a fundamental conflict between "the fiber and the form of Brahms's music."[26] By individualizing his material to an extraordinary degree — by refining each work with painstaking care, by increasing the integrity of the individual line through counterpoint, by avoiding clichés and rhetorical gestures, and above all, by making virtually every note thematically significant through a technique Adorno terms "total development"[27] — Brahms actually emphasized the arbitrariness of the connections between this material and its largely traditional forms of organization, which was not commensurately individualized. And individual configurations characterized by arbitrary connections cannot be considered necessary.

Adorno implies that Brahms might have come closer to achieving a "binding suprapersonal formulation of the personal"[28] — that is, proof derived from the individual itself of its own necessity — if he had systematized a formal technique that not only reflected completely the individuality of his material, but also allowed this individualized material to show the logical consistency of all its connections. Adorno is clearly thinking of Schoenberg's row. Yet even in Schoenberg's twelve-tone music, according to Adorno, there is no necessary connection between material and form, despite all Schoenberg's efforts to make his individually created system convincingly binding, and even despite all the historical inevitability that both Schoenberg and Adorno would grant this system. The layering and juxtaposing of rows remains arbitrary and hence only clarifies the discontinuity between row material and row technique.[29] Indeed, this discontinuity is now glaring because in Adorno's terms a spatial mode of composition has become an absolute replacement for a temporal one, in that the material no longer in any sense implies the form.

By contrast with logical implication, as embodied in the syllogism, musical implication, as Adorno understands it to occur in the classical style, is a temporal rather than a formal process. This is the case not only because music has traditionally distinguished itself from logic through its concreteness, but also because musical implication makes itself fully known only in terms of an actual and hence subsequent resolution, since it involves a degree of freedom impossible in a syllogism. Thus Adorno would probably agree that classical implication achieves its force not because there is only one possible resolution to a classical premise, but because the style conveys a sense that the resolution actually used has been freely chosen as the "right" one from among many possible and often far more likely, alternatives.[30] Certainly there is no doubt that from Adorno's standpoint the force that classical implication does achieve is the force of necessity — or a remarkably good simulation of it — brought about by temporal means.

It is equally clear that from the same viewpoint, the power to imply a necessary course is initially lost not in Schoenberg's twelve-tone music, but in music at the very onset of romanticism, with the growth of individuality as a discrete and dominant factor in composition. In fact it is possible to view individuality itself as the most immediate cause of this loss. For classical implication establishes its own necessity by creating an impression of freedom through reference to a more general set of alternatives not taken; and this is a type of reference not available once individuality emerges as a distinct and self-absorbed entity. Beethoven's second-period music conveys a sense of individual necessity because its individuality, as Adorno interprets it, inheres in the very process of working out implication, that is, of development. But when individuality feels compelled to concretize itself into distinct, self-contained themes, the authority of its power to generate a course of seamless development out of itself gets lost — so that as in Schubert's finales "*das Beethovensche Muss*" disappears.[31] Once crystallized, the representative of individuality in nineteenth-century music loses its certainty about where to go next in time; a gap or hesitation becomes palpable between an idea and its continuation, at once undermining the grounds for belief in any necessary connection between the two. Moreover the appearance of necessity is rendered still less credible by a series of gaps that appear concomitantly, so to speak, over the entire piece — as though the very dismantling of implication had found its own anti-implicative way of determining structure. Adorno has something of the sort in mind when he claims that lack of binding force becomes an organizing principle in Weber's *Freischütz*.[32] This fragmentation, which Adorno considers endemic in nineteenth-century music from Schubert on, not only shatters the illusion of a single controlling quasi-Beethovenian persona, confidently and continuously developing, turning it into something more like a stammer.[33] It also explodes the image of the individual work as a necessary configuration. It even casts doubt on the relevance of the question "What next?" to musical construction.

Indeed, Adorno encourages his reader to formulate such notions as the simultaneous appearance of successive gaps in nineteenth-century music precisely because he associates the loss of implicative power in this music with a shift from temporal to spatial modes of organization, notwithstanding the status that Beethovenian development through time continued to enjoy as an ideal throughout the century. Time enters into Schubert's music only in essentially atemporal guises, such as a "temporal series of timeless cells."[34] The equal importance (in Adorno's terms, the "exchangeability") of individual themes that are complete in themselves destroys the relationality of history and suggests an ahistorical, synchronic mode of existence; this holds for Schubert's music generally, as it does also for the potpouris that were based upon it and for contemporaneous miniature landscape painting. The same undercutting of temporality through the dissolution of relationships can, by Adorno's account, be found in all romantic music.[35]

Even in the work of Brahms, where Adorno at times points to surviving elements of Beethovenian temporality,[36] the "totality" of the developmental process, the "universal economy" with its elimination of the nonfunctional and hence of genuine contrast, really amounts to a kind of nondevelopmental sameness. The result is a sort of static inventory of equivalent variations or

structural transformations, identically (because in all respects wholly) significant and, as it were, superimposed upon a model.[37] Wagner's music is constantly presented by Adorno in terms of such images as a form "congealed
in space" or a "gigantic container," the contents of which reveal an essentially
nontemporal "coexistence in time."[38] Mahler may seem momentarily to
resuscitate the illusion of necessary development in time. But Mahler's suggestion of "teleological regularity,"[39] as Adorno calls it, must be placed in the
context of the cryptic phrase that he applies especially to Mahler's, though
also to other late romantic, music: "as-if."[40] Mahler's teleology is no longer
a real possibility, any more than Mahler's music, in contrast to Beethoven's
second-period style, can be taken to manifest an insistence by some individual subject that things "must be so and not otherwise."[41] For even Mahler finds it necessary to replace Beethovenian development with a network
of "variants," which bear on each other not in terms of temporal relationships
but in terms of the formal "likenesses and differences" so commonly used in
twentieth-century criticism to describe structures. Rather than developing
form and material simultaneously over time, Mahler gives the individual
components of each work such a markedly distinct character that he is able
to establish among them and their variants a sense of aggregate structure existing out of time at some purely formal level.[42] Where time is evoked in
Mahler's music, according to Adorno, it is evoked negatively, through atemporal resistance to time or through the "temporal layering of its individual
fields."[43] And when Schoenberg makes final the end of implication, he is only
treating time at the level of music history in the way Mahler treats it at the
level of the individual composition: he is negating time by carrying out an
early implication of the breakdown of implication.[44]

Adorno sees time at every level of nineteenth-century music as given over
to an atemporal condition of structure where implication, and indeed all
devices for demonstrating the necessity of a particular self-realization, becomes impossible. As a result, grounds for belief in the necessity of any actual
individual are undermined in nineteenth-century music, for in this music individual necessity is revealed as not necessarily anything more — and, indeed,
in all likelihood, nothing more — than a subjective illusion. And in failing to
demonstrate its own necessity in music, Adorno would almost certainly add,
human individuality puts its own objective reality in grave doubt.

Individual Freedom

In view of this alleged futility of trying to prove individual necessity, it may
seem odd that Adorno praises Wagner for being the first composer who

grasps fully the need to seek universally binding principles (notably, necessity) in the particular or individual.[45] What Adorno in fact admires is Wagner's recognition of the artistic (which for Adorno is indistinguishable from the moral) "need" to resist the limitations of his own artistic situation. Predicated as they are on a theory of art as social or moral criticism, Adorno's musical writings naturally show high regard for gestures of resistance to externally imposed or current norms, even though at times he seems to identify such gestures, as in the case of what he calls Wagner's critique of myth, through a process of circular reasoning.[46]

Adorno argues that no composers fought harder to establish individual necessity in music than Wagner and Brahms. Both composers went farther than any before in treating individuality as a wholly binding principle; this they did by devising their own individual rules of composition and making these rules quite rigorous. Adorno concedes both men a measure of greatness for giving the self-made rule a considerable semblance of authority on a social scale.[47] This is not to deny that he has incomparably less sympathy for the entire Wagnerian ideology than for Brahms's enterprise (although it is Wagner whom he finds the irresistible object of study). In terms of their effect, however, the differences of motivation between the two composers can have no more significance for Adorno than similar differences between Adorno and Lévi-Strauss are likely to have for some future scholar. Both Wagner and Brahms, in Adorno's judgment, were doomed to fail in the defense of individual necessity, just as neither really had a choice about the way to approach the genre or medium in which he worked.[48] What Wagner really grasped in the "need" to seek the necessary in the individual was not a requisite means of establishing the necessity of the individual, but only the absence of any alternative source of necessity for the serious German opera composer. His free acknowledgment of this need not only forced him into a futile quest but also made evident his own lack of freedom.

As we have seen, Adorno's negative dialectic suggests that nonimplication becomes the implication of nineteenth-century music and that individual necessity is rendered undemonstrable by individualization. In a similar way, he appears to find evidence in this music that individuality uses its own most definitive characteristic, freedom, to effect the destruction of individual freedom. It is as though individuality, having liberated itself through the process of Beethovenian conflict from the absolute authority of externally imposed norms, finds its own survival gravely imperiled without such absolutes and is forced to look for their replacement. But is Adorno sees it, the way back to older sources of authority, especially the rational norms of the Enlightenment, is barred. Even so great a composer as Brahms cannot reunite classical forms with the individual material of the nineteenth century. Individuality has no choice but to transform itself into a new absolute principle, removed from relationships to anything general, that is, to anything truly "other" than itself, and this brings about the condition that Adorno labels nominalism.

But absolutism of any kind, even absolute individuality, is antithetical to individual freedom. This is true, from Adorno's point of view, whether the elevation of individuality is conceived as coming about through a conferral of absolute status on each musical component, which would produce un-bridgeable discontinuity, or through the rendering absolute of one single musical element or technique, which would minimize differences to the point of insignificance. (Different as they may seem, discontinuity and insignificant difference — the two characteristics that Adorno in effect associates with in-animate objects — tend to converge in their inability to generate interaction, and hence in their tendency to rigidify into structures, as we have seen.) Thus on the one hand Adorno can liken Wagner to Hitler in the effort by each to make his own individuality absolute and binding on every element in his domain — for Wagner, the music drama.[49] And on the other, he can trace the incompatibility between freedom and total thematic consistency that he finds in Schoenberg's twelve-tone music back to Brahms's "universal economy." Individual freedom in nineteenth-century music entails the loss of individual freedom, not only in the sense that the individualistic composer's course of action is limited, but also in the broader sense that musical individuality of every kind is forced to submit to a self-negating absolutism.

Probably the most persuasive sign for Adorno that individual freedom has negated itself in nineteenth-century music is the loss he finds in that music of a particularly vivid manifestation of process, the sense of *progress*. Not sur-prisingly, this loss is similar to the loss of implication that cost nineteenth-century music its guarantee of individual necessity, for the notions of musical progress and musical implication have much in common, at least from Adorno's standpoint. Both processes must occur in time because both require genuine interaction. And both use this interaction in time to define freedom. Thus progress, like implication, is clearly a process that can be perceived only in terms of relationships, in this case between the supposedly progressing element — and progress interests Adorno only insofar as it benefits the individual — and elements of an environment "other" than itself. And pro-gress, too, is to be intimately associated with the notion of freedom, because it constitutes the course that will be chosen by any rational being capable of self-determination (which is essentially Adorno's definition of an individual). So inseparable, indeed, are these two notions for Adorno that he thinks any music that fails to project a sense of progress shows itself incapable of in-dividual self-determination or freedom at any level.

In Beethoven's second-period style, where it is definitively embodied for Adorno, progress might be imagined as the process through which the musically subjective or individual resolves a conflict inherent in its relation to the outside world or "other," a conflict involving differences between timelessness and change. One thinks, for example, of the conflict between the timelessness associated with the subjective experience of individual identity and the constant change of external circumstance; or, at another level, between individual transience and cosmic eternity. Beethoven succeeds, at least momentarily, in establishing the timelessness of individual identity precisely through this continuous insistence on relationships or interaction, which produces a large-scale progress through time toward some self-determined goal.[50] In effect, Adorno indicates, the element of individuality in Beethoven's second-period style resolves the tension between timelessness and change not by denying or undercutting the contradiction between them, which the living individual actually experiences, but by fusing the two principles together within itself through an emphatic affirmation of the temporality that defines life. Beethovenian individuality demonstrates its timeless substantiality (and thereby defeats the limitations of time) by centering attention upon its own temporal nature.

In this way Beethoven manages (somewhat like Hegel) to suggest that the most timeless reality is temporal change, and hence that the free individual defines reality through its progress toward the full development of its capacities. He remakes the world, so to speak, through the eyes of the self-developing individual or persona. Through the interaction of timelessness and change, then, Beethoven's music, and by implication (not analogy) every individual life, has access to an objectively valid meaning through the individual capacity for self-realization. And the clarity with which Beethoven maintains the sense of relationship between a progressing individual and a large-scale musical whole reinforces the idea that the relationship between the individual and its universe is at bottom intelligible, that is, rational.

In nineteenth-century music, by contrast, neither the individual freedom implicit in Beethovenian progress nor the universal rationality associated with it seems capable of being sustained. For already by Schubert's time, the sense of progress, like the process of implication, has given way to essentially nonprogressive (i.e., nontemporal) modes of movement, such as circularity, an image evoked with particular frequency in connection with the music and texts of Schubert and Wagner.[51] As early as Schubert, the impression given by the Beethovenian subject of "going somewhere" has been replaced by a situation in which the individual element, stripped of subjective dynamism and cut off within itself, comes to be repeated without significant change and, as it were, atemporally — a phenomenon for which Adorno uses Nietzsche's phrase "the recurrence of the same."[52]

Adorno seems to consider invariant return the archetypal sort of recurrence in all nineteenth-century music after Beethoven. Even where this music does admit changes in recurring material, or where the thematic material is potentially developmental — Adorno cites Schumann and Wagner in this connection — the effect is not one of progressive development but rather of a nonprogressive shifting about of the same idea, variations of which do not prove significant.[53] The latter seems to hold true even in the account of Mahler's music, where Adorno actually takes pains to assert the opposite; for he himself admits that the sense of progress between Mahler's variants — a temporal sense that should in Adorno's terms make the differences between these variants significant — turns out to be only part of a "ghost-pull," a negative image of a progressive development that can no longer occur.[54] Moreover, Adorno himself associates Mahler's variant technique with the essentially unchanging recurrences of pretemporal oral traditions.[55] Repetitions of sameness, with their insignificant variances, seem to have an analogue in the nontemporal or paradigmatic dimension of the structuralist model, in which elements are grouped together not by virtue of any actual contiguity that could define time, but rather as abstractly available equivalents for a single element that exists out of time.

A particularly characteristic example of Adorno's view of recurrence in nineteenth-century music is furnished by his suggestion that the continuous rise to a climax characteristic of the classical sonata yields in Wagner's music to the discontinuous adjacency of numerous climaxes — to what could be called the continual repetition of climax not as a process but as a systematized technique. Adorno has especially in mind here Wagner's sequential repetition of small motives at successively higher pitches (as at the opening of the *Tristan* prelude), where rhetorical exaggeration has replaced genuinely dynamic growth.[56] Such repetition could go on indefinitely since it involves still another sort of romantic circularity that prevents the music from going anywhere — alternation, in this instance the alternation of intensification and abatement. In a sense, such repetition *must* go on indefinitely, since it is central to Adorno's notion of circularity (in this context he calls pointed attention to *The Ring* as a title) that it admits of no way out or resolution.[57]

Thus Schubert's texts, according to Adorno, turn cyclically to the topic of death — a "way out" only in a nontemporal sense that exposes progress as futile[58] (and one might add that these texts do not turn to life-affirming resolutions, such as the Countess's forgiveness of the Count or Leonora's rescue of Florestan). As for Wagner, his mature texts try to come to terms with the historical transience of the human not by direct Beethovenian confrontation but by a retreat into what Adorno, sounding very much like Lévi-Strauss, calls the "permanent catastrophe" of myth.[59] Schubert's instrumental finales, in sharp contrast to Beethoven's, can in their most effective interactions with time provide only a joyously sensuous experience of the stasis that for Adorno has replaced the possibility of resolution.[60] And Wagner's musical attempts to regain some rational sense of time, as Adorno understands them, cannot get beyond a technique such as that of the leitmotiv, which he considers reiterative rather than developmental. In essence, an isolated and unchanging recurrence of sameness contributes to a large-scale sense of circular futility.[61] From the rational freedom of the Beethovenian subject with its self-engendered linear progress, the individual in nineteenth-century music has become entrapped in the unbreakable circle of a prerational, and hence irrational, fate.

In the music that followed Beethoven, by Adorno's account, individuality seems altogether incapable of sustaining progress because it is too weak to exercise its freedom by determining its own course. One might even go farther and say that from this view, individuality in nineteenth-century music has such a fragile identity that it cannot risk movement or change of any kind; even at the cost of its own freedom, it elects what seems to be a safer immobility. In any case, Adorno certainly considers stasis, of which circularity is but one manifestation, to be a fundamental condition of nineteenth-century music. At times he seems to mean this almost literally. Certain finales of Schubert and symphonies of Mahler renounce all semblance of the dynamic relationships that define the forward movement of time and offer an experience close to pure duration. In such instances, it seems, time as a relational construct, a construct of reason, disappears from music to be replaced by a musical tendency, palpable in Schubert's "heavenly lengths," or perhaps in Wagner's evocation of the cosmos (as at the opening of *Rheingold*), to fill up or approximate almost physically some raw, brute dimension — a noumenal dimension that exists outside of human reason and, like the experience of duration associated with it, is for Adorno not temporal at all, but spatial.[62]

More common, however, in Adorno's conception of nineteenth-century music is a less literal but similar condition of stasis that emerges from the making absolute of an individual element or elements at the expense of relationships. What is lost, to be more specific, is functional differentiation. Adorno's account suggests a number of ways in which this loss and its corollary stasis might occur. The loss may consist, for example, in a kind of entropy, arising from the dominance of invariant, or only slightly varied, materials or techniques.[63] But such a loss could also result from a state of distinction among the various individual components so thoroughgoing that the continuous (and thus progressive) sense of time within a work becomes fragmented into a series of discontinuous moments, experienced as essentially immobile and spatial.[64] For if, in such a case, the components of a composition differed wholly from each other, then the common bonds necessary to the very definition of function would disappear. Functional differentiation and its associated propulsive quality, after all, are as irreconcilable with total difference as with total sameness.[65] In the sense that its absence of interaction precludes "significant" differences, total differentiation (a form of total individualization) could be said to converge with total sameness.

But if the process of musical distinction were carried to a point of high refinement (as, say, in Adorno's conception of Mahler's "variants"), rather than being presented as bold or coarse, it might result in differences that were below the threshold of perception. So in this way, too, difference could converge on sameness, or, to use Adorno's own words, "highly differentiated means . . . [could] come to resemble each other and become indistinguishable."[66] For on the one hand such highly individualized entities might each be characterized by so much surface detail that the perceiver could for the most part retain only the basic similarity between them. This might be true of certain complex instrumental sonorities, symmetricalized scales, or chordal combinations; certainly Adorno has something of the sort in mind when he refers to the equalization of consonance and dissonance in Wagner's music, and to the elevation of dissonance by Wagner to a position of qualitative supremacy.[67] Such might also be the case where a theme is transformed subtly into variants. Thus variance can be thought of as a technique exemplifying either minimum or maximum differentiation.

On the other hand, individual entities might be reduced to discontinuous moments or points with only slight differences, yet with too few characteristics to be clearly identified in themselves, as in the case of highly differentiated dynamic markings. In such cases the discontinuities between points, though never bridged, would be perceived as part of a collective tendency by such points to approximate the condition of a static, quasi-spatial continuum—very much the sort of continuum that Lévi-Strauss tries to construct out of self-contained structural units.[68] Such are the terms in which Adorno describes Wagner's sequences, his chromaticism, and in essence— despite references to feats of reforging and resynthesis—his orchestration, which Adorno himself compares with the pointillism of French Impressionist painting; far from contributing to any sense of movement forward, the more such differences are refined, the more they approach what Leonard Meyer has called the state of "fluctuating stasis."[69]

In short, once functional differences give way to individual identity (or formal differences) as the fundamental organizing principle of music, as

Adorno believes happens in the nineteenth century, the result is stasis. Whether the variances among musical elements are nonexistent, small, or considerable, the result is an absence of significant change or progress and hence an absence of freedom. The differences that one perceives in nineteenth-century music, together with the promise they hold out of providing a basis for rational distinction and interpretation, turn out to constitute, in something like the manner of what Adorno calls Schubert's "changes of mood,"[70] an illusory facade on the surface of a vast, essentially irrational structure of invariance. And because of its invariance and its apparent imperviousness to accident, this structure seems far more convincingly real than events on its surface. Adorno's criticism, moreover, suggests not only the image of an invariant structure but also a concomitant anti-image: an image of individual entities and differences existing on a surface, which precisely by virtue of their particularity—their uniqueness, their momentary definition, the very quality of their existence—are precluded from belonging to the structure underlying them. Hence the individualized surface diverges from its structure and becomes its antithesis. To the extent that the invariant structure is real, its surface is unreal.

This could explain why nineteenth-century music, as it is presented in Adorno's critical writings, seems so pervasively deceptive. This is the repertory that in terms of style appears to be the musical vindication of individuality. Instead, Adorno indicates, it exposes individuality in any meaningful sense—individual necessity, freedom, power, and even significance—as a principle that cannot be distinguished, ontologically, from an illusion. This appears to be music generated by notions of historical progress. Instead, it constitutes a static structure. And very interestingly, although the musical repertory that Adorno discusses is quintessentially a German art, it exhibits characteristics that are most readily associated with French and Russian music from Berlioz on—the absence of progress, the absence of a single controlling persona, invariant repetition, and preoccupation with surface rearrangements or "transformations."[71]

The analogy between nineteenth-century music, so interpreted, and all things human seems obvious. From Schiller's classical restatement of the ancient conviction that the individual is accidental and hence unreal, the nineteenth century had appeared to shift radically, redefining the real precisely in terms of the particular.[72] But the actual message of nineteenth-century culture, one can infer from Adorno's criticism, had not changed significantly after all from ancient conceptions of an immutable reality. For in music the particular or individual, lacking a guarantee of both the necessity and the freedom needed to sustain it—a guarantee it would enjoy in a rational world—remains accidental: that is, not necessary and immutable, as Beethoven for one moment was able to suggest, but only actual. And even nineteenth-century music cannot find a way of equating the accidental rather than the necessary and immutable with reality. It is through music after Beethoven that all things actual, including all things human—individuality, history, time, and above all, life—are revealed, at least by analogy, as surface phenomena with no more objective reality than the natural cycles of earth have when viewed from a distant star, than conflicting choices (such as those of Wagner and of Brahms) in one cultural system have when viewed from another, or than stages of a single life have when viewed from its end.

Time, nineteenth-century music indicates to Adorno, and hence all that must exist in time, is an illusion. In the end all the differences that at one moment seem to be time-defining changes will be perceived in terms of a single static spatial structure. In the same way, the Beethovenian process is assimilated into a single, nontemporal, and virtually corporeal conception of the Beethovenian "work," and, later, succession becomes indistinguishable from simultaneity in the concrete denseness of Schoenberg's twelve-tone system. Hence time, with its associated concepts of development and change, is to be understood as dissolving into space, with its formal samenesses and differences; historical "anticipations," such as Adorno not infrequently notes in nineteenth-century music itself, must in the long run be viewed not as indications of continuing progress but as miniature versions of general formal types.[73] Music itself, defined through Beethoven's second-period style as the archetypal temporal art (and thus, perhaps, given the temporality of all things human, the archetype of all art)—music seems to sense, as it were, the unreality of the temporal and to set about transforming its temporality into what it hopes will be an immutable condition of stasis. It is as if this music, acting by analogy for the human individual, tried to escape the unreality inherent in its own transience by becoming nontemporal. But music can no more guarantee its own reality by becoming atemporal than the individual can do so by dying. All it can do is pass from the ontologically unreal (temporality) to the humanly unreal (atemporality). The two kinds of reality cannot be reconciled; looked at from the point of view either of humanity or of ontology, nineteenth-century music suggests that the real is the unreal.

Thus whereas Beethoven sets forth change as the essence of reality, nineteenth-century music reveals this essence as invariance. Whereas Beethoven presents invariant authority as a human construct that the free individual can overturn, nineteenth-century music reintroduces invariance as a characteristic of reality existing at a level too deep for the individual to reach. And whereas Beethoven constructs a temporal and rational universe to accommodate the free individual, nineteenth-century music constructs (or, more accurately, defines in spite of itself) an inanimate and irrational universe that the impotent individual can enter not by virtue of any self-determination but only passively, through the invariance of its death. Mahler's music suggests to Adorno the notion that "every life proceeds obliquely to its own premises."[74] Nineteenth-century music in general suggests that what all human life proceeds to is a static manifestation of its own unreality.

Metaphysical Meaning

Interpreting nineteenth-century music as itself an interpretation of reality, one that takes the form of a structural homologue to reality, Adorno discerns in this music the message that humanity has not progressed beyond its historical beginnings. In this music individuality is presented as no more viable a force than it has been in most of Western civilization. From this exposure of individuality as an apparently illusory force, numerous corollaries might be drawn, all with a similarly negative import for humanity. But Adorno himself seems especially concerned, almost obsessed, with a particular corollary — one that seems to provide a context for understanding the collapse of individuality (and thus of the human concept) as real possibilities. It is a message that concerns the very possibility of messages. More precisely, it concerns the capacity of art to embody grounds for meaning, through which individuality, and thereby humanity in general, can make sense of its place in the world.

Individuality in nineteenth-century music, Adorno would say, defined itself into a state of discreteness or apparent autonomy. But in contrast to Beethoven's music, where individual autonomy seemed to have a general basis of validity, autonomy in the music of the subsequent period amounted to nothing more than a condition in which the individual demonstrated its lack of self-sufficiency. Much as Mahler seemed to discern that artistic form in itself was not ontologically privileged, that is, that it embodied no reality,[75] Adorno himself interprets individual autonomy in nineteenth-century music as a reduction of the individual to a state of self-contained isolation from which it could not form any substantive relation with the world outside itself.

But given the inseparability, in Adorno's philosophy, of relationships and meaning, this lack of secure outward connections in the individual has tremendous significance. Above all it seems to mean that nineteenth-century art music, in contrast to all preceding Western music, including in the end even the more persuasively autonomous classical style,[76] carries with it no authoritative metaphysical content. That is, it carries no convincing revelation of meaning in the universe outside of music, nor any assurance that such meaning exists. Rather than constituting some transparent modes of access to a world of meaning beyond subjective human experience, nineteenth-century music seems merely to crystallize Western doubts about the correspondence, or the necessity of any correspondence, between human images of reality and any reality beyond those images.

This condition of doubt, of course, did not end with German romantic music, nor did the latter establish any definitive aesthetic response to it. Indeed, Adorno's own criticism suggests that the prevailing modern aesthetic response to such doubts was spearheaded toward the end of the century outside of Germany. This was done particularly by Debussy and other French artists, in what Adorno considers a postindividual artistic tradition, a tradition that has stopped seeking grounds on which to make sense of the experience of individuality. From Adorno's standpoint, "French music . . . renounced all metaphysics — even the metaphysics of pessimism."[77] The rationale for such a renunciation seems evident enough. If no connection can be proven between art and metaphysical reality, then art can maintain its truth only by ceasing to concern itself with metaphysical reality and by restricting its attention to the posing and solving of technical problems.[78] In effect this art has rejected the assumption of analogues between itself and the human individual on the one hand, and between itself and metaphysical reality on the other.

Now, remembering Adorno's emphatic opposition to metaphysics in philosophy,[79] it might be supposed that he would approve of music that explicitly denies all interest in metaphysics. Because it allows no place for a self-determining, rational humanity, metaphysics is rejected by Adorno in favor of history as the ground of all philosophical investigation. Yet precisely the anguished humanism that leads Adorno to treat history as ontological reality prevents him from renouncing all thought of a metaphysical reality, and therewith, all possibility of hope in an ultimate ground of rationality. In his very rejection of metaphysics, one could say, Adorno retains an unmistakably metaphysical thrust.

Indeed, beginning with Adorno's characterization of the *Missa Solemnis* as "balanced on a point of indifference which approaches nothing,"[80] there is such an obvious analogy between the constant references in Adorno's music criticism to the nonbeing of God and the almost palpable metaphysical longing of nineteenth-century German music, that it seems simplistic to accuse Adorno, as some do, of insensitivity to religious matters.[81] Far more adequate to the ambiguous character of Adorno's outspoken atheism and rejection of metaphysics would be some formulation such as Karl Löwith's attribution of the idealistic basis of Karl Marx's materialism to "the old Jewish messianism and prophetism . . . and Jewish insistence on absolute righteousness."[82]

To Adorno, in short, the humanistic impulse behind the desire to retain metaphysics, if only an entirely negative metaphysics, is greatly preferable to a disregard of the entire category. Consequently, his reaction to the stance taken by music that turns it back altogether on metaphysics is distinctly negative. On one level, he suggests, by reducing itself to "mere art," music limits its own significance to a triviality unthinkable in any great musical tradition of the past. And beyond that, such music has a way of turning into falsehood, the falsehood of nonhuman art. For it not only refuses to make the individual subject its center, and dismisses individuality, which is for Adorno the fundamental category of the human; what is worse, it divorces itself explicitly even from the hope of any metaphysical basis for defining the "human" as a morally distinguished species, or for claiming art as a moral force in that it contributes to such a definition. This means that even where the renunciation of metaphysics reflects an honest acknowledgment of the individual artist's limitations — and indeed, Adorno himself in one instance praises this renunciation as "a corrective against the German [Wagnerian?] art religion"[83] — such music constitutes a lie so long as it holds itself out as art. For it denies the very purpose for which the notion of art, as Adorno conceives it, came into being — the purpose of defining the human as a morally superior species.

To follow Adorno's criticism one step further: nonmetaphysical music also falls easily into the double lie of using humanistic conventions to resuscitate metaphysics surreptitiously in a nonhumanistic form. Thus he derides the notion that "through the fastidious consistency of its style, aesthetic structure is supposed to conjure up [*beschwören*] a metaphysical meaning, the substance of which is lacking in the demystified [*entzauberten*] world."[84] He would doubtless have the same reaction to structuralist attempts at reinvesting self-contained, impersonal musical structures (or for that matter linguistic structures) with universal significance, as for example in Jean-Jacques Nattiez's "automatic documentary" of Debussy's *Syrinx*.[85]

But Adorno's objections to nonmetaphysical art go even further. It seems clear that from his vantage point the "nonhuman" slips all too readily into the "antihuman." Adorno has some such idea in mind when he characterizes the late nineteenth-century French rejection of metaphysics as a "preform" for the release of "barbarism" in the music of another important non-German composer, Stravinsky. By Adorno's account Stravinsky liquidates the individual, and thus humanity itself, by reducing music to a pure, "objective," material phenomenon existing at an irrational level beneath that of individual meaning.[86] What Adorno seems to argue here is that reference to the notion of metaphysical meaning cannot be abandoned in music without at bottom abandoning rational meaning as well.

In the context of Adorno's own unyielding humanism, such a thesis makes sense. For to him, the idea of metaphysics as well as the principle of rationality are both primarily concepts for defining the human—the latter through its close connection with the sustenance of free individuality, the former through its ability to suggest at least the glimmer of an ultimate ground of reality for rationality, and thereby also for meaning. Hence for Adorno, reference to both metaphysical and rational meaning is necessarily present in any genuinely human art.

This is not to deny that from Adorno's perspective, art can be fully *humane* only in relation to the concreteness of history. It would contradict everything Adorno stands for if he were to countenance justifying inhumane art through reference to the mysteries of an unknowable and very possibly irrational or nonexistent metaphysical reality. In addition, however, art would also have to acknowledge in some way the humane impulse in the desire for a meaningful connection between the individual and the cosmos, and thus for a basis in reality for rationality in history. To do otherwise would be to abandon all hope that either rationality or meaning has any status in reality, thereby setting up the art in question for delivery over to irrationalism, which for Adorno means not only nonhumanism but, far worse, explicit antihumanism as well.

Of course, nonmetaphysical art might well claim to avoid this bind precisely by sustaining rational meaning on a nonhumanistic basis. For Adorno, however, rationality is no less human a construct than metaphysics. Consequently the assertion of a nonhuman rationality in music amounts to nothing more than a false front of the antirationalist or irrationalist position already signaled in the denial of metaphysics.

There can be no question that in taking such a line of argument, Adorno is refusing to accept nonmetaphysical music on its own terms. Instead he insists that all music, even music that "renounces of its own accord any claim to meaning,"[87] will continue nevertheless to project some basis for interpretation that can be called meaning. He goes so far as to assert that "all modern music constitutes itself as a vehicle for meaning," and that the renunciation of meaning may itself constitute the objective meaning of certain music.[88] In the context of nonmetaphysical music, Adorno no doubt speaks primarily of unwitting levels of cultural significance such as might be uncovered through hermeneutical exegesis. But it is also possible, within the general framework of Adorno's criticism, to imagine even in nonmetaphysical music a certain residual authority as art which allows this art to convey the sense of interpreting reality for humans. To the extent that this authority is retained, non-metaphysical music, by turning away from the human condition, would depict ultimate reality as an antihuman, meaningless, irrational state of being to which the music itself contributes. Understood thus, nonmetaphysical music would continue to suggest, albeit in wholly negative terms and in spite of itself, an identity traditionally assumed in music between the human perception of reality and the structure of reality itself.

Adorno is never more German than in this tendency to find a metaphysical significance even in the nonmetaphysical music of non-German countries. The German humanist tradition from which Adorno's musical writings stem is incapable of surrendering either of two related things: the search for a metaphysical meaning that would establish the significance of individuality, and the notion of some necessary connection, beyond mere analogy, between human constructs and a transcendent reality that would guarantee the validity of such a metaphysical meaning—even if this connection must be understood to join nothing more than parallel negative entities. "It was by metaphysics that German music became great music," Adorno comments, even though "as a carrier of metaphysics it is a bit of usurpation like metaphysics itself"; and he adds that it was necessary for "the great music of that German style which makes for unity from Beethoven down to the Schoenberg exiled by Hitler" to try to constitute itself as "a warrant of transcendence," even if "ideology" or falseness was inherent in this source of greatness.[89] Thus, for example, at the very moment when doubt about access to metaphysical meaning through the individuality of art was making itself felt in German culture, German music was concerning itself intensely with such meaning, if only to question its reality. "*Lebt kein Gott?*" is for Adorno the central question of an early nineteenth-century work such as *Der Freischütz*; Wagner's music drama seems to embody metaphysical despair; and still later, Adorno says in essence, consideration and rejection of the ontological proof of God come to constitute the basic content of Mahler's work.[90] If only in a negative sense, nineteenth-century German music could not abandon metaphysics any more than Adorno himself could resist attributing the problems of post-Beethovenian composition to a concomitant metaphysical problem (which in the end, he concludes in Hegelian fashion, art is not adequate to solve)[91] rather than simply to technical difficulties.

Of course, precisely by virtue of the negative sense in which he relates nineteenth-century German music to metaphysics, Adorno suggests that this music undermined not only the concept of individual necessity but also whatever belief remained in the metaphysical foundation for any concept of necessity at all. Whereas a medieval theorist could conceive of an ontological identity between musical and divine law so close and so binding that a forbidden interval could be referred to as "the devil in music" or a "deadly sin," by the early nineteenth century the very notion of external authority in music had broken down under the revolutionary force with which it had been challenged in Beethoven's second-period style. And once the concept of external, objectively existing grounds for the necessity of any choice had been challenged, as perhaps symbolically in Beethoven's twilight *"Muss es sein?,"* these grounds could not be convincingly reconstructed, Beethoven's affirmative replies notwithstanding. It is at such a moment in history that the concept of necessity begins to seem more a construct of reason, as it does to Adorno, or a linguistic construct, than a metaphysical reality. But if necessity itself cannot be shown to be demonstrably necessary, then precisely by virtue of its definition through linguistic usage it can be thought of as converging on the accidental or random and ceasing in reality to exist. If the necessary is not necessary, linguistic usage might ask, then is it not actually impossible?

In an analogous way, we can see how the inability of nineteenth-century music to reestablish a viable musical definition of necessity could be taken to correspond (though, of course, not necessarily!) to the actual nonexistence of such a principle. According to this line of thought, the apparent exercise of individual freedom in nineteenth-century music, as for example in matters of harmony or form, actually brought with it a sense that no restriction in music was inviolable, that no genuine taboos remained in music, because there was no objectively existing authority to bind the individual through its principle of necessity. Commonly associated with art of the twentieth century, this idea was in fact present throughout the nineteenth too.

And yet the individual, as analyzed by Adorno, scarcely exercises any real freedom of choice about what happens to it in nineteenth-century music. On the contrary, the German music of this period presents the individual not as free but as fundamentally insufficient, lacking the possibility of choice—in a word, as heteronomous, determined by something outside of itself. What differentiates this "something" from its counterpart in earlier, less individualized or even preindividual music is the sense it conveys of constituting not a presence but an absence. Thus nineteenth-century music suggests by analogy that the individual is governed not by a God or by any other potentially reasonable principle, such as humanity might invent for itself, but rather by an absence of rationality that neither binds the individual in any active sense nor permits it to be free. The individual is put forward as preordained, so to speak, by a blind, indeed a nonexistent, necessity. This means, once again, that the underlying structure of reality suggested in nineteenth-century German music is nothingness, the absence of all that would make the human real. And from Adorno's standpoint, this nothingness emerges not as morally indifferent but as actively evil. For although the distinction between rationality and irrationality seems to disappear at such a level of reality, the absence of rationality continues to exist there, providing grounds for irrationalism; and, again, irrationalism, from Adorno's viewpoint, is always, and above all, inhuman.

Nowhere does Adorno suggest more effectively, though often obliquely, that nineteenth-century German music conveyed just such a sense of metaphysical nothingness than in his allusions to the use of individual expression in this music to evoke an irrational underside to everyday phenomena — the very phenomena that through their familiarity should seem the most uncomplicated and benign of realities. The image is already present in Adorno's discussion of early nineteenth-century German music, not only where one might expect it, say in connection with the forest realm of *Der Freischütz*, but also in the somewhat cryptic notion of Schubert's ability to project in a single instant the geographical nearness and yet the unbridgeable and terrifying remoteness between the worlds of Austrian and Hungarian dialect.[92] The same theme reappears with particular frequency in Adorno's analysis of Mahler's music, as for example in his characterization of bare tonal chords and banal gestures in Mahler's symphonies as Kafkaesque.[93] It is Adorno's contention that Mahler deliberately "breaks" musical language, causing a gap between musical appearance and reality,[94] or, one might say, a lack of identity between the musical intention (*signifiant*) and the musical message (*signifié*). Mahler's purpose here, it would seem, is to force a duality between the musically expressive individual and the world to which this individual refers — thereby preventing the process of musical signification from collapsing into a self-enclosed (nominalistic) tautology; thereby reinforcing, at least by analogy, the sense of a substantial reality outside of humanity; and thereby preserving a condition favorable to the process of correspondence, and hence to the establishment of grounds for meaning, between people and their universe. The same purpose, one can infer, is at work in Mahler's insistence — despite Adorno's view that the romantic symphony is historically untenable — on retaining not only the individual voice associated with this genre but also its cosmic proportions. This insistence is far more attractive to Adorno than is the flight, as he sees it, of Brahms as well as Debussy into the merely private sphere of the intimate.[95]

    But in trying to avoid the tautology and solipsism inherent in romantic musical "autonomy," what Mahler achieves is not a classical correspondence between his *signifiant* and his *signifié*, but rather a lack of this correspondence so unmistakable that for the individual, who requires a rational connection to the universe, it amounts to a frightening divergence between the two. This is a divergence that Mahler probably understood and anticipated but that he did not want and, in the end, could not control. Thus, by Adorno's own account, Mahler's efforts to preserve the metaphysical frame of reference necessary for a humanistic music fail. He becomes the first composer not only to despair in his music of finding metaphysical meaning but actually to acknowledge therein the impossibility of doing so.[96] And the force of this acknowledgment is felt precisely because Mahler's music is able to project with such clarity its own anguished need to establish a reality that goes beyond mere physical being.[97] But despite this projection, Mahler's works, scarcely less than Schoenberg's, are no longer wholes but structures, demonstrating the impossibility of guaranteeing any sort of meaning through the arrangement of sounds. (In contrast, Beethoven seemed able to construct models of the universe that corroborated Hegel's aphorism "the whole is the true" in metaphysical as well as in musical terms.) Indeed, like the German music that preceded it, and for that matter like the French music that pointed into the twentieth century, Mahler's music remains stubbornly enclosed in the human experience of the real, unable to break through the latter into another, more enduring level of reality, unable to provide a model of a transcendent reality that does not negate humanity. Mahler's music sends up an agonized question to the universe, in a way that French music generally chooses not to and probably cannot. But no more than French music is it capable of transcending the known world (the *Lebenswelt*) in which the act of the individual takes place.

Of course, the presence—even the impotent or negative presence—of the individual questioner makes a considerable difference to Adorno in his own comparative evaluations of the German musical critique of metaphysics and of nonmetaphysical French music. It is of no small importance that in the face of overwhelming grounds for nihilism, a composer such as Mahler, rather than turning his back on metaphysics, could manage to conjure up the ghost of a necessary correspondence between music and metaphysical reality, that is, of a valid metaphysical meaning—if only to confirm the impossibility of finding such meaning, or to suggest that no grounds for such meaning exist. But like other such differences between what could be called French and German modes of thought, this is a difference not of results but of intentions, real only to the extent that any aspect of the fragile notion "human" is real. Adorno's own exegesis of nineteenth-century music demonstrates that such differences are ultimately to be read as insignificant. Thus even in Adorno's terms it can be doubted that nineteenth-century German music provided any real alternative to the nonhumanistic models of art that followed it.

Adorno and Structuralism

In many respects, Adorno is clearly aware of the extent to which the nineteenth-century German musical tradition, of which his own criticism forms a part, converges on modern French thought. It is Adorno who constantly calls attention to the presentation of reality as irrational, both in German music after the Enlightenment and in more modern French and Russian music. It is Adorno who calls attention to the symmetry between the "art-religion" of the nineteenth-century Germans and the "style-worship" of more modern French music.[98] It is Adorno who encourages the inference of a parallelism between the French assumption of no meaning and the German insistence on "no meaning."

Still, on the basis of Adorno's criticism of nineteenth-century music, one may be permitted to wonder whether Adorno himself gauged the full extent to which his own work confirmed the structuralist view of reality. In spite of his critical sophistication, Adorno probably shared some of the secret hope that he attributed to such German predecessors as Mahler and Freud,[99] for he seems to have been driven by a need of his own to rid the individual configuration of its contingency and retain for it something of the metaphysical status of necessity. Hence he too finds it necessary to purge art of its "accidental" subjectivity and to develop a method of interpreting reality that consists essentially in the analysis of depersonalized and demystified autonomous formal structures, structures that he himself often likens to Leibniz's "windowless monads." This is an enterprise not very different, in the end, from the nonhumanistic undertakings of French structuralism.

Moreover, Adorno's critical method, like so many contemporary critical methods, seems unable to free itself from the need for some theory of structure that permits its application to highly particularized musical works and enables it to propose convincing isomorphisms between such works and other elements within the same culture. One of the most striking impressions to emerge from a study of Adorno's criticism is the extent to which he assumes characteristics to cohere in structures — not only of actual nineteenth-century music (discontinuity, circularity, invariance, stasis, space, self-negation, structure, antistructure) or even of nineteenth-century German music as it might have idealized itself (individualization, metaphysical meaning, rationality, humanism), but of classical music as well. Adorno may present classical music as intrinsically historical, "processive," and dialectical, but the manner in which the terms he uses in connection with the classical style (wholeness, objectivity, individuality, relationship, time, rationality, necessity, freedom, and, perhaps, humanity) constantly evoke each other, not so much causally as by association, or what a structuralist might call "syntagmatically"—all this is highly suggestive of a structure. It is almost as if Adorno's musical criticism assents to the notion that history is really a "temporal series of timeless cells," a Schubertian series of structures, and that it finds in the stylistic shift to romanticism merely a way of returning from the aberration (and illusion) of classical temporality to a musical condition more conformant with reality.

By this line of reasoning, the musical tradition derived from classicism, like the coeval dialectical critical tradition that extends classical values well into the twentieth century, does no more than make it likely that post-Enlightenment German music, along with the civilization it has helped to define, will be identified by some future civilization as the *historical* structure. In other words, one can infer from such a reading of Adorno's criticism that the historical (and humanistic) self-consciousness that has suffused Western civilization since the Enlightenment will be seen as merely an accidental characteristic, useful in distinguishing one particular epistemic system from another. Nineteenth-century music, then, can be imagined as nothing less — or more — than a microcosmic example of how, like human life, the Hegelian *Geist*, a human construct of history and dialectics, "proceeds obliquely" to the premises of a structure that is very likely real, but lifeless.

Within this model of history derived from Adorno, moreover, Adorno's own criticism can be imagined as a structural variant of nineteenth-century German musical values or as a "recurrence of the same." It is merely a historically tinged strand such as might decorate the surface of an ahistorical structure where the direct force of linear history or progress (like its analogue, classical tonality) has given way to the systematized treatment of history (or the tonal relationship) as a distinct self-contained object, capable of emerging at numerous levels of a structure but no longer possessing, or regarded as possessing, any real power to effect change. Hence it bears no inherent significance. Adorno's criticism could, indeed, be taken as evidence of a tendency by music to give up on a purely musical solution to its own problems, a solution such as the historical ideal of progress would require, and to resign itself instead to unending attempts at reformulation within verbal or critical analogues to music, any number of which might coexist in a structural arrangement. And in thus implicitly acknowledging temporal progress and resolution as unreal, this criticism might well reinforce the notion that criticism and all the hierarchies of metacriticism verify among themselves the accuracy of the atemporal, and essentially negative, image of reality proposed by structuralism. Adorno, to be sure, cannot prove a necessary connection between this negative image of reality and reality itself, any more than he can guarantee the epistemological validity of art. What he does is perhaps all that any good structuralist can do: present a model of reality that some may find convincing.

In the light of such striking affirmations of the structuralist position, Adorno's criticism, and studies based upon it, can perhaps be forgiven for characterizing French movements such as structuralism not only broadly but also parochially, through German eyes. Especially since, in the end, Adorno reveals even his own existential agony as no more than an illusory phenomenon on the surface of the negative metaphysical structure that French structuralism posits as reality.

Chapter 12

Individualism in Western Art Music
and Its Cultural Costs

In teaching the introductory music course at the University of Chicago, I have generally opened the first class by playing recordings of two pieces, asking the students to observe similarities and differences between them.[1] The first is John Philip Sousa's "Washington Post March"; the second is the "Soldier's March" from Igor Stravinsky's *Histoire du Soldat*.[2] Except for some foreign exchange students, virtually no one fails to find the former piece at least somewhat familiar. The majority can name the composer, and occasionally one or two students even know the name of the particular piece. Very seldom, on the other hand, does anyone in the class recognize the latter piece.[3]

The unfamiliarity of the Stravinsky piece has certain pedagogical advantages. Above all, perhaps, it prevents the class from approaching it with the cultural preconceptions ordinarily aroused by a printed concert program, preconceptions that might get in the way of a direct response to this music and cut off at the outset any real belief among my students, nurtured as they are on electronic mediums and rock concerts, that I have anything to tell them that they will care about. By allowing each piece to present itself anonymously, I make it possible for the two to be heard on an equal basis.

Now the sophisticated listener might suppose that in simply lining up the two pieces side by side, I imply that the qualitative superiority of the second piece is so self-evident as to need no commentary. This is not, however, the reaction of the musically uneducated students in Music 101. For them, the equal presentation of the two works has generally had the initial effect of suggesting that the second piece — heard in the context of the first — isn't really so bad and may even offer elements of interest not altogether different from those offered by the first.

At the outset, at any rate, the class quickly begins to perceive that the two pieces have certain noticeable features in common. Both, for example, seem to assume as some kind of norm the practice of measuring music evenly with respect to time, and more particularly, the possibility of organizing music into units of two beats, units that can be counted 1–2, 1–2, et cetera. Both pieces give some prominence to brass instruments and drums. And these two features, in turn, are soon recognized as signs that both pieces represent a common genre: the march. It is from this classification as march music that the class first grasps the idea that the Stravinsky piece is probably not totally meaningless or lacking in connection to the notion of a genuine function, any more than the Sousa piece is. It is an idea that seems to come as a revelation to most of my students.

With a bit of prodding on my part, the class can further begin to recognize that the two pieces share certain structural characteristics that allow certain common features of style to be discerned in each. Though qualifications can be made in both cases, each piece seems to have a relatively marked beginning and end; both pieces also have recognizable internal elements of repetition and contrast. Together these characteristics seem to mark off each piece as a rather clearly defined object, a status that seems to have some bearing on the fact that both can be recognized as Western rather than, say, as East Asian or African. Both pieces seem, in fact, to be objects precomposed by an individual rather than patterns of sound that are improvised on the spot. The class is even willing to acknowledge that each piece *may* exemplify a characteristic individual style of composition, though here reactions are confused and uncertain. The first piece is clearly recognized as by Sousa, whether or not its actual name is known (generally it is not). The second piece is recognized as somehow the more individualized *structure*: it is more irregular, less predictable, and therefore presumably less easily confused with other pieces of its kind and less easily simulated by imitators of its composer. And yet this individuality cannot be associated by my students with any individual *style* of composition. Almost always, the stylistic character of the Stravinsky piece seems less attractive to the class than that of the Sousa piece. Still, after analyzing some relationships between the two, including the possibility that the Stravinsky piece is in some way a parody of the tradition represented by the Sousa piece, the class will generally concede that both pieces can be considered "music" in some positive or normative sense, that is, music as opposed to "noise" or "cacophony." This concession does not come easily, even though I have deliberately chosen this march from *L'Histoire du Soldat* as a relatively accessible piece of its kind and period (it appeared in 1918).

Paradoxically, however, any reservations that the class may have about calling the Stravinsky piece "music" seem to vanish when it comes to calling this piece "art." When the question of the relative *value* of the two marches arises, as sooner or later it always does, the norm invoked by the class is not that of "music" but that of "art." And except for a few holdouts (frequently young men with fond, fresh memories of playing tuba in the high-school band who will call attention to the staying power of Sousa's marches in American band repertories and American life), the class will cheerfully acknowledge that the Stravinsky piece is superior because it is art. But what do they mean by this?

Most of my students recognize that they have no basis for judging the merits of the Stravinsky piece in terms of its own kind. Suppose that Stravinsky were to come back to life tomorrow and announce that the march from the *Histoire du Soldat* was a failure. Perhaps he had decided that it didn't carry out his own vision of it adequately, that it didn't work properly in relation to the whole piece from which it was taken, or even that he had gone about composing it with erroneous compositional or aesthetic ideals. My class would be perfectly willing to take Stravinsky at his own word, but they would not, in their present state, really be privy to any of the reasons on which Stravinsky's revised judgment was based. Certainly my class has no inkling of actual critical traditions, such as those fostered by Theodor W. Adorno and other admirers of Schoenberg, traditions in which it would be argued that Stravinsky's allusions to tonality and other accessible conventions expose the artistic sterility and cultural failure of pieces such as the *Histoire du Soldat*. No, my class makes its value judgment about the "Soldier's March" on the basis of some general characteristics that have little to do with the particularity of Stravinsky's piece or compositional style. The Stravinsky piece is called "art" for precisely the same reasons that it is recognized as "classical," reasons that are worth examining here in a little detail.

First of all, then, the Stravinsky piece, as opposed to the Sousa one, makes my class feel uncomfortable. It is an unfamiliar piece, it doesn't bring immediate and unmitigated pleasure, the students are not sure how to listen to it, how to respond to it, how to talk about it. It doesn't have a continuous melody line that they can follow or whistle or remember. It doesn't have a foot-tapping regularity they can absolutely count on. The piece *is* a march of sorts, or at least it is *about* a march, but yet it doesn't quite seem to be a *functional* march: it doesn't impel the desire to march in the same way as Sousa's piece does, or even call to mind the spectacle of a good parade. (Most of my students are surprised to learn that the Stravinsky march is associated with a narrative text and comes from a work that can be physically staged, though a few, on learning this, have made the telling comment that they felt when they first heard the piece that it was missing something.[4] The Stravinsky piece cannot be associated with any of the more self-gratifying uses to which an occasional college student these days may be putting music. One doesn't, for instance, think of it as music to make love by or get high to. In fact, from the point of view of my students, this piece seems to be quite useless, providing them with an experience that is essentially superfluous to their own lives. Thus, though Stravinsky himself may well have intended the piece to have a positive social function, say of giving musical pleasure, for most of the students in Music 101, its primary function seems to be that of making them feel uncomfortable. It is music that these students could expect to listen to after they had donned a three-piece suit or basic black dress, pearls, and heels and squeezed themselves into the balcony of Orchestra Hall, where they would have a distant view of the orchestra, and a somewhat closer one of the connoisseurs, society matrons, and other holders of season tickets to the symphony. (This may sound like exaggeration, yet it is in just such terms that they describe their preconceptions in the concert reports they write for me. For most, the concert involved is the first classical concert they have ever attended.) The Stravinsky piece is also music that my students might expect to hear in an introductory music course that has been forced upon them in a college curriculum. But it certainly isn't *their* music.

Oddly, it is this very lack of a sense of ownership, of a personal stake in Stravinsky's music, which seems to persuade my students most effectively that the Stravinsky piece is art where the Sousa one isn't. This is music that is defined for them as art not by themselves, their peers, or, in most cases, their families, but by Sir Georg Solti, the University of Chicago faculty, the programmers at the public television stations or at WFMT, a highbrow Chicago FM station. And such a definition of musical art—as the music of a repertory deemed "classical" by its association with professional experts and a social elite—is one that my students accept readily. They are no more prepared to question this definition than they would dream of questioning the post-Newtonian concept of physical reality defined for them by their physics professors. Very seldom does it occur to my students that "art" could be something that they themselves had a hand, or a stake, in defining, even after it becomes clear during the course of the class that in fact our current notions of art in the West depend overwhelmingly on social conventions, such as deference to aesthetic judges drawn from certain segments of society, and not at all on any universally recognized metaphysical truths.

Again, my class seems to designate Stravinsky's work "art" because it is somehow more "complex" than the Sousa piece. When pressed, my students will acknowledge that this impression of complexity stems partly from an awareness of their own inability to make much sense of the Stravinsky piece, and from a suspicion that they will never be able to make *complete* sense of it. Since the piece is recognizably Western, its relative inaccessibility cannot be attributed to an ethnically alien identity. Therefore what they cannot understand must be a function of their own intellectual inadequacy to the music; and since pre-med students at the University of Chicago do not ordinarily think of themselves as intellectually inadequate (at least until they take their Medical Boards), the cause of this incomprehension must be musical complexity.

But beyond this broad definition of complexity lie other, more subtle ones. Eventually, for example, the class comes to associate its impression of complexity with the notion that relative to the Sousa march, the Stravinsky march is a far more fixed, inviolable object. One could imagine one's good friend—someone born, say, during the Vietnam War, more than a century after Sousa, and thus a total stranger, personally, to Sousa and his circle—one could imagine such a friend picking up the tunes, rhythms, and harmonies of the Sousa march on the piano and presenting a version of the piece that, though lacking the character and effectiveness of Sousa's band version and therefore not identical with it, was nevertheless recognizable as an aesthetically defensible version of that march. In the process of translating the Sousa march into new mediums or performing circumstances, that is, no catastrophic loss of identity need result if the performer failed to execute every detail left by the composer in his score. Indeed, it is conceivable that the performer might not even be able to read music at all.

Of course, it is also true that occasional deviations of a certain kind from the original version—certain distinct or violent changes of pitch, rhythm, or harmony, for example, would be widely recognizable as wrong, as errors. This latter may seem to signify a paradoxical rigidity in the form and identity of the original version, but this paradox is more apparent than real; for recognizability of error does not, in fact, signify an absolute and inflexible fixing of the musical object by its composer. On the contrary, widespread recognizability of error points to the same underlying condition that allows performers to take considerable liberties with Sousa's march. It points to an identity that is not altogether fixed in its individuality, that is, to an individual identity sufficiently dependent on collectively used musical language and form that it can preserve its widespread recognizability in the face of numerous reinterpretations or even assaults upon it in society at large.[5] And for this same reason, one could even imagine a group of skilled amateurs getting together and improvising upon a piece like the "Washington Post March" in a jam session, making it the basis of active musical fantasy, and still not utterly destroying its continued identifiable presence.

All this, clearly, is not the case with the Stravinsky piece. Generally my students find it more or less self-evident that the Stravinsky piece must be performed in exact accordance with the musical instructions written out in

Stravinsky's score, and that it in fact requires considerable previous rehearsal to achieve such an accordance. Far less freedom is permitted by the Stravinsky march for translation or reinterpretation by society at large. This restriction is evident even in the simple fact that far fewer people are in a position to tamper with Stravinsky's own conception of his work than with Sousa's. If nothing more, my class will generally acknowledge — always with the exception of the trombonists and cornettists, joined occasionally by a jazz aficionado — that the Stravinsky piece requires more skill of its players than does the Sousa piece, and that the Stravinsky piece, therefore, limits the extent to which music-makers in society can make it their own. Barring a virtuoso jazz or folk instrumentalist with the phenomenal musical ear of a Mozart, instrumentalists who can't read music are not going to play the "Soldier's March." It is simply too complex. The players who perform this sort of work have necessarily undergone a musical discipline imposed by others who are considered musically educated. And this sort of musical training, it is worth noting, does not incline performers to reinterpret a Stravinsky's wishes in accordance with their own wishes or circumstances.

Nor, of course, does Stravinsky's piece lend itself very readily to extensive reinterpretation by the performer. Again, it is too complex: too rich, too individualized, and too nearly complete in its own detail. In this respect too, then, Stravinsky's march, in its relative imperviousness to violation, seems also to have precluded its own inclusion in spontaneous, actively imaginative music-making. Now, presumably, the fixity of form that entails all these effects is itself something that Stravinsky wanted. Indeed, the students in Music 101 will acknowledge, on reflection, that Stravinsky has almost surely taken deliberate advantage of the existence of a complex system of musical notation — a notation that permits the exact transmission of numerous diversified instructions — precisely in order to write a piece that cannot be violated by society at large, a piece that assumes the presence of performers disciplined to submit their skills as completely as possible to Stravinsky's bidding.

This isn't to say that Stravinsky writes as he does in order to make life difficult for performers or to keep his music out of the hands of proletarian rabble. What interests Stravinsky, it seems clear, is to make a firmly fixed individual statement, that is, to externalize some internal configuration that he finds worth communicating in its precise particularity. With this desire, and its corollary, the right of the composer to control his or her work and protect it from the performer, my class has no quarrel. After all, whose music is it? Even if the composer's copyright has run out, it is still the composer who owns the piece, not the performer or audience. Or at least this is so in the opinion of my students. My class is sometimes a bit startled to discover how readily it invokes the notion of ownership in connection with its definition of art. Nevertheless, its convictions about such ownership are as deeply grounded as its fundamental contempt for any composer who borrows a tune from another composer (a widely honored practice before the complete ideological victory of private ownership in Western art music and the reinterpretation of such borrowing as stealing). A composer, to my students, is at bottom a property owner, and hence, the composer's rights are paramount, beyond those of the performer or listener — especially if he is a renowned property owner like Stravinsky, one of the socially and culturally "elect." (I leave aside here any discussion of the complex and extended litigation over Stravinsky's manuscripts that took place after his death, a conflict of no little relevance in a culture that defines the composer as a property owner.)[6]

My class, then, has no trouble recognizing and even admiring in Stravinsky's piece a kind of ideological preoccupation with the individual identity of the composer's vision. And yet where Stravinsky is concerned, as opposed to Sousa, there are paradoxes involved in the conception of individual musical identity that are unquestionably real and troubling, paradoxes that become clearly evident if one considers the relation of my Music 101 class to the Stravinsky piece in question. Let us put aside, for the moment, the inability of my students to determine for themselves whether Stravinsky's vision is *worth* communicating. These students cannot even decide for themselves with certainty whether the piece *has been* communicated precisely in any performance. To be sure, they will assume this is the case in any particular performance, for where are they likely to hear the work? On commercial recordings, or in concerts by professional groups, contexts in which they suppose that every effort has been made to render the composer's intentions faithfully.

Now, of course, not all recordings or concerts are in fact so faithful. But let us hypothesize that in such a performance, substantial errors were actually made or great liberties were deliberately taken with the composer's instructions. How sure could the members of my class be of detecting either situation? Certain gross errors might no doubt be apparent — especially if the students could see that the clarinet player had lost the place or the double-bass player had broken a string. Disruptions of the metric regularity in the bass line would be noticeable. But by and large the tolerance for errors, especially of pitch, would be far greater in the case of Stravinsky's piece than of Sousa's. The class could count little on any irrefutable common musical logic or well-established set of musical conventions as a reliable check on deviations of performance from composition. (And it should be evident, I might add, that anything I say about Stravinsky in this context can all the more readily be applied to the hundreds of twentieth-century composers who are far less generally accessible than he.)

Or again, let us suppose that it were possible, from a compositional standpoint, for a performing group to improvise a polished fantasy on the "Soldier's March" from the *Histoire du Soldat*. It seems clear that the point would come considerably earlier in the case of this piece than in the case of Sousa's when the audience would cease to recognize deviations from the original — because it would no longer be able to identify the original.

Here I cannot resist a brief digression. Anton Webern paid homage to Bach by reinterpreting a ricercare from Bach's *Musical Offering* more or less in his own instrumental idiom, in effect turning it into a new piece while preserving the living identity of the original, just as Mozart once did with Handel's *Messiah*. But — my students always laugh when I ask this question — who will Webernize Webern in this fashion? How could it be done? And who in society would know or care? These two properties, of compositional inflexibility and collective unrecognizability, are clearly related.

Indeed, despite all the self-conscious neo-classical plundering of older repertories that has gone on since the nineteenth century,[7] it is probably against the interests of contemporary composers to reuse older works in a way that is popularly recognizable and that solidifies a continuity with the past. Such a practice might well reinforce the popular preference for older methods of composition over newer ones, and encourage commercial movie-makers, for example, to return to older composers, thereby avoiding the costs of salaries and royalties to living ones. At least, it is fairly uncommon to see much attention given in academic compositional (or scholarly) circles to commercially viable reworkings of older works. I myself know of no composition class that investigates the compositional significance of using old music in films such as *A Clockwork Orange* or *2001*, and a recent academic article on Barry Manilow's "Could It Be Magic," which reuses the Chopin C-Minor Prelude, is distinctly exceptional.[8] This avoidance of recognizable reuse fits in well with continuing historicist notions of purity, in academic circles, whereby one either leaves an older work totally intact or destroys it utterly in an artistic reworking. But by the same token, of course, it is to be expected that works written today will not lend themselves to a future life through compositional borrowing or reworking as did music of an earlier time. There is a loss here for contemporary composers in terms of the resultant historical disposability of their historically inviolable works, but there is also a potential gain, since this kind of thinking, which tends to put a patent on compositional originality, may help to sustain the illusion of a continuing social need for the musically new. And certainly it is axiomatic today that each musical artwork must be new in an absolute sense that was simply not contemplated in earlier centuries, when ironically, the social need for *more or less* new compositions was more genuine and constant.[9]

But in any case my class cannot rely on itself very far to determine even *whether* Stravinsky's intentions have been executed accurately; for this sort of assurance my students must rely on the good faith, the honesty, or perhaps the lack of imagination of someone who intervenes between them and the composer. Thus in one respect, oddly, Stravinsky in limiting the freedom of his performers is actually more vulnerable than Sousa is to any license that performers may take in mediating his intentions to the public.

Nor is this the only paradox involved here. Relative to Sousa's piece, it is clear, Stravinsky's piece does communicate to my students a far greater emphasis on the theoretical value of transmitting individual constructions with precision. And yet, ironically, it is Sousa, with his lesser interest in fixing individual expression, who stands the far greater chance of having the actual character (which is to say, the original intended meaning) of his individual piece communicated to my students and thus, we can assume, to society at large. Still, my students are willing to concede the qualitative superiority of music that idealizes the importance of individuality, even if the very embodying of this ideal precludes them from fully understanding the individual piece on its own terms, or from judging it by standards securely related to its own individuality. They concede this superiority for much the same reasons as they concede the superiority of "classical" over "popular" performing skills or the validity of the composer's claim to complete control over the fate of his or her piece. In every case, qualitative superiority is attributed to that conception of music which, at least in theory, gives ideological precedence to the composer's individuality of expression; for at bottom, whether one thinks of the students' discomfort with Stravinsky's piece or their emphasis on its complexity, it is really upon the notion of service to individualized expression that my class rests its highest qualitative designation for music, the designation of art.

Now, obviously, respect for the freedom and uniqueness of individual expression is a cultural value that contains a great deal of good. In Beethoven's lifetime, when notions of individual worth were just beginning to attain real power in society after centuries of deference to ideals oppressive of individuality, the unqualified pursuit of individualistic values was undoubtedly of great importance for the betterment of society. And certainly, to the degree that it took place, in music and elsewhere, this pursuit brought with it a nexus of associated values from which I myself as well as most of those reading these words still benefit today — for example, an increase in the importance assigned by society to education.

Such respect for education reflects and serves a cultural respect for individuality in notable ways. By emphasizing the need for education in order to understand music, or any system of signs, we corroborate the value of differences between ourselves and other individuals, and we discourage uneducated pre-judgment, that is, prejudice, the wholesale rejection of differences that can result in xenophobia or racism. Through an insistence upon disciplined learning, we put limits on the unlimited and irrational gratification of our own individuality in the interests of making room for other individualities, while preserving a cultural space in which our own individuality of expression can flourish, as it did in the case of the great romantic composers. Education thus seems to enhance a state in which our own individual expression as well as our neighbor's, and that of a stranger or even an enemy, can be preserved, and perhaps successfully communicated.

Nevertheless, there are some dangers far too seldom recognized in continuing to cultivate and expand nineteenth-century ideals of individuality without subjecting them to critical reflection. The same set of individualistic values that has produced our principal concert repertory and given the West its cultural hegemony in much of the world also has a negative underside that extends through the entire breadth of our musical culture and probably of our civilization as well. This underside can be illustrated concisely through reference to the concept of art that is apparently at work in my introductory music class. The title of art may be the accolade that my students confer upon music of the highest quality, but what a dreary honor this title seems to be, reserved as it is for music that can be recognized by the discomfort it brings, for music that excludes these same students in no small measure from a relationship to itself, for music that my students hesitate, in some instances, to call music!

Whether or not they recognized it, the great nineteenth-century composers (Beethoven, Berlioz, Wagner, Verdi) fought for the autonomy of the individual artwork — its protection from corrupting social effects — as a symbolic means of strengthening the cultural and social reality of individual freedom of expression. In winning this fight, however, Western composers also experienced the obverse side of autonomy in the sense that as artists, they were cut loose from the economic power structure within society and began to produce works so autonomous, so free of society, that society came to question its own need for those works. And certainly for the students in Music 101, the archetypal autonomous art work is one that exists apart from the social fabric of actual life; it is a dead object, in need of exhumation, resuscitation, and interpretation, by teachers or by critics. Or, to change metaphors, for these students such a work is not only useless, as we assume that any purely aesthetic object must be (since we continue to hold to the Kantian notion of the aesthetic as involving a disinterested pleasure, unbound, say, by

political or commercial ends); beyond this, the autonomous piece is also re-
mote, a system of esoteric symbols, a manifestation of a more or less private
language that these students feel they can never fully understand.

But incommunicability of individuality is not only a self-defeating attitude, destructive to the real existence of the individuality in question; it may
also have adverse effects on a social scale as well. Thus, to take but one example, though a degree of elusive meaning may spur listeners to educate themselves about individual stylistic differences, there is a point beyond which the
impenetrability of a musical structure leads listeners to so denigrate their own
intelligence and claims upon good music that it demoralizes them, encouraging them to abandon self-education as futile and to make a virtue of the sort
of self-contented philistinism that, unchecked, can lead to death by trampling
at a concert of The Who.

Perhaps in every society there exists a perpetual tension between individualistic and collective sorts of value, a tension too fraught with contradiction ever to be fully dispelled, a tension that must, rather, be maintained
at something near a state of balance, however uneasy, if individual needs and
values within that society are to be served. This last hypothesis may sound
contradictory; yet it probably is the case that individualistic elements in society, which are far more contingent and precarious than collective forces, are
threatened by cultural exaggeration of *either* individualistic *or* collective sorts
of values. To illustrate, if the musical responses of my students are at all
representative, it would seem that the notion of "art" has come to connote
a disproportionate emphasis on individuality within our own system of cultural values. And yet the individuals most directly involved today in sustaining an artistic musical tradition on the whole do not seem to exert very much
power over our collective social life or cultural institutions. On the contrary,
it would seem that our continuing and uncritical collective reverence for the
idea of individuality — our transformation of respect for individuality into an
ideology of individualism, one might say — has contributed to intensifying
the force with which our present collective life as a society represses individualized expression, and other values of the very champions of individuality. Some sense of this repression can be gained by a brief look at some
characteristic features in three current domains of musical art, those of the
composer, the performer, and the scholar.

Composition

There can be little doubt that at the culturally most prestigious levels of our
musical life, there exists an ideal of compositional individualism so nearly ab-

solute that it might well satisfy that premier megalomaniac Richard Wagner. It is an individualism succinctly formulated in the composer Milton Babbitt's famous challenge, "Who Cares if You Listen?"[10] Ideally, today, the best composers write totally for themselves, without significant regard for audience or even performer. No changes comparable to those that a Mozart or even a Beethoven sometimes made for performers or audience are to be contemplated in the contemporary art object. Some composers are very explicit about trying to control every variable in their works (for example, replacing the performer with a computer), thereby turning their works into fixed, hermetically self-contained worlds, impervious to the vagaries of performance or the structuring forces of socially recognized convention. But even among composers who in fact use their talents to acquire social patronage or fellowship support, few would openly admit to giving much consideration in the compositional process to any interests of a performer or an audience that might conflict with the composer's unbridled—or as the composer would say, uncompromised—self-expression. Certainly no composer would make such an admission who had any hopes of being taken seriously in academic musical circles, where the history books are written. At such prestigious levels of composition, the works of unquestionably talented composers who do try to effect some accord with academically unsanctioned performing or listening traditions (I think always of Leonard Bernstein, whose hesitation to compose really "serious" music may well be a sign of exceptional musical intelligence and historical sensibility, or perhaps of George Rochberg, in his recent turn back toward tonality) may well be greeted with the question, "Do you call that *music?*" (Ironically, this is the very question that confronts the dogmatically individualistic composer today, in Music 101 and in society at large.)

The only type of contemporary composition that can openly incorporate some deference to the performer without seriously endangering a claim to academic recognition is so-called chance music, music that gives over some or all of its ultimate formulation to random and unrepeatable choices and relationships among the players. Without question, such music represents an effort to break away from the closed world of the individual composer. On the other hand, as a solution to the problems I am describing, it is a troubling one, both insofar as it concedes that the cohesive force of recognizable, collective convention in music has been completely supplanted by random, openly incomprehensible principles of combination and insofar as it suggests that the only alternative to the tyranny of individualism is the abandonment of individual control and responsibility. To an important extent, chance music proclaims its despair of actually integrating individual and collective values within itself.

It should not be overlooked, in any case, that at bottom, chance music remains a highly individualized form of music since those who compose it, as a rule, not only provide the materials for combination but also define the bases on which random combinations can be allowed to occur. It is as if composers, realizing their inability to establish a living bond between their interests and those of their performers and audience, have elected to maintain control by turning that very inability into an element of their compositions. And certainly it has become a truism that the sound of total chance music is impossible to distinguish from that of total serial music, in which composers try to leave no parameter of the piece to chance.[11]

At the level of "serious" musical aesthetics, then, the values of individuality reign supreme; but what are the effects of this supremacy? First of all, composers have forfeited the prospect of any direct relationship between their music and the public at large; and conversely, we in society have forfeited our rights as individuals to make our own judgments about contemporary music. If we don't like what we hear, we are branded as uneducated or vulgar, even if there is no reasonable way of understanding what we hear, indeed, even if it is central to the composer's aesthetic and moral integrity that we not like what we hear. Occasionally, a clever musicologist will assert that we are not really in a position to judge early art music (meaning medieval, renaissance, or even early baroque music) on purely aesthetic terms: that we are too dependent on chance factors that have allowed only certain scores to survive physically (though heaven knows musicologists are doing their best to combat selective survival); that we are too impressed by mere chronological age, that our opinions are preformed by the perspectives and opinions of scholars involved in the revival of early music. Assuming this is so, it is interesting to note that our situation does not seem to be very different in relation to the art music of our own culture. Today, ordinary listeners have little control over which contemporary art works will actually reach their ears, especially since they have so little chance of being able to perform even the smaller works that they might run across. Today, the only socially safe course in judging contemporary art music is to rely on the intervention of classes of experts—scholars, critics, other composers—who perpetuate their standards of expertise, standards we are seldom any more competent to judge than we are to judge the music they mediate for us.

And even learned musical figures have their troubles understanding contemporary art music. Many a survey course in the history of Western music is run in such a way as to leave very few sessions for music of the twentieth century. I have heard a well-known musicologist, speaking in private, of course, deride composition today as a skill that is as obsolete as that of the blacksmith. (The reference, naturally, was to classical Western composition, the only kind that most of us in academic circles give much thought to.) If my own experience is any guide, moreover, few and brave are the scholars on music faculties today who do not defer, more or less automatically, to the composers among them when judging the compositional talents of prospective students. Likewise, on a more advanced level, even in learned circles, it is too often the composer's credentials—the list of commissions and fellowships—rather than the music itself that is judged.[12] (Would Mozart's adult résumé been good enough for a Guggenheim fellowship? Mozart's music did not fare well among the Viennese elite during his last years, no doubt for political as well as aesthetic reasons. Yet even in its seemingly unconscionable rejection, Viennese society of the 1780s probably had more direct access to Mozart's individuality as a composer than would have been possible if Mozart himself had been regularly preceded by his own curriculum vitae, and the mass of depersonalizing, nonmusical information it would have contained.) The modern reliance on credentials, of course, is often deadly for the unknown artist, as any unestablished poet will testify who has received a machine-written rejection from the *New Yorker* stating that the editors do not even *read* the works of unknowns.[13]

Of course, the case could be made for a kind of aesthetic Darwinism, according to which that music survives and comes to the fore which deserves to survive. If this viewpoint is right, then the composers who succeed in contemporary society thereby show themselves to be aesthetically the fittest. But this, unfortunately, is a theory that cannot be validated. The IRS can attest to the composer's bankroll but not to the aesthetic value of his music. Moreover, disturbing moral overtones intrude themselves into the application of Darwinism to contemporary musical life in a way that they do not when we equate the survival of past music with aesthetic quality. For every individual composer who succeeds in our society, there are many more who despair of surviving as composers, and who are probably worse off musically (and more isolated socially) than their counterparts in previous centuries, since there are now so few institutions or activities at any level of society, least of all at any local level, that really *need* new art compositions, especially when so many old ones are now available.

Ironically, most of the genuine social need for new musical works today does not coincide with any need for musical artworks. By far the greatest real need for new musical works in our society exists in two sorts of commercial milieus. On the one hand there is a need—a need no doubt manufactured by the pop music business but nevertheless felt as such by millions of consumers—for popular compositions in themselves (especially if the definition of their structure is expanded to include a video aspect). By this I mean that there is a need for an endless supply of new pieces to feed into the music videos, the Walkmans, and the social landscape of American teenagers. On the other hand, there is a need for music that serves various commercial functions, mainly that of contributing to the total effect of movies, television programs, and above all, television advertisements. In neither of these milieus, even the latter, is there much concern with musical claims to artistic status.[14] And in fact, most music today with an uncontested claim to the status of art — a category that currently includes far more works of an "artlike" appearance than incontestable masterpieces — is produced outside of the commercial context that I have just described.

What social need is there for art music today? On the whole it must be admitted that whatever need manifests itself in our society for new musical artworks is an artificially created or self-perpetuating need, a situation that is scarcely surprising in a society where the need for music, among the socially elite, has given way so extensively to the need for musical artworks *as such*. Universities, for example, decide that they have a need for composers who produce autonomous works, that is, works for which there is no social need. Or composers get together and form groups that are defined as "needing" the kinds of music written by their own founders. In both cases, the social foundation for such a need is neither broad nor deeply grounded in contemporary life and cannot support more than a handful of individuals. Can any of us argue with moral comfort that composers who fail in a society that has so little need for them do so because they lack talent?

The organization of society in a manner that supports a few individual composers at the expense of many others is a second ill that can be associated with an exaggerated cultural emphasis on the values of individuality. Yet even those few individual composers who do succeed in contemporary society seem to suffer in terms of individualistic values as such values once worked in the past. What composer of art music who is alive today can be said to have impressed his or her musical individuality on the life of society with anything like the impact of Beethoven or Wagner, or even the aging Haydn in London? Who can imagine the biography of any contemporary composer opening with words comparable to those with which Stendhal began his *Life of Rossini*:

> Napoleon is dead; but a new conqueror has already shown himself to the world; and from Moscow to Naples, from London to Vienna, from Paris to Calcutta, his name is constantly on every tongue. The fame of this hero knows no bounds save those of civilization itself.[15]

Today we recognize the cultural self-centeredness in Stendhal's words and, at least in theory extend the notion of "civilization" beyond the West and its colonies. Even in their own cities, however, do even the most committed individualists among our own composers, in their wildest dreams, imagine achieving such a triumph for individual expression? Is it conceivable that a composer of art music could ever again be viewed as even a local hero?

Ours is no longer an age of world-historical figures, at least in art music. Yet we continue to define our demands of music in terms of an individualism more suited to the ethos of an earlier age, with results that circumscribe the effectiveness of even our most successful composers of art music. For again, once the property of individual expression is idealized beyond the point of any possible counterbalance by collective musical values, musical "expression" tends to lose its character of "expressiveness" as well as its corollary capacity for communication. What remains, as we can hear in the large number of formally self-conscious but expressively impotent works produced in our own half-century, is music that constitutes evidence of individualized formal concerns and standards that are no longer "expressive" in the sense of either individually revelatory or socially effective.

And this is a condition from which not even our best-known composers are exempt. They too find themselves far too often caught in a vicious circle wherein it becomes necessary to cultivate their own musical individuality more or less in social isolation, with the result that social support for their music remains restricted. In some ways, indeed, it seems clear that not only the unsuccessful but also the successful twentieth-century composers have actually lost ground in their relation to society compared with their predecessors, and that some of the technological disadvantages we tend to associate with music of an earlier time seem to have crept back into the lives of even our more respected composers. I allude here not merely to the comparable remoteness of medieval and contemporary music from the current general audience, which I mentioned before, but also to the return of certain limitations of a preindustrial society. Thus, just as widespread access to piles of computerized information about everyone in our society has not kept our less successful composers from working in almost total social obscurity, so too in our world of satellite communications and instant replays, there is so little demand for Western art music that we have largely annulled for such music the benefits of the printing press, forcing many composers, even well-regarded ones, to have copied out by hand scores that no publisher finds it profitable to underwrite.[16] And likewise, despite the possibilities of global jet travel, performances of new art compositions are so infrequent that composers often list such performances on their résumés.[17] It is not unthinkable that the minor composer of some past age, whose world may have been restricted to a few towns that could be reached by horse-drawn coach, may have been able to anticipate as many performances of his works as can the average major composer living today.

Moreover, the restriction of a secure place for "serious" music in our society to the works of a relatively small number of individuals past and present is undoubtedly related to another unfortunate tendency in contemporary Western musical life. I speak here of the relative failure within those circles that value art music to identify either individuality or other sources of value in the music of cultures outside those circles. Today the study of music is pretty much divided into "regular" musicology, so to speak, which studies Western art music, and ethnomusicology, which studies everything else. Relatively few "regular" musicologists today receive any significant education about music outside the European art tradition that began with medieval Catholic chant; and such education is not yet a standard part of the music major at all of our leading colleges and universities.[18] Why do we accept this isolation of Western art music, and what are the reasons for this academic neglect of other music? One of the main reasons may well be that music outside the Western art tradition cannot readily be associated, in a number of academic circles, with established individual artists. Do such artists exist? Undoubtedly they do, but so far neither their individuality nor their artistry has achieved anything like the degree of recognition among mainstream musicologists that is accorded to individual artists of the European art tradition. All individuals are equal, but some are more equal than others.

A second reason that other musical traditions do not attract attention in musicology is very likely that many or most of these traditions embody values about individuals and society that in fact cannot be readily accommodated by the "great man" theory of history so prevalent in so much American humanistic study even today. In fact, it seems rather probable that the relative neglect within American musicology of music outside the domain of European art bespeaks a general disdain within much of our cultural elite for value systems that lie outside the traditional Western aesthetic of individualism.[19] Certainly such disdain is suspected in some quarters of our society, and, understandably, it breeds resentment among individuals whose music can never gain recognition in our society as art, not because it is judged as lacking individual merit but because it is never judged individually at all, because the ethos of an entire culture in which an individual may be working is simply rejected out of hand.[20] If this is the case, then the respect for individual difference that has distinguished Western cultural values has also led, in terms of Western attitudes toward composition, to an undifferentiated rejection of whole systems of cultural values different from our own, and to a denigration of individuality within such foreign cultural systems.

Performance

Let us turn now to the effect of extreme and uncritical individualistic values on the performance of art music. The philosopher Nelson Goodman recognizes the absurdity in everyday terms of his notion that, strictly speaking, a piece maintains its identity only if every last one of its pitches is performed in accordance with the composer's notational instructions (so that one mistake, for example, changes the identity of the piece).[21] But is this notion really absurd in relation to the demands that we actually put upon performers of art music today? We can still think of some notorious individualists among our leading conductors, divas, pianists, etc., of the recent past, especially among an older generation of performers that is now just about gone; but often the performer today, whether of old music or of new, seems to be held by educated aesthetic ideals in a state of total bondage to the wishes of the individual composer, as reconstituted, if necessary, by the musicologist. No doubt, critics still use terms like "powerful personality" and "full-blooded musicality" when writing about performers (just the other day I passed a poster at Lincoln Center that quoted from a review [in the Spanish paper *El Pais*] of a particular pianist as "powerfully persuasive . . . enormously poetic . . . real musical magic"). Yet very often the ideal against which performers are actually measured is one that may well conflict with such terms, that of transparency to the composer's wishes. I am not saying that reasonable efforts to interpret the musical wishes of the composer necessarily destroy the performer's individuality. What I am saying is that when efforts to preserve the autonomy of the composer's vision are unbounded, the performer is turned into a kind of automaton. Most of us have some sense of the fact that a good deal of contemporary art music is written in a way that restricts the individual expressiveness of its performers. Again, even in chance music, where certain kinds of initiative are allowed, indeed demanded of the player, performers may well feel that their efforts do not result in individual expressiveness, first because the composer's systematizing of chance elements severely limits the ways in which the performer can make either spontaneous or deliberate choices—in fact, within the range of alternatives left to chance, the performer may be as much at the bidding of the composer as ever—and, second, because the performer's efforts are not likely to be perceived as individually expressive by the audience.

But what about the performance of older music today? No more cadenzas for us in an anachronistic but highly personal style; now our ornamentation must be strictly authentic in terms of its historical period, just as our instruments, according to our most educated ideals, must be historically authentic, even if they cannot be heard in a large modern concert hall or be acquired by amateur music makers, and even if they sound a bit thin or off-putting on modern electronic equipment. Ideally, the boy soprano, where historical authenticity requires him, replaces the mature female soprano, even if her voice produces what seems to the modern ear a more pleasing musical result. And amateur performers of Bach's *Well-Tempered Clavier*, if they have a good musical education, sit down at their historically inauthentic pianos a lot more uncomfortably than they used to.

Today we scoff at the ethnocentricity of the nineteenth-century performer who turned older music into a vehicle for personal self-expression; and yet, which culture had the greater, more immediate and vital love of musical performance, that of the historically naive nineteenth-century amateurs, with their histrionic rubatos and four-hand piano transcriptions, or that of the twentieth-century American listening passively to authentic performances in the concert hall, in the classroom, or on the living-room sofa? What has happened to the living art of improvisation by the performer, and to the enthusiastic, if not necessarily authentic, performance of music as a central activity in the home?

In a well-known essay entitled "Narrate or Describe?" the Hungarian critic Georg Lukács has extolled the superiority of Tolstoy, who narrates a horse race as if from the standpoint of a participant, to that of Zola, who describes such a race from the standpoint of a disinterested observer.[22] Every detail in the Zola description is accurate — or authentic, let us say — and yet by standing outside of the race, Zola fails to connect it in any vital way to a surrounding human context. Is this not the position in which exaggerated deference to the wishes or at least cultural assumptions of any particular composer puts the modern performer? (And is it, of course, not possible that care for authenticity of performance, when carried to an extreme, may become so conspicuous as to overshadow the individuality of a composition, so that the work is perceived principally as "rococo," "baroque," or just plain "antiquated"? Is there not a point when the ideal of historical authenticity brings about that very violation of musical individuality that it set out to overcome?)

It seems ironic that in oral traditions — say, in religious rites or epic poetry — where the rights of a collective culture seem often so rigidly antithetical to individual self-expression, individual deviations from a cultural norm, up to a certain point, are regularly tolerated, precisely because they are considered so insignificant, so transparent in relation to what really matters, the collectively defined substance. In our own culture, by contrast, individual deviations are recognized as so significant, as so important in themselves, as potentially so opaque, that we must repress them vigorously.

Writing about Mozart's compositional revisions of works by Handel, a respected modern biographer notes that to us, with a keener historical sense than Mozart and his contemporaries, the arrangements may seem a travesty of Handel and an unconvincing mixture of styles. But by the canons of his own day, Mozart was not guilty of a lapse of taste: to him it could only have seemed that he was bringing up to date, as far as possible, some works which were rather primitively scored.[23]

The passage means to defend Mozart, and yet in its way it is patronizing, since it never really considers the possibility (a particularly plausible possibility when the subject is Mozart) that a lack of absolute historical authenticity in ideals of composition may in fact allow the survival of certain vital musical values that are no longer with us. The ideals of performance, today, are much the same as those of composition; and here, too, attempts are seldom made to discern positive musical value in any aesthetic of performance that is or was less strict with respect to authenticity.[24]

And yet, such looser ideals of performance were culturally dominant for most of Western musical history, and even after historical self-consiousness began to increase in Western culture, they held their own for some time against an aesthetic shaped to the individuality of the composer alone. In 1635, in his preface to his *Fiori musicali*, a well-known collection of organ pieces, the fine Italian composer Frescobaldi admitted his preference for having his piece played from the score "because in this way true masters can most surely distinguish themselves from the ignorant."[25] But he also began his preface as follows:

> I have always striven, with what talent God has given me, to help, in their profession, according to the best strengths, those eager to learn . . . . It is my warm wish that everyone who obtains and studies my work shall draw satisfaction and profit from it. Of this new volume I say merely that my chief aim was to help the organists in that I have composed pieces of the kind that one uses as verses for mass and vespers; they will be of great use to the organists, who otherwise can use the versets *as they think fit*, and in the canzonas and ricercares can make a conclusion out of an [internal] cadence, if [the piece] seems too long [italics added].[26]

And among his more specific instructions to the player can be found the following remarks:

> In short, the toccatas shall be played according to the discretion and taste of the player. . . . From the Kyries, some can be

played quickly and others slowly as seems right to the player.
. . . The cantus firmus shall be played legato, but where that
causes awkwardness for the hands, [the player] can also discon-
nect [the notes]. I am always concerned for the greatest possible
facility to the player.[27]

Here we have what amounts to historically authentic permission from Frescobaldi to place limits on our concern with faithfulness to his wishes; yet how
many performers today, in playing from the *Fiori musicali*, would dare to give
this element of Fresobaldi's own aesthetic precedence over the historical pur-
ism of our own culture?

At a later time in history, Mozart, Beethoven, and Rossini all placed a far
greater value on the integrity of their compositions and on authenticity of
performance, as can be seen, for example, in the greater specificity of their
notational instructions relative to those of earlier composers. Yet, as I have
earlier indicated, all were known, on a varying number of occasions, to re-
write parts of works in accordance with the needs of performers or listeners.
Mozart may actually have preferred the second version of the slow movement of the *Paris* Symphony (K. 297) that was forced upon him by Le Gros,
the director of the organization for which the Symphony was written.[28] Rossini was not in a position to control the performances of his work all over
Europe, nor does his concern for authenticity of performance ever seem to
have reached the point of obsession. Yet his works were indeed performed
all over Europe and played a far more vital role in the musical life of
nineteenth-century Europe than they do today. Could there be some connection between the flexibility of Rossini's own attitude and the place of his
works in an earlier society? And if Rossini could compare the role of his
operas then with that role today, is it clear that he would choose the system
of cultural values that gives absolute priority to his own wishes over those
of his performers or potential audience?

Again, with Wagner and Verdi, the ideal of a fixed artistic object seems
to have incorporated itself into the very concept of the operatic composition;
and the construction of Wagner's theater at Bayreuth certainly signifies an interest in total control by the composer over the conditions of performance.
And yet, though opera seems to be one genre where the ability of the performer (and not just the conductor) to project an ego still seems to rival that
of the composer, what has happened to the vitality of the operatic tradition
since the enshrinement of the genre in a museum-like concept of repertory?
How many alternatives do singers with operatic voices have today to express
their individuality besides looking for new ways to serve old masters? How
much opportunity do they have to participate actively in the shaping of mu-

sic rooted firmly in the life of contemporary society? For that matter, why does the cutting edge in operatic performance seem so often these days to involve neither singing nor even music more generally but, rather, the set-design, costumes, and lighting of operas past? Composers such as Beethoven, Wagner, and Verdi contributed mightily to the triumph of individualistic values in Western culture, but it seems this was not a victory without a price, even for the performance of their own chosen medium and genres.

Scholarship

The effects of an unbalanced veneration of individualistic values on musical scholarship are closely related to the effects of this ethos on performance. Today, the dominating concern of American musicology is to reconstruct, with painstaking accuracy, authentic editions of works by the older masters. The purpose of such work is usually taken to be self-evident, and yet perhaps it ought to be questioned in that its effects are not always what one might expect. Authentic editions are welcomed by other musicologists for purposes of study, for example; and yet the broader intellectual kind of study for which such editions are supposed to be indispensable seems to be constantly postponed as a goal of American musicology, in favor of getting to work on still other critical editions.[29]

Another prime purpose of textual reconstruction is to improve and encourage performance of the works in question, but oddly, the effect on performance may not be altogether salutary; or perhaps not so oddly. The current musicologist is much like the museum curator who carefully removes centuries of varnish and dirt, or, conceivably, restores bits of lost color, to reveal an old masterpiece in its original form. But painting and music are not totally comparable arts. In our culture at least, an original painting consists in a physically existing object that invites mental responses, whereas an original composition consists in a mentally existing object that invites physical response.

In painting, that is, the identity of a work necessarily inheres in a physically fixed and unique object. In music, by contrast, except perhaps in the case of certain taped or computerized music, there is no need for such a literally physical existence as long as performers exist who can imagine the work and put together a performance out of their own heads. In this respect, obviously, an original piece of music is, at least in theory, directly accessible to far more people than a painting is.

Furthermore, painting, at least in Western culture, has not ordinarily been defined as an art involving active participation, least of all on any extensive social scale. There is, in fact, a necessary conflict between the physical existence of an original artwork, such as a painting enjoys, and most sorts of interpretation that require physical participation in the work by observers. The original painting—call it x—cannot coexist in any meaningful sense within its own physical reinterpretation, which amounts to a *not-x*; it is either one or the other. (I do not speak here, of course, of reinterpretations by means of new paintings, which are something quite different.) We can, to be sure, imagine a mode of responding to painting whereby the viewer feels compelled to alter or improve upon the original; perhaps it is to some extent the results of such activities, and not just the effects of physical age on paintings, that keep the modern curator busy. But in Western art, at least, it is apparent that this sort of participation has been limited over history, since if all viewers had been in the habit of responding so actively to painting, there would be nothing resembling an original artwork left. For most Western viewers, it seems safe to guess, it has not been customary to do much more with a painting than look at it. And though looking may well involve the active critical use of the imagination as well as endless mental violations of the artist's intended meaning, it is a physically passive activity that does not threaten the physical integrity of the original but instead leaves intact a constant basis for new critical interpretations of a similarly passive physical sort.

In music the situation is somewhat different. Again, up until the advent of the tape recorder and computer, music in Western culture has traditionally been defined as an intrinsically participatory art, in which the survival of the composer's original construction (by way of notation) did not discourage but actually required active physical participation by others besides the composer, that is, by performers. Still, in this medium, too, there remains a tension between the ideas of the composer and the interpretation of the performer; and the more actively performers are involved in re-creating a work, the more opportunity they have to make changes, whether accidental or deliberate, in an original. In music, as in painting, it is certainly possible for physical response to destroy the original identity of an artwork.

In music, however, at least until now, our culture has found it neither necessary nor desirable to restrict its mode of response so as to prevent such destruction, even in the case of art music. For just as the development of the concept of art music in the West has been virtually inseparable from the development of notation, so, too, Western art music has almost by definition been notated music. And within boundaries of cultural continuity, a notated musical composition is far sturdier than a painting is with respect to its original identity.[30] As defined in our culture, that is, identity can endure incomparably more physical reinterpretation in notated music than in painting without getting altogether lost. For in our culture, that identity derives from the definition of music as an art that in its very essence is dialectical, surviving and thriving on a kind of tension that is essentially fatal to the original identity of a painting.

But since such tension seems to be a necessary condition of most Western art music, it could well be argued that restoring the musical composition to a state of absolute authenticity actually undermines an essential part of its character and brings it closer to the state of a painting. Carried to an extreme, restoration may discourage attitudes conducive to active participation in music and favor inclinations toward passive contemplation. This is the less pleasant side of the benefits wrought by our historical reconstruction of the authentic. Thus it is possible to imagine levels at which the uncritically obsessive production of so-called critical editions may actually inhibit performance, for much the same reason that the difficulties of contemporary music turn away demoralized listeners instead of spurring them to educate themselves. The director of the amateur church choir, who once reveled in putting together a Bach cantata, gloriously oblivious to errors and anachronisms in the eventual performance, might well sink into lethargic gloom when confronted with the so-called *Kritische Bericht* that accompanies the new critical edition of each Bach work, that is, the volume of alternative markings and commentary on authenticity of various notational choices. In its very density one of these volumes may impress upon amateurs their historical naivete as well as the hopelessness of their ever mastering all of the information needed to insure the absolute authenticity of a performance. In short, by overwhelming performers with a sense of their inadequacy to the intentions of the composer, the modern scholarly edition may in some respects weaken the living force of the composer's music.

Such editions may also have some such effect on those students of music who wish to involve music in other sorts of study than the reconstruction of authentic texts. Indeed, it may in no small measure be the very existence of the authentic edition that accounts for the strikingly slow development of intellectual breadth in American musicology that I mentioned earlier. Is it professionally safe, after all, to ascribe social or humanistic meanings to a work by Bach without having mastered all of the information bearing on the authenticity of a text? And who would dare to try and ascribe such meanings to music, even well-known music, for which no authentic edition is yet available?[31] What value would one's own interpretive musings have if it turned out that they were based on a score that contained a couple of wrong notes? Again, whose music is it, anyway? In such ways, then, authentic editions may actually discourage those ends of performance and scholarship for which they are intended, and may well exacerbate the lack of integration of art music into current social life.

The very fact that musical scholarship exists no doubt signals a loss of living tradition with respect to the music—primarily Western art music—that is involved in such scholarship. This loss is not the fault of any particular individuals or any one group, such as composers, performers, or scholars; as I have tried to show, many people in our society who would seem to be well served by the cultural system of individualistic values that has led to this loss of tradition have also been hurt by the system. Nor are the corollaries of this loss of tradition, including the growth of scholarship and the preservation of authentic scores, by any means an unqualified evil. (If I do not dwell on their good points, it is because I assume that they are taken for granted by educated people, and that as a culture we have more to learn at this moment from questioning such trends than from defending them.)

Nevertheless, there are trade-offs and limitations attendant upon exclusive allegiance to any value system, and by questioning the exclusivity of our own cultural system of values, it may be possible to counteract some of its more unfortunate effects. In particular, if scholarship is an inescapable fact of modern Western culture, a reorientation of our ruling ideology, or at least an increase in tolerance for other ideologies, might allow us to open musical scholarship to a wider range of music and intellectual problems. More encouragement might be given to the study of minority and non-Western musical traditions. More incentives might be offered for attempts to relate the Western art tradition to the social structures and cultural values, not only of an older time, but of our own time as well, attempts that supplement efforts simply to know as many facts as possible about original musical structures. More encouragement might be given to young scholars to combine their respective fields of expertise in joint collaborations that go beyond the scope of what any individual scholar can reasonably be expected to produce alone. And perhaps the field of musicology might back away from an unfortunate tendency to equate the value of scholarly work with the greatness of the composer studied, as if a scholar somehow partakes of a composer's greatness, and as if the documenting of every event in a great Western composer's life and restoring the authenticity of every detail in that composer's work were the only imaginable or significant task of a humanistic musical scholarship.

To a certain extent, restoration of authenticity and active participation are mutually exclusive activities;[32] churches that are still in use are not normally turned into museums. And to a certain extent, restoration is a safer pursuit than attempts to integrate music into a living social and cultural context. For restoration is subject to objective standards of empirical accuracy, which in a sense help limit the burden of active responsibility that is placed on an individual's judgment, whereas integration opens up a wide path for mistakes of individual judgment. On the other hand, to the extent that we decide that we ourselves, and not just restored artifacts of the past, are a legitimate object of humanistic study, such mistakes may actually prove illuminating.

Moreover, just because a thing is difficult does not mean it should be avoided, especially if it holds out even a small hope of creating a musical ethos, and a society, that is a bit more humane than what currently exists. A musical attitude that allowed us in society, as listeners, performers, improvisers, students, and amateurs in the best sense, to participate in socially valued music far more fully than we do — and that placed more social value on the music in which we did participate actively — might well challenge the sanctity of individual authenticity as a cultural value and the social privilege of a certain art repertory; but such challenges might well be healthy for us, and conducive to the social integration of far more individual musical and human interests than is currently the case. The American system at its best, after all, is supposed to consist in an uneasy accommodation of conflicting interests through the dynamic of checks and balances. Is it not possible that Mozart's culture allowed the creation of unquestionably great music precisely because that culture did not yet insist on the absolute rights of individuality, with all the concomitant values of inviolate expression and historical authenticity, but rather permitted an uneasy truce between the identity of an individual's work on the one hand and the claims of society upon that work on the other? At the very least it seems to me worth our questioning seriously, both as individuals and as collective institutions, the extent to which our current notions about the absolute value of individual expression and our associated designation of certain music as art are actually a good thing, either for ourselves or for music.

Chapter 13

The Challenge of
Contemporary Music

Introduction: The Historical Situation

The self-contained music of the tonal system clearly defines normal music for our civilization, and constitutes accordingly a sort of world of music with a character of its own . . .

The challenge of contemporary music is not to society but to itself.[1] The challenge is to recognize its own lack of autonomy and to use this recognition as an opportunity for contributing to a new paradigm for music that would preserve its own most humane values.

This challenge is historically conditioned. It is accessible to analysis in philosophical terms, but only insofar as such an analysis acknowledges the particularity of the cultural context in which the challenge operates. One could ignore this context, and attempt an abstract, ahistorical account of the challenge posed by any new music only by assuming that all music comes into being as new music. But in fact many of the world's musical structures have existed only momentarily, as variants of a culturally fixed archetype, in relation to which their own physically unique, "new" characteristics are perceived, if at all, as accidents. And the assumption breaks down entirely when the term "new music" is replaced by "contemporary music." For the latter concept, even in its purely musical aspect, is bound to a historically specific cultural situation which has no exact counterpart, even in the periods of Western music history that immediately preceded the concept, and that in important respects engendered it.

At the center of this situation lies a widely recognized dichotomy between two post-Kantian modes of connecting humankind to reality, a dichotomy that developed from the breakdown of culturally common metaphysical assumptions and an ensuing reduction of reality itself, as an object of thought, to the status of a relativistic concept.[2] These modes can be envisioned as two polarized theoretical models that Westerners have devised for defining and evaluating the humanly accessible domain: a generalized or objective model, rooted on a need for order; and an individualized, or subjective, model, rooted on a need for freedom.

Both models aim at encompassing within their own frameworks the very dichotomy that distinguishes them, that is, aspects of experience that, in the West, are deemed either general or individual. And it is especially important here to recognize that any genuinely individualized vision of reality sustains the force it needs to actualize itself by taking on something like the status of Kant's categorical imperative. Though its conviction of its own validity is subjective, it imputes to itself a quality of necessity that entails the possibility of general affirmation. To be fully itself on its own terms, the individualized construction must be able to assume its own general validity.

Equally important, both models depend on what I would call the ideal of an autonomous significant structure, that is, both assume the possibility that humans can build structures or domains that are complete and meaningful within themselves. Based equally on a turn away from an inaccessible metaphysical reality, both models locate evidence of their own validity in the necessity of the connections formed in the semiotic (or, to use Francis Sparshott's term, "messagelike")[3] structures based upon them. Hence, the models themselves are characteristically justified through reference to internal structural laws.

Because such models rely so fundamentally on the principle of structural necessity, both tend to exclude as accidental and extrinsic the quality of contingency that characterizes the domain of concrete existence. Hence both models encourage a theoretical disregard of the sensuous particularity *as such* of structures based upon them. And the recognition of validity in such a structure is not thought to depend on the particular identity, power, habits, or values of those who create or receive the structure in question. Rather validity is supposed to inhere in the ability of a structure to carry out its own laws with consistency; and the execution of these laws is assumed accessible to all people, on the basis of a common faculty of reason and human identity.

This ideal of autonomy, I believe, is itself a fiction. In my judgment, Kant's efforts to preserve a universal basis for human communication have proven futile against the power of irreducible differences in perceptions, structuring principles, and values among differently situated individuals and cultures.[4] The ideal amounts to a notion of abstract, ahistorical, meta-physical truth, that is, truth at a level that the relativistic and historicizing culture of the post-Kantian West has long acknowledged as inaccessible.[5]

Nevertheless, the abiding power of this ideal over both models is clear in the paradigms we have developed for each. The cultural paradigm for the general model is science, which is commonly viewed as a self-contained intelligible structure, the inner connections of which have a self-evident necessity. (This structure is in turn assumed to derive its validity from its grounding in some sort of deep-seated, preestablished mental structure, not unlike Kant's transcendental reason, existing at an abstract and universal level.) This image of epistemological certainty has given science a culturally privileged status that is tantamount to a guarantee by Western society of its very existence. However dubious its potential moral effect may be, American scientific research usually manages sooner or later to get funded, for example.[6]

Indeed, relegating moral, like aesthetic, judgment to a merely subjective realm of freedom (and thereby thwarting Kant's efforts to preserve the universal basis of both), Americans in particular have tried to protect what they consider the purely general necessity of many structures — science, the American Constitution, the Invisible Hand — by excluding them from explicit considerations of morality. Instead, they have viewed such structures with attitudes that are assumed to be general and objective, for example, ideological neutrality and relativism.

But as this recognition of moral relativism indicates, alongside the scientific ideal there has developed in the West a deep-seated, in some senses antiscientific commitment to free subjective conviction as the ultimate tribunal for assessing structures. Pressed by the same metaphysical uncertainty that nurtured the development of science as a more restricted but also more reliable domain of knowledge than metaphysics, individuals have felt compelled to justify their own constructions of reality on a quasi-Cartesian ground: the clarity and distinctiveness of the connections formed in one's own mind, through its own free exercise. Half a century after Heisenberg and Gödel, ideas of natural science itself turn up regularly as topics of hot dispute on Phil Donahue's show.)

The cultural paradigm for this second model of construing reality is the concept of "art." This concept, which crystallized in the late Enlightenment,[7] gained such high cultural prestige in the nineteenth century that it took on an aura of mystification once reserved for the Church. And the paradigm for mystical art in nineteenth-century Europe was undoubtedly music.

Romantic music was thoroughly permeated by assumptions and values that showed its lack of autonomy — for example, its reliance on particular cultural associations among listeners, its interaction with other sensuous mediums, and its emphasis on personal style.[8] It was probably the first Western musical style to make explicit the dependence of musical configuration on the identity and values of a specific cultural situation. Nevertheless, like science, it too involved an illusion of autonomous significant structure.

Lacking culturally secure means of establishing what linguistic scholars call the "double articulation" of *signifiant* and *signifié*, music in the nineteenth century could not promise to signify anything outside the immediacy of its own structure. Because of this condition, music became the paradigm of a (syntactic) medium that need not "point" (in semantic fashion) but need merely be. This paradigm was enshrined in the romantic idealization of (untexted, purely instrumental) "absolute music."

According to this latter ideal, the individual composer of genius imagined a kind of transcendently existing, self-determined musical structure, which he translated into physical terms for society. The power of "absolute music" derived precisely from its status as an abstractly evocative, yet concretely bound metaphor for an ideal of self-contained significant structure. This ideal conditioned thinking about all romantic music. However much its actual persuasiveness owed to the forcefulness of a confident and coherent personal style or to other nonautonomous elements, romantic music located its own ultimate basis of validity in what the composer Carl Maria von Weber called its "inner connections," that is, the necessity of its own internal structure.[9]

Moreover, since the origins of this structure were subjective, the composer, in trying to establish its objective validity, felt obligated to set the highest standards of responsibility for the use of his own newly acknowledged state of imaginative freedom. Not trusting to any standards but his own unmistakable conviction as to "what comes next," and answering only to himself rather than fearing external sanction, the romantic composer recognized a need to safeguard the integrity of his imagined structure. He tried to actualize it in physical terms with a degree of honesty and precision that generalized structures neither required nor encouraged.

As a result, in an age of disintegrating artistic and moral consensus, the musical structure became a perfect paradigm for the concept of integrity, in the sense not only of wholeness but also of honesty based on inner conviction. This status was also served, of course, by the reluctance of romantic music (continuing the Kantian tradition of aesthetic disinterestedness) to define itself through an externally determined functionality and thereby subject itself to the possibility of corruption for ulterior social purposes. Given the theoretical incorruptibility of self-knowledge, the individualistic structure, such as the musical artwork, came to seem the last remaining safeguard for the very possibility of integrity in society.

This sense of duty on the composer's part reflected some perception of the tremendous disparity in post-Enlightenment culture between society and the individual. This disparity is a matter not only of power but also of character: individualistic structures are heavily strained by the contradiction between their own structural ideals and their concrete actuality. Unlike a generalized structure—say, the U.S. Constitution (or even the U.S.S.R. *Constitution?*)—an individualized expression, which requires the precise articulation of a vision, stands to lose its integrity and identity if even minor changes are imposed on its actual physical structure. Thus it is relatively easy, even without the use of brute force, for society to threaten the existence of an individualized structure.

Furthermore, it is not just the existence of particular individualistic structures but the very category of such structures that is jeopardized by society in Western culture. True, in countries committed in principle, by way of ideological neutrality, to political tolerance, any particular individualized expression has at least a theoretical chance of coming into socially recognized existence. Yet even in such countries, the social existence of individualistic constructs is secure only as a general principle. At an individual level, the public existence and integrity of any particular structure are not any less contingent, or any less subject to external ideological considerations, than those of a letter to the editor. But if an individual structure cannot count on persuading society of its necessity even through the most scrupulous realization of its own inner laws, then the essential force of such a structure is undercut, and the grounds for existence that the very category of individuality has chosen for itself are challenged. And indeed, as the actual obstacles to such persuasion have become increasingly apparent in twentieth-century Western culture, entire categories of individual enterprise have in fact become threatened with extinction. This, I would argue, is the current situation of contemporary music.

For almost 200 years, Western art music has tried to secure a social guarantee of its own existence, precisely as if it were as "self-evident" a structure as science. Basing its case on the realization of its own internal laws, Western art music has tried to project the necessity of that realization by defining itself, in its individual manifestations, with an ever-increasing degree of precision. Thus composers have moved toward transforming their compositions into authoritative texts. They have tried to avert misreading by filling their scores with increasingly detailed instructions or, in some electronic works, by eliminating the vagaries of human performance altogether. To the extent possible, they have tried to control the printing and production of their works; where they have failed, their agents (the musicologists) have labored to repair what is seen as the resultant social damage.

And for a period of time, beginning with the Haydn of the London Symphonies and exemplified especially by Beethoven, this demand actually worked. Taking advantage of structural conventions, including tonality, which still had considerable general intelligibility, and of external cultural associations as well, composers for the next century or so managed to make personal style itself a vehicle for guaranteeing the social value (and hence the existence) of an essentially individualistic category, Western art music. Furthermore, through the enormous impact of Beethoven, the romantics were even able to establish the notions of the standard repertory and the masterpiece, which preserved specific examples of individual musical art. Though not every work survived, of course, the success of the category and the success of the individual work tended to reinforce each other. In successfully projecting the illusion of itself as a self-evidently necessary structure, Western art music gave itself a privileged status in Western culture, comparable to that of science.

During the twentieth century, however, the contemporary composition has refined the principle of individualization to such an extreme as to shatter social illusions of its own internal necessity. Requiring each element in a work to be structurally necessary — in Webern's case conferring so much value on the individual element that the latter in itself suggests self-contained (if not isolated) significance — the contemporary composer has come to place a very nearly absolute burden of responsibility on each compositional decision.[10]

As a result, in spite of its own essentially abstract structural ideal, the contemporary composition has increased to a degree unprecedented in Western history the importance of particularity *as such* to its own conception. Starting with the attempts of such early twentieth-century figures as Debussy, Schoenberg, and Stravinsky to distance themselves in their various ways from romanticism, the contemporary composer has generally avoided presenting his or her composition either as a vision of genius or as an argument that works primarily through stylistic persuasiveness. Attributing a quasi-objective necessity to the demands of their craft, contemporary composers have in fact taken a romantic tendency to its extreme: they have located musical significance not just metaphorically but literally — coextensively and exclusively — in the structure of their works.

In so doing, the contemporary composer has demystified the metaphysically evocative romantic artwork into a self-contained piece of craft, with no further claims to a sacred place in society. Moreover, even when drawing upon materials from a common social sphere, contemporary composers have located the meaning and value of a composition so completely in its own actual physical structure that the latter has become totally vulnerable to the slightest social activity that comes near it.

Recognizing the danger, contemporary composers have sought to render the composition tamper-proof by individualizing each structure, encoded in a variety of private languages, to the point where it is protected against even the simple social activity of comprehending. This attempt to preserve the composition inviolate has largely succeeded, yet the danger has not abated.

A radically individualistic artwork is not an assault on a general archetype. Unlike a scientific experiment, which upon failure can be replaced by another without jeopardizing the category of science, a radically individual artwork, which claims to be necessary and complete in itself, embodies the very principle of individuality. Hence in exposing to doubt the necessity of its own internal structure the contemporary composition has also opened to question the need for itself and for its category altogether.[11] Not only have the concepts of "repertory standard" and "masterpiece" disappeared in relation to contemporary music;[12] in addition, contemporary music, viewed collectively, is engaged in constant battle to achieve performance. And it is so difficult to get new contemporary scores published and recorded that the physical preservation and dissemination of this music seems scarcely less tenuous than in the days of the isolated medieval scribe.

From the standpoint of individualism, contemporary music has come closer than any in Western history to achieving a state of structural autonomy: more than any of their predecessors, contemporary composers have felt free to make their musical case to society on a basis of internal merit. But an enormous gap exists between the necessity posited by composers in their structures and the claim such structures have been able to make on a compelling social interest to hear it through.

At most, what the contemporary composition, with its hermetically self-contained rationale, communicates to society today is not a self-evident structure or even the illusion of one. Rather it is a sense of the piece as a fragment that might potentially have meaning for society in a context that contemporary music, insisting on its autonomy, refuses to provide. To answer its own challenge, and to reclaim that possibility of social validation which its own values require, contemporary music must find a way to reintegrate those values with some larger and present context.

The Inability of Contemporary Music to Challenge Society Directly

The Composer

> *What replaces the pleasure principle is an absolute demand for holiness of the will, as shown in a sort of Kantian reverence for the sense of aesthetic duty.*

It might be supposed that, given the criticism of general values implied by its rigorous, even radical individualism, contemporary music sets out to challenge the assumptions and priorities of society simply and directly. With respect to the commonly imagined effect of contemporary music, this supposition has a certain persuasiveness. Starting with Schoenberg's systematic disallowance of traditionally defined consonances and tone-centers and Stravinsky's early rhythmic violence, the massive rejection by contemporary music of conventional syntax and expectations has often suggested that such music wants to shock the public into paying attention to it. Whether by startling, angering, disorienting, or even temporarily alienating its audience, much contemporary music can be imagined as trying to challenge listeners in ways that will draw them back, however reluctantly (like Salieri returning obsessively to the darkened balconies on the film *Amadeus*) for further hearings, and perhaps even for a change of consciousness. Tempting as such an argument may be, however, it runs counter to the generating impulses of contemporary music.

Admittedly, to assert that a direct social challenge is inconsistent with the generating impulses of contemporary music is not the same as arguing that old, wholly uncritical modes of musical response are acceptable to contemporary music. True, a good deal of twentieth-century composition, even apart from explicitly popular music, has not renounced those modes. But then, not all of this music can properly be called "contemporary."

Contemporary Western audiences do recognize and like works by such composers active in the twentieth century as Sibelius, Ravel, Vaughan Williams, Orff, Copland, Shostakovich, Barber, and Britten. As a category of positive value, however, the concept of "contemporary" music was created and developed not by the general public but within a musically and intellectually elite tradition of specialists. And within the domain of that tradition, which today, especially in the United States, is heavily academic, the contemporary status of such popular favorites is uncertain. Certainly their music occupies a less prominent place in the American musicological curriculum than does that of such less generally well-known composers as Varèse, Messiaen, Carter, Babbitt, Stockhausen, or Penderecki.

Over the course of this century, to be sure, contemporary music has developed not as a monolithic but as a quintessentially pluralistic enterprise, with a diversity of schools and interests that allow many sorts of interpretation. Nevertheless, a strong argument can be made that the contemporary musical aesthetic was shaped above all by the ideas of the most strikingly unpopular of its early important figures, Arnold Schoenberg.

True, a number of composers, notably in the first half of the twentieth century, and notably such non-Germans as Debussy, Satie, the so-called Les

Six, Bartók, Prokofiev, and possibly Ives, along with the Viennese Berg, came closer than Schoenberg to producing "contemporary masterpieces"— works that can claim support from both contemporary aestheticians and the general public. Yet a college survey course with limited time in which to present an account of twentieth-century music history would most likely not focus first on these composers.[13]

Stravinsky's early ballets are among the most widely successful works acceptable to the contemporary aesthetic; in particular the *Rite of Spring* had unusually broad impact as a symbol of newness in musical art. In his writings as well as his music, moreover, Stravinsky defined an antihistorical, demystified credo of rigorous "objective" craftsmanship which contributed substantially to the development of the contemporary aesthetic. Nevertheless, I would argue that Stravinsky's musical philosophy, with its strong strain of pragmatism, is insufficiently systematic and comprehensive to bear the weight of defining and unifying the contemporary aesthetic movement in music. Moreover, despite his great stature and influence both musically and aesthetically, Stravinsky did not have the same commanding presence in the history of contemporary music that Picasso, to whom he is so often compared, did in modern art. In the end, especially after his turn to neoclassicism and later serialism, Stravinsky might, in an overloaded survey course, be studied mainly as a foil to Schoenberg (whereas the reverse is almost unthinkable). In this sense, the role assigned him might be little less conditioned by his relation to Schoenberg than would be that of Schoenberg's disciple Webern.

Webern would be difficult to cut, not even so much because of his tremendous musical influence as because of the degree to which he surpassed Schoenberg himself in crystallizing the musical implications of Schoenberg's aesthetic theory. There can be little doubt, on the other hand, that even the most inefficient instructor would feel compelled to discuss Schoenberg as the archetypal representative of the contemporary musical aesthetic and, on that account ultimately of the history of Western art music in the twentieth century. Though Schoenberg may in one view seem to represent an extreme case of ideological consistency and purity rather than the middle ground of twentieth-century composition, it is precisely his ability to delineate the outer reaches of the twentieth-century composer's situation that allowed him to lay down terms that forced a response, and thus to serve as a touchstone in definitions of the contemporary musical aesthetic.

Whatever the distance between other contemporary composers and Schoenberg's own position as last heir to the nineteenth-century German cultural tradition, Schoenberg's ideas as set out both in his music and in his numerous aesthetic writings had a historically decisive impact on the formation of the concept of contemporary music. And from the vantage point of his powerful legacy, "contemporary music" cannot be considered a chronologically descriptive term, encompassing all newly created twentieth-century art music. It is a historically normative term, with aesthetic, intellectual, and even moral implications. The reason that the most popular twentieth-century composers fail to qualify as indisputably contemporary is not that experts consider their music bad. On the contrary, most experts would probably agree that this music is well crafted, and good of its kind; and they would place that "kind" squarely in the camp of artistic rather than of popular or commercial music. The difficulty is that this music is felt to have sidestepped the central historical problem of contemporary music as laid out by Schoenberg, which is to evoke a response solely on the basis of its fidelity to uncompromising self-determined standards of good and bad.[14]

From the standpoint of the contemporary aesthetic, any other construction of the terms "good" and "bad" is artistically suspect.[15] This is why experts do not evaluate twentieth-century music in Darwinian terms. During the nineteenth century, though abandoning the tradition of the fixed general archetype and exposing the public with unprecedented speed to the musical adaptations required by an individualistic aesthetic, Western art music was still able to establish a genre, the masterpiece, which could satisfy both composer and a relatively broad public. Even today, contemporary elitists assume a survival of the fittest in the nineteenth-century standard repertory, and are prepared to interpret the absence of a work from that repertory as a sign of compositional weakness. The individual structure of the forgotten work is presumed internally inadequate to the task of validating itself socially.

But no such assumption is made about the twentieth-century repertory; if anything such absence is taken for a mark of compositional virtue. For popular success, from a contemporary aesthetic viewpoint, almost by definition entails a process of misconception and improper evaluation. To be fully contemporary, a composition must be able to vouch for its own integrity as a structure *sui generis*; it must discourage efforts to understand it as an example, no matter how excellent, of a preexisting kind.[16] But since general understanding almost invariably involves reference to some sort of preestablished structure, what the public validates when it accepts a twentieth-century work tends to be not the value inherent in a unique structure but the nonbinding force of such value. It validates its own ability to draw on extrinsic, preexistent standards and thereby to interpret a structure as something other than what it specifically is. And this last violates the very *raison d'être* of individualistic enterprise.

The contemporary aesthetic has refined the relativistic aspects of historicism to such an extreme that it has negated the hopes of contemporary music as a whole for historical vindication as a standard repertory and locked it into a self-contradiction. Unable to achieve secure social status on strictly structural grounds, contemporary music has left itself only one legitimate way to draw a relatively broad public. Its one rather wan hope is to coerce the public, through a sense of moral obligation based on faith in the composer's integrity and in the authority of experts, into supporting contemporary music for the fact, rather than the substance, of its individualistic virtue.

In effect, the contemporary aesthetic has loaded relativism, a supposedly value-free position, with a complex value system of its own. Its demystification of art to craft is deceptive because this has simultaneously served a need to mystify, at an intensified level, the seriousness of the composer's structural duty and thereby preserve the concept of "art" itself. Contemporary music considers itself aesthetically superior to other new music because of a belief that it has kept alive the idea of individuality and thus the possibility of art.

Indeed, not just modern painting (as Tom Wolfe laments on popular grounds) but also contemporary music (as Adorno laments on other grounds) has in effect worked out a Hegelian process of *Aufhebung*, whereby the idea has surpassed the medium as a locus of artistic value.[17] More than anything else it is this priority that has given Schoenberg his towering historical importance in contemporary music; for Schoenberg "the *idea*," as prior to sound and style, generates and indeed *is* "the totality of a piece."[18]

This priority of the conceptual is evident not just in Schoenberg's career or in schools of so-called concept art music. It is evident also in the characteristic incorporation of discursive elements into the generating principle of contemporary compositions. At bottom, even music that seems to denigrate structure in favor of new sensuous or experiential definitions of music generally manages to retain the primacy of structure that vouches for its validity, by expanding the notion of autonomy to include the idea of that experience. No Western musical structure has ever lent itself so readily to verbal "explanation" as the contemporary one — or felt so keenly the need to be able to do so.

Of course, the priority of the idea is not new in the history of Western art music. One could argue that it dominated music from the Middle Ages through Bach, until the secularization of culture decisively liberated the sensuousness of sound. In that earlier period, however, the parameter of "idea" worked precisely to counter any claim by music to an autonomous aesthetic value. Far from conferring any superiority, the presence of "idea" underscored the subordination of music to a higher metaphysical order. Nor is this priority new in terms of listening habits; the acceptance of any music probably involves a process of "neutralization," to use Adorno's term, whereby the audience ends by hearing not so much a musical structure as its own idea thereof. In contemporary music, however, this priority has a theoretical status that is ultimately used to support the claim of this music to the highest aesthetic significance of its century and, on that account, to a moral significance as well.

For the supposed neutrality of relativism and its cultural manifestations has indeed been used by contemporary music to stake out a position of moral superiority for itself. Believing itself to have kept alive the category of art music for all new works, even those that have lapsed in their historical responsibility to art, the radically innovative contemporary aesthetic allows its partisans, not excepting Adorno, precisely the same satisfaction as that felt by Orthodox observers who maintain an unchanging faith not only for themselves but also for the sake of their fallen coreligionists.

Now there is little doubt that it is more difficult today than it would have been thirty years ago to characterize the enterprise of new composition as in some sense Schoenberg's legacy. Serialism itself, as both a method and a philosophy of composition, has lost a good deal of its former hegemony. Moreover electronic music, multimedia efforts, tonal revisionism, and various strains of popular art music have all developed musical sources distinct from Schoenberg, and in many cases distinct from traditional Western art music.[19] In fact, to the extent that composers in these and other schools have relinquished the ideal of structural autonomy and tried to alter the character of the purposes, occasions, and audiences for which they create music, their work clearly signals the emergence of a new, postcontemporary aesthetic, which is rapidly extending its domain. That aesthetic may be one of neoconservativism or philistinism; it may be one of activism or advocacy; it may be one of post-art or non-art; it may also be one of fake art, or trash. Apart from a commitment to the discipline of structural autonomy — that is, to the terms of the contemporary aesthetic — new music has not yet found a basis for guaranteeing its own honesty. It can only point to a broadened accessibility to judgment by others, which in itself is not enough to satisfy the criteria for integrity and value, or to overcome the objections, of an individualistic aesthetic.

But even including such schools, the majority of current composers still work as heirs to the ideals and contradictions of Schoenberg's norm of radical autonomy in the sense of preparing painstakingly constructed pieces for presentation at traditional occasions as potential masterpieces (not, to be sure, in the heroic nineteenth-century mold, but nevertheless, as repertory staples). Some, in the tradition of the romantics down through Schoenberg himself, may periodically step outside the music into journalism or other enterprises through which they can bark for the carousel.[20] But from the standpoint of Schoenberg's legacy, such promotional efforts are only ancillary to a main event (not integral or even identical to it as in the case of most PR hype). Any effort *within* the music to engage an audience directly is still open to charges of charlatanism. It reduces composing from an artistic to a political activity; and as an individualistic counterpart to the general concept of government by law, contemporary music can no more recognize political purposes than the American Constitution (at least in theory) can recognize political crimes.

Ultimately the way in which a composer addresses the audience makes no difference. The taint of charlatanism has affected political music, which is accepted and discussed as contemporary only insofar as its political aspect is ignored.[21] It affects socially ingratiating music; though Leonard Bernstein's popular tone may be no less motivated by sincere conviction than was Ralph Shapey's onetime decision to pocket his new works rather than violate them through public exposure, Bernstein is often dismissed as "packaging" his work for commercial sale and profit. The taint affects "happenings" and other "gimmick" music, often associated with John Cage and his tradition;[22] by definition, in terms of the individualistic aesthetic, it must affect any sort of challenge addressed directly to an audience. To a system of values as dependent as the contemporary aesthetic is on the composer's good faith, charlatanism is a capital charge. Committed, as an expression of individualistic values, to vouch for its own honesty, contemporary music cannot issue a direct challenge to society without invalidating its own concept.

The Audience

We have so little time that whatever takes a lot of time seems unjust.[23]

Contemporary music is precluded by its own aesthetic from challenging society directly not only in terms of its own intent but also in terms of the specific kind of musical response it can afford to permit itself. To defend its own autonomy, contemporary music, unlike earlier new music, requires a particular mode of listening that reinforces its isolation from society.

This mode, as set forth by Schoenberg and Adorno among others, can be called "structural listening," a process that amounts to following and comprehending the unfolding realization, with all its inner relationships, of a musical conception.[24] Developed out of the formalistic doctrine crystallized in Eduard Hanslick's classic, *The Beautiful in Music*, and marking in effect Hanslick's historical last laugh on Wagner, structural listening is today the elite form of listening *par excellence*. It is, for example, the method of listening almost exclusively taught in American college music departments, which unlike their European counterparts have no tradition of mingling musical with philosophical analysis. Indeed, the method serves to justify the very need for higher education in music since innate competence in structural listening is almost universally assumed in the West to be a rare gift.

Nor is any amount of sheer listening experience, which *is* widely available today in Western culture, deemed sufficient to develop such competence. For since its conceptualization around 1800 as a medium of "art," music has been recognized in the West as presenting extraordinary cultural obstacles to a knowing of itself in this structural sense.[25] Thus the precise naming of the components in a musical structure, which has become fully standardized and characteristic of musical discussion in our century, requires technical education for its mastery. Moreover, unlike architecture, which also has precisely nameable parts, art music has become so radically defunctionalized that no appreciation of structure can be gained through encounters with functional adequacy or inadequacy. Furthermore, to the extent that it operates as a physically opaque medium, without the semantic capacity to point at a more familiar correlative domain of meanings, Western music circumvents short-cuts to its structural comprehension. Though counterparts to the Monarch plot outlines are not unknown in music, their inadequacy to their medium is even more patent than in the case of literature. These obstacles all limit the social base of structural listening.

Structural listening focuses intensely on its musical object, the definition of which is assumed to owe nothing to the individual or cultural biases of its users. Rather than requiring self-criticism, the method treats the individual user's mental framework, in a Kantian sense, as a kind of universally grounded, and hence ideologically neutral, epistemologically transparent structure. In short, structural listening is seen to offer an objectivity that makes it an exact counterpart to scientific method, and as such it is regularly applied by experts to music of all periods in Western history.[26]

Without question, this method has opened up a kind of relativistic perspective on earlier music that was previously lacking. Not surprisingly, given the clear affinity of structural listening to products and values of the Enlightenment, music based on the thoroughly relational concept of classical tonality seems particularly to invite the method, and could even be said to have set up the conditions that engendered it. Yet the degree to which this method, by failing to recognize post-Kantian cultural insights, remains culturally limited and limiting should not be overlooked. Structural listening is not sufficient to account for all the generating aesthetic principles, much less for the individual and cultural values of a composer (not to mention those of the listener) that bear on the definition of earlier musical structures.

To some extent, in fact, the method actually violates the original conception of such works. For even apart from the social functionality that shaped

Western music in a fundamental way up to the end of the eighteenth century, almost no Western music outside the classical style ever presented itself as a fully autonomous significant structure. On the contrary, most music has expected to be perceived in the context of a larger cultural scheme of ideas and values (for example, medieval religious symbolism, baroque "affect," or later, romantic poetic association). Before the onset of tonality, moreover, when the very notion of autonomy had yet to establish itself, distinctions between style and form are at best problematical. And not even in the classical period, at least until Beethoven began to place rhetorical emphasis on many of his main structural junctures (in effect questioning the self-evidence of structure), is there reason to suppose that composers rejected the ideal of seemingly artless art, as articulated by Kant.[27] Rather, one can suppose that Haydn and Mozart preferred to manipulate structural detail by sleight of hand; while sufficient convention was provided to make complex structures, especially in Haydn's case, seem persuasively and generally intelligible, the secrets of their guild, like Mozart's Masonic references, may well have been assumed a private matter.

In a sense, moreover, like Schenker's "deep" analysis, which is closely related (though more explicitly limited in scope to certain kinds of tonal music), structural listening could take place through intelligent score-reading, without the physical experience of an external sound source. By Schoenberg's own testimony (see note 18 in this chapter) this method tends to relegate to a secondary role all other modes of response, including sensuous experience and stylistic appreciation. And even if we leave aside style (a notion still too seldom subjected to rigorous reflection in musical scholarship), as an unconsciously produced and problematical parameter of music, there can be little doubt that as the anticorporeal bias of religious mysticism was left behind, Western composers, including the Viennese classicists, came to place a high value on the sensuous actuality of their music.[28] By the nineteenth century, specificities of instrumental color were in no small measure constitutive of the musical configuration.

In this respect too, then, structural listening constitutes a cultural violation, which may do more harm than good to the status of Western art music. Hanslick did his work well. Far more than the neutralizing effects of time and familiarity, Hanslick's formalism has distanced its heirs from the overwhelming sensuous (not to mention sexual) immediacy of music that many besides Nietzsche likened, in the case of Wagner, to the hypnotic and addictive effects of a drug. It has inhibited such self-indulgence as "irrational" and "irresponsible." Thus, with whatever social power it has, structural listening has encouraged the loss of one of the most popular attractions of art music.

Whatever its historical shortcomings with respect to earlier music, however, there can be little doubt that structural listening, with all its distancing effects, is not only appropriate to contemporary music but also essentially required by it. Demanding to be accepted for what it is, and committed to guaranteeing its own honesty and validity through the necessity of each structural decision, contemporary music (including chance music to the extent that it subsumes contingency itself under a species of structural necessity) really has no choice but to require a structural response. Contemporary music demands not just intelligent selective perception but a unifying structural understanding. And since every element must have a structural necessity in a contemporary work, the proper and adequate understanding of the latter demands a degree of structural concentration on the listener's part equal to that which the composer put into its construction. The entire structure, or more precisely the entire piece *as structure*, must be audible to a listener who is actively and continuously attentive.[29] To the composer's painstaking exercise of responsibility the listener has the same sort of moral obligation as you do reading this essay.

To be sure, many modern composers (George Crumb is a fine example) are exquisitely sensitive and deeply committed to elements of timbre. But to the extent that a composition projects itself as a purely sensuous impression — as a kind of sound — or, as so often happens even in specialized publications, that it elicits only stylistic modes of comprehension, it has disqualified itself as contemporary music and opened up its status to doubt.[30] It has failed to establish the one condition, structural necessity, through which it could fulfill the promise that defines and justifies contemporary music, that of guaranteeing its own validity. The mere arousal of sensuous pleasure, a process long recognized as offering no grounds for defining general as opposed to individual necessity, is not enough to sustain its claim to the privileged social status of "art."

If structural listening became a general habit, it would force society to judge new musical structures on their own terms. This situation would have the social value claimed by the individualistic principle: an honest individual's position in society would in many ways be improved if that individual's arguments were judged strictly in terms of their own internal consistency rather than in terms of extrinsic ideological or stylistic biases. (Make no mistake, though — in other ways the depreciation of ideology and style would constitute a serious loss.) Ideally, structural listening as a basically general, "objective" attitude applied to individually designed structures might maximize the benefits of cultural relativism, and even reconcile the demands of freedom and social order, giving all individual expression access to a scrupulously fair public.

Such achievements remain unrealized, however, because genuine structural listening is itself a fiction. In its pure state it would require the possibility of defining (and assessing) autonomous significant structures, without allowance for individual and cultural differences in perception, ordering principles, style, and values, an illusion that an enterprise based on radically individual principles is singularly ill-equipped to sustain.

What the demand for structural listening actually does is to alienate society from contemporary music in two respects. First, it requires a conscious expenditure of time devoted exclusively to itself, both for its mastery and for its exercise; Schoenberg suggests the potential size of the investment in the very title of his essay "Eartraining through Composing."[31] In a culture accustomed to the speed of mass technology, with its instant disposability and dial-flipping, the bias of the individual against an expenditure of "quality time" can be overcome only by some far more positive inducement to self-interest than the moral force of structural autonomy. Hence, despite the resistance of painting to generalized dissemination (a print hardly has the adequacy of a recording), and despite the cost of maintaining art galleries, modern painting, at least in the United States, is less financially dependent than contemporary music on an academic environment, and far more "fully integrated in the cultural life . . . of society,"[32] for it requires only space. In direct contrast to the experience provided by music — that is, by *art* music — the painting sits still while the audience moves on.

Secondly, the demand for structural listening cuts off the general public from its accustomed sensuous and stylistic modes of listening, which if encouraged might enlarge the audience for contemporary music. Uninitiated college students, for example, almost always write more intelligently about live performances of contemporary music than about those of older music. Precisely because they lack the cultural perspective and preestablished associations which condition (often negatively) their response to older music, and which lead them often to evaluate performances at the expense of hearing a composition, they react with considerable directness to contemporary music. Though they do not find the music structurally transparent, they do find it culturally accessible in much the same way, though not on the same grounds, that earlier listeners must have found the music of their own time. Because they share with contemporary music a cultural sensibility, they are able to some extent to interact with it, not as an object of reverence but as an element in an ongoing cultural conversation. When allowed to relinquish the oppressive responsibility of structural comprehension, and asked only for the degree of reflectiveness needed to write a short paper, they show themselves sensitive to raw elements,[33] cultural affect, and even conceptual suggestiveness. Instead of assuming ideas about the music that replace the musical experience, they make ideas to fit the musical experience. They show themselves stimulated by the sensuous abrasiveness or even the conceptual irreverence to authority they hear. At times they even seem to experience a sense of liberation from the excessive familiarity, the aura of grand metaphysical vision, the cultural optimism, or the cloying beauty of various older styles, qualities they cannot integrate into their own cultural experience. They become a willing audience.

But even if such modes of listening were adequate to the self-demands of contemporary music, there is probably no way in which they can any longer be used to draw a sizable willing public to that music. No figure in society at large has the cultural authority of a college instructor to "permit" the indulgence of nonstructural listening, an indulgence regularly exercised by the public with styles where intelligibility is not an issue. Nor can the coercive force of a course requirement, which is in any case antithetical to the spirit of individualism, be employed to create an audience in a free secular society. And as suggested by its ultimate indifference, for all its self-consciousness, to its own stylistic aspect — like the Beast's demand that Beauty see only its noble character — the contemporary composition that is true to its own aesthetic has no way itself of authorizing terms for survival that deny its own identity.

Ultimately, the conditions that demand structural listening have resulted in its social irrelevance. The audience of the converted to whom contemporary music genuinely appeals, or for whom it at least serves some direct nonfinancial need, is so small and socially insignificant that it does not even encompass a secure majority of musical experts. (One could argue that centered as it is on composers themselves, and on performers and critics with a stake in contemporary music, the audience for this music represents more an extension of self than an authentic other.) And the public at large, unable to perceive the structure of contemporary music, which would be tantamount to understanding it, has formed its own "idea" of contemporary music, as something to be avoided.

Finally it does not matter whether Francis Sparshott is right to posit "a 'sense for' music," which allows the listener a relationship even with music of a wholly unfamiliar sort.[34] Nor does it matter to the social situation of contemporary music whether public incomprehension bears out an underlying cultural contradiction, so that the more a composer refines the individuality of a structure, the less generally audible that structure becomes. To an audience that refuses its presence, it makes no difference whether a composition stays true to its creator's principles or screams for attention. The musical habit that contemporary music has established is not structural listening but no listening at all.

For most contemporary music, the prospects of broad support are at best something like those of an X-rated movie scheduled for presentation on the Public Broadcasting System. Not even the self-culpatory tonal revisionism of a George Rochberg can hope to achieve sell-out status in any but a negative elitist sense. Avoiding even the occasion to hear contemporary music, the public has renounced any interest in validating its structure. For the supposed neutrality of cultural relativism, the contemporary aesthetic has allowed the public to substitute the neutrality of total indifference.

As a result, contemporary music has imperiled the availability of a general public not only for itself but for other new music as well, especially in the United States, which has come to rival Europe as a source of new music. Negative public presumptions about new music have become so automatic that on the whole even composers seeking to break out of individualistic constraints and establish some sort of league with society against their own predecessors still face formidable obstacles to attracting a sizable audience.[35] Having collapsed into a condition of solipsism, which undercuts the force of its own self-defined right to exist, contemporary music threatens other new music with the self-negating aspects of a Hegelian *Aufhebung*, while offering other music no help in defining compensatory, self-transcending aspects of that process. Far from protecting the viability of "art" as a social category for all new music, contemporary music has confirmed the historical obsoleteness of that category. Even if contemporary music were suddenly somehow able to withdraw its demand for structural listening, the social damage has been done. So long as any new art music continues to present itself as a traditional occasion for admiring art, it is unlikely to issue any challenge to society that will be heard.

Contemporary Music: The Challenge of Its Historical Situation

It is time to . . . look at . . . ways in which the relation of music to life is something that the notion of an art misses entirely.

Contemporary music is scarcely the first genre of Western music to define or even to champion itself as something new. This situation has many cyclically reappearing precedents even before romanticism: the fourteenth-century Ars Nova, Tinctoris's brief for the composers of the past forty years (in 1477), the ferment of the Florentine Camerata and Monteverdi's *seconda prattica* in the late fifteenth and early sixteenth centuries, the reaction against "learned" counterpoint in the first half of the eighteenth century, and so on.

Before romanticism, however, the recognized basis for partisanship in these cases was some substantive change in style, not the condition of newness *per se*; indeed, alongside such periodic changes in stylistic values, the idea of establishing aesthetically prior archetypes for new composition retained its force.

Nor is contemporary music the first genre in Western history to encounter initial resistance. Up until the nineteenth century, however, even new styles could generally count on the support of some economically powerful religious or social group. Even after the Council of Trent, as the vested interest of socially privileged classes in conservative musical styles became increasingly apparent, and as Court patronage declined and middle-class participation in a public musical life grew, the power of some elite still constituted the principal guarantee of income for European composers, innovative or not, who wished to maintain the inherited standards of their craft.

Initial resistance to new music began to seem characteristic of Western culture only toward the end of the eighteenth century. The emergence of this cultural change seems well symbolized by Mozart's last three symphonies (written in 1788), for which no intended performing occasion is yet known. Even if such an occasion was intended, these works make retrospective sense, in a way that earlier works typically do not, as conceptions that no longer count on an audience. They are among the first Western compositions to begin their existence by surviving as museum masterpieces.

In historical terms, the catalyst for this cultural change was the interaction of a new aesthetic with a new set of social conditions, both of which contributed to the newly emerging conception and differentiation of general and individual principles. On the one hand, the romantics prized the newness of individual creativity in itself. And on the other hand, a clear shift was occurring in the balance of power between old elite groups and a newly urbanized mass public. With the storming of the Bastille, the right of small groups to control social and economic power was definitively recognized as contingent rather than necessary. Concomitantly, as the claims of the previously ignored social majority gained increasing social recognition, cultural power began to gravitate toward a larger general public. Against the latter, romantic individualism defined its own free necessity, and a distinction between elite art and mass entertainment began to harden.

It was at this point that the social contingency of art music began to seem a normal state of affairs. Faced with a broad public that valued novel versions of the familiar, but not individualistic newness, romantic composers could not count on the massive popular support that by exception was granted to Weber's opera *Der Freischütz* (1821). Instead, they had to take their chances on the development of a new powerful elite that, either through genuine understanding or through blind faith would see their works through an initial period of uncertainty.

And in fact an elite devoted to art did gain and hold sufficient cultural power to influence the tastes and habits of society from the top down. The "trickle-down" effect of nineteenth-century art music, epitomized in its own time, perhaps, by the fondness of organ-grinders for Rossini tunes, can still be felt today in the periodic use made by popular recording artists of old art music.

Evidence of this impact could be found on the physical scene of nineteenth-century Europe, both out of doors and within. Outside, the construction of public concert halls and opera houses, under way in the eighteenth century, went forward with increased intensity and ambitiousness.[36] True, a number of the works presented therein were enshrined masterpieces of the past (baroque choruses, Mozart operas, Beethoven symphonies). Yet the museum concept did not yet signify the extinction of new art music; though composers faced a lifetime of struggle and many failed projects, some degree of coexistence was maintained in the claims of old and new works on public musical life.[37] Virtuoso composers played their own works to large audiences, and Wagner had a theater built for his exclusive use. Likewise in the private domain, the popularity of the modernized piano spread rapidly. And though the music played most often on the piano certainly diluted standards of compositional individuality, its cultural impetus, unlike that, say, of the zither, a folk instrument, came from "above," not "below." Many distinguished romantics contributed to the development of salon music.

Similarly, the new artistic elite, again expanding on eighteenth-century developments, succeeded in securing a time as well as place for art music in European life. True, art music was no longer integrated into social life in the same characteristically functional sense as earlier music had been. Rather, time was now set aside exclusively to hear and perform art music. Instead of submitting to predetermined social functions, nineteenth-century art music defined a new kind of social function, and with it a new social need. And this function, in turn, solidified the identity of the new artistic elite as a group with the money and leisure to devote exclusively to art music. Thus art music in the nineteenth century integrated itself into the life of society by dint of the very separateness it established as normal for its own domain. If new music well into the classical period continued to present itself as functional (in a sense that was both social and artistic), art music thereafter achieved a socially functional functionlessness.

In short, contemporary music is not the first Western genre either to designate itself as new or to encounter initial social resistance. Nevertheless, however ones looks at it, its cultural situation is markedly different, and worse, than that of its nearest counterpart, the new music of the romantics. This is especially clear in the United States, where for a variety of reasons the alienation of even an educated public from contemporary music has defined its own extreme case in a way that crystallizes the difficulties of this music in Western culture, and ultimately the difficulties of the culture itself.[38] In this country, for example, the main public impetus for erecting new music buildings still comes from a general desire to hear not new but old art music (which also permeates, and not just for copyright reasons, the "contemporary" mediums of film and television advertising). Modern art seems to have done better in securing public recognition of its need for space: Is there a contemporary recital hall as widely known as the Museum of Modern Art, the Guggenheim, or the Hirshhorn? Similarly the private American interior, which now includes the automobile as well as the home, is dominated not by the piano but by the stereo, the compact disc player, the tape deck, the Walkman, the video cassette recorder, even the television set, in the sense that it carries music videos. The impetus for these does not come from any art music at all. And it is certainly easier to think of Americans who own contemporary prints but never listen to contemporary recordings than it is the reverse.

Likewise, contemporary music, which is designed principally for old notions of musical place, time, and occasion—the "enclosure,"[39] which, as Sparshott notes, "is the normal condition of our art music"—has evoked no generally felt need for its functionlessness. By contrast contemporary popular music, which requires no exclusive place, time, or occasion for its existence, has redefined the relation of music and society so as to insinuate itself into every space and activity that defines a day in the life of the modern American. And though this pervasiveness entails a musical inaudibility of its own, popular music has created such a powerful sense of need for itself that it regularly uses every aspect of the existing public landscape—concert hall, nightclub, sports stadium, park—to capitalize on more traditional notions of musical occasion as well.[40]

In fact, it is not so much the definitive victory in the twentieth century of old masterpiece over new art music that differentiates the situation of contemporary music from that of any earlier new art music. Today even a revered institution for older musical art, such as the Boston Symphony Orchestra, may be in trouble whether it performs contemporary music or not. If it does, the public gets restless. If it doesn't, it suffers the effects of decline.[41] Either way it is handicapped by its perceived inability to provide the kind of vital connection that links a society to the music of its own culture. And the music of contemporary American culture is popular music. What ultimately gives the situation of contemporary music its historical distinctiveness is the emergence, most notably in the United States, of a clear and reversed imbalance between general and individual kinds of power in the cultural domain, an imbalance that favors popular over artistic culture.

Popular tradition is not a new phenomenon in Western culture; over the course of the eighteenth and especially the nineteenth centuries, popular music gained unprecedentedly widespread recognition as an aspect of European musical life. Throughout most of Western music history, however, popular music (in the social sense) lagged far behind what we would now call art music in its access to the economic and technological resources of society. The lower-class, so-called suburban Theater an der Wieden, which launched Mozart's *Magic Flute* in 1791, could not hope to match the pomp of the coronation festivities surrounding the premiere, in Prague during the same year, of Mozart's *Clemenza di Tito*. Of course, as precisely this example indicates, lesser dependence on vested wealth was not necessarily detrimental to compositional imagination; the eighteenth-century *opera buffa* was musically a far more innovative genre than the aristocratic *opera seria* was. Nevertheless, works of a popular genre rarely enjoyed the cultural prestige of a *Magic Flute*; up until the twentieth century, relatively inferior resources generally insured that European popular music did not overtake art music as the most significant in its own culture.

Clearly this limitation on popular resources no longer applies in Western culture. Just as the center of Western culture has shifted over the twentieth century from European elitist tradition to the American marketplace, so, too, the most sophisticated resources and technology for musical production, reproduction, and dissemination are controlled not by contemporary art music, which until fairly recently was dominated by European composers, but by popular music, an essentially American phenomenon. This shift in control has given popular music a significance in Western culture which exceeds that of contemporary art music not just in a quantitative but even in a qualitative sense.

This is not to say that popular music is structurally better than contemporary art music, or even that it is necessarily more characteristic of its culture. Rather, to assert such a significance is to recognize the extent to which the direction of cultural influence has changed and become a "trickle-up" effect, whereby art music benefits from gains made in the commercial domain. And it is to suggest that contemporary popular music does better than contemporary art music at characterizing the expressive parameters of style in its culture in the sense of defining the stylistic strengths, as opposed to the weaknesses, of that culture. It is even to suggest that as a genre, contemporary popular music is better popular music than contemporary art music is art music because it is in the refinement of general values that modern

Western culture permits a capacity for excellence. It is to suggest that in a culture no longer committed to the elitism that nurtured great art, popular music does well what its culture allows to be done well.[42]

Through its preoccupation with electronic effect, popular music has changed the very conception of sound in Western culture to an extent that no contemporary electronic or computer art music has come close to matching. As a group, commercial sound engineers typically have a more sophisticated technological knowledge about the production of sound — and far more opportunity to draw on such knowledge — than do those whose primary concern is with the structural integrity of art music. And just as "recording artists" have replaced singers (witness the posthumous career of Elvis), so too the production of sophisticated high-tech sound, from the concept of which it is no longer possible to exclude video, has replaced composition as the primary musical activity in Western culture.[43] This is one reason that, despite the British origins of many of the most important rock stars, popular music is perceived as fundamentally American (another being, of course, that popular music is so clearly and deeply rooted in American black music). Elitists may criticize the structural crudity of most popular music, but what the public hears in such music is what is always heard, not autonomous structure but the sensuous manifestation of particular cultural values. What it hears, very prominently, is the presentation of sound at a technological level that in its totality is far more explicitly sophisticated than that which is characteristically available in art music, or which has ever before been available in any music. It hears that refinement of general principles through which American mass technology, for better and for worse, has come to dominate and define Western culture, and indeed various cultures outside the West, in the latter half of the twentieth century.

This is not to deny that much, possibly most popular music has established itself at the expense of many values central to an individualistic aesthetic. Just as the strengths of mass technology are by no means all necessarily strengths in a humane sense, so too popular music has involved many of the abuses of power that are so difficult to combat in a generalized structure: among others the manipulative use of market research, the glorification of drugs, electronic trickery, the violent aspects of heavy metal groups, or even in some instances, the use of texts that are offensive to particular racial, religious, or ethnic groups, or to women (see note 46, this chapter). Popular music has not resolved the fundamental contradiction in post-Kantian Western culture; it remains subject to many of the limits that condition both sides of that contradiction.

On the other hand, in part because it enjoys the superior social power of a generalized structure, popular music has been able to make more effective use than has contemporary art music of human strengths that are implicit (Adorno notwithstanding) in its situation. Whereas art music has been unable to make a socially compelling case for individual values, popular music has persuaded millions of individuals, in a way that is not felt to be coercive, of an advantage to be found in general values. It has turned its own state of mere nontranscendent physical existence into a sensuously valued experience. And in a post-masterpiece era, well symbolized by the physical transience of computerized information (scarcely more useful to future historians than the islands of medieval documentation), it has turned its own disposability into an occasion for continuous musical productivity. Yet at the same time, despite the historical tendency of generalized structures to replace each other, popular music has produced a standard repertory of its own; some of its works have actually won critical praise on structural grounds.[44]

In fact, an argument could be made that beyond just exploiting the advantages of power characteristic of generalized structures, popular music may have gone further than contemporary art music toward resolving some of the contradictions in Western culture. However much popular music through its immediate gratification may (as Adorno argued) dull the sensitivity of individuals to their own powerlessness, looked at another way it is also the only contemporary music that offers any continuity between public and private preference, or any actual sense of alternative to a contradiction between general and individual interest. Through its ability to integrate progressive, impersonal technology with traditional musical conventions, including not just tonality but also the affective appeal of sound and the opaque human performer, especially the human vocalist, popular music may in some of its guises have led the way in suggesting an alternative to the self-negating force of the Western historical imperative.

One could further argue that by acknowledging more willingly than contemporary art music does the nonexistence of autonomous significant structures, popular music has been able to draw into its domain a diversity of ethnic as well as social traditions and values that have long been excluded from a European-dominated Western art music. In this important sense, its pluralism has been more encompassing, and its relativism more positive, than their counterparts in art music; its relativism, one might say, is a concept that at least is in a position to serve an ideal of community rather than of individuality.[45] In fact one might argue that rather than advocating totalitarianism, as it could do, or, alternatively, demeaning the individual, popular music offers a critique of rugged individualism; at its politically most responsible it substitutes for the latter the cooperative, humane vision of "We Are the World."[46] And finally, though it has not been able to restore the concept of "new 'art' " in a society dominated by mass culture, popular music may have rendered a service even more important to music. By finding a way to sustain a sense of powerful social need for itself, popular music may well be what keeps alive a cultural inclination to perceive new organizations of sound as defining a medium called "music."

These arguments are offered tentatively; since popular music is not an autonomous significant structure, it is as subject as contemporary art music is to many plausible interpretations. And certainly these arguments, in attempting no distinction between "good" and "bad" popular music, bypass a question fundamental in any relativistic system of values, a question that is central to an individualistic aesthetic, and which no doubt keeps many composers from leaving the contemporary mainstream. That question is this: Barring individual structural responsibility, who or what is to vouch for the value of new music? If to answer this question, however, one is willing to go back beyond Aristotle and to readmit some of Plato's concern with the moral effect of music itself, then it could be argued that by developing not just the commercial but also the humane potentiality of mass technology, the music of Bob Dylan, or Bruce Springsteen, or the Talking Heads, or Tracy Chapman is the sort of music that one would most want to put in the time-capsule of latter twentieth-century Western culture.

If, nearing the centennial, or at least the diamond jubilee, of contemporary music it seems fair to view that music as an experiment that failed, it seems unfair to place all the blame for that failure on the music itself. The failure of contemporary music to establish close ties with society is symptomatic of underlying contradictions in a cultural value-system that has propelled this music toward a self-definition on untenable terms, and indeed encouraged it in the illusion that total self-definition is possible in society at all. This is not to consider contemporary music powerless to contribute to its own definition, or to hold it utterly blameless for its own predicament. Like other components of its culture, it has done its bit to perpetuate the contradiction from which it suffers. Nevertheless, to avoid embracing nihilism, contemporary music would be well advised to consider the value-system of modern Western culture itself as the principal failed experiment. If in the past contemporary music has constituted an indirect critique of the generalized sorts of values it opposes, it should now turn itself whole-heartedly to a critique that is already under way of its own participation in a cultural malaise, through its interpretation of such notions as integrity, success, art (the work, the text, the canon), and, ultimately, humanity itself.

For contemporary art music to sustain the humane purposes for which it came to champion imaginative freedom and honesty, it must struggle toward a new basis consistent with such purposes. It must find some way around the terms of the post–Kantian contradiction that has sapped it of its social vitality. This cannot be done by continuing to ask how an individual can create a complete musical universe and protect it against the depredations of an incomparably stronger society;[47] this question merely perpetuates the terms of the contradiction.

Instead, composers who start out from the contemporary tradition will almost certainly have to renounce the ideal of complete structural autonomy in favor of values associated with community, including communication.[48] They will have to recognize the ways in which all human statements actually operate within society, not as abstract structures with varying degrees of truth content but as elements in an ongoing discourse, inseparable from interpretation on all sides (the listener's and also the speaker's) in terms of numberless concrete values, associations, and needs. Hard as it seems, contemporary composers have an interest in finding a way, without abandoning altogether the virtues of historical consciousness and critical (as well as self-critical) reflection, or the possibilities of rational judgment, to move toward a condition of music closer to process than to structure. (Undoubtedly this will make it more difficult to produce the conventional enterprises of current musical scholarship, and for that matter all analyses that, like the present one, treat music as an "it.") Such composers will almost surely have to acknowledge limits on the powers, and even on the value of individuality. In short, they will have to develop a humane definition of "community," and take steps to reintegrate their music into a socially broader context of meanings and values.

Thus contemporary music would probably do well to give vigorous cooperative[49] reinforcement to efforts already under way to establish a post-contemporary aesthetic. Having more or less finished off the possibility of attracting a general public directly through the traditionally defined formal enclosed "occasion" for art, composers have more to gain than to lose by turning away from such occasions. Probably they would benefit from rejecting the notion of autonomy in a second sense,[50] by aiming at a rapprochement of their music with environments and mediums that have already secured a place in popular cultural life, such as electronic mediums (especially the video and cinema), dance, and nature.

Similarly, contemporary composers probably stand to benefit, as some composers already do, from putting aside their artistic heritage altogether for a while, and starting out from a popular basis of composition into which elements of their heritage might gradually be absorbed. Conceivably this could take them into a middle ground between art and popular music, which seems already to be populated by some reflective, articulate rock and jazz musicians as well as a growing number of adventurous "serious" composers. Even if the dichotomy between popular and art music—which is to say, that dichotomy between general and individual values which has impeded the development in the West of a concept of musical community—cannot be swiftly overcome, composers would still do well to ponder the wisdom of trying to individualize general values instead of trying to institutionalize individual ones. Certainly composers, and musicologists as well, should not encourage their students in the prevailing elitist ignorance of popular musical culture. If we in the academic musical elite don't know popular music, we should learn about it from our students (and our children).

Contemporary composers might also find it desirable, as popular music regularly does, to readmit social and political function as proper and central to the domain of music; likewise they might consider reinstating self-conscious moral reflection, on other issues besides compositional integrity, into that domain. Instead of assuming the impossibility of keeping communicative music honest,[51] or denying the positive needs that created general as well as individual principles, or insisting on the ideological neutrality of semiotic structures, they might contemplate the relationship between purpose and effect. Redefining music as a kind of "purposiveness *with* purpose," they might move away from the Kantian aestheticism of structure, with its indirect moral implications, to an explicit concern with moral effect as a basis for justifying music. The assessment of such effect would not necessarily require the services of a philosopher-king. On the contrary, this tense and messy task, which eludes easy general dictums, and which demands the unending exercise of honest, self-critical judgment, is ideally suited to those susceptible to the values of individuality. Possibly, then, contemporary composers could direct some of their sense of responsibility toward trying to keep humane the purposes and uses that their music does and can serve. Even if such refunctionalization, at least initially, helps only to define and serve communal rather than global needs, the effort to intensify and expand the kinds of relationships their music might have with society could help composers establish a more powerful and promising sense of social need for imaginative music, and hence a social stake in such music, as clear evidence that human life is worth sustaining.

In changing its self-conception in such ways, contemporary music would surely find not only that it had yielded the right to absolute self-definition in favor of a communal effort to define music but also that it had transformed itself into a nonautonomous construct of sound that could be called post-contemporary and perhaps even post-music. On the other hand, to the extent that contemporary music continues to dig in, abandon the musical life of society at large to commercial music, and turn inward on its private base, the legacy it leaves is also likely to be something that is not just post-contemporary but post-music as well, in a somewhat different sense.

Whatever it does next, contemporary music is almost certainly facing its own demise. Unless survival is equated with self-negation, one cannot imagine a new definition of contemporary music with which the latter can live. The opportunities available to it are not easy; but then, contemporary music has never leaned toward easy solutions. These opportunities, moreover, are far from insignificant. Contemporary music has the chance to salvage the human good in individuality in a way that does not require the illusion of individual omnipotence. In choosing how it enters what could well be an era of post-music, contemporary music will decide whether it can rise to its own primary challenge.[52]

Notes

Introduction

1. "New Music: My Music" (1930), *Style and Idea*, ed. Leonard Stein, trans. Leo Black (Berkeley and Los Angeles, 1984), p. 104.

2. I was luckier than most in my generation since in my very first semester at Columbia I was able to take a superb course on historiography from Edward Lippman, an uncommon musicologist deeply knowledgeable in many humanistic disciplines.

3. The arguments raised by Edward Lowinsky's scholarship, for example, were typically of this kind.

4. Old-fashioned music theory included a variety of courses in harmony, counterpoint, and sometimes formal analysis. In recent decades, Heinrich Schenker's reductive system of analysis, twentieth-century set theory, or other systems have become standard in a variety of programs.

5. My first article was "Lortzing and the German Romantics: A Dialectical Assessment," *Musical Quarterly*, 52 (April, 1976), 241–64. In this article, the first and last I published of a substantially empirical sort, I provide a good deal of information about the German opera repertory in the first half of the nineteenth century. Here also appeared my first published work on Adorno. In fact, I was able to cut this piece down to manageable size and complete it only after I had come into possession, through Adorno, of a tangible way in which to select, organize, and interpret historical facts. With the help of Adorno's theory, I was able finally to present a concise analysis of some relationships between popular taste on the one hand and notions of art on the other, as they pertained to German opera of the period. This article has not been included in the present collection because its focus on the composer Albert Lortzing seemed to restrict its potential interest.

6. *Philosophy of Modern Music*, trans. Anne G. Mitchell and Wesley V. Blomster (New York, 1973). A project I never completed was to publish a list of mistranslations I found in this edition. In many instances I found that passages that failed to make sense in English involved the translation of a German word into precisely the opposite of what seemed to be its original meaning. Before ridiculing these pioneering translators, however, we should each try our own hand with a passage or two

from Adorno's original texts. His German, as he intended, is fiendishly difficult to translate. This former paucity of translations accounts for the direct references, in my earlier articles, to Adorno's original German texts.

7. Intimidated by this unequivocal warning, I never even allowed myself to formulate the project that would have been natural for me at this point in my career, a full-length book on Adorno's musical writings (to my knowledge, it would have been the first such book in English). Ironically, the enterprise to which I turned instead, an intensive reading of Kant's *Critique of Judgment*, and an analysis of its structure as if it were a work of art, posed an even greater danger to my career, of which I was naïvely unaware. Just as I did not realize ten years later, when I was at the City University of New York Graduate Center (where, for some years now, Jacques Derrida has had a regular visiting appointment in comparative literature but none in philosophy), that the very act of studying Jacques Derrida's work would get me in trouble with a number of analytic philosophers, so too, at this earlier time, it did not occur to me that philosophers had a traditional manner of interpreting Kant that I would be expected to know and follow. At the time, I actually thought I was as free to read Kant's third critique and think about it for myself as Beethoven had been.

8. Scholars who have come to develop an expertise in critical theory are still sufficiently uncommon in music that there is seldom more than one, or occasionally two, in a given department; rarer still is the scholar who was hired from the beginning as an expert of this kind. No doubt this situation is beginning to change; yet even today one searches the College Music Society's *Music Faculty Vacancy List* in vain for openings purely, or even primarily, in critical theory and aesthetics. I myself refer inquiries from students to the University of Minnesota, the one place I know where, thanks to Susan McClary in music and Richard Leppert in humanities, it is possible to pursue a first-rate graduate program of critical studies in music.

9. On Schoenberg's concept of "developing variation," see for example, the following essays in *Style and Idea*: "Bach," p. 397, "Linear Counterpoint," p. 290, and "Connection of Musical Ideas," pp. 287–88. Both aspects of this concept were important to Schoenberg: "developing" connoted logical progress; "variation" connoted an utter resistance to simple repetition and redundancy. My subtitle is, of course, meant to evoke the title of Schoenberg's whole collection. From Schoenberg's perspective, it is the abstract timelessness of "idea" that is to be valued in music, as opposed to the ephemeral concreteness of "style," which is to be disdained as trivial. (See "New Music, Outmoded Music, Style and Idea," *Style and Idea*, esp. pp. 118–24.) I analyze this relationship at length in my essay "Toward A Deconstruction of Structural Listening: A Critique of Schoenberg, Adorno, and Stravinsky," *Explorations in Music, the Arts, and Ideas: Essays in Honor of Leonard B. Meyer*, ed. Eugene Narmour and Ruth A. Solie (New York, 1988, pp. 87–122), which will be reprinted in the companion volume, described in n. 24 of this introduction. From my own perspective, as I try to clarify in this introduction, though "style" and "idea" signify contrasting images and ideals of great power, neither can be defined apart from mediums conditioned by cultural experience, viewpoints, and values. In an epistemological sense, therefore, the realm of "idea" cannot be distinguished incontrovertibly from that of "ideology."

10. I refer, that is, to pure reason (which involves cognition, science, theory); practical reason (which involves moral responsibility); and the configuration of reason that is invoked in aesthetic judgment.

11. My own preference, shared by some of my advocates in musicology, would have been to publish the essays in this volume in chronological order. But perhaps it is a bit narcissistic to desire a chronologically accurate version of one's own intellectual development. In any case, I have deferred in this matter to the judgment that

readers in a variety of fields would find a topical arrangement here more useful. For those who wish to read these essays in the same order in which they were written — which cannot always be safely determined from the original dates of publication — a chronology is provided in the preface to this book.

12. For example, both allow recognition of a tension between two views of humanly created structures: as texts (the poststructuralist term) that *mean* in relation to culturally or historically positioned viewers; or as autonomous semiotic structures that *are* in some purely abstract sense. By contrast, Anglo-American empiricism typically offers no basis for considering epistemological positions other than its own.

13. Each man insisted in his own terms on the need for humans to aim at a condition of self-determining historical development, as the only relationship to time through which rationality could be conceived of as able to dispel the power of irrationality.

14. To be sure, Schoenberg's traditionally German conception of abstract reason involves a good deal more cultural concreteness than does its counterpart in empiricist schools of thought. In the sense that "structural listening" constitutes a model of reason, this difference is discussed in my essay, "Toward a Deconstruction of Structural Listening," particularly in the section entitled "The Case for Structural Listening," *Explorations in Music, The Arts, and Ideas*, pp. 89–99. My essay "The Closing of the American Dream? A Musical Perspective on Allan Bloom, Spike Lee, and Doing the Right Thing," which will appear in my companion volume, is also concerned to distinguish between more and less abstract ideals of reason, and to clarify the moral isolation of purely abstract ideals of reason.

15. From a telephone conversation reported by Max Berley in connection with James Gleick's review of Gould's book *Wonderful Life: The Burgess Shale and the Nature of History*, *New York Times Book Review*, October 22, 1989, p. 40.

16. Of course, in his refusal to reduce the concreteness of history down to some abstract theoretical conception of reality, Adorno incorporates a recognition of contingency into the very foundation of his thinking. For both Adorno and Schoenberg, however, who place individual autonomy at the very center of any rational process of historical unfolding, contingency is a ground for despair, for it lies outside the nexus of order and freedom, the rational principles through which individual autonomy defines itself. A central task for Western thought today, I believe, would be to develop a view in which allowing for the force of contingency in the human condition does not entail renouncing either the ideal of reason, however much that ideal must be rethought, or the binding force of moral responsibility.

17. For insight into the resemblances between my own enterprise and Schoenberg's concept of the developing variation, I am deeply indebted to David Bain, a doctoral candidate of extraordinary originality and articulateness in the music program at the City University of New York Graduate Center.

18. In this respect I must also acknowledge a debt to Leonard Meyer. Many years ago I waited outside a classroom at the University of Chicago where he was teaching a course called "Music as a Model for History," and thought to myself that the gimmick here was dazzling but, after all, merely fictional. It *was* fictional, but I was wrong in considering that an epistemological limitation. Like Schoenberg, though in a very different way, Meyer refused to undervalue the significance of music and, more generally, of aesthetic models for making sense of human knowledge and experience. Like Schoenberg's enterprise, though in very different ways, Meyer's criticism is responsible in a profoundly moral as well as intellectual way.

19. This entire line of reasoning is obviously indebted to Derrida's concept of *différance* as well as to other ideas developed in poststructuralism, a movement dis-

cussed at length in the essays that will appear in the companion volume to this one (see n. 24, below).

20. Again, apart from this introduction, the essays I have written since encountering poststructuralism will appear in my companion volume. I am, of course, aware that many other critics and traditions outside these movements have focused on the reader and on reading in various ways; I think particularly of those presented by Terry Eagleton in a chapter entitled "Phenomenology, Hermeneutics, Reception Theory" (*Literary Theory: An Introduction* [Minneapolis, 1983], pp. 54–90). Had I stayed on in academia during the 1980s, I would have given a high priority to studying these movements closely, in relation to music.

21. Schoenberg himself, of course, suffered such great disappointments in the reception of his music that in a sense he became obsessed with the public; the entire collection *Style and Idea* can be understood as an extended and tremendous effort at public education. On the other hand, Schoenberg's interest in the problem was not of the sort that led him to focus at length on the public's relation to art as an abstract, ahistorical problem. Nor, given the cost of his ferocious efforts to maintain the integrity of his compositions without the taint of any concession to popular taste, was he well situated to sympathize with a view that attributes much of the shape in any artwork or text to the act of interpretation.

22. A question posed by Fred Friendly on a PBS program entitled "Hard Drugs, Hard Choices: The Crisis Beyond our Borders," illustrates that others, too, seem to find this dynamic enlightening: "Are our lives so barren because we use drugs? Or do we use drugs because our lives are so barren?" (The program aired on WNET, Channel 13, in the New York area, February 26, 1990.) The question is dialectical to the extent that it enables one to grasp the two opposed priorities as simultaneously valid.

23. Since dialectic in Adorno's sense is not an abstract pattern but a process inseparable from the self-conscious mind of the interpreter, every relationship at bottom involves a "text" (or object) and an interpreter (or subject); and the simultaneous priority of text and interpreter has to be understood as coexisting with a more fundamental priority of the interpreter. (In other words, the "otherness" of the text must itself be acknowledged as ultimately defined by and within the consciousness of the thinking subject; whether or not one accepts Kant's concept of the subject as universal, to think of this otherness as existing apart from the subject is to set it outside the limits to accessible knowledge as set by Kant.) Though they represent different cultural values and are used in different ways, this notion of dialectic and the deconstructionist notion of infinite regress obviously have much in common.

24. This companion volume (tentatively entitled *Deconstructive Variations: Music and Reason in Western Society*), to which I have referred several times in preceding notes, will also be published by the University of Minnesota Press in the not-distant future, and will reflect work done on poststructuralism and some study of Bakhtin. It is expected to include one previously published essay, "Toward a Deconstruction of Structural Listening: A Critique of Schoenberg, Adorno, and Stravinsky" (published in *Explorations in Music, the Arts, and Ideas*; see n. 9 above), and three unpublished ones of varying lengths, all of which began as lectures. These are "How Could Chopin's A-Major Prelude Be Deconstructed?" "Whose *Magic Flute*?" and "The Closing of the American Dream? A Musical Perspective on Allan Bloom, Spike Lee, and Doing the Right Thing."

25. Though Adorno was an outright snob, he was repelled by the hardening of artistic expression into an object of cultural worship, an attitude that in his terms neutralizes the force of social criticism in art (see, for example, his essay "Cultural Criti-

cism and Society," *Prisms*, trans. Samuel and Shierry Weber [London, 1967], pp. 19–34). Thus it is interesting to speculate on the position Adorno might have taken in the current American debate over the place of the Western canon in the college curriculum.

26. I also reviewed a book by János Maróthy entitled *Music and the Bourgeois, Music and Proletarian* (Budapest, 1974), in the *Journal of Aesthetics and Art Criticism*, 22 (Spring, 1975), pp. 356–58.

27. Since it is in this broad sense that I myself understand and use the term "ideology," it is important to indicate at the outset the distance between my own usage and Adorno's. Adorno regularly uses the term "ideology" in its negative Marxist sense, to mean "false consciousness," that is, viewpoints that serve to sustain the status quo in society at the expense of the disadvantaged, typically through producing an illusion of harmony and stability. See, for example, his essay, "Classes and Strata," in his *Introduction to the Sociology of Music*, trans. E. B. Ashton (New York, 1976), p. 63. At the same time Adorno emphatically rejects doctrinaire ideologies of any kind in art, including vulgar Marxist ones (see his harsh judgment of "socialist" cultural criticism, "Cultural Criticism and Society," p. 32), while also rejecting the "dilut[ion]" of ideology into a "universal relativism," whereby, in effect, resistance to ideology in art gives way to morally detached, purely intellectual modes of analysis that themselves serve ideology (ibid., p. 30). This latter is a criticism that in recent years has been leveled often at deconstructionists, as critics who play abstract analytical games wholly removed from any notion of moral responsibility.

28. This isn't to suggest that the ideological assumptions embedded in an expression by the writer or composer are necessarily identical to those extracted by a reader, but simply that expression cannot escape a fundamentally ideological condition of existence.

29. See n. 23.

30. Again, though Adorno himself would equate the most "critical" music with the least degree of "ideology"—i.e., ideology in the sense of lies that serve the social status quo— his presentation points toward the possibility of characterizing music as "ideological" in my own more general sense.

31. This isn't to deny that *within* this restriction one can make useful and important distinctions of kind and degree. On the other hand, one could not expect, in my judgment, universal assent to one's own distinctions of this kind; nor is it self-evident that work that affects the greatest claim to objectivity in its choice of problems, attitudes, and styles is necessarily the freest of self-serving ideological prejudices. What is crucial for the approximation of such freedom is a self-critical capacity.

32. An amusing sign of a shifting balance in this argument seems worth mentioning. After years of trying unsuccessfully to explain to old friends the nature of my divergence from traditional American musicology, I found the problem suddenly solved at the twenty-fifth reunion of my college class, in 1988, when a classmate's husband, the dean of a law school, greeted me with the remark, "Say, I hear you've been doing 'critical legal studies' in music." At once everyone present understood the course my career had taken; the issue as it affected musical scholarship had finally been placed on a more generally readable map.

33. For a developed account of the notion, see Paul de Man, *Blindness and Insight: Essays in the Rhetoric of Contemporary Criticism*, 2nd ed. rev. (Minneapolis, 1983).

34. The kinds of standards involved in such rigor, such as standards of intellectual honesty, are rejected with scathing contempt by Allan Bloom as wholly inappropriate to the university, as an institution devoted purely to cognitive reason. See his book, *The Closing of the American Mind* (New York, 1987), e.g., p. 201, or p. 261: "Intellec-

tual honesty," "commitment" and that kind of thing have nothing to do with the university, belong in the arenas of religious and political struggle, only get in the way of the university's activity." Since Bloom's concept of a rational relation to oneself invariably involves self-interest (e.g., p. 288)—even his concept of wisdom involves no self-sacrifice (see p. 327)—it doesn't occur to him that intellectual honesty, or perhaps even commitment, could involve rigorous self-criticism.

35. These provisional analogies are subsequently developed in the essays "Evidence of a Critical Worldview in Mozart's Last Three Symphonies" and "Toward a Deconstruction of Structural Listening."

36. Or, as the very phrase "rigorous moral sensibility" may suggest, I have come to see aesthetic sensibility (as opposed to scientific certainty) as the only ground on which scientific ideals of rigor could be reconciled with moral ideals. By this I mean that one can imagine the possibility of such a reconciliation, for example in scholarship, so long as its presence were measured "only" by aesthetic, not scientific, standards. The possibility of such a reconciliation seems well worth the cost involved in restricting scientific certainty as a measure of scholarly value; for what is at stake in such a reconciliation is nothing less than the kinds of "truth" one can hope for in scholarship. At the time I left the University of Chicago, one of my colleagues passed on to me the opinion that my work used "too many qualifiers" ("probably," "almost," "so to speak," and so on). Having puzzled on this objection for more than a decade, I think I can finally attribute it to the difference between my colleagues' scientific criteria for truth in scholarship and my own acceptance of more aesthetic ones as the condition for balancing scientific against moral requirements of truth. And in a sense, aesthetic criteria are even more rigorous than scientific ones: very often my qualifiers (like my copious quotation marks, which my excellent copy editor, Ann Klefstad, has battled valiantly) reflect my need to acknowledge that the existence of an absolute principle is open to doubt.

37. For help in defining this theme in my work, I am indebted to Dr. Lief Carter, of the Department of Political Science at the University of Georgia. His study "Die Meistersinger von Nürnberg: Aesthetic Theory in Constitutional Jurisprudence" (*Polity*, 18 [Winter, 1985], pp. 272–94), takes the possibilities of musical parallelism in an especially intriguing and important direction.

38. Robert Winter, "A Musicological Offering," *New York Review of Books*, 32 (July 18, 1985), p. 26.

39. My essay "How Could Chopin's A-Major Prelude Be Deconstructed?" continues this enterprise in somewhat modified terms.

40. Very concentrated attention was later given to this same relationship in my essay "Toward a Deconstruction of Structural Listening."

41. My reason for not tapping other repertories is simply that I am less familiar with the music, or at least the traditions, and have not wanted to increase the strain I find in this kind of thinking by taking on still more unknown quantities (cf. the Subotnik syndrome, n. 38. above).

42. *Fondements d'une sémiologie de la musique* (Paris, 1975); the review appeared in the *Journal of Aesthetics and Art Criticism*, 35 (Winter, 1976), pp. 239–42.

43. That is, for the first time, chronologically, in my own career; as the chronology in my preface clarifies, chapter 3, which works along similar lines, was written after chapter 11, which is under discussion here.

44. They are, in structuralist terms, metaphorical equivalents; on the other hand, "The Challenge of Contemporary Music" has a far closer metonymical relation to the piece "Toward a Deconstruction of Structural Listening," which grew directly out of it.

45. This article was delivered as a lecture on March 26, 1980, at Brown University as part of the Marshall Woods Lecture Series. My decision to include it here stems from reports of the vigorous discussion it has evoked in introductory music courses at Brown, where David Josephson uses it regularly in his teaching.

46. By the same token, in the four years since I began work on this essay, signs have been rapidly proliferating that a postcontemporary (postmodern) aesthetic is in the process of replacing the contemporary (modern) one; and it goes without saying that the more techniques and aims change in composition, the less point this essay will have as a critique of the present. Where the essay may not lose all of its point is precisely as a "period piece," that is, as a critique that, in its own configuration no less than in its focus, points to a specific time, place, and culture. Here, in other words, is an instance of how the contingent and transient aspects of a culture can become the locus of a value that, while not timeless and unchanging, is at least continuing. As my entire enterprise should make clear, I believe the reversal of ancient priorities thus implied, between the categories of the changing and of the lasting, has become characteristic in modern Western conceptions of the humanly significant.

Chapter 1. The Role of Ideology in the Study of Western Music

1. Despite the parallelism available in these two pairs of terms, I speak mainly of "Continentalists" and "empiricists" in the following discussion, partly because the term "metaphysicist" is easily misconstrued and partly because the primary import of the term "Anglo-American" is ideological rather than geographical. A version of this chapter was first given at the annual meeting of the Society for Ethnomusicology, November 20, 1980, in Bloomington, Indiana.

2. Professor Arthur Mendel and his students, as I understand it, matched up pinholes (made through binding) in Bach manuscripts as part of a process of establishing chronology and provenance. The question raised here is not whether this process produced something of value but whether the study of music should be restricted to such processes.

3. This assertion was made at the Adorno Symposium held at the University of Southern California on May 18, 1979.

4. An intensive analysis of the difficulties involved in qualifying the First Amendment is presented by Ronald Dworkin in "Is the Press Losing the First Amendment?" *New York Review of Books*, 27 (December 4, 1980), pp. 49–57. See also chapter 5, n. 12, this volume.

5. Finding alternatives to the scientific method of study that do not sacrifice intellectual rigor is perhaps the principal task facing any intellectual community that recognizes the limits of scientific method. It is, of course, a formidable task, but it should not on that account be given up as hopeless. At least as far back as Kant's *Critique of Judgment*, foundations have been offered for construing nonscientific modes of mental activity as potentially rigorous. The difficulty, as Kant's work itself (more or less unintentionally) makes evident, is to define bases for an individual rationale or exercise of discretion that can be accepted as generally valid. In a paper delivered, as one of the Thalheimer Lectures, at the Johns Hopkins University on May 4, 1979, I argue that Romantic music itself constitutes one major Western attempt to solve this very difficulty. (This paper, "Romantic Music as Post-Kantian Critique," is published as chapter 7 of this volume.) Some of the problems attendant on an exercise of discretion in humanistic disciplines are usefully discussed in a review by Denis Donoghue, in the November 9, 1980, issue of The *New York Times Book Review* (pp. 11 and

32–33), of Geoffrey Hartman's book *Criticism in the Wilderness: The Study of Literature Today.*

6. See Ralph Vaughan Williams, "Some Thoughts on Beethoven's Choral Symphony," *National Music and Other Essays* (London, 1963), p. 84. For my own offending passage see my article "Adorno's Diagnosis of Beethoven's Late Style: Early Symptom of a Fatal Condition," chapter 2 in this volume, p. 34.

7. Today in 1990, eight years after this piece was first written, the situation has to some degree improved. A small number of scholars deeply versed in Continental (or another alternative) traditions of scholarship, such as Susan McClary (after years of suppression of her work), Carolyn Abbate, Ruth Solie, Janet Levy (without institutional support), and Jann Pasler, have begun to achieve prominence; and the number of young scholars at the junior faculty level who are now daring to pursue new intellectual directions (Fred Maus, of the University of Virginia, and Julie Cumming, of Wellesley, are good examples) has greatly increased. Here and there whole conferences have provided opening for those working outside of the ideological mainstream; for example, the annual meeting of the American Musicological Society in New Oreleans, in October 1987 (organized by Gary Tomlinson and David Josephson) and the conference "The Musical and Verbal Arts: Interactions," at Dartmouth College, in May, 1988 (whose musical organizer was Joe Kerman). On the other hand few American faculty positions or programs have yet opened up in these areas of musical scholarship. (And it might also be added that among those who are now presenting papers in such areas, it is not yet altogether clear how many are deeply committed to broadening the ideological framework of American musicology and how many have simply jumped on what has suddenly become a bandwagon.) See also chapter 5, n. 12, this volume.

Similarly, there are now many more opportunities to study traditions other than those of Western art music, and at least a degree of exposure to such courses is increasingly becoming a requirement for majors. On the other hand, a complete division between programs in Western art music (musicology) and in other traditions (ethnomusicology) is still the norm in American universities. The graduate programs at Brown and Wesleyan (Connecticut) Universities are unusual in that they offer degrees in ethnomusicology only; the undergraduate program at Wesleyan is probably close to unique in that it was designed from the start as a program in world music, of which Western art music was considered simply one branch. See also chapter 12, n. 18, this volume. This is not to deny that, both theoretically and specifically, Adorno himself recognized no musical value outside the post-1600 Western art tradition; nevertheless, his viewpoint offers useful ways of understanding musical value more inclusively.

8. This distinction between Catholicism and Protestantism is derived from a lecture I heard in 1970 by the American sociologist Robert Bellah. I use it solely as a metaphorical distinction, based on historical generalities, not as a critique of any Christian religion today. The metaphor seems revealing in many contexts. Consider, for example, one similarity between that brilliant bearer of the Protestant spirit, the U.S. Constitution as originally written, and Nazi doctrine. Both gave high place to laws of a general or scientific character; each excluded various groups of people from its own definition of human society.

9. Theodor W. Adorno, *Introduction to the Sociology of Music*, trans. E. B. Ashton (New York, 1976), p. 195. Professor David Josephson, of Brown University, finds Adorno's imagery here inapposite in the sense that terrorism nowadays connotes the activities of guerrillas, fighting outside of a dominant power structure, rather than those of the power structure itself. The objection is intriguing. But let us not forget

the historical realities behind Adorno's choice of words. Terrorism, defined by Webster as "the systematic use of terror especially as a means of coercion," has all too often been institutionalized as law by groups in power, no less in our time as in any other.

10. See, for example, *Beiträge zur musikalischen Hermeneutik,* ed. Carl Dahlhaus (Regensburg, 1975).

11. In "Romantic Music as Post-Kantian Critique," chapter 7 in this volume, I develop at length the distinction between internal structure and external context, associating the former with structure and perception, the latter with style and interpretation. It is my contention in this essay, which aims at defining two different modes of understanding a musical composition, that the classical style proposes the possibility of understanding a musical structure or message wholly on its own internal terms, because its premises and modes of argument are universal, and that musical romanticism in effect presents a critique of that proposal by acknowledging explicitly the role played in musical communication by various sorts of specific contexts, contexts that cannot be reduced to general principles, contexts that are extrinsic to inner structural connections, and contexts that make necessary an element of discretion in any act of understanding. These contexts include personal style, cultural identity, and even the physical character of the musical medium. In short, as I suggest above in n. 5, the romantic composition takes on the task of establishing the validity of a rationale, in this case a musical rationale, that is unmistakably shaped by particular contexts or ideologies rather than assumed to be universally true. As such I argue that this music constitutes an archetype for all human utterances. See also chapter 12, no. 12, this volume.

12. *Introduction to the Sociology of Music,* p. 194.

Chapter 2. Adorno's Diagnosis of Beethoven's Late Style: Early Symptom of a Fatal Condition

1. Adorno took such an active role as musical adviser in *Doctor Faustus* that virtually all of the principal discussions of music in the novel can be considered as much his as Mann's. A number of such passages were taken almost literally from Adorno's *Philosophy of Modern Music,* and Mann admitted making philosophical as well as technical changes upon Adorno's advice. See Thomas Mann, *The Story of a Novel: The Genesis of "Doctor Faustus,"* trans. Richard and Clara Winston (New York, 1961); and Gunilla Bergsten, *Thomas Mann's "Doctor Faustus,"* trans. Krishna Winston (Chicago, 1969). Because the novel is so close in theory to Adorno's own work, and since the connection with Adorno is well documented, *Doctor Faustus* can be used judiciously as a source of Adorno's own musical thought.

It must be added that since the initial appearance (in 1976) of the present essay (and I would like to think at least in part because of that appearance), English-language scholarship has taken a much greater interest in Adorno's work on music than it did before 1976.

2. Adorno's own term for Hegel's texts (Fredric Jameson, *Marxism and Form* [Princeton, 1971], p. 48).

3. T. W. Adorno, *Einleitung in die Musiksoziologie* (Reinbek bei Hamburg, 1968), p. 7. In the English translation (*Introduction to the Sociology of Music,* trans. E. B. Ashton [New York, 1976]), which is not cited in this chapter, corresponding page references are about ten to fourteen pages lower than in the German edition.

4. T. W. Adorno, "Spätstil Beethovens," *Moments Musicaux* (Frankfurt, 1964), pp. 13–17; "Verfremdetes Hauptwerk: Zur *Missa Solemnis,*" ibid., pp. 167–85. For a

translation of the latter see Duncan Smith's "Alienated Masterpiece: The *Missa Solemnis*," *Telos*, no. 28 (Summer, 1976), pp. 113-24.

5. Thomas Mann, *Doctor Faustus*, trans. H. T. Lowe-Porter (New York, 1948), pp. 51-56. Unless otherwise indicated, all references in the following discussion to *Doctor Faustus* will be to this English translation. It should be noted, however, that an important passage adapted from Adorno, on the role of fugue in Beethoven's late style, appears only in the original German version of *Doktor Faustus* ([Stockholm, 1947], pp. 91-94). It was deleted from the English translation apparently at Mann's own request (see Robert Craft, "The 'Doctor Faustus' Case," *New York Review of Books*, 22, no. 13 [August 7, 1965], p. 20, fn. 5). If restored, the passage would appear on p. 58 of Lowe-Porter's translation, just preceding the second paragraph, which begins, "Thus Kretschmar, on 'Beethoven and the Fugue.' " I am grateful to Professor Joseph Kerman for guiding me to the precise location of this missing passage.

6. See T. W. Adorno, "Bach Defended against his Devotees," *Prisms*, trans. Samuel and Shierry Weber (London, 1967), p. 137; and Mann, *Doctor Faustus*, pp. 485-86.

7. Adorno, "Verfremdetes Hauptwerk," p. 172; *Einleitung*, pp. 105-6.

8. See T. W. Adorno, "Arnold Schoenberg, 1874-1951," *Prisms*, p. 157; *Philosophy of Modern Music*, trans. Anne G. Mitchell and Wesley V. Blomster (New York, 1973), pp. 67-71; "Modern Music Is Growing Old," trans. Rollo H. Myers, *Score*, no. 18 (December, 1956), p. 26; Mann, *Doctor Faustus*, pp. 189-94; Jameson, *Marxism*, pp. 34-38; and Ferenc Feher, "Negative Philosophy of Music—Positive Results," trans. Zoltan Feher, *New German Critique*, no. 4 (Winter, 1975), pp. 102, 107-8.

9. See, for example, Adorno, "Growing Old," p. 24; and "Thesen über Tradition," *Ohne Leitbild* (Frankfurt, 1968), p. 35.

10. See Feher, "Negative Philosophy," p. 102.

11. See Adorno, *Philosophy*, pp. 60, 102; and *Einleitung*, pp. 57-59. This is an important theme in *Dialectic of Enlightenment* by Adorno and Max Horkheimer, trans. John Cumming (New York, 1972). See pp. 35-36. A similar conception of history is reached in a strikingly different manner by Leonard Meyer in *Music, The Arts, and Ideas* (Chicago, 1967), pp. 87-232.

12. Adorno, "Cultural Criticism and Society," *Prisms*, p. 34.

13. Feher, "Negative Philosophy," p. 109. Note the similarity of Adorno's own image in "Growing Old," p. 20.

14. Adorno, "Spätstil," p. 17.

15. See Adorno, *Einleitung*, pp. 72, 223-28, 232; and "Ideen zur Musiksoziologie," *Klangfiguren* (Berlin and Frankfurt, 1959), p. 25. Although he is generally taciturn on the historical events themselves, Adorno's understanding of them is probably not far from the views of Romain Rolland and Harry Goldschmidt as set forth in the latter's "Der späte Beethoven—Versuch einer Standortbestimmung," *Bericht über den Internationalen Beethoven-Kongress 10-12 Dezember 1970 in Berlin*, ed. Heinz Alfred Brockhaus and Konrad Niemann (Berlin, 1971), pp. 48-49.

16. Georg Lukács, *Writer & Critic* (New York, 1970), p. 86.

17. See Adorno, *Einleitung*, pp. 23-33, esp. p. 225 on the "windowless monad" and p. 229 on the ontological or essential character of the parallelism that does emerge between art and society. It must be stressed that Adorno categorically rejects any one-to-one correspondence between artistic components and particular events.

18. See Adorno, *Einleitung*, pp. 227-30; and "Ideen," p. 22. On the relationship between form and matter, especially in this context, see Adorno, *Philosophy*, pp. 32-33. The reference in Heinz-Klaus Metzger, "Intermezzo I (Just Who Is Growing Old?)," *Die Reihe* [English edition], no. 4 (1960), p. 64, to this last passage in the

German edition of *Philosophy* (*Philosophie der neuen Musik* [Frankfurt, 1958]) is wrong; it should read "pp. 36 et seq." See also n. 37, this chapter.

19. See esp. Adorno, *Einleitung*, pp. 227, 230–33. See also chapter 3, n. 8, this volume.

20. For the discussion of Beethoven's second-period style see esp. Adorno, *Einleitung*, pp. 223–25, 232; *Philosophy*, pp. 55–56; and "Verfremdetes Hauptwerk," pp. 182–83; also Mann, *Doctor Faustus*, p. 190; and Jameson, *Marxism*, pp. 39–44. For different elaborations of Beethoven's work as dialectical synthesis, see Christopher Ballantine, "Beethoven, Hegel and Marx," *Music Review*, 33 (1972), pp. 34–46; and Philip Barford, "The Approach to Beethoven's Late Music," *Music Review*, 30 (1969), pp. 106–17.

21. Feher, "Negative Philosophy," p. 106. On the categories of totality and self-movement, see Adorno, "Verfremdetes Hauptwerk," p. 180.

22. Although this term is now often associated with Adorno, who developed it fully, Adorno openly derives it from Schoenberg. See Adorno, "Bach," p. 139; "Schoenberg," p. 154; and Arnold Schoenberg, *Style and Idea* (New York, 1950), p. 43.

23. The coincidence of the individual and the general in Beethoven's second-period style is a recurrent theme in Adorno's writings, which is echoed in *Doctor Faustus*. See Adorno, *Einleitung*, pp. 78, 223–24, 227–28, 237; and "Verfremdetes Hauptwerk," pp. 182–84; also Mann, *Doctor Faustus*, pp. 190–91, 240–41. (It should be noted, however, that Adorno does not examine empirically the actual response to Beethoven in the latter's own lifetime, so that he misses certain subtleties which enrich the work of other nonpositivist scholars. For examples of the latter, see Georg Knepler, "Das Beethoven-Bild in Geschichte und Gegenwart," *Beethoven-Kongress Berlin*, p. 27; and "Zu Beethovens Wahl von Werkgattungen," *Beiträge zur Musikwissenschaft*, 12 [1970], pp. 319–20.) See also nn. 36 and 96, this chapter.

24. See Adorno, *Einleitung*, p. 232; Jameson, *Marxism*, pp. 38–39; and nn. 67 and 104, this chapter.

25. On the work of art as criticism, see Adorno, "Verfremdetes Hauptwerk," pp. 184–85; "Ideen," p. 29; *Einleitung*, p. 226; and "Growing Old," p. 26. See also the remarks on cognition [*Erkenntnis*] in *Einleitung*, pp. 72, 227; and in Mann, *Doctor Faustus*, pp. 239–40; and n. 67, this chapter.

26. Adorno, "Verfremdetes Hauptwerk," pp. 183–85. For a fine, though by no means sympathetic, discussion of this section (and of the extension of its ideas by Peter Gülke), see Goldschmidt, "Der späte Beethoven," pp. 43–44.

27. Adorno, "Verfremdetes Hauptwerk," p. 183.

28. For the following discussion, see esp. Adorno, *Einleitung*, pp. 224–25, 228–29; "Verfremdetes Hauptwerk," pp. 183–84; and Feher, "Negative Philosophy," pp. 100–101, 106; also Adorno, "Verfremdetes Hauptwerk," p. 174, and Mann, *Doctor Faustus*, p. 487, on static variation; and Adorno, *Einleitung*, pp. 38, 73, on invariant return. It should be noted that with his characteristic impatience with empirical detail, Adorno gives little attention to the problems of defining precise boundaries between Beethoven's style periods. He does call attention to a kind of "law of uneven development" in Beethoven's treatment of the various genres, particularly evident in the progressiveness of the chamber music relative to the symphonies (see "Verfremdetes Hauptwerk," p. 172, and *Einleitung*, pp. 104–8). He shows little interest in specific chronological overlappings, however, and apparently accepts Wilhelm von Lenz's well-known periodization more or less as given.

29. Adorno has in mind the giving way of belief in freedom to the acknowledgment of force when he asserts, "[The fact] that the affirmative gesture of the recapitu-

lation in some of Beethoven's greatest symphonies takes on the power of the repressive dashing down, the authoritative 'It is thus' [*so ist es*], and gestically, decoratively exceeds what is happening musically [*schiesst über das musikalisch Geschehende hinaus* — i.e., goes beyond what a logical unfolding would entail] is Beethoven's forced tribute to the ideological essence, into whose jurisdiction falls even the most supreme music that ever intended freedom under enduring unfreedom" (*Einleitung*, p. 225). (Unless otherwise stated, all translations from the German are my own.) Credit for deciphering the most obscure aspects of the preceding passage belongs to Mr. Lawrence Fuchsberg, a former graduate student at the University of Chicago. On "ideological essence," see *Einleitung*, p. 73, and below, pp. 24 and 31, and n. 37.

30. Adorno, "Verfremdetes Hauptwerk," pp. 179, 182, 185; and *Einleitung*, p. 229. See also Robert L. Jacobs, "Beethoven and Kant," *Music & Letters*, 42 (1961), 242–51. See also nn. 37 and 95, this chapter.

31. Adorno, *Einleitung*, pp. 224–25. See also his "Verfremdetes Hauptwerk," p. 183.

32. See Sang-Ki Kim, Review of *Drei Studien zu Hegel* by T. W. Adorno, *New German Critique*, no. 4 (Winter, 1975), p. 176. On the limits of bourgeois society, see also Adorno, *Einleitung*, pp. 51, 229.

33. See Mann, *Doctor Faustus*, p. 68; and Adorno, *Aesthetische Theorie*, Gesammelte Schriften, vol. 7 (Frankfurt, 1970), p. 10. I should like here to express my gratitude to Professor Martha Woodmansee of the English Department at Case-Western Reserve University for access to her unpublished work on Adorno's *Aesthetische Theorie*, "Rede über Lyrik und Glaesellschaft," and *Dialectic of Enlightenment*.

34. See Adorno's "Growing Old," pp. 19–20: " . . . an art that accepts without discussion . . . a repression . . . has given up trying to be true and has renounced what is, in fact, the only justification for its existence."

35. The necessity of double negation, it should be noted, is a principal theme of both Adorno's *Aesthetische Theorie* and Mann's *Doctor Faustus*. For an example of its application to Beethoven's music, see Adorno, "Verfremdetes Hauptwerk," pp. 184–85; also his entire article "Spätstil." In Adorno's view, it is in a sense prefigured by Bach, especially late Bach, who was no more in harmony with his society than was late Beethoven (see Adorno, "Bach," pp. 136–39; and *Einleitung*, p. 237); but see also the qualification of this similarity in Adorno, "Verfremdetes Hauptwerk," p. 175. On contradiction as the essence of authentic modern art (from Beethoven on) see Adorno, "Verfremdetes Hauptwerk," p. 183; *Einleitung*, pp. 80, 220; and "Cultural Criticism," p. 32.

36. See Adorno, *Einleitung*, pp. 51–52, 223: "If Beethoven is already the musical prototype of the revolutionary bourgeoisie, he is simultaneously the prototype of a music which has escaped from its social guardianship, [is] aesthetically fully autonomous, no longer 'in service' [*bedienstet*]." The two had to diverge in the third period, Beethoven choosing the latter.

37. For further discussion of the "accidental," in this sense, see Adorno, "Verfremdetes Hauptwerk," pp. 179, 181; and *Philosophy*, p. 59; also Feher, "Negative Philosophy," p. 109; and Célestin Deliège, "Une incidence d'Adorno," *Arc*, 40 (1969), p. 106. To describe this problem in more philosphical terms, the subject needs to prove the rationality of objective reality in order to establish the objective reality of its own rationality, the principle on which its own distinguishing characteristic, autonomy, depends. But since the subject has no access to objective reality except within the framework of its own perceptions, it cannot establish this proof. Therefore, through the very act of pointing toward the object, the subject shows itself to be fragmentary rather than autonomous; that is, open to the power of irrational exter-

nal forces, and therefore without the self-determining capacity crucial to its own definition. At issue here, obviously, is the problem that constitutes the core of Kant's philosophy. The urgency of this problem becomes apparent in romantic efforts to define the individual as the locus of the universal. As suggested by Martha Woodmansee in "The Genius and the Copyright" (*Eighteenth-Century Studies*, 17 [1984], pp. 447–48), whereas the Enlightenment poet might expect to create a world that was universally recognizable, romantic reading involved one in "the exploration of an Other, in penetrating to the deepest reaches of the foreign, because absolutely unique consciousness of which the work is a verbalized embodiment." In effect this indicates that in romanticism, the self had become the only available source of an "Other," a situation that cast grave doubt on the subject's access to any genuine sort of otherness, unless the objectivity of an individual inner vision could somehow be guaranteed. This issue is relevant to a number of others discussed elsewhere in this volume, such as the following: the heteronomy of the individual (this chapter, nn. 29 and 30); the relation of subjectivity to form (this chapter, n. 18, and chapter 4, e.g. n. 20); the relationship between the form envisioned by the artist and the form the artist transmits (chapter 7, n. 6, and chapter 9, n. 22); the objective significance of musical and other forms of individuality (e.g. chapter 3, p. 47, chapter 9, n. 24, chapter 11, pp. 221ff., and chapter 13, pp. 266–71.); and the tension between images of metaphorical replication and metonymical contiguity (chapter 3, nn. 8 and 9, chapter 4, n. 12, and chapter 6, n. 34: Does the great artist's inner world complete one's own or does it at bottom merely replicate the limits of one's own?).

38. See Adorno, "Verfremdetes Hauptwerk," p. 178; "Schoenberg," p. 164; *Einleitung*, p. 73; and *Philosophy*, pp. 56–57; also Mann, *Doctor Faustus*, pp. 189–91. Closely related is the notion that unlimited development of a subject, be it a musical subject or bourgeois society itself, leads (through the dialectical workings of history) to the ultimate negation of the subject. See Adorno, *Einleitung*, pp. 51, 229.

39. See, for example, Adorno, "Verfremdetes Hauptwerk," p. 184: "Out of freedom the autonomous subject, which otherwise no longer knows itself master of objectivity, yields itself to heteronomy." See also Adorno, "Schoenberg," p. 164; and Ronald Weitzman, "An Introduction to Adorno's Music and Social Criticism," *Music & Letters*, 52 (1971), 292.

40. See Adorno, "Verfremdetes Hauptwerk," pp. 182–83; also see esp. the closely related passages in Adorno's "Spätstil," pp. 16–17; and Mann's *Doctor Faustus*, pp. 52–56.

41. See Adorno, "Spätstil," p. 14; and "Bach," pp. 137–42; also Mann, *Doctor Faustus*, pp. 53, 281. The idea is implicit throughout Adorno's "Verfremdetes Hauptwerk."

42. On the dangers, see Mann, *Doctor Faustus*, pp. 59–60, 367, 373. On the values, see ibid., p. 63; Adorno, *Einleitung*, p. 230; and *Philosophy*, pp. 38–39. See also the original version of *Doktor Faustus* (Stockholm, 1947), p. 93, on the relation of the cultic and the cultural, and p. 94, on the "never extinguished homesickness of emancipated music for its cultically bound [*kultisch gebundenen*] origins"; also Kurt Oppens, "Zu den musikalischen Schriften Theodor W. Adornos," *Ueber Theodor W. Adorno* (Frankfurt, 1968), p. 22.

43. Adorno, "Schoenberg," pp. 156–57; *Einleitung*, pp. 104–8. Bach, on the contrary, as a result of his lesser self-consciousness, was able to square considerable individualism with counterpoint (Adorno, "Bach," pp. 137–39). On Beethoven's relation to Bach, see also *Doktor Faustus* (Stockholm, 1947), pp. 92–93.

44. For comparisons, on this basis, between harmony and counterpoint, see Adorno, *Philosophy*, pp. 58–59; and Mann, *Doctor Faustus*, pp. 74, 76, 193, 321.

45. Adorno, "Verfremdetes Hauptwerk," pp. 184, 178, 175.

46. Ibid., pp. 180 (avoidance of specificity), 173 (sonata), 176 (fugue), 174 (development), 174 and 177 (avoidance of motive and segmentation), and 174 (Netherlands polyphony). For somewhat more specific suggestions of renaissance models for the *Missa Solemnis*, see Mann, *Doktor Faustus* (Stockholm, 1947), pp. 93–94.

47. Adorno, "Verfremdetes Hauptwerk," p. 185.

48. Ibid., pp. 174–76.

49. Ibid., pp. 178–80. It is as if, Adorno notes (pp. 178–79), Beethoven wanted to push human suffering into the past (where, in contrast to the present, he could conceive of a meaningful source of authority). Passages of a related nature can be found in Mann, *Doctor Faustus*, pp. 177–78 (expressiveness of the archaic), 357 (on the expression of despair through figures learned by rote), and 485–89. See also *Doktor Faustus* (Stockholm, 1947), p. 94 (on the struggle of the "emotionalist" with the "cool[ness]" of the fugue on the "far side of the passions"); Mann, *Story of a Novel*, pp. 46, 155; and Martin Jay, *The Dialectical Imagination* (Boston, 1973), p. 200 (on Walter Benjamin's high regard for literal quotation).

50. Adorno, *Einleitung*, p. 72; "Spätstil," pp. 14–15; and Mann, *Doctor Faustus*, p. 53.

51. And it is only in this sense — not in a direct psychological sense — that the late works can be said to embody Beethoven's acknowledgment of his own approaching death (Adorno, "Spätstil," pp. 15–16). On the "resistance of convention," see ibid., p. 16; and Mann, *Doctor Faustus*, pp. 53–54. See also R. T. Llewellyn, "Parallel Attitudes to Form in Late Beethoven and Late Goethe: Throwing Aside the Appearance of Art," *Modern Language Review*, 63 (1968), pp. 410–11. (For a quite different view of convention in Beethoven's late work, see Barford, "The Approach to Beethoven's Late Music," p. 114.) On the later fate of musical convention, see Adorno, "Schoenberg," pp. 153, 161. On the relation of convention and death, see Adorno, "Spätstil," pp. 15–16; "Verfremdetes Hauptwerk," p. 182; Mann, *Doctor Faustus*, p. 53; and *Story of a Novel*, p. 46.

52. Adorno, *Philosophy*, pp. 55, 119; also p. 120 on the dissociation involved; and Mann, *Doctor Faustus*, p. 488.

53. See esp. Adorno, "Verfremdetes Hauptwerk," pp. 179, 184; and n. 29, this chapter.

54. See Adorno, "Verfremdetes Hauptwerk," pp. 183–85; and Mann, *Doctor Faustus*, p. 53.

55. See Adorno, "Ideen," p. 22; "Growing Old," p. 23; and "Verfremdetes Hauptwerk," p. 184 (on Beethoven's turn to "*gebundener Stil*"); also Mann *Doctor Faustus*, pp. 191, 193, 369; and Metzger, "Intermezzo I," pp. 70–71. See also nn. 29, 65 this chapter.

56. See Adorno, "Verfremdetes Hauptwerk," p. 174; and n. 28, this chapter.

57. See Adorno, "Spätstil," p. 17; "Verfremdetes Hauptwerk," p. 183; and "Bach," p. 142. A similar *musical* analysis is offered by Paul Henry Lang in *Music and Western Civilization* (New York, 1941), p. 771.

58. See Adorno, "Spätstil," pp. 14, 17; "Le style tardif de Beethoven," trans. Steffen Deutschbein and Dominique Jameux, *Arc*, 40 (1969), p. 31, fn. 14; and Mann, *Doctor Faustus*, p. 57. For another interpretation of the fugal directions, see Rey M. Longyear, "Beethoven and Romantic Irony," *The Creative World of Beethoven*, ed. Paul Henry Lang (New York, 1971), p. 154.

59. See Adorno, "Spätstil," p. 17; "Verfremdetes Hauptwerk," p. 183.

60. Mann, *Doctor Faustus*, p. 53.

61. See, for example, Adorno, "Spätstil," p. 17; and Mann, *Doctor Faustus*, pp. 54, 376.

62. Adorno, "Spätstil," p. 17; idem, "Verfremdetes Hauptwerk," pp. 172–73, 180.

63. See esp. Adorno, "Verfremdetes Hauptwerk," p. 183.

64. Here, of course, Adorno cuts himself off completely from traditional Marxist historical theory; see the criticism in Goldschmidt, "Der späte Beethoven," p. 48. But see also n. 116, this chapter.

65. Again, the logical conclusion of this contradiction for Adorno is the situation of Schoenberg's twelve-tone music, in which a system set up by the composer to free himself from external influences only reveals the virtual impossibility of free individual action in Schoenberg's world. See esp. Adorno, *Philosophy*, p. 69; and Jameson, *Marxism*, pp. 34–35.

66. Adorno, *Philosophy*, p. 35; and Mann, *Doctor Faustus*, p. 239. See also Adorno, *Einleitung*, p. 73.

67. See, for example, Adorno, "Ideen," p. 24; *Einleitung*, pp. 79, 174, 230, 236, 239–40. Lawrence Fuchsberg has suggested, in this connection, that criticism, in Adorno's view, is the only remaining medium through which the fragments of the modern world could conceivably be viewed as a (meaningful) totality; hence, Adorno's association of a utopian function with authentic art—which is criticism, as pointed out above, n. 25, this chapter.

68. *Einleitung*, p. 79; see also pp. 225 and 238 on the vulnerability of all art to ideology.

69. See Adorno, *Einleitung*, pp. 63–64, 80; Feher, "Negative Philosophy," p. 111; Donald B. Kuspit, "Critical Notes on Adorno's Sociology of Music and Art," *Journal of Aesthetics and Art Criticism*, 33 (1975), p. 322; and Douglas Kellner, "The Frankfurt School Revisited: A Critique of Martin Jay's *The Dialectical Imagination*," *New German Critique*, no. 4 (Winter, 1975), p. 147.

70. Adorno, "Beethoven im Geist der Moderne: Eine Gesamtaufnahme der neun Symphonien unter René Leibowitz," *Süddeutsche Zeitung*, 20 no. 306 (December 22, 1964), p. 9; *Einleitung*, p. 136; Hans Heinrich Eggebrecht, *Zur Geschichte der Beethoven-Rezeption*, Akademie der Wissenschaften und der Literatur Mainz, Abhandlung der geistes- und sozialwissenschaftlichen Klasse, 1972, no. 3 (Mainz, 1972), p. 20; and Heinz-Klaus Metzger, "Zur Beethoven-Interpretation," *Beethoven '70* (Frankfurt, 1970), pp. 7–13. It is worth noting that Knepler, a strong critic of Adorno, shows sympathy for this idea in "Beethoven-Bild," pp. 29–30, 34.

71. See esp. Adorno, "Verfremdetes Hauptwerk," p. 169. On the virtually limitless capacity of modern society to neutralize all art eventually, see *Einleitung*, pp. 50, 225, 238; and *Aesthetische Theorie*, p. 339.

72. See Adorno, *Einleitung*, p. 139; "Growing Old," pp. 18, 25. The words "growing old" in the latter title seem to mean, essentially, "becoming neutralized."

73. See Adorno, *Einleitung*, pp. 73, 78; "Ideen," pp. 11–13, 24.

74. Adorno, *Philosophy*, pp. 9–10; *Einleitung*, pp. 52, 79.

75. This does include the *Missa Solemnis*, presumably because society, in Adorno's judgment, has accepted the work as a creation of Beethoven's but has never been able to penetrate its exterior and assimilate its content; it has had to swallow the work whole, so to speak. On resistance in Beethoven's late work, see esp. Mann, *Doktor Faustus* (Stockholm, 1947), p. 92.

76. On resistance generally, see Adorno, *Einleitung*, pp. 51, 130, 238–39; "Schoenberg," pp. 150, 158; and "Growing Old," p. 18. Especially important in this

context is Adorno's landmark essay, "Rede über Lyrik und Gesellschaft," *Noten zur Literatur*, vol. 1 (Frankfurt, 1958), pp. 73–104. For Adorno's (elitist) typology of musical listeners, see "Typen musikalischen Verhaltens," *Einleitung*, pp. 12–30. See also *Einleitung*, pp. 107–8, on the innate resistance of chamber music; and "Growing Old," p. 25, on "the absence of expression . . . [as] expressiveness."

77. Adorno, "Bach," p. 145; "Schoenberg," p. 156. Like "subcutaneous structure," these concepts are indebted to Schoenberg's musical theory.

78. See Adorno, *Philosophy*, p. 34. The idea is developed at length in his "Lyrik und Gesellschaft." See also Mann, *Doctor Faustus*, pp. 239, 372.

79. See Adorno, *Philosophy*, p. 67: "The question which twelve-tone music asks of the composer is not how musical meaning is to be organized, but rather, how organization is to become meaningful." See also Adorno, "Schoenberg," p. 158; "Growing Old," pp. 23–26. Knepler is at pains to deny precisely this dichotomy in Beethoven's music (*Musikgeschichte des 19. Jahrhunderts* [Berlin, 1961], 2, pp. 589–90).

80. "The shocks of incomprehension, emitted by artistic technique in the age of its meaninglessness, undergo a sudden change. They illuminate the meaningless world. Modern music sacrifices itself to this effort" (Adorno, *Philosophy*, p. 133). (It is interesting that the same image of illumination appears in the final metaphor of Adorno's "Spätstil.") Even Schoenberg, according to Adorno the modernist most dedicated to individual freedom, fails to communicate to society either the meaning of his self-expression or the rationality of his form. Hence total freedom (self-expression) and total enslavement (formal order) converge in modern music and are subsumed into the larger category of meaninglessness. See, n. 86, this chapter.

81. See Adorno, "Verfremdetes Hauptwerk," p. 182; also Weitzman, "An Introduction to Adorno's Music and Social Criticism," p. 298, on intelligibility.

82. Adorno, "Verfremdetes Hauptwerk," pp. 170–71.

83. It is interesting that Mann speaks of artistic "imploring" in the context of discussing Beethoven's close association of words and music (*Doctor Faustus*, p. 163).

84. Adorno, "Ideen," p. 29.

85. Adorno, *Einleitung*, p. 52. Relevant to this entire discussion is the poignant passage in which Leverkühn "takes back" the Ninth Symphony and with it "the good and noble, what we call the human," because he has discovered that all this "is not to be" (Mann, *Doctor Faustus*, p. 478).

86. See Adorno, *Philosophy*, p. 133; *Aesthetische Theorie*, p. 13; Mann, *Doctor Faustus*, p. 54; and Alan Lessem, "Schönberg and the Crisis of Expressionism," *Music & Letters*, 55 (1974), p. 434. The result is the same, it might be added, whether the subject embraces the principle of form or tries to fight off its tyranny (on the latter, see Adorno, *Einleitung*, p. 230).

87. Adorno, "Verfremdetes Hauptwerk," pp. 180–81.

88. See esp. Adorno, "Schoenberg," pp. 164, 171; also *Philosophy*, p. 29; and Mann, *Doctor Faustus*, pp. 180–82.

89. For the utimate result, see Adorno, *Philosophy*, p. 69: "The new ordering of twelve-tone technique virtually extinguishes the subject." See also "Growing Old," p. 26.

90. On this move away from the traditional class orientation of Marxism and its implicit rejection of Marx himself, see especially Jay, *Dialectical Imagination*, pp. 256–59. It is interesting that Lukács, probably the greatest Marxist literary critic of this century, ended his life with a similar extension of the class concept to all industrialization. See Neil McInnes, *The Western Marxists* (New York, 1972), pp. 127–29; also Feher, "Negative Philosophy," p. 111.

91. Jameson, *Marxism*, p. 56.

92. Adorno himself brings in the term "ontology" when he asserts that the *Missa Solemnis* asks "whether ontology, the objective and mental [*geistig*] ordering of being is possible at all any more" ("Verfremdetes Hauptwerk," p. 179). See the same essay, p. 185 (on the work's "Kantianly rigorous question about what after all is still possible"); also Kuspit, "Critical Notes," p. 325 (on Adorno's fetishizing of the dialectic); and Peter Demetz, *Marx, Engels, and the Poets: Origins of Marxist Literary Criticism* (Chicago, 1967), p. 235.

93. See Adorno, "Verfremdetes Hauptwerk," p. 184. To Beethoven and Hegel Adorno might add Goethe; see "Spätstil," p. 16.

94. In the same way that the bourgeoisie, having gained for itself the advantages of individualism, could not let itself be negated into some ensuing form of social organization (Adorno, *Einleitung*, pp. 51, 229).

95. On the self-conscious equaling the impossible, see Mann's remark in *Doctor Faustus* (p. 115): "A form of life that discusses and examines itself thereby dissolves as form, and only direct and unconscious being has true existence." See also *Doctor Faustus*, pp. 365–66; and Adorno, *Einleitung*, p. 60 (on the empirical impossibility of the individual) and p. 230 (on the eventual futility of the subject's fight against the form principle).

96. As Professor Robert L. Marshall of Brandeis has astutely suggested in a private communication, it is this historical coincidence of individual and generic death that distinguishes Beethoven's late style from the more general phenomenon of late styles to which Adorno alludes in the article "Spätstil."

97. Note, for example, the consolation Adorno perceives in Beethoven's Op. 111 (Mann, *Doctor Faustus*, p. 55), but which he directed Mann to remove from Leverkühn's last work (ibid., p. 491; Mann, *Story of a Novel*, pp. 222–23).

98. See Kim, Review of *Drei Studien*, pp. 177–78; and Goldschmidt, "Der späte Beethoven," p. 47.

99. Adorno, "Thesen über Tradition," *Ohne Leitbild* (Frankfurt, 1968), p. 35. The passage goes on to discuss the "march into inhumanity."

100. Adorno, "Verfremdetes Hauptwerk," p. 183.

101. Adorno, *Minima Moralia: Reflexionen aus dem beschädigten Leben* (Frankfurt, 1951), p. 80.

102. Eggebrecht, *Zur Geschichte der Beethoven-Rezeption*, p. 18. "Semblance" because Eggebrecht is subsequently at pains to show Adorno's underlying conformity with critical tradition (p. 83).

103. For example, Goldschmidt, "Der späte Beethoven," p. 43; Knepler, "Beethoven-Bild," p. 35; Konrad Boehmer, "Adorno, Musik, Gesellschaft," *Die neue Linke nach Adorno*, ed. Wilfried F. Schoeller (Munich, 1969), pp. 118–34, passim; Kuspit, "Critical Notes," p. 325; and Kim, Review of *Drei Studien*, p. 178.

104. Mann, *Doctor Faustus*, p. 491, a passage written to Adorno's specifications. Despite Adorno's numerous references to the utopian prefiguring of social harmony in art, his theory of modern society (for example in *Dialectic of Enlightenment*) offers no basis for a belief in the possibility of such harmony. See Kuspit, "Critical Notes," p. 325; Jay, *Dialectical Imagination*, pp. 278–79; Kellner, "The Frankfurt School," p. 147; and Kim, Review of *Drei Studien*, pp. 177–78. Even Eggebrecht (*Zur Geschichte der Beethoven-Rezeption*, pp. 83–84), whose use of the term "utopian" is misleading, especially when applied to Adorno, is willing to admit at least an inconsistency in Adorno's use of the concept. See also Adorno, *Einleitung*, p. 153, on the simultaneous need for and rejection of utopia by society; and the conclusion of "Growing Old," where Adorno is utterly unable to suggest, even vaguely, any legitimate way out for modern composition.

105. See Feher, "Negative Philosophy," p. 104; and Demetz, *Marx, Engels, and the Poets*, p. 235. For an introduction to Lukács's theory of realism, see Georg Lukács, *Writer and Critic*, pp. 75–82; *Studies in European Realism* (New York, 1964), pp. 43–46, 58–60 (on Balzac), 80–87 (on Zola); also the introduction by Fredric Jameson to Henri Arvon's *Marxist Esthetics*, trans. Helen Lane (Ithaca, 1973), pp. xxi–xxii; G. H. R. Parkinson, "Lukács on the Central Category of Aesthetics," *Georg Lukács: The Man, His Work and His Ideas*, ed. G. H. R. Parkinson (New York, 1970), pp. 132–34; and Roy Pascal, "Georg Lukács: The Concept of Totality," ibid., pp. 167–68. For a many-sided view of Lukács's conception of realism, I am also indebted to discussions with Professor George Bisztray of the University of Toronto. On Adorno's actual indebtedness to Lukács, see esp. Jay, *Dialectical Imagination*, pp. 174–75; also Feher, "Negative Philosophy," p. 100.

106. Adorno, "Verfremdetes Hauptwerk," p. 185.

107. "Music, and art generally, which acquiesces to what is socially possible for it and perfects that fully within itself ranks, even primarily in terms of social truth content, higher than an [art] which, through a social will external to the thing [i.e., to the art work], seeks to go beyond the dictated boundaries but thereby fails. Music can become ideological even when, on the strength of its social reflection, it takes up the standpoint of a consciousness [which is] correct seen from the outside [but] which contradicts its own inner construction and its necessities and therewith what is open to it to express" (Adorno, *Einleitung*, p. 74). Here Adorno is emphasizing not only the autonomy of art but also the same primacy of artistic results over artistic intention worked out in detail by Lukács.

108. Adorno, *Einleitung*, p. 73; see also pp. 230, 239.

109. See esp. Adorno, "Growing Old," p. 26; and *Einleitung*, p. 236; also Feher, "Negative Philosophy," p. 106.

110. Adorno, "Verfremdetes Hauptwerk," p. 170.

111. See for example Metzger, "Intermezzo I," pp. 66, 71, 79 (Metzger also points to a number of philosophical inconsistencies in Adorno's music criticism); and Albrecht von Hohenzollern, "Gedanken zu Beethovens 'Missa Solemnis' und zu Adornos Aufsatz 'Verfremdetes Hauptwerk,'" *Musica Sacra*, 90 (1970), pp. 263–70. In Adorno's defense it should be noted that few of his arguments are the sort to stand or fall on empirical grounds. Thus Goldschmidt ("Der späte Beethoven," p. 46) appeals to the work of Warren Kirkendale ("New Roads to Old Ideas in Beethoven's *Missa Solemnis*," *The Creative World of Beethoven*, ed. Paul Henry Lang [New York, 1971], pp. 163–99) to refute Adorno's analysis of the *Missa Solemnis* empirically. But even though Kirkendale can show, for example, that the double statement of the Credo had eighteenth-century precedents ("New Roads," p. 180, fn. 80), this does not invalidate Adorno's interpretation of such a usage in the *Missa Solemnis*, that Beethoven is trying to convince himself of a belief that has been lost ("Verfremdetes Hauptwerk," p. 179). Adorno's resistance to empirical attacks, as well as the virtual impossibility of isolating his individual arguments, have led Kurt Oppens (who accuses Adorno of "sight-reading" classicism) to conclude that the only way to react to Adorno is to object to him altogether ("Zu den musikalischen Schriften," pp. 23, 15).

112. Jameson, *Marxism*, p. 54.

113. On the former, see Feher, "Negative Philosophy," p. 107; on the latter, see Boehmer, "Adorno, Musik, Gesellschaft," p. 119.

114. In this connection, one should not overlook Eggebrecht's observation of the frequency with which the notion of "subject" occurs in Beethoven criticism (*Zur Geschichte der Beethoven-Rezeption*, p. 61).

115. "Critical Notes," pp. 321–22.

116. See especially Goldschmidt, "Der späte Beethoven," pp. 51–52 (on the meaning of the style change in Beethoven's last period); and Eggebrecht, *Zur Geschichte der Beethoven-Rezeption*, p. 85 (on the creation of a new concept of art in which Beethoven would negate himself).

117. See Kuspit, "Critical Notes," pp. 325–26; Kim, Review of *Drei Studien*, p. 178; Oppens, "Zu den musikalischen Schriften," p. 15; and Eggebrecht, *Zur Geschichte der Beethoven-Rezeption*, p. 84 (on Adorno himself).

118. Special thanks are due here to several former graduate students of mine at the University of Chicago who have shared with me their own written work about Adorno: Ann Feldman, Jann Pasler (now of the University of California, San Diego), Karen Thorkilsen, and above all, Lawrence Fuchsberg (now in the U.S. Foreign Service), whose uncanny sensitivity to Adorno's work was a vital source of the preceding discussion.

Chapter 3. Why Is Adorno's Music Criticism the Way It Is? Some Reflections on Twentieth-Century Criticism of Nineteenth-Century Music

1. For further information, see, "The Historical Structure: Adorno's 'French' Model for the Criticism of 19th-Century Music," chapter 11 in this volume. In case it is not obvious, I should stress that the structuralist reading of Adorno both in the article just cited and in the present article is most definitely my own experiment, written "against the grain" of Adorno's self-conception.

2. For an elaboration of this point see, "The Cultural Message of Musical Semiology," chapter 9 in this volume.

3. Adorno does not treat Brahms's attempts to "reuniversalize" the bases of music as an essentially "post-individual," postmodern phenomenon any more than he so treats Schoenberg's music. On individual identity vs. choice, see also chapter 7, n. 27, this volume.

4. Obviously Adorno exaggerates his case in implying that every particular pitch or interval is predetermined by the row. On the other hand, it is difficult to deny that the notion of responsibility for every pitch, that is the rejection of "accidental" or "irrelevant" (i.e. "unnecessary") choices of pitch, is implicit in the row system.

5. T. W. Adorno, *Philosophy of Modern Music*, trans. Anne G. Mitchell and Wesley V. Blomster (New York, 1973), pp. 40–41.

6. "Nachwort" to Schumann's *Liederkreis*, op. 39 (Wiesbaden, 1960).

7. Roughly speaking, "paradigmatic" (or, "metaphorical") elements in structuralist terms are all those elements that could be substituted as equivalents for one element in a configuration (say, harmonies that could replace IV in a IV–V–I cadence); "syntagmatic" (or "metonymical") elements are elements that have a contiguous or complementary relationship within a configuration (say, IV, V, and I in the above cadence).

8. In fact, Adorno does not subscribe ultimately to this conception of classicism, which I have evoked (for clarifying purposes) as a contrast to romantic incompleteness. In his *Introduction to the Sociology of Music* (trans. E. B. Ashton, [New York, 1976], pp. 69–70), although Adorno admits the difficulty of teasing out social meaning from Mozart's music with its "detachment from empiricism," he simultaneously emphasizes the urgency of doing so. (See also, ibid., p. 204: "While autonomous music, by virtue of that distinction, also has a place in the social totality and bears its mark of Cain, the idea of freedom lives in it at the same time"; and p. 69: "[To object] that

representation itself is reconcilement already, and is thus ideological, would touch upon the wound of art in general.") See also chapter 4, nn. 37–38, this volume.

Utimately, in much the same sense as I do in chapter 7 in this book, Adorno views the classical style as simply a variant of the semiotic incompleteness that Beethoven's late work established as inescapable by *any* style. From this viewpoint, a condition of wholeness analogous to that of the universe is to be understood not as a state that the classical musical structure actually achieved, but only as an image or theme to which the music points by drawing on culturally concrete conventions and values extrinsic to "purely abstract" musical structure. Viewed in this way, classical music did not give objective reality to homologous universes, autonomous semiotic structures, or an identity between sound and meaning. At bottom these concepts are no more than constructs of human language, which utimately point back at the language that evoked them, and which are therefore useful, finally, as guides to understanding the stylistically distinctive (and irreducibly cultural) ways in which classicism thought about the universe. Or to put it another way, one that may even shed light on Adorno's concept of mediation (see chapter 2, n. 19, this volume), the art incorporates its ideal into its concrete formal means, which thereby become the theme of that art; and as this process becomes increasingly explicit and self-conscious, we as interpreters feel more and more free to argue that the composition (the poem, the painting) "is about" its own form. See also chapter 10, n. 5, this volume.

9. One example will illustrate the pervasiveness of this incompleteness as an explicit characteristic of nineteenth-century style. What is being suggested here is that classical music encourages a model of criticism as a metaphorical analogue to music, whereas romantic music encourages a model of metonymical incompleteness. A strong argument can be made along the same lines that the conception of various relations in opera (music and text, character and orchestra, stage and audience) changed from one of metaphorical, homologous universes in Mozart (and in Beethoven's *Fidelio*) to one of a metonymical merging between two incomplete entities, say in Weber's *Freischütz* and in Wagner. This imagery is consistent with Dahlhaus's conception of a romantic shift away from architectural to dynamic form (see the passage quoted below, chapter 10 in this volume, n. 13); it also accords with the picture of the typical classical work as a particular universe (see, for example, chapter 6, p. 104, this volume, and also chapter 4, pp. 74–75).

At the same time it must be acknowledged that to associate images of analogy or metaphor with the completeness of a universe, and of contiguity or metonym with the incompleteness of a finite world, is to define the polarity metaphor-metonym in a poststructuralist sense that reverses my usage elsewhere in this volume (chapters 4, 6, and 7), which, based on readings in structuralism, emphasizes the rational connectedness of metonym, and the disjunction of metaphor. For more on this reversal see, in this volume, chapter 4, n. 12, and chapter 6, n. 34. In this connection, it may also be worth noting that besides indicating a shift away from classical linear conceptions of time, my description of criticism at this point in chapter 3 strikingly evokes elements of Jacques Derrida's thought, and deconstructionist images more generally, for example, in its suggestion of an infinite regress in thought, and its attention to absences or traces.

10. T. W. Adorno, "Wagners Aktualität," *275 Jahre Theater in Braunschweig* (Braunschweig, 1965), p. 95.

11. Ibid., p. 97.

Chapter 4. Kant, Adorno, and the Self-Critique of Reason: Toward a Model for Music Criticism

1. Immanuel Kant, *Critique of Judgment*, trans. J. H. Bernard (New York, 1951), section 49: page 157. (Henceforth, the terms "section" and "page" will be omitted from references to this work. Section numbers in roman numerals refer to the Preface.) Reference in the following discussion to Kant's critical philosophy is based largely on a close analysis of the *Critique of Judgment*, both in Bernard's translation and in the original German (*Kritik der Urtheilskraft*, hrsgbn. v.d. Königlich Preussischen Akademie der Wissenschaften, Kant's gesammelte Schriften, Bd. 5 [Berlin, 1913]). It must be stressed from the outset that my reading of Kant's third critique, like that of many post-Kantian thinkers, though probably not of most analytic philosophers, draws epistemological conclusions that Kant's whole critical enterprise was at bottom designed to stave off. Thus my references, here and throughout, to "Kant's presentation [account, and so on]," are not to Kant's own conception of what he had preserved for rationality in this critique but to my own understanding of the losses entailed by his position for the status of rationality. Of interest in connection with my opening quotation is Goethe's statement that "the philosopher might indeed be right who states that no idea is fully congruent with experience, but admits that idea and experience can, indeed must, be analogous," quoted in Karl Löwith, *From Hegel to Nietzsche: The Revolution in Nineteenth-Century Thought*, trans. David E. Green (New York, 1964), p. 6.

2. Rosemary Dinnage, "No Surrender," *New York Review of Books*, 26 (April 19, 1979), p. 16. The article is a review of Bruno Bettelheim's *Surviving and Other Essays*, and the remark, which manifests a strongly Kantian sensibility, actually refers to Bettelheim, though it also captures a fundamental attitude in Adorno's existential attitude.

3. Theodor W. Adorno, *Introduction to the Sociology of Music*, trans. E. B. Ashton (New York, 1976), p. 56.

4. See especially *Sociology*, p. 209.

5. Adorno, "Bach Defended Against His Devotees," *Prisms*, trans. Samuel and Shierry Weber (London, 1967), p. 146; and Charles Rosen, *The Classical Style* (New York, 1972), p. 107. This attitude can be directly related to what will later be called "analogy of difference."

6. See *Critique of Judgment*, VI: 25; though Kant did not distinguish explicitly here between rational "limits" (*Schranken*) and empirical "bounds" (*Grenzen*), such a distinction is clearly the point of this passage. For clarification of this distinction see Allan Janik and Stephen Toulmin, *Wittgenstein's Vienna* (New York, 1973), p. 148. On the subjectivity of reason see Richard Kroner, *Kant's Weltanschauung*, trans. John E. Smith (Chicago, 1956), p. 68.

7. *Weltanschauung*, p. 112, n. 1.

8. Involved here is the enormously complex problem of the relation between the rational and the real, a relation suggestive of a pattern that is often evoked in analysis of the *Critique of Judgment*. This is a pattern in which each of two disjunct principles, in presenting itself as in some sense primary or ultimate, can be interpreted as simultaneously (or even as thereby) indicating the other as still more fundamentally primary or ultimate. A similar pattern can be discerned, for example, in the relation between God and moral law as Kant presented the two (see *Weltanschauung*, p. 35), or between the *Ding an sich* as something existing in itself and for us (see *Weltanschauung*, p. 51). Nothing within this pattern, which shall be called here the pattern of infinite regress, suggests a manner of resolving the contradiction between its two members;

and characteristically, Kant himself proposed no synthesis or identity of the rational and the real in the *Critique of Judgment*. On the one hand, he renounced the possibility of cognitively establishing the rational as (metaphysically) real; on the other hand, he proceeded on the moral assumption that the ground of reality must be rational. See, for example, *Critique of Judgment*, 88: 308; and also 78: 260 and 91:338.

For interesting commentary on aspects of this problem see the following: *Wittgenstein's Vienna*, p. 148; Adorno, "Arnold Schoenberg, 1874–1951," *Prisms*, p. 168, and "Cultural Criticism and Society," ibid., p. 31; Arthur O. Lovejoy, *The Great Chain of Being* (Cambridge, Mass., 1936), pp. 52, 148–49, and 152: *Weltanschauung*, p. 74; *Hegel to Nietzsche*, p. 115; and Karsten Harries, "Hegel on the Future of Art," *Review of Metaphysics*, 27 (1974): p. 688. The sort of pattern described here has something in common with that suggested by the Epimenides paradox (see Douglas Hofstadter, *Gödel, Escher, Bach: An Eternal Golden Braid* [New York, 1979], p. 17); and also with deconstruction.

9. The ground on which the faculties may be resolved must be imagined as existing in a sphere of reason beyond human experience and, finally, beyond knowledge that meets its own standards for cognitive certainty (see, e.g., *Critique of Judgment*, 57: 186–87, and 83: 279). The impossibility of knowing wholes except from a vantage point external to cognition is a central theme in the *Critique of Judgment*, especially in part two, where Kant called attention to the paradoxical contingency of autonomous wholes and distinguished decisively between mechanistic cause and purpose, a noncognitive kind of causality involving the apprehension of wholes.

10. The contradiction between self-containment and incompleteness — a polarity that corresponds generally to that of limits and bounds — can readily be associated with the contradiction between the completeness of logical necessity or structure and the incompleteness of time as it is experienced or defined empirically. Many analyses of the classical style of music, including Adorno's, allude in some way to the synthesis of this particular contradiction; see also *Classical Style*, p. 44, on the simultaneity of surprise and logic. Of relevance to the notion of levels within levels is the discussion in *Gödel, Escher, Bach*, pp. 644–46, which appears under the heading "Frames and Nested Contexts."

11. The conflict is especially apparent when analogous elements are conceived of as reciprocal in their effect, as in *Critique of Judgment*, 34: 128.

12. Kroner suggested the priority of the analogical over the complementary in noting that "the real opposite of subjectivism is . . . not objectivism but absolutism" (p. 74). For more on the disjunction involved in analogy see below, especially n. 21, this chapter. In this chapter, as in chapters 6 and 7, I view complementary (equated with metonymical) structures as amenable to logical connection, and analogical (equated with metaphorical) structures as disjunct and, therefore, not amenable to such a connection. (See, for example, chapter 6, n. 34, and also chapter 3, n. 9.) This imagery, formed during my readings in structuralism, is substantially (though not precisely) reversed in the essays of my companion volume, where I take up the poststructuralist view of metonym as a merely contingent (not complementary) contiguity, and metaphor as a formal relationship of similarity, the very discernment (or definition) of which points to the activity of an intelligence. The two usages are not necessarily incompatible, for they occur at two different levels of analysis: in the first case, referring to formal characteristics through which analysis can make sense of structures, and in the second, referring to formal characteristics that make sense in relation to the act of structural analysis itself. At times, in fact, the second usage is already visible in the present volume. Though I have not yet attempted a direct con-

frontation between these two usages, I assume the deconstructionist notion of infinite regress would help to clarify such a process.

13. See *Critique of Judgment*, 10: 55 and 22: 78; also 9: 52. It should be noted that a comprehensive account of Kant's notion of judgment in all of its modes, determinative and reflective, or even of his notion of aesthetic judgment cannot be attempted here. In general, aesthetic judgment as manifested in determinations of beauty is construed throughout this discussion as having an archetypal structure of judgment, an interpretation I believe warranted within the third critique itself.

14. From a precritical (or everyday) standpoint, cognition appears to work by actual connections between disparate but complementary realms (see, e.g., *Weltanschauung*, pp. 97–98). What Kant made clear, however, is that this pattern of complementary connections (including its clear distinction between subjectivity and objectivity, and the cognitive necessity associated with this pattern) is wholly intrasubjective. Not wishing to relinquish a necessary basis for cognition, Kant in effect asserted a necessary analogy between the structures of the mind and those of the laws of nature (e.g., *Critique of Judgment*, V: 19–21) by redefining the grounds of necessity as subjective. Thus cognition is allowed to derive the necessity of its own internal connections from its own need for those connections (again, the pattern of infinite regress comes to mind). But cognition cannot establish either its own necessity or that of analogy. The fundamental relationship between the human mind and nature must now be recognized not as a connection at all but only as a contingent (and in a sense aesthetic) analogy between two structures, each subjectively construed as internally necessary. See *Critique of Judgment*, VI: 24; also Morse Peckham, *Beyond the Tragic Vision* (New York, 1962), p. 65.

15. For explicit evidence of such relationships, see especially *Critique of Judgment*, III: 13, and IX: 34.

16. See, for example, *Critique of Judgment*, 61: 206; and 28: 260 and 263; see also in this volume chapter 6, p. 101.

17. On the special status of moral reason see *Critique of Judgment*, II: 12, IX: 32, 28–29; 101–5, 42: 142–43, 57: 189, 59: 200, 60: 201–2, 65: 222, 88: 309–10, etc.; also *Weltanschauung*, pp. 70–71.

18. Thus, for example, descriptions of the moral realm constantly make use of terms proper to the theoretical, such as "concept" (*Critique of Judgment*, I: 7), "knowledge" or "cognition" (91: 327, and 59: 198), "cause" (87: 301) and "the intelligible" (59: 199). See also ibid., 91: 336 (on the categories) and 88 (Remark): 310 (on noncontradiction). The line of reasoning that follows bears a clear resemblance to poststructuralist notions such as the "chain of signifiers."

19. For the quoted assertion see *Critique of Judgment* 59: 200; see also ibid., III: 13 (*Mittelglied*) and IX: 33 (*vermittelnder Begriff*); and *Weltanschauung*, pp. 111–12.

20. "Relatively particular" in the sense that Kant, who defined judgment as "in general . . . the faculty of thinking the particular as contained under the universal" (*Critique of Judgment*, IV: 13), showed little interest in extreme forms of individuality, either aesthetic or organic. (This is not to deny that the *Critique of Judgment* can be construed, in spite of Kant, as signaling a historical reversal in the priority ascribed to generality and particularity relative to each other.) More than the "object" of aesthetic judgment it would, from Kant's standpoint, appear to be the exercise of judgment in each determination of beauty that constitutes the archetype of particularity — and, in a sense, of the autonomous individual structure. On the discussion preceding this note see chapter 2, n. 37.

21. Indeed, within a series of analogues, it is not necessarily possible to identify any one as an archetype (any more than the variation process in music implies the ac-

tual presence of an archetypal theme). Thus, in the case of Kant's conception of the mind, there is a sense in which each of the faculties can be construed as a structural archetype of the other two; Kroner, for example, treated the moral faculty, in effect, as such.

22. See the discussion of "perspectivism" in E. D. Hirsch, *The Aims of Interpretation* (Chicago, 1976), p. 27. Earlier (p. 13) Hirsch notes that "for . . . cognitive atheists, all principles are subject to a universal relativism except relativism itself," and asks, "But whence comes *its* exception? What is the sanction, in a world devoid of absolutes, for *its* absoluteness?" And, indeed, no absolute status can be claimed, with cognitive certainty, for relativism. All that the relativist can assert, as Kant so often did in other contexts, is that one's reason allows one to posit as cognitively valid no other assumption about the relations between people's minds.

23. See especially *Critique of Judgment*, 47: 151 (on the genius's limited knowledge of his own work).

24. See Charles Rosen, "The Origins of Walter Benjamin," *New York Review of Books*, 24 (November 10, 1977), p. 31; also Carl Dahlhaus, "Zu Kants Musikästhetik," *Archiv für Musikwissenschaft*, 10 (1953), p. 341, n. 3.

25. Quoted in "Origins," p. 33.

26. See, for example, "Hegel on the Future of Art," pp. 681–83, and Harries, "Metaphor and Transcendence," *Critical Inquiry*, 5 (1978): pp. 75–76. See also "Zu Kants Musikästhetik," pp. 344–46, and Giselher Schubert, "Zur Musikästhetik in Kants 'Kritik der Urtheilskraft,' " *Archiv für Musikwissenschaft*, 32 (1975), pp. 24–25. Though Dahlhaus and Schubert are both right in stressing Kant's association of the aesthetic and the moral, it is nevertheless so that the relation between these two realms, as presented in the *Critique of Judgment*, remains one of disjunction; see, for example, *Critique of Judgment*, 29: 111–12, 42: 143, and 59: 199–200.

27. See *Critique of Judgment*, 47: 152, 49: 160–62, and 60: 200–201; Rosen, "The Ruins of Walter Benjamin," *New York Review of Books*, 24 (October 27, 1977), pp. 32 and 35, and also *Classical Style*, p. 22; Harold Rosenberg, *The Tradition of the New* (New York, 1959); and Harold Bloom, *The Anxiety of Influence* (New York, 1973). Bloom's study could profitably be used as a model for a study of Beethoven's influence on nineteenth-century music, on which see also Carl Dahlhaus, "Zur Problematik der Musikalischen Gattungen im 19. Jahrhundert," *Gattungen der Musik in Einzeldarstellungen*, ed. Wulf Arlt, Ernst Lichtenhahn, and Hans Oesch, (Bern and Munich, 1973), p. 880. See also the discussion of "formal imitation" in nineteenth-century aesthetics in Walter Serauky, *Die Musikalische Nachahmungsästhetik im Zeitraum von 1700 bis 1850* (Munster, 1929), e.g., pp. 160, 181–82, 245, 247, 260–61, and 265–66; this concept is defined (though not by name) in *Chain of Being*, pp. 303–4. See also "Arnold Schoenberg," pp. 164 ("the genre of the masterpiece"), and 166 ("to be true to Schoenberg is to warn against all twelve-tone schools"); and Jacques Barzun, *Classic, Romantic and Modern* (Garden City, N.Y., 1961), pp. 141–42.

28. *Classical Style*, p. 325.

29. See in this connection "Origins," pp. 35–36.

30. *Critique of Judgment*, 9:52. (This is another sort of connective pattern that seems to be characteristic of cognition; see n. 14, this chapter.) On significant differences see Adorno, "The Radio Symphony: An experiment in Theory," *Radio Research 1941*, ed. Paul F. Lazarsfeld and Frank N. Stanton (New York, 1941), pp. 116 and 123. Because this article crystallizes in a useful way many of Adorno's ideas about classical and romantic music, it has been used as an immediate source of reference for much of the discussion that follows. I am grateful to Professor Jurgen Thym, of the Eastman

School of Music, for calling it to my attention and lending me his own copy. See also
Classical Style, pp. 59, 77–78, and 100, on classical repetition.

31. *Sociology*, p. 69.

32. Ibid., p. 214. Ashton renders *Einheit* as "unit" here; for the original German
see *Einleitung in die Musiksoziologie* (Reinbek bei Hamburg, 1968), p. 228.

33. *Classical Style*, p. 33.

34. Ibid., p. 83.

35. *Sociology*, p. 214.

36. Adorno tended to minimize or overlook, for example, the degree to which
Haydn created a paradigm of logical development and economy or to which Mozart
individualized a general language (though on the latter see *Sociology*, p. 161).

37. See, for example, the remarks on Haydn in *Sociology*, p. 69; and cf. "Cultural
Criticism and Society," p. 32.

38. See Adorno, *Philosophy of Modern Music*, trans. Anne G. Mitchell and Wesley
V. Blomster (New York, 1973), p. 96, where Adorno applied the term "precritical"
to various traditional (though not specifically pre-Beethovenian) genres.

39. On the importance of thematic material see "Radio Symphony," pp. 116 and
129–30; on timbre see ibid., pp. 123–26 and 134. On the "systematic composition"
see *Sociology*, p. 214; and compare the description of such a piece, in "Radio Symphony," pp. 115–16, with Kant's definition of the organism, in *Critique of Judgment*,
66: 222. See also *Classical Style*, pp. 399 and 406.

40. See, for example, *Philosophy*, p. 55, on freedom, and Adorno's essay "Schubert,"
Moments Musicaux (Frankfurt, 1964), p. 34, on the "must." See also n. 76, this chapter.

41. *Sociology*, p. 214.

42. "Radio Symphony," p. 134.

43. And the concretizing of conceptions of reason and of modes of rational discourse, it is clear, which continues through romantic music and into the twentieth
century, emerges as a principal means by which post-Enlightenment Western society
criticizes the Enlightenment ideal of reason. See, for example, Claude Lévi-Strauss,
The Savage Mind (Chicago, 1966), pp. 11–22 and 266–68; and Ch. Perelman and L.
Olbrechts-Tyteca, *The New Rhetoric: A Treatise on Argumentation*, trans. John Wilkinson and Purcell Weaver (Notre Dame, Ind., 1969). It is, of course, the explicit concreteness of musical thought that gives the study of musical sketches its fascination
and its point.

44. "Radio Symphony," p. 117. Note his allusion, in the same place, to a "suspension of time consciousness." See also his remarks in *Philosophy*, pp. 100–101, which
resemble observations made about Mozart by Edward E. Lowinsky in "On Mozart's
Rhythm," reprinted in *The Creative World of Mozart*, ed. Paul Henry Lang (New York,
1963), p. 39; and Löwith's discussion of Hegel and time, *Hegel to Nietzsche*, pp. 207–8.

45. For more on the untenability of this synthesis see "Adorno's Diagnosis of
Beethoven's Late Style: Early symptom of a Fatal Condition," chapter 3 in this volume. Adorno's remarks in "Radio Symphony," p. 115, n. 8, show clearly that he
viewed the "systematic composition" as a norm rather than as an achievement.

46. Cf. *Classical Style*, pp. 76–77 and 276; suggestive also in this context is Rosen's
notion (ibid., p. 29) that the isolation of elements within the artwork has tended to
erode larger-scale aspects of isolation (though Rosen had in mind here only technical
sorts of isolation).

47. See "Radio Symphony," pp. 128–30, especially the remarks on Beethoven's
Fifth Symphony and Schubert's *Unfinished*.

48. See ibid., p. 138 (on Brahms's First Symphony).

49. For a graphic illustration of the processes involved in the apprehension of for-

eign semiotic structures, see the reproduction entitled "A Meaningful Story in Arabic" in *Gödel, Escher, Bach*, p. 624.

50. In other words, the rhetoric obscures the temporal drive. Cf. Rosen, *Arnold Schoenberg* (New York, 1975), p. 32.

51. "Radio Symphony," p. 120.

52. On the passivity forced on the listener by romantic music, see Friedrich Blume, *Classic and Romantic Music*, trans. M. D. Herter Norton (New York, 1970), p. 11.

53. This notion of time differs markedly from the self-defining notion discerned in classical music by Tovey (see *Classical Style*, p. 78). See also Adorno's remarks on the romantic (or romanticized) symphony and empirical time in "Radio Symphony," pp. 117 and 126–27. On romantic treatment of time see also in this volume chapter 3, n. 9; chapter 7, n. 32; chapter 10, n. 13; and chapter 11, nn. 34 and 62.

54. *Classical Style*, p. 277.

55. See *Sociology*, p. 64.

56. Adorno's remarks on Brahms in *Sociology*, pp. 64–65, and the extension of these remarks to Schoenberg in "Arnold Schoenberg," pp. 167–68, and *Philosophy*, p. 96, can without difficulty be applied to most nineteenth-century romantic music.

57. To the extent, of course, that romantic music suggests the pattern of drive toward an unattainable limit, one could say it keeps alive the notion of norms and meaning. From Adorno's standpoint, however, it is probably more consistent to argue that because romantic music, unlike classical music, no longer embodies (even in an illusory sense) its own unattainable norm, it presents itself as essentially isolated, with the same disjunct relation to the norm of a supraempirical meaning as the aesthetic has generally to the metaphysical in nineteenth-century post-Kantian culture. For Adorno, one can suppose, the romantic drive toward a norm would have constituted a surface phenomenon, like romantic rhetorical propulsiveness. For exceptions see "The Historical Structure: Adorno's 'French' Model for the Criticism of Nineteenth-Century Music," chapter 11 in this volume, pp. 219 and 234–35.

58. See, for example, "Arnold Schoenberg," pp. 169–70.

59. *Philosophy*, p. 104.

60. See, for example, *Philosophy*, pp. 97 and 110, and "Arnold Schoenberg," pp. 167, 168, and especially 171, on the destruction of the "work" as a category.

61. *Sociology*, pp. 69–70. In fact, an analysis of the sort I propose here is carried out in chapter 6 in this book.

62. On classicism and quasi logical norms see *Classical Style*, for example, pp. 69, 82–83, and 120.

63. See, for example, *Classical Style*, p. 100, on the characteristic relaxation of tension over the movements of a classical work; and cf. the concluding remarks of Hermann Abert's analysis of Mozart's Symphony No. 40, as translated and reprinted in Mozart, *Symphony in G Minor, K. 550*, ed. Nathan Broder, Norton Critical Scores (New York, 1967), p. 83. Abert's description of the "liberating solution" with respect to Mozart's work strongly evokes Kant's image of the metaphysical as beyond the limits of the knowable and suggests Mozart's work as "critical" in relation to the metaphysical (though also as pre-Hegelian in its refusal to simulate within itself an attainment of the metaphysical).

64. The quotation is from *Classical Style*, p. 43. See Edward E. Lowinsky, "Taste, Style, and Ideology in Eighteenth-Century Music," *Aspects of the Eighteenth Century*, ed. Earl R. Wasserman (Baltimore, 1965), p. 181; this latter should be read in conjunction with Lovejoy's account, *Chain of Being*, pp. 55–58, 229, and 241.

65. On contrast within themes see *Classical Style*, p. 82. Of course, periodization

tends to break down under the pressure of development; see in this connection ibid., p. 50.

66. The quotation is from *Classical Style*, p. 68; interesting also in this connection are remarks, ibid., pp. 31, 33, 70–71, and 81.

67. It is of importance since (however loudly analytic philosophers argue to the contrary) all initial principles must be considered irrational in that they cannot demonstrate their own rationality and must be established by fiat. Suggestive in this connection are *Critique of Judgment*, 55: 182, n. 1; and *Chain of Being*, pp. 147–58.

68. Of interest in this context is Rosen's remark on the "exciting rhythmic power of pure repetition" (*Classical Style*, p. 253).

69. In an unpublished analysis of Schumann's *Carnaval*, Frank Retzel, the composer, applies this term to the piece "Pierrot"; the term is taken from an article by Herbert H. Simon, "The Architecture of Complexity," *Proceedings of the American Philosophical Society*, 106 (1962), p. 469. See also the discussion of this notion in Leonard Meyer, *Music, The Arts, and Ideas* (Chicago, 1967), pp. 309–10.

70. See *Classical Style*, p. 91, on symmetry of material and of form.

71. Ibid., p. 80. The C-# in mvt. IV, mm. 17–18 of Beethoven's Eighth Symphony defines a similar situation.

72. Ibid., p. 68.

73. See *Chain of Being*, pp. 279–80.

74. *Sociology*, p. 214. Compare Constant Lambert, *Music Ho!*, 3rd ed. (London, 1966), pp. 264–65.

75. Ibid., p. 210. Adorno made clear in this context the moral ambiguity of any principle that presents the emphatic self-reassertion of the free subject as if it were the necessary resolution of tensions between the subject and what is "other" (ultimately, society).

76. Involved here, clearly, is the ambiguity of Hegel's dialectical *Aufhebungen*, that the highest stage in a synthesis can be taken either to preserve or to negate the identity of a preceding individual moment.

77. *Classical Style*, p. 81. The whole philosophical tradition of recapitulation is in need of analysis by critics of classical and romantic music. As points of departure see *Chain of Being*, p. 285 (on Bonnet), *Hegel to Nietzsche*, pp. 61 (on Hegel) and 225 (on Goethe), and Joan Stambaugh, *Nietzsche's Thought of Eternal Return* (Baltimore, 1972).

78. See *Classical Style*, pp. 82 (on dynamics) and 59–60 (on rhythm and melody); also pp. 44 and 64.

79. *Chain of Being*, p. 332. I wish to express here my gratitude to the American Council of Learned Societies and the Guggenheim Foundation for supporting the research on which this essay is based.

Chapter 5. Musicology and Criticism

1. A version of this chapter was first given at the annual meeting of the American Musicological Society, November 13, 1981, in Boston.

2. I agree with those scholars who argue that not even an originating artist's interpretation of his own work is epistemologically definitive or, for that matter, necessarily privileged. See Richard Taruskin's essay "The Musicologist and the Performer," *Musicology in the 1980s: Methods, Goals, Opportunities*, ed. D. Kern Holoman and Claude V. Palisca (New York, 1982), pp. 101–17, and compare Charles Rosen's assertion that "not even the author's own exegesis can ever attach itself permanently to [a text], or pretend to be an integral or necessary condition of experiencing it" ("The Origins of Walter Benjamin," *New York Review of Books*, 24, November 10, 1977, p. 37). This

viewpoint, prominent in current post-structuralist thought, is, to be sure, opposed by some of our most humane scholars, for example, E. D. Hirsch in *The Aims of Interpretation* (Chicago, 1976), chapter 5 (see also p. 7). On the whole I fear that in epistemological terms, Hirsch's argument rests on a kind of wishful thinking that overestimates the rationality of utterance, interpretation, and communication while underestimating the irreducibly individual or indeterminate aspects of such processes. At the same time, however, I do believe that a strong case can be made for the moral and epistemological value of trying to approximate, through a dialectical process, the original meaning of an utterance, so long as the ineradicable and ultimately governing role of the interpreter's own consciousness in any act of interpretation is openly acknowledged. The value seems especially clear when the originator of an utterance is alive and available for questions.

3. "The Ruins of Walter Benjamin," *New York Review of Books*, 24 (October 27, 1977), p. 32.

4. Ibid. For insight into this monumental upheaval in Western thought, as well as into the concomitant decline of Western ethnocentricity and the emergence of that relativistic outlook that produced modern criticism, there is still no better guide than Arthur O. Lovejoy's *The Great Chain of Being* (Cambridge, Mass., 1936), chapters 10 and 11.

5. Thomas S. Kuhn, *The Structure of Scientific Revolutions*, 2nd ed. (Chicago, 1970).

6. Morse Peckham, *Beyond the Tragic Vision* (New York, 1962), p. 76.

7. It is the presence of this scientific ideology that accounts for the "modernist" character of what Richard Taruskin terms the "reconstructionist" attitude, the very attitude that has established itself as traditional in what I call "mainstream" musicology. Taruskin is certainly right to identify Hanslick as the point of departure for current American musicological thought, though I would view Hanslick's philosophy not as an "astonishing" precursor of Stravinsky's but as part of the same cultural configuration that led to the prominence of positivism, empirical science, and industrial technology well within the nineteenth century. See also this chapter, n. 11, on ideology and "nonideology."

8. Charles L. Seeger, "On the Moods of a Music-Logic," *Journal of the American Musicological Society*, 13 (1960), pp. 224–61; see particularly 258–61.

9. Igor Stravinsky, *Poetics of Music* (New York, 1960), Lesson 3, "The Composition of Music," pp. 66–69.

10. Clearly I am advocating an extension of the sensibility underlying modern criticism to all of musicology. Thus, whereas Taruskin in effect associates the mainstream musicologist with a traditional scientific ideal, "the establishment of generalizing criteria," I would argue that *any* humanistic scholar is far closer to the artist in terms of activities, or, for that matter, to Taruskin's own model of the performer. In all three of the latter categories, I believe, works that can be fully accounted for through general principles are as limited in value as those that aim no higher than at "getting it right."

11. As my conception of "ideology" aroused controversy during the original presentation of this essay, it may be worth restating that conception. I think of ideology not, in positivistic fashion, as an unfortunate dogmatism that invalidates all intellectual achievements except those based on the nonideological truth of Western science, but rather as the context of particular ideas and beliefs that define (and thereby shape and restrict) the mental domain of *all* human beings. I have elaborated on this conception in "The Role of Ideology in the Study of Western Music," chapter 1 in this volume.

12. Leonard Meyer, an open-minded scholar by any standard, has cautioned in re-

sponse to this essay that the genuine right to freedom of speech must not be confused with the specious right to a platform or audience. And I would agree that none of us can automatically blame our failure to achieve publication or acceptance of a paper proposal on ideological prejudices rather than on our own inadequacy. But I would also argue for the converse: that incompetence ought not to be automatically accepted as the actual basis on which traditionalists deny the nontraditionalist a platform or professional footing, especially when there seems to be a pattern of ideological discrimination. For an unusually thoughtful analysis of the ways in which the context for free speech has changed since the ideal was formalized in the First Amendment of the U.S. Constitution, see Monroe E. Price, *Shattered Mirrors: Our Search for Identity and Community in the AIDS Era* (Cambridge, Mass., 1989), pp. 50–60. Of particular interest is the analysis of changes caused by technology: "Now, we must worry about a marketplace that casually maintains and reinforces the existing power structure through the prohibitive expense of entering the competition. This poses serious problems in democratic theory" (p. 51). Is this description altogether irrelevant to the current world of scholarship? True, in most (though not in all) instances, entering the *academic* competition for a hearing does not require the payment of any money. But today adherents of a growing number of viewpoints have concluded that they cannot get a hearing in academia unless they stifle their own interests, viewpoints, or convictions in favor of those held by "the existing power structure" in their disciplines. If their perception is accurate, isn't the denial of one's own intellectual (and perhaps moral) identity indeed a "prohibitive expense of entering the competition"?

13. Again, I am in agreement with Taruskin, here with his suggestions that "any authentic, which is to say authoritative performance" must incorporate the sensibility of its performers, and indeed that antiquarian attempts at presentation may well violate the eternal essence (not Taruskin's term) of an artwork. This same notion, that art is falsified by attempts to remove it from the temporal flux of the human condition, is one of Adorno's principal tenets. He takes it up explicitly with reference to performance practice in his essay "Bach Defended Against His Devotees," in *Prisms*, trans. Samuel and Shierry Weber (London, 1967), pp. 142–46.

Chapter 6. Evidence of a Critical Worldview in Mozart's Last Three Symphonies

1. In such a consideration, one would want to assess such suggestions as Walter Benjamin's that stylistic extremes yield more informative interpretations than do stylistic norms (see Charles Rosen, "The Origins of Walter Benjamin," *New York Review of Books*, 24 [November 10, 1977], p. 33).

2. Jan LaRue, *Guidelines to Style Analysis* (New York, 1970); David B. Greene, *Temporal Processes in Beethoven's Music* (New York, 1982), a methodologically fascinating book.

3. The categories of the present analysis as well as the terms "critical" and "precritical" stem from my comparative study of Immanuel Kant's *Critique of Judgment*.

4. *The Great Chain of Being* (Cambridge, Mass., 1936), p. 294.

5. See the speech of the Little Monk in Scene 7 of *Galileo*, in the English version by Charles Laughton (*Seven Plays by Bertolt Brecht*, ed. Eric Bentley [New York, 1961], pp. 366–67).

6. Manfred Bukofzer, "Allegory in Baroque Music," *Journal of the Warburg and Couriauld Institutes*, 3 (1939–40), p. 21; Edward E. Lowinsky, "Taste, Style, and Ideol-

ogy in Eighteenth-Century Music," *Aspects of the Eighteenth Century*, ed. Earl R. Wasserman (Baltimore, 1965), p. 192.

7. Paul Henry Lang's insistence on the secularity of Handel's religious music goes to the heart of the matter: the ability of music to project, through purely formal means, a significance that may be quite different from the meaning of an associated text (*George Frideric Handel* [New York, 1966], pp. 215–18 and 383–93). Consider also the interpenetration of sacred and secular meaning so often remarked in Mozart's last opera and Mass.

8. I would further argue that this belief became radically, indeed, irreversibly problematic in Beethoven's music as well as irreconcilable with romanticism.

9. In his article "The Mirror of Tonality," *19th Century Music*, 4 (1981), p. 192, Lawrence Kramer misrepresents my theory of music history. My point is not that the classicists are better composers than their successors but simply that the distinctiveness of the classical style derives from the value placed by classicism on the general intelligibility of an implicitly logical system, by virtue of the way classicists formulated tonality. The romantics and Schoenberg undoubtedly still wanted general intelligibility, but in using a syntax that became increasingly more individual than general, both in character and in formal significance, they traded the primacy of implicit intelligibility for that of precision of expression. In short, they faced the difficulty of achieving general intelligibility with basically individualized means. For them, persuading others of the rationality (especially in the sense of inner logical necessity) of their system meant making explicit the rationality not of a conventionalized system but rather of individualized choice. They had to redefine rationality as an individual rather than as a general principle, much as Mozart began to do in his mature style; and with this shift arose an undeniable tension, to an extent definitive of romanticism, between the desire for the universally recognizable logical necessity that classicism had successfully projected as an ideal, and the actual contingency (or, at most, the rational plausibility rather than necessity) projected by a style that entertains doubts about the universal validity of individual choices. See chapter 4, n. 34, of this book.

10. On the sequence, see Charles Rosen, *The Classical Style* (New York, 1972), pp. 48 and 58.

11. See Hermann Abert's remarks on finales in the Norton Critical Score of Mozart's *Symphony in G Minor, K. 550*, ed. Nathan Broder (New York, 1967), p. 83.

12. See Max Weber, *The Rational and Social Function of Music*, trans. and ed. Don Martindale et al.. (Carbondale, Ill., 1958), pp. xxiv–xxx and 8–10.

13. For clarification of significance, see the first movement, mm. 26–40 (theme 1) and 98–101 (theme 2), and the fourth, m. 41ff. (theme 2). For demarcation, see the first movement, mm. 181–83 (announcement of the recapitulation), the second, mm. 27–29 and 53–64 (framing of a contrasting section), and the obvious contrast between minuet and trio themes. For reconciliation of earlier themes, see the second movement, m. 72, and the fourth, mm. 152–54 (union of expository variants in the recapitulation). Note also the prominent use of repeated-note motifs in all four movements and the pattern moving from pitch center G to C at the opening of the outer-movement development sections (first movement, mm. 143–60, and fourth, mm. 104–21). This pattern has a counterpart in the use of D minor in the outer developments of Symphony No. 40: first movement, mm. 134–38, and fourth, mm. 131–37.

14. Rosen, *Classical Style*, p. 44.

15. Norton Critical Score of the *Symphony in G Minor*, p. 72.

16. Ibid. p. 69.

17. See the first movement, mm. 20–22 (restatement of theme 1), mm. 102–5

(opening of the development), mm. 160–65 (return to the recapitulation), and even mm. 281–86 (approach to the coda); also the third movement, mm. 36–38 (joining of the coda), and the fourth, mm. 133–35 (return to "convention" in the development); and compare with Symphony No. 39: first movement, mm. 22–25 (end of the slow introduction) and mm. 180–83 (return to the recapitulation).

18. Rosen, *Classical Style*, p. 68.

19. Note also the prominent enharmonic shifts; for example, in Symphony No. 39, fourth movement, mm. 48–52 (beginning of the harmonic parenthesis) and mm. 112–14 (in conjunction with parallel major-minor shifts).

20. For sudden transpositions or abrupt stepwise movement, see Symphony No. 39, first movement, mm. 141–46 (which involves an augmented fourth), and fourth movement, mm. 104–9; No. 40, second movement, mm. 55–57 (opening of the development, with D♭ conceivably "prepared," though by no general rules of tonal logic, by m. 29); and No. 41, fourth movement, mm. 158–66 (opening of the development), and, in a sense, first movement, m. 123 (opening of the development as opposed to the G-major statement at m. 101).

21. Note the heavy doubling of C and D in mm. 30 and 34 in the minuet. Though the chain is broken harmonically at m. 34, E defines the melodic peak at m. 40.

22. On row, see Heinrich Jalowetz's comments in the Norton Critical Score of the *Symphony in G Minor*, pp. 99–100. David Josephson has pointed out to me another intriguing example of the C–E relationship in this symphony. The theme of the trio seems to be a retrograde variant of the minuet theme, starting with the leading tone to tonic cadence at m. 3 of the minuet. And in a sense the final cadence of the trio (ending in C–E–C, m. 87) completes the thematic transformation by alluding to m. 4 of the minuet.

23. See Symphony No. 41, first movement, mm. 173–77 (here E, D, and C are supported by the harmony, but with parallel major-minor shifts), and fourth movement, mm. 245–49 (in a highly complex harmonic-contrapuntal context).

24. Hans T. David, "Mozartean Modulations," *The Creative World of Mozart*, ed. Paul Henry Lang (New York, 1963), pp. 68 and 73.

25. Rosen, *Classical Style*, pp. 82–83.

26. See Symphony No. 39, first movement, mm. 160–79 (V of C minor), and fourth movement, mm. 120–37 (V of C minor); No. 40 (in addition to the outer movements, which are about to be discussed), second movement, mm. 64–70 (V of C); and No. 41, second movement, mm. 56–58 (V of D Minor), fourth, mm, 207–19 (V of E minor), and even the third movement, trio, mm, 68–75 (V of a minor).

27. Rosen, *Classical Style*, p. 79, though also pp. 73 and 80.

28. First movement, mm. 81–85; second, mm. 18–27; and fourth, mm. 127–32.

29. Though F minor and C minor are the nominal equivalents of F major, the key of this movement, and C, its dominant, they are obviously not their functional equivalents, since the dominant must be on the major form of V. The "preparation" of this passage by earlier allusions to the minor mode, starting with D minor (see the C# in mm. 6–9) — itself a process that works by adducing similarities, not through logical tonal connection — in no way mitigates the effect of an assault, here, on the notion of a logical tonal goal. On the other hand, the half-cadence on V of F that immediately precedes this episode (m. 18) contributes to that assault; for coming as it does, after some leisurely chromaticism and bits of modulation, it suggests the tonic itself, F, as the point of destination in which a new area of conflict (V) is "supposed to" be presented. (A similar cadence, on the dominant seventh of the original tonic, C, precedes the first-movement episode in the exposition, m. 79, which appears well within dominant "territory.") And the assault is strengthened when this V of F ca-

dence (i.e., a cadence on C major) is abruptly followed by a triad on C minor (functioning momentarily as a new, unprepared, and unrelated tonic, and noticeable, therefore, above all for its effect of coloristic shock).

30. Here and elsewhere in this analysis, as in the analysis, throughout this book, of Kant's solutions to the problem of preserving rationality as a universal principle, one encounters a shifting of epistemologically definable levels that evokes the deconstructionist dynamic of infinite regress as well as, of course, Hegel's dialectic.

31. First movement, mm. 269–75; fourth, mm. 325–32.

32. It is intriguing to note that the strikingly similar moment of recalcitrance, or stalemate, in the first-movement exposition episode of the G-minor symphony (mm. 58–62), which also occurs within the second key-area (here, the area of the relative major rather than the dominant), *also* centers on the pitches C and Db, in still a different key (Ab) and in reverse order. This episode is in turn prepared by the appearance of the same two notes in a V of Bb context at mm. 34–42. Can it be that these pitches were fixed at this time in Mozart's inner ear as a kind of free-floating color, independent of tonal moorings?

33. Interestingly, when it plays the actual pitch C over I (m. 334), the violin drops an octave in register below the initial melodic C (over F minor, m. 326) and Db (m. 328), as if in anticlimax.

34. This entire chapter constitutes the extreme distillation of an extended comparison of Kant's *Critique of Judgment* and Mozart's last three symphonies, a study that was subsidized by fellowships from the American Council of Learned Societies and the Guggenheim Foundation. Again, especially because the whole argument here has drawn on the notion of "metaphor" both in an ordinary sense (as a figure of speech) and in a structuralist one (as analogue), I would call attention to chapter 4 in this volume, n. 12, which notes a reverse sense in which poststructuralism construes the terms "metaphor" and "metonym" (the latter of which I have here associated with complementarity).

Chapter 7. Romantic Music as Post-Kantian Critique: Classicism, Romanticism, and the Concept of the Semiotic Universe

1. On types of sonata movement see Charles Rosen, *The Classical Style* (New York, 1972), pp. 99–100. Though the present chapter, which presents a detailed foundation for all of my remarks elsewhere on Kant, was originally written before I encountered poststructuralism, it seems to anticipate so many of the positions I developed by way of deconstruction that it has seemed useful to point out some of these convergences.

2. On counterparts to a *signifié* in baroque music see Manfred Bukofzer, "Allegory in Baroque Music," *Journal of the Warburg and Courtauld Institutes*, 3 (1939–40), pp. 2–4, 20–21.

3. See, for example, Douglas Hofstadter, *Gödel, Escher, Bach: An Eternal Golden Braid* (New York, 1979), p. 458.

4. Reference in the following discussion to Kant's critical philosophy is based largely on a close analysis of the *Critique of Judgment*, both in English translation and in German. See Immanuel Kant, *Critique of Judgment*, trans. J. H. Bernard (New York, 1951) and *Kritik der Urtheilskraft*, ed. Königlich Preussischen Akademie der Wissenschaften, Kant's *Gesammelte Schriften*, vol. 5 (Berlin, 1913). My analysis is not, by and large, of his own intended meanings but rather of those that, in retrospect, seem to me inherent in his argument.

5. As with any system, that is, no amount of theoretically rational internal consistency can establish the rationality of the system as a whole.

6. See, for example, *Critique of Judgment*, section 34, page 128, where Kant argues, in effect, that the job of art criticism is to refer various configurations back to the structure of judgment to see if the apprehension of these configurations involves a state of internal analogy (between the capacities for perception and for comprehension) within the structure of judgment. That criticism, however, can never locate or define the common structure underlying all actual, individual faculties of judgment or, hence, deduce "correct" judgments of beauty from such an archetype. (Hereafter, references to the *Critique of Judgment* will omit the words "section" and "page" and simply cite the number of each. Section numbers in roman numerals refer to the Preface.) For another formulation of the epistemological problem broached here see my essay "The Cultural Message of Musical Semiology: Some Thoughts on Music, Language, and Criticism since the Enlightenment," chapter 9 in this volume, p. 176, especially the following statement and its attendant note: "in calling attention to the dependence of objective knowledge on language, Kant had provided a basis for questioning the objectivity of the knowledge obtained through language, that is, for doubting the power of language to reach any such objective truth as did exist." See also chapter 2, n. 37 in this volume.

7. On problems connected with the notion of cultural structures see especially Bukofzer, "Allegory in Baroque Music," p. 1; Charles Rosen, "The Origins of Walter Benjamin," *New York Review of Books*, 24 (November 10, 1977), pp. 33–34; and E. D. Hirsch, *The Aims of Interpretation* (Chicago, 1976), pp. 46–49.

8. The sorts of meanings I am assuming to be imposed on semiotic structures comprise what could in broad terms be called *perceptual* meanings (static structural wholeness and surface detail as they are perceived or recognized by the interpreter) and *conceptual* meanings (internal connections that are imagined to lie at a deeper internal level of the semiotic structure than surface detail, a level from which they must be extracted in a temporal process of following or reconstituting connections, which amounts to an exercise of discursive understanding). This distinction between types of meaning implies a distinction between perception and understanding, the dual "moments" that Kant locates in the faculties of both cognition and aesthetic judgment (albeit with certain differences, as evidenced in *Critique of Judgment*, 59: 197 and also in Hirsch, *Aims of Interpretation*, p. 75).

On the basis of my analysis of Kant's third critique, I am in fact positing such a distinction, not only because the two capacities define themselves according to relatively different norms, but also because, as Kant makes explicit in the case of aesthetic judgment, understanding cannot, through any absolute cognitive status, absorb and negate the contingencies of sensory perception, any more than a necessary connection can be established in any cognitively absolute sense between a sensory perception and a given cognitive interpretation that is attached to it. At the same time, however, both perception and understanding turn out to be concrete and subjective, and hence cognitively contingent faculties, so that with respect to cognitive value, there seems to be no *significant* difference between them. In short, as in Kant's account of judgment, the two moments appear to be distinct or disjunct in the manner of analogy: they are (much as deconstruction might describe them) irreconcilable and yet not significantly different, with each, in a sense, containing its own moments of perception and interpretation. (An electrifying neurological ground—or at least analogy!—for such a distinction is suggested by Oliver Sacks and Robert Wasserman in "The Case of the Colorblind Painter," which concerns a man who "could discriminate wavelengths"—i.e. take in physically [via the retina] all the quantitative differences projected by the various colors—but "could not *go on* [italics theirs] from this to 'translate' the discriminated wavelengths into color, could not generate the cerebral or mental construct of color." That is, he saw only shades of black and white, because the conscious identification of color depends on a different, "associational" area of the brain. See the *New York Review of Books*, 34 [November 19, 1987]: p. 30.)

Clearly, perceptual meaning becomes acknowledged as a kind of archetype of cognitive sorts of meaning in nineteenth-century music, precisely as it does in the faculty of judgment, where, by Kant's account, the cognitive value of understanding is undermined openly and shifted, essentially, onto perception, which has its own interpretative moment (see *Critique of Judgment*, 35: 129: "comprehension" *[Zusammenfassung]*). This shift could be said to signify a transition from a cultural preference for cognition, with its inviolable moment of understanding, as the archetypal cognitive (and semiotic) faculty, to a preference in this respect for aesthetic judgment, which in effect not only puts cognitive weight on a sensory moment—perception—but also makes explicit the ultimate dependence of understanding in *both* cognition and judgment on a cognitively problematical, and no more than aesthetically "verifiable," transcendental structure of reason. In other words, the shift of cognitive weight to perception seems to involve recognition of precisely the same sort of relation between cognition and aesthetic judgment as that noted above between understanding and perception, the latter member being archetypal in each case. See also this chapter, nn. 14, 27, and also 17, on the clearly related shift in the nineteenth century from logical to empirical models of knowledge.) It is precisely such a shift that figures in the second reading of my deconstructionist analysis, "How Could Chopin's A-Major Prelude Be Deconstructed?" (See my companion volume.) See also chapter 4, p. 73, and chapter 7, p. 127, this volume.

9. Rosen, *The Classical Style*, p. 100.

10. Ibid., p. 33.

11. This is essentially Leonard Meyer's point when, in connection with a harmonic digression in the finale of Mozart's Symphony No. 39, he observes that no general rules can be made for particular musical events; he is pointing out the absence of logical determinism within individually designed semiotic structures. See his *Explaining Music* (Berkeley, 1973), pp. 10–12.

12. Jacques Barzun, *Classic, Romantic, and Modern* (Garden City, N.Y., 1961), p. 38.

13. See *Critique of Judgment*, 53: 174; also Walter Serauky, *Die musikalische Nachahmungsästhetik im Zeitraum von 1700 bis 1850* (Münster, 1929), pp. 5–6.

14. See especially *Critique of Judgment*, 22:78, 35:129, and 57:185. It should be noted here that although Kant associates aesthetic judgment with the sublime as well as with the beautiful, I have throughout this discussion construed that structure of judgment manifested in determinations of beauty as archetypal for all aesthetic judgment, a construction I believe warranted within the *Critique of Judgment*. I would further argue that in spite of Kant's indication to the contrary (*Critique of Judgment*, 1:37, n. 1), the structure of judgment associated with beauty actually suggests itself in the *Critique of Judgment* as archetypal for every sort of judgment considered by Kant in this work, including teleological judgment and even determinant (that is, logical or objective cognitive) judgment.

15. See espcially *Critique of Judgment*, 22:78, 35:129, and 57:185. On the whole, in the *Critique of Judgment*, cognition points toward two discrete realms, subjectivity and objectivity, though it cannot link them with cognitive security and in the end can define them only as analogous forms within a single realm, subjectivity. This latter sort of definition is the normative condition within aesthetic judgment, which offers no illusion of a connection between the subjective and objective worlds, and which,

even within subjectivity, isolates perception in the sense that it can refer a specific percept to no specific concept of the understanding (though it can refer it to a state of analogy between the faculties of perception and understanding). Assuming that the aesthetic structure, as argued here, replaces the cognitive as the archetypal semiotic structure, one can plot a progress from the complementary dualities that seem necessarily connectable through cognition to the state of intrastructural and contingent analogy, which appears actually to obtain in cognition as well as in aesthetic judgment, to the potential isolation of the fundamentally aesthetic percept. Such a progress is highly suggestive as a model for the history of musical structure in classicism, romanticism, and post-romantic formalism, respectively. See also chapter 2 in this volume, n. 37; and chapter 9, n. 24.

16. Cf. Rosen's assertion that Schlegel and Novalis turn criticism from an act of judgment into an act of understanding ("The Ruins of Walter Benjamin," *New York Review of Books*, 24 [October 27, 1977], p. 32). The entire preceding line of argument might also be cast in terms of a poststructuralist viewpoint, whereby analogy is construed as a contingent form of adjacence, contiguity, or association, and metaphor as a relationship of structural similarity defined through the activities of the (subjective) intelligent observer. See chapter 3, n. 9, and chapter 4, n. 12, in this volume. Though I wrote the present essay with no knowledge of poststructuralism, I converge on its view of metaphor in the discussion that follows (see p. 122, following n. 18); and in turn the discussion at this point, as more explicitly further on, p. 126, points to a similarity in the shifting of levels suggested as an epistemological strategy not only in my own work but also in poststructuralism and in Hegel's dialectic (see chapter 6, n. 30, in this volume).

17. If classical syntax suggests logical deduction, these cumulative processes seem more akin to empirical induction, a difference with clear analogues in other intellectual and technological developments during the nineteenth century. Clearly, there is some sort of analogical relationship between the suggestion of empirical induction at this level of temporal structure in romantic music and the suggestion, in this same music, of the need for an accumulation or series of analogical interpretations to approach a total understanding of a semiotic structure, a suggestion brought about through stress on what will be called "stylistic meaning"; see also Hofstadter, *Gödel, Escher, Bach*, p. 582. (As discussed in my essay, "How Could Chopin's A-Major Prelude Be Deconstructed?" this imagery comes close to the hopes defined in deconstruction for a chain of metaphors.)

18. A good place in Beethoven's works to observe many elements of the techniques noted here is in the first movement of the *Waldstein* Sonata, op. 53.

19. On the whole, this is likewise so if competence is defined as the ability to perform rather than as the ability to comprehend.

20. See Friedrich Blume, *Classic and Romantic Music*, trans. M. D. Herter Norton (New York, 1970), pp. 108–9, on the transformation of all critics of romantic music into dilettantes.

21. Though in a sense it may seem strange to equate this sort of surface perception with linguistic competence, it is precisely the point of this discussion to suggest that even ostensibly cognitive semiotic structures, such as those making an ordinary use of language, engage at most faculties of concretely logical apprehension that like perception operate by analogy with structures in subjective, concretely defined minds, and thus are cognitively no more verifiable or secure than the faculty of perception.

22. There is, indeed, a rather broad school of thought today, that, without embracing irrationalism, is trying to redefine reason concretely, in terms quite different from those of traditional Western cognitive theory, by directing attention to sensuous

devices (such as rhetoric) and perception, much as romantic music itself can be con-strued as trying to do. See, for example, Chaim Perelman and Lucie Olbrechts-Tyteca, *The New Rhetoric: A Treatise on Argumentation*, trans. John Wilkinson and Pur-cell Weaver (Notre Dame, Ind., 1969)), beginning with the remarks on pp. 2–4, which define an attack on "the idea of self-evidence as characteristic of reason (p. 3). See also Claude Lévi-Strauss, *The Savage Mind* (Chicago, 1966); and my own essay "Kant, Adorno, and the Self-Critique of Reason: Toward a Model for Music Criti-cism," chapter 4 in this volume. In a sense, of course, the *Critique of Judgment* is itself an attempt to secure the rationality of the aesthetic on grounds other than the strictly cognitive which would yet satisfy certain rational requirements of cognition; see es-pecially 15:64, where the absence of cognitive value in an aesthetic judgment is ad-mitted, and 9:51–53, 57:184–86, and 59: 197–200, where, in effect, Kant offers com-pensation for that absence. On space see chapter 11, n. 62, of this volume.

23. This is not, clearly, an unconscious apprehension of wholes, where one knows the end has been reached because one has understood an internal rational argument, but a conscious perception of wholes, where one recognizes the end from isolated "external" cues—or from previous hearings.

24. Though when I orginally wrote this sentence, I intended merely to emphasize that romantic signification pointed toward the concreteness of style (as I define it), it makes equal sense to indicate a shift toward language itself (a projection of the hu-man mind) as the content of romantic music, an idea I take up at length in chapter 9 in this book, and also (citing the work of Mikhail Bakhtin) in my essay, "Whose *Magic Flute*?" (in my companion volume).

25. (In essence this is what Hofstadter means when he asserts that "hiddenness is of the essence in semantic properties" [*Gödel, Escher, Bach*, p. 583].) This relationship defines a clear instance of that paradoxical state of autonomy to which the *Critique of Judgment* calls attention, in which a structure is at once free of and dependent on a governing mind. In connection with the relative advantages and disadvantages of stylistic competence, it is worth pointing out that Berlioz, an archetypical romantic critic, vacillated continually concerning the benefits and limitations of education for an understanding of romantic music. The cultural significance of this vacillation is analyzed with great insight in a doctoral dissertation on Berlioz and Delacroix, enti-tled 'The Romantic Artist's Dilemma," written by Kineret Jaffe for the History of Culture Committee at the University of Chicago.

26. Thus, though more Western listeners today probably have some stylistic com-petence in romantic music than in any other style of art music, few have structural competence; conversely, the formalism of most contemporary analysis exemplifies a loss of access among the structurally competent to distinctive nineteenth-century modes of hearing and meanings. See Carl Dahlhaus, "Fragmente zur musikalischen Hermeneutik," *Beiträge zur musikalischen Hermeneutik*, ed. C. Dahlhaus (Regensburg, 1975), p. 161, and "Thesen über Programmusik," ibid., p. 189.

27. Given the central importance of analogy in *Critique of Judgment*, it is worth not-ing that the relationship described here between understanding and perception is in some ways precisely analogous to that described by Kant in his third critique, be-tween the theoretical, or nature, and the moral, or freedom (II: 12, and IX: 32). The dichotomy described here between physical and semiotic autonomy recalls chapter 6, pp. 105–6 of this volume, and also the dichotomy between individual identity and choice suggested in chapter 3, p. 47. It may also be worth noting that what I am describing here is the shift from a musical style (classical) based on an ideal of abstract universal logic as its paradigm to a style (romantic) based on a paradigm of concrete language. The social ramifications of this shift in paradigms are a focus of my article

"Whose *Magic Flute?*" which will appear in the companion volume; see also chapter 9, n. 67, in this volume.

28. In fact, the two melodic phrases in mm. 3–4 and 5–7 are actually analogous variants. See example 1 of the analysis from Leonard Meyer's *Emotion and Meaning in Music*, as reprinted in the Norton Critical Score of Chopin's *Preludes, Op. 28*, ed. Thomas Higgins (New York, 1973), p. 76. Here the relationship of analogy seems graphically indicated, though Meyer himself characterizes it simply as a relationship of similarity. Again, although the second Prelude represents a harmonic extreme in relation to the other preludes, the latter can likewise be analyzed fruitfully in terms of analogy, identity-difference, and arbitrary succession; and, of course, other nineteenth-century works (Beethoven's Ninth Symphony, Schuman's *Dichterliebe*, Wagner's *Tristan und Isolde*) present harmonically ambiguous openings. See also chapter 11, n. 31, of this volume.

29. Meyer, *Preludes*, p. 79. This formulation calls to mind Jacques Derrida's "always already." See, for example, the passage quoted in "Critical Factions/Critical Fictions" by Josué V. Harari in his book *Textual Strategies* (Ithaca, 1979), p. 37. See also T. W. Adorno's essay on Schoenberg in *Prisms*, trans. Samuel and Shierry Weber (London, 1967), p. 160: "With Schoenberg, 'the first time' is always 'once again.' "

30. Ibid., p. 78.

31. See the comparison of the harmonic structure of mm. 12–23 with that of the earlier and shorter segments, as analyzed by Meyer, *Preludes*, p. 78; again, Meyer himself describes the relationship simply in terms of similarity.

32. On the distinction use/mention, see Jonathan Culler. *On Deconstruction: Theory and Criticism after Structuralism* (Ithaca, 1982), p. 119, n. 5.

This aspect of my analysis obviously differs from the emphasis in Meyer's analysis on aspects of process; yet, to the extent that process can be distinguished from implication, the two analyses need not be mutually exclusive. What I am suggesting, in effect, is that processes of change that call attention to particular states of identity or difference rather than submerging themselves in generally established functional patterns tend to undermine their own temporal force. Change is not the same as movement. To put it succinctly, whereas classicism proposes an ideal situation in which temporal and logical unfolding are identical, romanticism acknowledges a cognitively irreducible gap between the two. See also chapter 4, pp. 73 and 82–83, chapter 8, pp. 160–161, and chapter 10, n. 8, in this volume.

33. On the volume in m. 12, see Thomas Higgins, "Notes Toward a Performance with References to the Valldemosa Autograph," in the Norton Critical Score of Chopin's *Preludes*, p. 62.

34. The effect of anticipation itself at this point represents an audible intensification of an analogous effect of anticipation at the beginning of the previous melodic phrase. Whereas the first melodic phrase enters on the first beat of the third measure on the same harmony that has been established in the first two measures of introduction—a harmony that appears to be more or less stable—the second phrase comes in (m. 8) on the third beat of its measure, after only half a measure of the new harmony involved. (As a transposition of the opening chord, this harmony is clearly the analogue of its predecessor, though its stability is now, by example, open to a doubt that is subsequently justified.) The last principal melodic phrase enters (m. 14) before the unstable diminished-seventh chord has resolved into a new version (now in six-four rather than root position) of the relatively stable chord that opened the piece. And though the bass pattern over which the melodic phrase enters has been going for a full measure before the melodic entrance, the first note of the melody does not wait this time for the third beat of the measure but comes in on the rhythmically weak second beat

of its own measure. Hence, by comparison with its counterpart in m. 8, the first melodic note in m. 14 seems to have entered too early, both in harmonic and in melodic terms.

35. This piece is a fine example of the narrowing down to units of one or two notes of the expressive burden in much romantic music. My essay "How Could Chopin's A-Major Prelude Be Deconstructed?" elaborates considerably on the kinds of meaning that can be drawn from such small differences, as on another aspect of the present analysis, to which the next note (n. 36) alludes: that when sufficient weight is placed on a nominal antecedent, its physical quality of instability becomes a focus of attention in itself, allowing us to construe the logical stability of resolution in an ensuing consequent as a characteristic of secondary significance. See also chapter 10 in this volume, n. 13.

36. Not only is it possible to view the whole piece as a study in avoiding the logical resolution of inconclusive harmonies. In addition, the constant reassertion of dissonance on a more localized level like other techniques that dwell on moments of harmonic instability, undercuts the very notion of resolution. In at least one critical instance, moreover, the rhetorical disruption of the resolving process is so striking that it undermines the connectedness and logical authority of a harmonically "correct" resolution and even suggests the latter as the breach of a rhetorical norm. I refer to the E-major triad of m. 21, which cannot fully counterbalance the pointedness with which the last bass-line dissonances and the accompanying pedal, in mm. 18 and 19, are broken off, or differentiate itself completely from the fundamental E, which permeates that dissonant blur, in part through sheer force of color. See also chapter 8, n. 17, this volume.

37. Note the accented octave progression from E to D in mm. 3–4 and from B to A in mm. 8–9; in the last phrase this progression, anomalous in tonal practice, is avoided.

38. On dual structure see chapter 9 in this volume, pp. 172, 174, and 178, e.g., n. 29.

39. See chapter 11 in this volume, nn. 30 and 31; also Theodor W. Adorno, *Philosophy of Modern Music*, trans. Anne G. Mitchell and Wesley V. Blomster (New York, 1973), pp. 39–41.

40. Meyer, *Preludes*, p. 78.

41. "Chopin's Preludes, op. 28, Analyzed by von Bülow," trans. Frederick S. Law, *Musician*, 16 (February 1911), p. 88. These analyses cannot be ascribed with complete certainty to von Bülow since they were transcribed by a pupil, Laura Rappoldi-Kahrer; in any case, the fundamental point here is unaffected. I am grateful to Susan T. Sommer of the New York Public Library for locating these notes to the *Preludes* on short notice.

42. I wish to thank here the American Council of Learned Societies and the Guggenheim Foundation for the fellowships that made possible the development of this piece.

Chapter 8. On Grounding Chopin

1. Jeffrey Kallberg, "Chopin in the Marketplace: Aspects of the International Music Publishing Industry in the First Half of the Nineteenth Century," *Notes*, 39 (1983), p. 819. This informative article won the Alfred Einstein Award of the American Musicological Society for 1983.

2. See, for example, the conclusion to Philip Gossett's article, "Beethoven's Sixth

Symphony: Sketches for the First Movement," *Journal of the American Musicological Society*, 27 (1974), p. 280.

3. "The Role of Ideology in Western Music," chapter 1 of this volume.

4. Nor is the failure even to approximate structural autonomy limited to such extreme cases. Insisting on the self-containment of any scholarly problem, the positivist school renounces recourse to nonmusical resources that might help these scholars to make distinctions concerning the importance of their musical materials and to define for them some significance. This spares them the messiness of trying to establish a dialectical relationship between the shape of an idea and the diverse materials to which it will be applied. But at the same time, lacking criteria for characterizing or assessing their materials, such studies, while needing a form, do not characteristically work out a problem in a genuinely autonomous fashion. Rather, they typically rely for their structure on models established in preceding studies of the same kind. This entire discussion is deeply indebted to the ideas of William A. Levine, a cultural theorist and software consultant at the Burroughs (now Unisys) Corporation in Chicago, where I worked at the time this essay was written.

5. This edition was published in New York by G. Schirmer, as vol. 8 of Chopin's complete piano works.

6. "Introductory," ibid., pp. 1–2.

7. Theodor Adorno, "Bach Defended Against his Devotees," *Prisms*, trans. Samuel Weber and Shierry Weber (London, 1967), especially pp. 142–46; Richard Taruskin, "The Musicologist and the Performer," *Musicology in the 1980s: Methods, Goals, Opportunities*, ed. D. Kern Holoman and Claude V. Palisca (New York, 1982), pp. 101–17.

8. See especially in this connection the study by Phyllis Rose, *Parallel Lives: Five Victoriian Marriages* (New York, 1983), p. 6.

9. "Romantic Music as Post-Kantian Critique: Classicism, Romanticism, and the Concept of the Semiotic Universe," chapter 7 of this volume.

10. See chapter 6, n. 1, of this volume, and Charles Rosen, *The Classical Style* (New York, 1972), pp. 21–22.

11. Essay on the twenty-four preludes, op. 28, Robert Schumann, *On Music and Musicians*, ed. Konrad Wolff (New York, 1946), p. 138. In another review (*Neue Zeitschrift für Musik*, 9 [1838], pp. 178) Schumann writes: "Chopin can hardly write anything now but that we feel like calling out in the seventh or eighth measure, 'It is by him!' " From Leon B. Plantinga, *Schumann as Critic* (New Haven, 1967), p. 230.

12. See Lawrence Kramer, "The Mirror of Tonality," *19th Century Music*, 4 (1981), p. 192.

13. Though it attempts no theoretical interpretation of this characteristic, Kallberg's "Chopin" (see n. 1) provides many useful examples of it.

14. "Evidence of a Critical Worldview in Mozart's Last Three Symphonies," chapter 6 in this volume.

15. In the bass, for example, one can note the propulsive lowered-VI to V pattern (on Cb to B). In the melodic line, always so crucial in Chopin's definition of structure, one can point out the movement downward, essentially by step, toward the tonic; the repetitive circling of the leading-tone, D#; the prolonged postponement of a conclusive cadence on the tonic, E; and the increasing truncation of the melodic patterns (stretto). In terms of chordal texture, one can point to the recurring stress on dissonance which gives way at the last possible second (m. 61) to clear consonance.

16. Ironically, this music points, among other things, to the positivist relations of succession and coexistence or what Comte himself called "succession and resemblance" (as quoted in the entry on Comte in the *Encyclopedia of Philosophy* [New York,

1967], 2, p. 174). This is not so surprising since the two men lived in France at the same time, in a century that came to be dominated by certain aspects of empiricism. For a more extended study of the shift in significance that results from emphasizing the physical qualities of antecedence, I refer the reader to my essay, "How Could Chopin's A-Major Prelude Be Deconstructed?" in my companion volume.

17. David Josephson of Brown University, whose help in preparing this essay was invaluable, differs sharply with my perception of this passage. For him, the functional pull of the passage outweighs its static sensuousness, which he concedes is substantial. He characterizes this passage as a study in intensified avoidances. This difference in interpretation, I would argue, which reflects no disagreement about the structural "facts," cannot be settled by any reference to the musical text. (See chapter 7, n. 36, for a similar analysis of the second Prelude. Josephson would also disallow interpretations based on an ex post facto knowledge of culture, whereas I believe such interpretations are not only inevitable but also, within limits of responsibility, desirable. In my view it is actually counterproductive to invest any text with the authority of an autonomous meaning, independent of its dialectical relation to reception.)

18. See "Romantic Music as Post-Kantian Critique," especially pp. 134–35. I was startled recently to learn that at the time this article appeared some colleagues took issue with its failure to "explain" Chopin's second Prelude as "a study in the circle of fifths." I had hoped it was clear that this analysis was trying to deconstruct such conventional labels, that is, to bore through their often dulling effect on actual musical experience and its analysis.

19. Unlike the self-absorption in the sensuousness of the moment or even the inescapable world-weariness suggested by Chopin's use of this device, the precipitate return of the tonic Eb on the horns just prior to an explosion on the dominant and the start of the recapitulation in the first movement of Beethoven's *Eroica* (mm. 394–98) seems anything but anticlimactic. See chapter 7, n. 32, in this volume.

20. When the material in this chapter was first delivered as a lecture, Susan McClary suggested a sexual interpretation of the analysis just given. Chopin's music, she noted, is often characterized as effeminate. Could this not be in part because its lingering sensuousness at such typical moments, in contrast to the masculine Beethovenian climax, evokes and affirms the quality and the rhythm conventionally associated with female sexuality? This imagery, once offered, lends itself almost irresistibly to many aspects of nineteenth-century musical style (not least the critique, suggested in so many romantic compositions, of the no-nonsense ending). A principal focus of my companion volume is the tie between a stylistic emphasis on particularity and demands for equality by women and other groups.

21. It has been pointed out that the putative function of the Berceuse, that of lulling a baby to sleep, could account for the technique of repetition at this point in this piece. The obvious value of this interpretation should not be allowed to obscure the need for further reflection on the significance of a device so pervasive in Chopin's music. An argument could be made, for example, for a dialectical relationship between the device described and the genre of the berceuse. The genre may welcome the device; but the sensibility that constantly fashions the device may also account for an attraction to a genre drawn from the womanly domain of experience.

22. The danger in our situation, of course, is that the presence of style can be taken for a sufficiency that precludes any further struggle to develop rational connections or structures. The television critic Marvin Kitman ("The Marvin Kitman Show," *Newsday*, April 15, 1986, Part 2, p. 13) recalls George Bernard Shaw's observation on style: "The effect of assertiveness is the alpha and omega of style. He who has nothing to assert has no style, and can have none." This is not to argue, however, that those

with style necessarily have anything to assert except their *possession* of that style; such a proposition was certainly doubted, for example, by those who referred sarcastically to President Ronald Reagan, in the 1980s, as "The Great Communicator." See also Friedrich Nietzsche, "The Case of Wagner," *The Birth of Tragedy and The Case of Wagner*, trans. Walter Kaufmann (New York, 1967), p. 167: "This is the point of departure for our concept of 'style.' Above all, no thought!"

23. Edward A. Lippman, "Theory and Practice in Schumann's Aesthetics," *Journal of the American Musicological Society*, 17 (1964), pp. 310–45. Roland Barthes suggests a modern counterpart when he connects Schumann's music with " 'diction,' " observing, "Schumann's music is always a *quasi parlando*" ("Day by Day with Roland Barthes," *On Signs*, ed. Marshall Blonsky [Baltimore, 1986], p. 115).

24. Quoted in Kallberg, "Chopin," p. 565.

25. The two words have a common Latin root, *complere*, to fill up.

Chapter 9. The Cultural Message of Musical Semiology: Some Thoughts on Music, Language, and Criticism since the Enlightenment

1. Jean-Jacques Nattiez, *Fondements d'une sémsiologie de la musique* (Paris, 1975).

2. See, esp., Peter Faltin and Hans-Peter Reinecke, eds., *Musik und Verstehen: Aufsätze zur semiotischen Theorie, Aesthetik und Soziologie der musikalischen Rezeption* (Cologne, 1973).

3. Roland Barthes, "The Structuralist Activity," in *The Structuralists from Marx to Lévi-Strauss*, ed. Richard and Fernande De George (Garden City, N.Y., 1972), pp. 151–52. Important also in this connection is Claude Lévi-Strauss's conception of the "gross unit" beneath which relationships can essentially be ignored; see his *Structural Anthropology*, [vol. 1], trans. Claire Jacobson and Brooke G. Schoepf (New York, 1963), pp. 211–12. For a more detailed illustration of this point, the reader is referred to my review of Nattiez in the *Journal of Aesthetics and Art Criticism*, 35 (Winter 1976), pp. 239–42.

4. Barthes, "Structuralist Activity," p. 151.

5. Roman Jakobson, "Linguistics and Poetics," in *The Structuralists from Marx to Lévi-Strauss*, p. 89.

6. Lévi-Strauss, *The Raw and the Cooked*, trans. John and Doreen Weightman (New York, 1970), pp. 18, 12. See also Peter Caws, "What Is Structuralism?" in *Claude Lévi-Strauss: The Anthropologist as Hero*, ed. E. Nelson Hayes and Tanya Hayes (Cambridge, Mass., 1970), pp. 205, 207–10. In retrospect one can already see in passages such as the one just quoted, as well as in other structuralist views cited throughout this essay, the beginnings of a poststructuralist position.

7. Nattiez, *Fondements*, p. 143; Leonard Meyer, *Emotion and Meaning in Music* (Chicago, 1956), p. 41.

8. See, e.g., M. P. T. Leahy, "The Vacuity of Musical Expressionism," *British Journal of Aesthetics*, 16 (1976), p. 146.

9. Nattiez, *Fondements*, pp. 27–28.

10. Lévi-Strauss, *Raw and Cooked*, p. 11.

11. Ferdinand de Saussure, *Course in General Linguistics*, trans. Wade Baskin (New York, 1974), p. 71.

12. Franz Boas, as quoted in Lévi-Strauss, *Structural Anthropology*, [vol. 1], pp. 19–20; Lévi-Strauss, *Raw and Cooked*, p. 11. (Since my original writing of these remarks, I have come, by way of poststructuralism, to find a good deal more persuasive this treatment of individual consciousness as insufficient to account for or control

all the structures of language produced for or by the individual. See, for example, Julia Kristeva, "The Speaking Subject," On Signs, ed. Marshall Blonsky [Baltimore, 1985], pp. 210–20. In looking beyond individual consciousness, of course, poststructuralism, unlike Kant [see chapter 4, n. 9, and chapter 7, p. 115], finds no basis, or even the possibility of any basis, for secure universal principles or knowledge. For a further overview of this matter, see n. 67 this chapter.)

13. Lévi-Strauss, Raw and Cooked, p. 12. The analysis by Lévi-Strauss and Jakobson of "Les Chats" appears in The Structuralists from Marx to Lévi-Strauss, pp. 123–46, and also in Introduction to Structuralism, ed. Michael Lane (New York, 1970), pp. 207–21; Lévi-Strauss's analysis of Boléro appears in L'Homme, 11 (April–June 1971), pp. 5–14, and also in his L'Homme nu (Paris, 1971), pp. 589–96. Since the analysis of "Les Chats" appears to be marred by an impassable discontinuity between the treatment of structure and that of meaning, it is not difficult to understand why Lévi-Strauss subsequently became interested in the analysis of music, where presumably "meaning" need not be considered. Lévi-Strauss seems at one point to believe that in analyzing an artistic structure that is self-contained rather than referential, he has moved one step closer to defining the unconscious structure of the mind (see Raw and Cooked; pp. 14–18). In actuality, his analysis of Boléro is difficult to distinguish from a good deal of positivistic formal analysis, which avoids broad humanistic generalizations.

14. Lévi-Strauss, L'Homme nu, p. 560; all translations of quotations from L'Homme nu are my own.

15. T. W. Adorno, Introduction to the Sociology of Music, trans. E. B. Ashton (New York, 1976), p. 4.

16. Lévi-Strauss's somewhat obscure account of double articulation in Raw and Cooked (p. 24) differs from standard accounts such as André Martinet's (summarized by Nattiez, p. 421) and John Lyons's in Noam Chomsky (New York, 1970), pp. 19–20. Lévi-Strauss appears to include both phonemes and morphemes in the code level, whereas it is more usual to oppose to the phonemic or sound level a level of meaning that is both semantic and morphemic.

17. Nattiez, Fondements, pp. 231–33 and 392–93.

18. Lévi-Strauss, Raw and Cooked, p. 18; Lyons, Noam Chomsky, p. 37.

19. See Lévi-Strauss, Raw and Cooked, p. 27 (where music is considered prior to myth, a position later rejected in L'Homme nu, p. 583, n. 1), and pp. 29, 15–18, 26; L'Homme nu, pp. 578–80, 585–86, 599–600, 583–84.

20. Lévi-Strauss, L'Homme nu, pp. 583–85.

21. See Hans Heinrich Eggebrecht, "Ars musica: Musikanschauung des Mittelalters und ihre Nachwirkungen," Die Sammlung: Zeitschrift für Kultur und Erziehung, 12 (1957), pp. 317–18; Robert L. Marshall, "Bach the Progressive: Observations on His Later Works," Musical Quarterly, 62 (1976), p. 331; and Peter Kivy, "What Mattheson Said," Music Review, 34 (1973), p. 139. (Compared to nineteenth-century music, to be sure, late eighteenth-century music is in retrospect often likened to poetry, a likeness I take up in my essay "Whose Magic Flute?" See also Carl Dahlhaus, Between Romanticism and Modernism, trans. Mary Whittall [Berkeley and Los Angeles, 1980], pp. 43, on poetry, and 59, on architecture.) For a summary of the discrepancy between Kant's low esteem for music as an art that produces no clearly defined ideas (see chapter 7, n. 13, of this volume) and the grounds implicitly provided in his Critique of Judgment for evaluating art in terms of structural coherence, see my essay "Toward a Deconstruction of Structural Listening," Explorations in Music, the Arts, and Ideas: Essays in Honor of Leonard B. Meyer, ed. Eugene Narmour and Ruth A. Solie (New York, 1988), p. 90.

22. This isn't to say that the artist's "self," so to speak, was to be taken in the classical sense as representative of all selves. Rather, a truly individual self, the creative self of the artist, could create an imaginary universe sufficiently coherent and encompassing to provide truth for others. On this shift in literature, see the discussion of Pope, Goethe, and Herder in Martha Woodmansee, "The Genius and the Copyright: Economic and Legal Conditions of the Emergence of the 'Author,'" *Eighteenth-Century Studies*, 17 (Summer 1984), pp. 447–48. See chapter 2 in this volume, n. 37.

On Kant and irrationality, see chapter 4 in this volume, pp. 62–63. Without doubt, and quite apart from the types of poetic theme and mood that attracted the romantics, romantic conceptions of the artist's imagination pointed in many ways toward irrationality: the mystery of the cosmic, indeed, metaphysical sources from which a vision comes into the artist's mind (a problem eventually analyzed for music in terms of Schopenhauer's concept of will); the ineffability of that vision (the inexhaustibility of its meaning, the extreme difficulty of embodying it with any adequacy), and so on. Yet for the romantics, the contents of subjective fantasy had an internal rigor as well as a vividness that persuaded the artist of their truth. Of interest in this connection is the discussion of Friedrich Schlegel and romantic tradition by Carl Dahlhaus in the latter's *Realism in Nineteenth-Century Music*, trans. Mary Whittall (Cambridge, 1985), p. 32. According to Dahlhaus, Schlegel interpreted music as " 'philosophy in sounds' " (a notion Schlegel contrasted with the " 'trite' " view of music as a " 'language of the emotions' "). From Schlegel's viewpoint, a "theme undergo[es] the same processes of development . . . in music as the object of meditation in a train of philosophical thought." See also W. H. Wackenroder, "The Remarkable Musical Life of the Musician Joseph Berglinger," in Oliver Strunk, *Source Readings in Music History* (New York, 1950), pp. 760–63; and chapter 13 in this volume, especially n. 9.

What frustrated the romantic artist was the difficulty of communicating the *rationale* of an inward vision, and thus, of persuading others not to dismiss that individual vision as irrational nonsense. The immensity of the difficulty can be gauged, in one sense, from the degree to which the romantics were willing to salvage the rationality of individual fantasy through the concept of the genius (see n. 34, this chapter).

For a wide-ranging discussion of such problems in connection with Tieck, Wackenroder, E. T. A. Hoffmann, and also Wagner, Schopenhauer, and Nietzsche, see Dahlhaus, *Between Romanticism and Modernism*, pp. 34–38, especially the reference on p. 37 to "the immanent dynamic and logic of [musical] sound"; and also Friedrich Nietzsche, "On Music and Words," trans. Walter Kaufmann, in Dahlhaus, ibid., p. 110 (on the artist's "disinterested contemplation"). With Schopenhauer and Nietzsche, of course, the critical attitude taken by romanticism toward reason has become a direct preoccupation with the irrational (as in terms such as "will" and "power").

23. For reasons of space, aesthetic functions of language will not be considered here, nor will communicative functions except to the extent that they become dissociated from epistemological ones. The latter will be taken here to represent the characteristic mediating powers of natural language.

24. In other words, in confining knowledge to a domain of human thought that does not extend to metaphysical reality, Kant essentially redefined all knowing as a subjective process. From this perspective, objective knowledge stands in danger of collapsing into the subjective thought of which it is a function (that is, into a state of external unverifiability), or even into a condition of solipsism, if the subjective mind cannot be proven a supraindividual structure. Though Kant's critical philosophy was designed to obviate these dangers, which it clarified, it could not by its own standards guarantee a cognitively verifiable connection between the subjective mind

and any realm of objectivity that is defined as wholly external to that mind, any more than it could guarantee the universal status of the subjective mind. On the relation of subject and object see also, in this volume, chapter 2, n. 37, and chapter 7, n. 15.

25. See esp. Michel Foucault, *The Order of Things* (New York 1970), pp. 162, 295–97; and Allan Janik and Stephen Toulmin, *Wittgenstein's Vienna* (New York, 1973), pp. 120–32, 197. Here lie the roots of Chomsky's assertion that "as for the fact that the rules of language are 'public rules,' this is, indeed, a contingent fact" (*Reflections on Language* [New York, 1975], p. 71).

26. See esp. Foucault's sections on language in chapters 4 and 5 of *The Order of Things*. On the isomorphism of nature and culture in Enlightenment thought, see also Morse Peckham, "The Dilemma of a Century: The Four Stages of Romanticism," in *Romanticism: The Culture of the Nineteenth Century*, ed. Peckham (New York, 1965), pp. 17–18. On the breakdown of the *signifiant-signifié* relationship in the nineteenth century, see also Thomas Weiskel, *The Romantic Sublime: Studies in the Structure and Psychology of Transcendence* (Baltimore, 1976).

27. Lévi-Strauss, *The Savage Mind* (Chicago, 1966), p. 268.

28. See esp. Ludwig Wittgenstein, *Tractatus Logico-Philosophicus*, trans. D. F. Pears and B. F. McGuinness (London, 1961), sec. 5.64: "Solipsism, when its implications are followed out strictly, coincides with pure realism."

29. Charles Rosen, *The Classical Style* (New York, 1972), p. 24.

30. Cf. Edward Cone's discussion of freedom and form in Mozart's operas in *The Composer's Voice* (Berkeley and Los Angeles, 1974), pp. 26–29.

31. See Rosen, *Classical Style*, p. 94.

32. Ibid., p. 98, italics added.

33. The sentiments expressed in Wackenroder, "Joseph Berlinger," pp. 759–61 are typical in this regard.

34. On the Romantic definition of genius as individuality capable of embodying universality, see Wulf Arlt, "Einleitung: Aspekte des Gattungsbegriffs," *Gattungen der Musik in Einzeldarstellungen*, 1st series, ed. Arlt, Ernst Lichtenhahn, and Hans Oesch (Bern and Munich, 1973), p. 39. For an interpretation of Beethoven's third-period style, which will receive little attention here, the reader is referred to my essay "Adorno's Diagnosis of Beethoven's Late Style: Early Symptom of a Fatal Condition," chapter 2 in this volume.

35. See for example, E. T. A. Hoffmann's "Beethoven's Instrumental Music" (in Strunk), pp. 779–80, and "The Poet and the Composer" (in Strunk), pp. 785, 787–88. See also Dahlhaus, *Realism*, pp. 25 and 28, and *Between Romanticism and Modernism*, pp. 37–38; and the notion of replete autonomy in my own article "Toward a Deconstruction of Structural Listening," pp. 90–92.

36. Cf. Cone, *The Composer's Voice*, pp. 163–64, on gestural aspects of utterance; for a somewhat different division of musical elements into logical or rhetorical categories, see Charles Seeger, "On the Moods of a Music-Logic," *Journal of the American Musicological Society*, 13 (1960), pp. 230, 237.

37. Rosen, *Classical Style*, p. 455.

38. Quoted in Joseph Kerman, *The Beethoven Quartets* (New York, 1971), p. 330.

39. Richard Wagner, *Beethoven* (1870), trans. Albert R. Parsons (Indianapolis, Ind., 1872), p. 67. Wagner's imagery recalls some of the poetic criticism studied by M. H. Abrams in *The Mirror and the Lamp* (New York, 1953).

40. Wagner, *Beethoven*, p. 73.

41. Cf. Arnold Salop, "Intensity as a Distinction between Classical and Romantic Music," *Journal of Aesthetics and Art Criticism*, 23 (1965), p. 365; also Rosen, *Arnold Schoenberg* (New York, 1975), p. 32; and Abrams, *The Mirror and the Lamp*, p. 151.

A stimulating interpretation of Beethoven's music as language is offered by Owen Jander in "The 'Kreutzer' Sonata as Dialogue," *Early Music*, 16 (1988), pp. 34–49.

42. Eggebrecht, *Zur Geschichte der Beethoven-Rezeption*, Akademie der Wissenschaften und der Literatur Mainz, Abhandlung der geistes- und sozialwissenschaftlichen Klasse, no. 3 (Mainz, 1972). For a good, early example see E. T. A. Hoffmann's review (1810) of Beethoven's Fifth Symphony, trans. and reprinted in the Norton Critical Score of that work, ed. Elliot Forbes (New York, 1973), p. 153.

43. On the collapse of external models for genre in the nineteenth century see Carl Dahlhaus, "Zur Problematik der musikalischen Gattungen im 19. Jahrhundert," in *Gattungen der Musik*, pp. 840–95. On "genre of the masterpiece," see Theodor W. Adorno, "Arnold Schoenberg 1874–1951," *Prisms*, trans. Samuel and Shierry Weber (London, 1967), p. 164.

44. The semitone, for example, can be seen as seminal both in Schubert's String Quintet in C and in Berlioz's *Symphonie fantastique*. For a somewhat different interpretation of repeated intervallic patterns in the works of Berlioz, see Edward C. Bass, "Musical Time and Space in Berlioz," *Music Review*, 30 (1969), pp. 220–24. See also chapter 11 of this volume, n. 31.

45. On the desires and difficulties involved in fusing eloquence with structural necessity, see Dahlhaus, *Between Romanticism and Modernism*, pp. 45, 46, 50 (on logic and rhetoric in Brahms), and 52–53.

46. According to Cone, in "Schumann Amplified: An Analysis," in his Norton Critical Score of the *Symphonie fantastique* (New York, 1974), pp. 249–77, the endings of movement I (mm. 494–527) and movement 3 (mm. 175–99) were later additions to Berlioz's original version, as was, in all probability, the closing reference to the *idée fixe* in movement 4 (mm. 164–69); note also the progressive accelerations at the end of movement 2 and the inherently premediated "counterpoint of themes" in the last movement beginning at m. 414. See also Rosen, *Schoenberg*, pp. 25–27, on the breakdown of the harmonic function of the cadence.

47. Robert Schumann, *On Music and Musicians*, ed. Konrad Wolff, trans. Paul Rosenfeld (New York, 1946), pp. 138–42; and Cone, "Schumann Amplified," p. 277. See also Cone's remarks on Wagner's persona in his operas, *Composer's Voice*, pp. 27–29.

48. Criticisms of literal "descriptiveness" in Weber's music (such as those noted in Dahlhaus, *Realism*, pp. 34–35) are directed precisely at such a language-like quality. See also, in this volume, chapter 8, n. 23 (Barthes on Schumann). Of particular value is the account given of "absolute music" in Dahlhaus, *Between Romanticism and Modernism*, pp. 32–39 (see also p. 55, on "narrow" melody).

49. Eduard Hanslick, *The Beautiful in Music*, ed. Morris Weitz, trans. Gustav Cohen (Indianapolis, 1957), e.g., pp. 67–70, 122.

50. In Hanslick see, e.g., pp. 108, 109, and 124. On Wagner, see Friedrich Nietzsche, "The Case of Wagner," *The Birth of Tragedy and The Case of Wagner*, trans. Walter Kaufmann (New York, 1967), section 8, p. 173: "*He has increased music's capacity for language to the point of making it immeasurable* [italics his]." See also Dahlhaus, *Between Romanticism and Modernism*, pp. 55–58 (and essentially also pp. 45–50), on the notion of discourse in sound as it pertained to Brahms and Liszt as well as Wagner.

51. On Schopenhauer's role in objectifying music as a symbol of the irrational, see Susanne K. Langer, *Philosophy in a New Key* (Cambridge, Mass., 1957), p. 219.

52. Cf. Philip Barford, *Mahler Symphonies and Songs* (Seattle, 1971), p. 42, and esp., Adorno, *Philosophy of Modern Music*, trans. Anne G. Mitchell and Wesley V. Blomster (New York, 1973), p. 49, on Schoenberg's music as "case study." See also Nelson

Goodman, *Languages of Art* (Indianapolis, Ind., 1968), pp. 186–92, on attempts at binding musical notation, another way of dispensing with the individual subject.

53. See Jakobson, "Linguistics and Poetics," pp. 93–95, and esp. Nattiez's commentary, *Fondements*, p. 424; also Abrams, *The Mirror and the Lamp*, p. 150.

54. Stanley Cavell, "Music Discomposed," *Must We Mean What We Say?* (Cambridge, 1976), p. 207. See also chapter 13 in this volume, n. 17.

55. See Adorno, "Modern Music Is Growing Old," *Score*, 18 (December 1956), p. 25; and Meyer, *Music, the Arts, and Ideas* (Chicago, 1967), pp. 292–93.

56. Or, for that matter, from the medium of myth as defined by Lévi-Strauss.

57. See Nattiez, *Fondements*, p. 32.

58. Lévi-Strauss, *L'Homme nu*, p. 581.

59. See Nattiez, *Fondements*, pp. 346–54.

60. Meyer, *Music, the Arts, and Ideas*, p. 296. [This essay, it is obvious, predated the clear emergence of musical minimalism and other postmodern schools.]

61. Lévi-Strauss, *L'Homme nu*, p. 621; see also *Structural Anthropology*, [vol. 1], pp. 224, 229.

62. See Georges Charbonnier, *Conversations with Lévi-Stauss*, trans. John and Doreen Weightman (London, 1969), pp. 66–67.

63. On the historical connection between the concepts of individual and society, see esp. Lionel Trilling, *Sincerity and Authenticity* (Cambridge, Mass., 1972), pp. 19–25.

64. For Adorno's views, see "Modern Music Is Growing Old," pp. 21–26. For those of Lévi-Strauss, see *Raw and Cooked*, pp. 25–26, and in *Conversations*, pp. 120–23; also, *L'Homme nu*, pp. 582–83 (on the dissociation of sound and form).

65. Lévi-Strauss, *Savage Mind*, p. 246.

66. Foucault, *The Order of Things*, esp. pp. 386–87; Lévi-Strauss, *L'Homme nu*, pp. 620–21.

67. Quoted from a private communication by Lawrence J. Fuchsberg, formerly of the New School for Social Research, now in the U.S. Foreign Service, whose commentary on earlier drafts of this essay was of extraordinary value. Though the preceding essay focuses on structuralism, much of the same critique could also be applied to poststructuralist positions, which so often seem already present here in embryonic form. The defense here of dialectics, with its concomitant insistence on the centrality of individual consciousness, was clearly undertaken in an attempt to preserve humane values — particularly historical as well as moral responsibility, and also resistance to nihilism as one's ultimate epistemological position. Restrospectively this enterprise still strikes me as worth doing, and as valid, assuming one starts with the premise that the notion of rationality must be centered on the notion of the autonomous subject, that is, of the individual with a wholly conscious, self-determining mind.

Yet, as I suggest in my introduction to this volume, the time has probably passed when I myself could again start out with these exact premises. Though I continue to believe that the infinite open-endedness of poststructuralism must be reconciled in some way with the focus of a historical dialectic on responsibility, I no longer consider the capacity of the individual mind for conscious control adequate to serve by itself as a basis from which to understand reason, either within that mind or as a general principle. (See Marshall Blonsky's Introduction to his *On Signs* [Baltimore, 1986], p. xiv, n. 3, on Rousseau and the limits to consciousness; also n. 12 in this chapter, and chapter 7 in this volume, nn. 8, 27 and also 17, on the paradigmatic shift from logic to language.) Today the kind of admission called for in the last sentence of this chapter — at least if the final word, "futility," were changed to "fallibility" — would strike me as to some extent true of all schools of thought, and for that matter of all styles (including classicism), given the inability of any position totally to escape its own blindness — and contingency.

Chapter 10. Tonality, Autonomy, and Competence in Postclassical Music

1. Lawrence Kramer, "The Shape of Post-Classical Music," *Critical Inquiry*, 6 (Autumn, 1979), pp. 144–52. The present chapter, requested by the founding editor of *Critical Inquiry*, Sheldon Sacks, originally appeared on the pages directly following Kramer's piece.

2. Kramer, ibid., p. 152.

3. See, for example, Immanuel Kant, *Critique of Judgment*, trans. J. H. Bernard (New York, 1951), section 9, page 52.

4. Richard Kroner, *Kant's Weltanschauung*, trans. John E. Smith (Chicago, 1956). The same effect can be noted with respect to the recognition of metaphysics as an activity of the human mind rather than as a science of the otherworldly; this is a point of considerable relevance to romantic notions of music as in some sense a metaphysical medium.

5. In a symposium on T. W. Adorno at the University of Southern California (May 19, 1979), Charles Rosen suggested that the classical style in particular lends itself to purely musical criticism, in abstraction from a cultural context, at least in part because this style in particular was designed to be autonomous in the sense of independent of society. In all such formulations, however, it is important to emphasize that even for classicism, autonomy (in the sense of a universally self-evident and necessary meaning) constituted an ideal, or even a stylistic *theme* (defined in structural terms), not an achievement. To put it simply, the classical style is *about* universal intelligibility; it is not itself universally intelligible. See n. 30, this chapter, and chapter 3, n. 8.

6. Kramer, "Post-Classical Music." p. 146.

7. Ibid., p. 149.

8. Ibid., pp. 149–50. Conceivably there is some connection between the shift in musical models (as I see it) from logical implication to repetition and the problems raised by Kant's notion of analytic a priori judgments (involving propositions where the predicate is implicit in the concept of the subject) and synthetic a priori judgments (where the predicate adds information not implicit in the subject). Kant's epistemology requires the latter to have the same universality and necessity as the former, even though logic alone cannot connect the two parts of a synthetic judgment. Perhaps the shift to musical techniques of repetition can be construed as reflecting doubts about the purely logical force of the physically concrete consequents that can be adduced through classical tonality, while also forcefully asserting a necessity of connections through structural mimicry of the redundancy that marks analytic propositions. See also chapter 7, nn. 8, 17, 27, and 32, and chapter 11, n. 30, this volume.

9. An interesting exchange on the relation of musical repetition and temporality can be found in Rudolf Arnheim's "The Unity of the Arts: Time, Space, and Distance" in the *Yearbook of Comparative and General Literature*, no. 25 (1976), p. 10, and Leonard Meyer's response (p. 16). Particularly pertinent to nineteenth-century conceptions of structure, as either an autonomous or a fragmentary condition, is this description of the Wagnerian motive: "[It] is neither a complete period in itself, nor will it tolerate the construction of a consequent clause to make it up to a period. . . . The only suitable means of continuing [it] is sequential repetition" (Carl Dahlhaus, *Between Romanticism and Modernism*, trans. Mary Whittall [Berkeley and Los Angeles, 1980], p. 45).

10. The quotations and material in this paragraph are all taken from Kramer, "Post-Classical Music," pp. 146 and 147.

11. Of interest here are discussions of Wagner and Brahms in Dahlhaus, *Between Romanticism and Modernism*, e.g., pp. 69, 71 (on retrospective analysis), and 73–75, which illuminate similarities (individualization of harmony) as well as differences ("centrifugal" vs. "centripetal" harmonic tendencies, p. 74) between the two, and clarify the now problematical status of tonal syntax for Brahms.

12. See chapters 4 and 7 in this volume; I am indebted to Kramer's invigorating response for helping me to shape questions in both.

13. One must, to be sure, distinguish between an actual or even imaginable ability to follow and analyze all specific tonal relationships (which could be attributed to very few listeners of romantic music) and the ability to respond affectively to culturally established shadings (stability, ambiguity, etc.) of the tonal system that one cannot conceptually analyze. No one would deny that tonal norms are still sufficiently perceptible in romantic music to allow what Leonard Meyer has analyzed as the "affective experiences . . . [that]result from a direct interaction between a series of musical stimuli and an individual who understands the style of the work being heard" (*Emotion and Meaning in Music* [Chicago, 1956], p. 256). But the impact is affective, leading to culturally specific associations of the music with emotional states and physical images outside the literal boundaries of the structure. The impact is not structural, or even conducive to forming an *idea* of music as an autonomous structure. The same associations can be made, for example, from hearing only fragments of a romantic piece, which is not surprising since with romantic music, listening tends characteristically to focus on the sensuousness of individual moments. Even ideally, one does not imagine it necessary to grasp a romantic structure in its entirety in order to make sense of the style, any more than one can imagine coming close to an adequate sense of that style through a purely structural mode of comprehension. (On the role of such an ideal in classicism see n. 5, this chapter.)

Useful in this connection are Dahlhaus's distinctions between psychological and phenomenological ways of analyzing the relationship of consciousness to tonality (*Between Romanticism and Modernism*, pp. 66–67), and between dynamic as opposed to architectural perspectives on form (ibid., p. 69). To an extent, the latter exactly reverses Adorno's imagery of form, asserting that Wagnerian (dynamic) form "draws the listener into it," whereas classical (architectural) form is viewed from without: "When the listener is sufficiently aware of classical form, all the musical events of a movement can utimately be perceived in an imaginary simultaneity." (See also chapter 3 in this volume, n. 9, on metaphorical vs. metonymical conceptions of musical structure.) Relevant, too, are descriptions of romantic music or its perception through images of empirical time or concrete space, including surfaces (see, for example, in this volume chapter 4, nn. 53, 54, and 69; chapter 7, nn. 32 and 35; chapter 9, p. 184; and chapter 11, nn. 34 and 62), and ultimately all imagery that points toward a concentration of meaning into smaller and smaller units. (This latter process is often associated by critics with a shift in paradigms for understanding music, from one of poetry to one of prose. See, for example, Dahlhaus, *Between Romanticism and Modernism*, pp. 52–53; Paul Henry Lang, *The Experience of Opera* [New York, 1973], pp. 28–29; and Charles Rosen, *Arnold Schoenberg* [New York, 1975], pp. 20–22.)

14. Kramer, "Post-Classical Music," p. 149.

15. See chapter 7 of this volume, above, p. 128.

16. Kramer, "Post-Classical Music," p. 145.

17. Ibid., pp. 146, 151.

18. See esp. Edward A. Lippman, "Theory and Practice in Schumann's Aesthetics,"

Journal of the American Musicological Society, 17 (1964), p. 336; and Carl Dahlhaus, "Thesen über Programmusik," *Beiträge zur musikalischen Hermeneutik,* ed. Dahlhaus (Regensburg, 1975), pp. 191–92 and 202; also in the same vol. Karl Gustav Fellerer, "Zur Grundlage hermeneutischer Musikbetrachtung," p. 27; Walter Serauky, *Die musikalische Nachahmungsästhetik im Zeitraum vom 1700 bis 1850* (Münster, 1929), pp. 237–84; Pauline Watts, *Music: The Medium of the Metaphysical in E. T. A. Hoffmann* (Amsterdam, 1972), pp. 15–17; and my "Why Is Adorno's Music Criticism the Way It Is? Some Reflections on Twentieth-Century Criticism of Nineteenth-Century Music," chapter 3 in this volume.

19. See chapter 9 in this volume, n. 22, on the significance of formal rigor.

20. Charles Rosen, *The Classical Style* (New York, 1972), p. 460.

21. Kramer, "Post-Classical Music," p. 150.

22. As reported by Rosen, *The Classical Style,* p. 78.

23. Kramer, "Post-Classical Music," p. 148. The three pieces cited are the Variations and Fugue on a Theme of Handel, the Passacaglia of the Fourth Symphony, and the Rondo of the Violin Concerto.

24. Rosen, "The Origins of Walter Benjamin," *New York Review of Books,* November 10, 1977, pp. 34–35.

25. "The Historical Structure: Adorno's 'French' Model for the Criticism of Nineteenth-Century Music," chapter 11 in this volume.

26. Kramer, "Post-Classical Music," p. 145.

27. Ibid., p. 148.

28. Ibid., p. 145.

29. Ibid., p. 152.

30. One could say that tonality is the "theme" of this piece in more or less the same literary sense that autonomy is the "theme" of a classical symphony; it is what the piece "is about." (See n. 5, above.)

31. Igor Stravinsky, *Poetics of Music* (New York, 1960), esp. chapter 2, pp. 37–41 (the lectures printed therein were originally delivered in 1939–40). In his lecture "Adorno and Stravinsky" (given at the Adorno symposium cited in n. 5, above), Rosen asserted that for Stravinsky it was crucial that the musical material (including tonality) sound like it came from without, lest the listener perceive inauthentic, "immanent" historical meanings in the music.

32. A sense that could be designated "merely" formal, as Wagner once dismissed Rossini's "absolute melody" as semiotically impoverished (Dahlhaus, *Between Romanticism and Modernism,* p. 33).

Chapter 11. The Historical Structure: Adorno's "French" Model for Criticism of Nineteenth-Century Music

1. For more information about Adorno's understanding of Beethoven and Schoenberg see "Adorno's Diagnosis of Beethoven's Late Style: Early Symptom of a Fatal Condition," chapter 2 in this volume.

2. See especially Michel Foucault, *The Order of Things* (New York, 1973), pp. 217–387.

3. This discussion will refer principally, though not exclusively, to the following works by Adorno, which will be cited by short titles as given in brackets: *Philosophy of Modern Music* (1948), trans. Anne G. Mitchell and Wesley V. Blomster (New York, 1973) [*Philosophy*]; *Introduction to the Sociology of Music* (1962), trans. E. B. Ashton (New York, 1976) [*Sociology*]; "Schubert" (1928), *Moments Musicaux* (Frankfurt, 1964), pp. 18–36 ["Schubert"]; "Bilderwelt des *Freischütz*" (1960/61), *Moments*

Musicaux, pp. 40–46 ["*Freischütz*"]; "Nachwort" to *Liederkreis, Op. 39*, by Robert Schumann (Wiesbaden, 1960), pp. 68–75 ["*Liederkreis*"]; "L'Actualité de Wagner" (based on a lecture given in Berlin, 1963), *Musique en jeu*, 22 (1976), pp. 80–93 ["Actualité"]. A German version of this article can be found in *275 Jahre Theater in Braunschweig: Geschichte und Wirkung* (Braunschweig, 1965), pp. 81–97; "Zum *Versuch über Wagner." Die Musikalischen Monographien, Gesammelte Schriften*, vol. 13 (Frankfurt, 1971), pp. 497–508 ["Versuch"]; "Zur Partitur des 'Parsifal' " (1956/57), *Moments Musicaux*, pp. 52–57 ["*Parsifal*"]; "Mahler: Wiener Gedenkrede" (1960) and "Epilegomena" [1960/61], *Quasi una Fantasia* (Frankfurt, 1963), pp. 115–54 ["Mahler"]; "Zu einem Streitgespräch über Mahler," *Musik und Verlag: Karl Vötterle zum 65. Geburtstag*, ed. Richard Baum and Wolfgang Rehm (Kassel, 1968), pp. 123–27 ["Streitgespräch"].

The articles cited here on Wagner and Mahler present and maintain essentially the same intellectual positions as Adorno's monographs on those composers, even though the latter are naturally far richer in detail and concerned with a wider range of problems (especially with respect to sociology). In each case, moreover, the articles represent a later viewpoint than the monographs, of which they often refine the central arguments. No reference will be made here either to the *Versuch über Wagner* (1939, 1952) or to *Mahler: Eine musikalische Physiognomik* (1960), both of which can be found in volume 13 of the *Gesammelte Schriften*.

4. More narrowly, "negative dialectics" involves the use of dialectical methods to criticize notions of synthesis inherent in philosophical systems since Kant. For a brief discussion of the term see Fredric Jameson, *Marxism and Form* (Princeton, 1971), pp. 55–59. An extended analysis of the concept, including a number of references to music, can be found in Susan Buck-Morss's study, *The Origin of Negative Dialectics* (New York, 1977).

5. See, for example, "Schubert," pp. 26 and 29–30. On one or two occasions, as in *Sociology*, p. 163, Adorno qualifies this view.

6. "*Freischütz*," p. 44.

7. "Actualité," p. 86; see also "Versuch," p. 501, on the relation of individuality and unity .

8. See "Actualité," pp. 83 and 86–87, and *Philosophy*, pp. 57–58; and Carl Dahlhaus, "Soziologische Dechiffrierung von Music: zu Theodor W. Adornos Wagner Kritik," *International Review of the Aesthetics and Sociology of Music* 1 (1970), pp. 144–46. Adorno and Dahlhaus agree about the dependence of Wagner's form and text, but Dahlhaus, taking a characteristically nondialectical view of nineteenth-century music, seems too disingenuous in removing Wagner's work to the realm of "opera," pure and simple. In doing so Dahlhaus divorces Wagner's music from the cultural field that was formed in nineteenth-century Germany through the idealization of absolute (Beethovenian) music—a field that was defined, in large measure through the tension between music and word in Wagner's music and in his theory.

9. See, for example, "Mahler," pp. 120, 129–31, and 137.

10. On criticism as a structural transformation (and hence, continuation) of music, see "Why is Adorno's Music Criticism the Way It Is?", chapter 3 in this volume.

11. *Philosophy*, pp. 73, 110.

12. *Philosophy*, pp. 191–92; "Mahler," p. 149.

13. "Schubert," pp. 22–25; for discussion of the crystalline image see especially p. 23.

14. See, for example, Claude Lévi-Strauss, *L'Homme nu, Mythologiques*, vol. 4 (Paris, 1971), pp. 618–19.

15. See, for example, *Philosophy*, pp. 39 and 79; also nn. 75 and 84, this chapter.

16. On nominalism see *Philosophy*, pp. 40–41, 58, 77, 179 (fn. 32), and 213; also "Actualité," p. 83.

17. See, for example, "Spätstil Beethovens" (1937), *Moments Musicaux*, pp. 13–17.

18. See *Philosophy*, pp. 77 and 163.

19. See "Schubert," p. 21.

20. See "Mahler," p. 147, also p. 126.

21. See "Schubert," pp. 18–22 and 25–26; and "Actualité," p. 81. See also "Mahler," pp. 125, 133, and 140; "Streitgespräch," p. 125; *Philosophy*, pp. 39–41, and 57; and *Sociology*, pp. 211–13 ("a composer is always a *zoon politikon*," and so on). This assertion is not incompatible with a recognition of the widespread tendency to understand nineteenth-century works through reference to their composers (see chapter 9, above, especially n. 47). Adorno's underlying argument is that nineteenth-century music never came close to guaranteeing whatever individuality it defined a universal status. Such a status would have insured that individuality a permanent significance. Instead what this music projected was a mere contingent individuality (meaningful only in specific cultural circumstances), a condition that, from Adorno's standpoint, falls far short of constituting (or even conjuring up unless negatively) a self-explanatory musical content. See also chapter 8, p. 151, this volume.

22. See *Philosophy*, p. 128; also Martin Jay, *The Dialectical Imagination* (Boston, 1973), pp. 60–61 and 87; and in this volume, chapter 2, n. 37.

23. See, for example, Adorno's "Wagner, Nietzsche and Hitler" [review of Ernest Newman's *Life of Richard Wagner*, vol. 4], *Kenyon Review*, 9 (1947), especially pp. 160–61; also *Philosophy*, p. 57, on force in Brahms and Wagner.

24. *Philosophy*, p. 166.

25. *Philosophy*, p. 56; *Sociology*, pp. 64–65. The latter, though highly concentrated, is probably Adorno's most extended discussion of Brahms.

26. *Sociology*, p. 65.

27. *Philosophy*, pp. 56–57. My understanding of "total development" was aided considerably by two former graduate students at the University of Chicago, Thomas Boyer and Thomas Stanback.

28. *Sociology*, p. 64.

29. See *Philosophy*, p. 61. Adorno refers to the row here as a "fundamental structure."

30. For discussions related to this point see *Philosophy*, p. 78 and especially pp. 40–41 ("Only at the outset where [binding] conventions guarantee totality beyond all question could everything in actuality be different; precisely because nothing would be different. Most compositions by Mozart would offer the composer far-reaching alternatives without foreefiting anything. . . . Schoenberg's compositions are the first in which nothing actually can be different. . . . There is in them no trace of convention which guarantees any freedom of play." Though Adorno hereby grants some such conventional trace to nineteenth-century music, it is only by exception, as in n. 60, this chapter, that he ascribes to that music anything close to the classical projection of an individual necessity based on universality). In addition see nn. 31, 35, and 41 in this chapter; also Carl Maria von Weber, "On the Opera 'Undine,' " *Source Readings in Music History*, ed. Oliver Strunk (New York, 1950), p. 806; Adorno's "Fragment über Musik und Sprache" (1956/57), *Quasi una Fantasia*, p. 16; "Interview with Easley Blackwood," by Richard Brown, *Grey City Journal*, February 4, 1977, p. 4; and Edward T. Cone, *The Composer's Voice* (Berkeley and Los Angeles, 1974), p. 29. See also, in this volume, chapter 7, p. 138 and chapter 10, n. 8 (on a possible connection to synthetic a priori judgments).

31. *Philosophy*, pp. 73–74, including fn. 31; 182, fn. 35; and 101–102; also

"Schubert," pp. 28–30 (though see also n. 60, this chapter). The quotation is from "Schubert," p. 34. It is important to distinguish clearly in this context between the characteristics attributed by Adorno to the classical and to the romantic styles. Adorno does not deny that the latter projects a sense of hypothetical tentativeness, of being merely contingent, of not being under any binding obligation to be exactly as it is. On the contrary, these are exactly the qualities he would attribute to nineteenth-century music after Beethoven, just as, according to my own analysis of Chopin's second Prelude (see chapter 7, p. 134), it is a quality of contingency that is evoked by the vivid, almost physical sense that the final cadence was just one plausible alternative. This contingency, which results from the vitiation of a connection to some persuasively universal structural principle, is very different from the appearance of necessity fused with freedom that classicism seems able to confer on individual choices. As noted in chapter 7 (p. 113, 138–39), by defining the individual as a choice made through reference to a (seemingly) binding system of universal, rational principles, classicism allows us to imagine that each individual element has been freely chosen, from among many others, to serve some necessary purpose. In classicism as opposed to romanticism, the theoretical exchangeability of any individual element is not experienced as the actual physical contingency of the concrete individual element. (See also n. 30, 35, and 41, and p. 233, this chapter, and chapter 9, the text leading to n. 44.)

32. *"Freischütz,"* p. 43: *"wird . . . Unverbindliches selber zu einem Stilprinzip."*

33. In this connection see *"Parsifal,"* p. 55; also "Mahler," p. 127, on the need of the listener to keep shifting positions.

34. "Schubert," p. 30: *"zeitliche Folge zeitloser Zellen."* See also n. 62, this chapter.

35. *"Vertauschbarkeit"*; see "Schubert," p. 24; also, pp. 26 and 28–29. See also *Philosophy,* p. 79, and *"Parsifal,"* p. 53. Again (as in n. 30), it is important to distinguish between Adorno's notions of classical and of romantic exchangeability. In classicism, exchangeability means functional exchangeability; since actual individual material (typically the motive) is always given an intelligible function in relation to the whole, it can be imagined as chosen from among many absent but possible functional equivalents. In romanticism, on the other hand, exchangeability means a physical exchangeability among actual elements that have no clear functional differentiation.

Because they no longer have an unmistakable relation to the whole, actual romantic elements try to make their meaning unequivocal by emphasizing their specific physical individuality. Hence one finds in a romantic composition the kind of self-contained, distinctive theme that one cannot mistake for the theme of another piece (or of another composer, for such themes are easily identified as property). The radio listener who "waits for the [famous second] theme [in Schubert's 'Unfinished'] would get the shock of his life if it were replaced by another," Adorno writes in "The Radio Symphony: An Experiment in Theory," (*Radio Research 1941*, ed. Paul F. Lazarsfeld and Frank N. Stanton [New York, 1941], p. 130). This is what Adorno means by "quotation" music (ibid., pp. 129–30): music that is meaningful only in the sense that it can be identified by one or more "tag" themes.

Ironically, however, precisely because the romantic element is forced to rely on the actuality of its configuration for meaningfulness (essentially as described in *Philosophy,* p. 41), it tends to be a matter of indifference *within* a romantic composition whether a theme is used in one part of a structure or another, or even, finally, whether it is physically similar to or different from other such individualized themes within that piece. See *Philosophy,* p. 80, where, commenting on a loss of capacity in romanticism for clearly perceptible, functional contrast, Adorno notes, "The themes of Romanticism—gauged according to the ideal of integral form in Viennese classicism—were for the most part all too lacking in a direct relationship, thus threatening to dissolve the form into episodes."

36. See, for example, *Philosophy*, p. 79.

37. On "universal economy" see *Philosophy*, p. 57. See also *Philosophy*, pp. 57–59, 73–74, and 70–71; "Mahler," pp. 132–33; and Gerald Abraham, *A Hundred Years of Music*, 3rd ed. rev. (Chicago, 1964), p. 171. Also interesting in this connection is Charles Rosen's discussion of theme, accompaniment, and function in *The Classical Style* (New York, 1972), pp. 116–17.

38. "Actualité," p. 87; *Philosophy*, pp. 190–91.

39. "Mahler," p. 134: *"teleologische Gesetzmässigkeit."*

40. "Mahler," p. 119, *Sociology*, p. 108.

41. "Mahler," p. 136. What is again at issue for Adorno, when he contrasts Beethoven's "must be so and not otherwise" with the Mahlerian "as-if," is the difference between Beethoven's projection of a universal necessity versus Mahler's projection of contingency (see nn. 30, 31, 35, and 62, this chapter). Clearly such contingency is in no way incompatible with the temporality in the sense of transience or temporariness that Mahler's music projects through its suffusion with cultural specificity. In this respect, it may be helpful to recall that Lévi-Strauss's structures, like the explicitly concrete models of rationality that he opposes to Western models, are also culturally specific in their characteristic state.

42. See "Mahler," p. 124.

43. "Mahler," p. 123; see also Adorno's "Verfremdetes Hauptwerk: Zur *Missa Solemnis*" [1959], *Moments Musicaux*, p. 185.

44. See "Mahler," p. 135.

45. See "Actualité," pp. 83–84.

46. See "Actualité," p. 84, also p. 88.

47. See, for example, *Philosophy*, p. 68, on Wagner.

48. See *Sociology*, p. 64.

49. See, for example, "Wagner, Nietzsche and Hitler," pp. 157–58.

50. See especially *Philosophy*, p. 56.

51. See for example "Schubert," pp. 26–27 and 30–33; "Actualité," pp. 89–91; and *"Parsifal,"* pp. 54–56.

52. See *Philosophy*, p. 64: *"Wiederkehr des Gleichen."* On this subject see especially "Schubert," pp. 27, 28, and 34; also Jay, *Dialectical Imagination*, p. 105.

53. On Schumann and Wagner see "Schubert," p. 28; on differences, see especially *Philosophy*, p. 77. Adorno does not exclude all significant differentiation from nineteenth-century music (see for example *Philosophy*, pp. 57 and 78–79), but he does constantly undercut this notion (see for example *Philosophy*, pp. 77, 79–80, and 189–90).

54. "Mahler," p. 137: *"Geisterzug"*; see also p. 134.

55. Ibid., p. 134.

56. "Actualité," pp. 85–86, see also *Philosophy*, pp. 189–91. For an extended discussion of such rhetorical techniques in nineteenth-century music see "The Cultural Message of Musical Semiology," chapter 9 of this volume.

57. "Actualité," p. 91.

58. See "Schubert," pp. 25 and 31–33; also "Actualité," p. 91.

59. "Actualité," p. 91. See "Actualité," pp. 84 and 89–91; and compare, for example, Claude Lévi-Strauss, *Structural Anthropology*, [vol. 1], trans. Claire Jacobson and Brooke Grundfest Schoepf (New York, 1963), p. 229. Adorno implies in this context a considerably earlier influence of Schopenhauer on the *Ring* than was actually the

case. See "Actualité," p. 90, and Jack Stein, *Richard Wagner and the Synthesis of the Arts* (Detroit, 1960), p. 115.

60. See "Schubert," pp. 30 and 33-34. Adorno excepts the Finale of the Great C-Major Symphony, which he considers genuinely dynamic.

61. See "Actualité," p. 84; *Philosophy*, pp. 57-58 and 189-91; "Versuch," pp. 497-98; and "Parsifal," p. 52.

62. See "Mahler," pp. 126-27; "Schubert," p. 34; and *Philosophy*, p. 56. Also important in this connection are Adorno's notion of "counted" time as a form of literalness ("Versuch," p. 497) and his notion of Wagner's harmony as approaching pure, nonfunctional sound and, thus, space ("Versuch," p. 499). See also *Philosophy*, p. 190, on Wagner: "In no case does sound go beyond itself in time; it rather vanishes in space." Paradoxical as it might at first seem, even this spatial imagery of time need not be incompatible with a definition of time as culturally specific and contingent. What the two concepts have in common is that neither fuses the universal necessity of abstract logic with the freedom of concrete individual choice, and thus neither can be imagined as constructed by a wholly self-determining individual, that is, by an individual that constitutes its own autonomous universe. (Already implicit here is Adorno's description of the way in which Schoenberg's later style negates time and ceases to recognize history: "The continuum of subjective time-experience is no longer entrusted with the power of collecting musical events, functioning as a unity, and thereby imparting meaning to them" [*Philosophy*, p. 60]. See also this chapter, n. 41; chapter 7, n. 32; and chapter 10, n. 8. On time more generally see chapter 3, n. 9; chapter 4, nn. 53, 54, and 69; chapter 10, n. 13; and this chapter, n. 34.)

63. See, for example, "Actualité," p. 90.

64. See *Philosophy*, p. 60, for a discussion of such an effect in connection with Schoenberg's music.

65. This despite Adorno's efforts to equate each of Mahler's "individual characters" with a different function. See "Mahler," p. 133, also pp. 135 and 124.

66. *Philosophy*, p. 79.

67. See "Actualité," p. 85, and "Versuch," p. 499; also Dahlhaus, "Soziologische Dechiffrierung," p. 139. Here again Dahlhaus seems too disingenuous in failing to acknowledge his fundamental agreement with Adorno. For if, as Dahlhaus insists, Wagner shifts the balance from consonance to dissonance (an assertion Adorno himself makes several times), then in effect Wagner moves in the direction of equalizing consonance and dissonance and, hence, of undercutting the difference between them. This is Adorno's essential point.

68. See, for example, *L'Homme nu*, pp. 604-5.

69. On Adorno and Wagner see "Actualité," p. 87. On Meyer see chapter 2, n. 11, of this volume.

70. "Schubert," p. 28.

71. See, for example, Edward C. Bass, "Musical Time and Space in Berlioz," *Music Review*, 30 (1969), p. 220 and passim; Philip Friedheim, "Radical Harmonic Procedures in Berlioz," *Music Review*, 21 (1960), pp. 283-84; Brian Primmer, *The Berlioz Style* (London, 1973), pp. 2, 14, 17, etc.; and Gerald Abraham, *A Hundred Years of Music*, pp. 22 and 144. See also *Philosophy*, p. 144, fn. 6.

72. See Arthur O. Lovejoy, *Essays in the History of Ideas* (New York, 1960), p. 208; also Lovejoy's *The Great Chain of Being* (Cambridge, Mass., 1936), pp. 297 ff., and Adorno's "Lyric Poetry and Society," *Telos*, 20 (Summer 1974), p. 67.

73. On the miniature, see Claude Lévi-Strauss, *The Savage Mind* (Chicago, 1966), pp. 23-34.

74. "Mahler," p. 144; see also "Actualité," p. 93.

75. "Mahler," p. 124.

76. See, for example, Morse Peckham, "The Dilemma of a Century: The Four Stages of Romanticism," in *Romanticism: The Culture of the Nineteenth Century*, ed. Morse Peckham (New York, 1965), p. 17.

77. *Philosophy*, p. 190: What the French got in their music, Adorno goes on, was "a mere here and now, [an] absolute transitoriness." This is explicitly contrasted with Wagner's "philosophical pessimism": "In Wagner, renunciation—the negation of the will to life—was the sustaining metaphysical category."

78. See—for example, *Philosophy*, p. 190; also Peckham, "Four Stages," pp. 30–31. The connection of this attitude to the decentering of the individual that takes place in French structuralism, and later in French poststructuralism, should be evident. See also this chapter, n. 86, on Stravinsky.

79. See, in this volume, chapter 2, pp. 35–36, especially n. 92.

80. "Verfremdetes Hauptwerk," p. 179.

81. See, for example, Ronald Weitzman, "An Introduction to Adorno's Music and Social Criticism," *Music and Letters*, 52 (1971), pp. 296–97.

82. Karl Löwith, *Meaning in History* (Chicago, 1949), p. 44; and see especially Jay, *Dialectical Imagination*, p. 56, on the possible "subterranean influence of a religious theme on the materialism of the Frankfurt School," and the possible relevance of the Jewish prohibition on naming God.

83. *Sociology*, p. 173.

84. "*Parsifal*," p. 57.

85. *Fondements d'une sémiologie de la musique* (Paris, 1975), pp. 346–54.

86. On the "preform" see *Philosophy*, p. 190. Adorno's entire critique of Stranvinsky's music in terms of its absence of intention, its similarity to phenomenology, its fetishism of means, and so on, is directly related to this notion of liquidation (see *Philosophy*, pp. 138–43, 145, 172–74, and so on).

87. *Philosophy*, p. 142.

88. *Philosophy*, p. 139, also p. 142.

89. *Sociology*, p. 172; see also "Schubert," p. 25, where Adorno asserts that "no art has itself for an object."

90. See "*Freischütz*," pp. 45–46; "Actualité," p. 90; *Philosophy*, p. 190; "Mahler," pp. 122 and 153; and "*Parsifal*," p. 56.

91. See, for example, "Actualité," pp. 91 and 93; "Versuch," p. 507; and "Mahler," p. 125. Also interesting in this connection is Adorno's statement that "only he may hope and grasp something essential in the work of art who perceives in the latter itself, as in a windowless monad, the universe the monad represents" ("Versuch," p. 506).

92. "*Freischütz*," p. 45; "Schubert," p. 35. See also "Mahler," p. 151, on the need to restore strangeness to convention, and p. 121, on the subject's inability to speak its own language.

93. "Mahler," pp. 122 and 132, and "Streitgespräch," p. 125.

94. See "Mahler," pp. 117–19, 121, and 126.

95. "Mahler," pp. 120, 126, and 137; also *Sociology*, pp. 64–65, and *Philosophy*, pp. 188–90.

96. "Mahler," pp. 122–23.

97. "Mahler," p. 131.

98. See "*Parsifal*," pp. 56–57.

99. See, for example, "Mahler," p. 154, and Jay, *Dialectical Imagination*, p. 105; also "Versuch," p. 508.

Chapter 12. Individualism in Western Art Music and Its Cultural Costs

1. This essay was originally delivered as the Marshall Woods lecture at Brown University, on March 26, 1980. Though 1980 was in fact my last year at the University of Chicago, I have decided this essay can be of most use for new students if it preserves the immediacy of the present tense, and of the local references to Chicago.

2. I use the version of Stravinsky's piece as it appears in the *Histoire du Soldat* Suite, which eliminates the spoken text of the original.

3. In earlier years, I used to use as my second example the Funeral March from Beethoven's *Eroica* Symphony, a practice I discarded because the movement requires so much time. This piece *was* recognized once or twice, but never by name; if identified at all, it was as the piece that some nameless "they" plays on the radio when a distinguished personage has died.

4. This sensation could also be explained by the inability of students unfamiliar with the style to grasp the piece, as if in overview, as a unified entity. At this point, many of the issues I discuss elsewhere in this book—for example, the relation of various kinds of musical structures to ideals of self-evident meaning, or the effects of specific cultural identity in music on modes of listening—come directly into play.

5. See, in this volume, chapter 11, n. 30.

6. A related issue is the extent to which Stravinsky should be considered the author of his own book *Poetics of Music*. However much of this material may actually have been written by Alexis Roland-Manuel and Pierre Souvtchinsky, it was Stravinsky himself who gave the lectures it contains (in 1939 at Harvard, in French) and he who put his name on them. I myself see no more difficulty about attributing this work to Stravinsky than about attributing to Ronald Reagan speeches written by Peggy Noonan. I recognize that not everyone shares this viewpoint. The notion of an "elect" is taken up in detail in my essay "Whose *Magic Flute?*" to appear in the companion volume (see the Introduction to the present volume, n. 24).

7. At the time I wrote this essay, I was particularly struck by a recent hearing of a work by Mauricio Kagel, which consisted in a reconstruction, or more accurately, a deconstruction of Brahms's piano variations on a theme by Handel.

8. Jon Finson, "Music and Medium: Two Versions of Manilow's 'Could it be Magic,'" *Musical Quarterly*, 65 (1979), pp. 265–80.

9. The modern demand for the new was given its definitive statement in music by Arnold Schoenberg in his essay "New Music, Old Music, Style and Idea," *Style and Idea*, ed. Leonard Stein, trans. Leo Black (Berkeley and Los Angeles, 1975), p. 115: "*Art means New Art* [italics his]." This position was worked out with great care by Schoenberg in a way that reflected his own tremendous artistic integrity. For more on this topic, the reader is referred to "The Challenge of Contemporary Composition," chapter 13 in this volume.

10. The article by Milton Babbitt, "Who Cares if You Listen?" (1958), has been reprinted in, among other places, *The American Composer Speaks: A Historical Anthology, 1770–1965*, ed. Gilbert Chase (Baton Rouge, 1966), pp. 234–44.

11. Clearly in the decade since I first wrote this essay, postmodern (e.g., "downtown") sensibilities more attuned to the value of communal accessibility have become far more prominent in the composition of art music, encouraging among other things considerable erosion of the barrier between art and popular traditions. On the other hand, the norm of total control has by no means passed yet from our universities; student composers in many programs are still vigorously discouraged from writing

chance music, or for that matter, music that depends on words or any other medium rather than on itself alone for its structure.

Having now experienced a wider range of aleatory music, I have become considerably more sympathetic to its premises and promise, at least within certain limits. The notion of allowing performers to jointly redefine a work over and over, never emerging twice with the same exact configuration, seems to me to have a great deal to recommend it. For one thing it seems to me that the concept of identity at work here takes both performers and listeners as well as composer into account. The performers develop the actual configuration through an enterprise of cameraderie; the listener learns to perceive the identity through repeated exposures to its numerous possible contingent forms. For reasons suggested in my introduction to this volume (when I clarified the nature of my divergence from Schoenberg), this process based on an acknowledgment of contingency seems to me far truer to the way perception actually works than are processes that require the listener to focus precisely and exclusively on the detail as well as the organization of a musical structure. Nor does music of this sort necessarily engender less musical responsibility than does music based on an ideal of total control by the composer. To the extent that this music does allow performers as well as audience to participate actively in the definition of the structure, especially when the music is defined in conjunction with other mediums and a vital context of performance, it may well point toward a great sharing of responsibility, that is, toward a notion of musical responsibility that involves not just individuals as lone creators but also individuals in a communal enterprise. For insight into the ideals behind aleatory composition I am particularly indebted to the composer Matt Malsky.

12. To be fair, far from being confined to musical composition, this phenomenon (captured perfectly by the distinction in an old Jewish joke between "eating-herrings" and "buying-and-selling-herrings") is rampant throughout the academic world and most of the rest of American culture as well. It is, after all, just an extension of the processes through which all communication works; that is, human expressions are interpreted not through the force of abstract argument alone but also through responses to the physical characteristics and to the cultural style and associations that embody argument. See chapter 1, n. 11, this volume.

13. Likewise, the morning news shows of the major television networks, which one would suppose present a representative slice of American life, are said not even to consider booking guests (except in the case of fast-breaking stories) who don't have agents. The refusal of the filmmaker Spike Lee to have either an agent or a manager is, in my judgment, directly related to Lee's ability to make a film that is outstanding for its integrity in both senses (i.e., its honesty and its artistry).

14. Avant-garde filmmakers are no doubt far more concerned with such claims than commercial movie makers are, but of course they are locked into a social bind only somewhat less confining than that of the modern composer.

15. Stendhal, *Life of Rossini*, trans. Richard N. Coe (Seattle, 1970), p. 3.

16. In the decade since this was written, some composers have gained access to computerized means of writing out their music. This technology obviously makes it far easier to reproduce scores; on the other hand, by comparison with commercial publishing houses and their distribution systems, such desktop publishing remains a kind of protoindustrial cottage technology.

17. This practice in turn suggests, once again, that prospective sponsors and critics will be more comfortable judging the list of performances than the compositions themselves.

18. At the time I wrote this essay, no courses were ever offered at the University

of Chicago in non-Western music, jazz, or black music, even though the music department had available to it the services of an acknowledged expert on American slave music. Clearly this sort of rigid ethnocentrism has changed considerably in the past decade; even Chicago now has an ethnomusicology "slot." Nevertheless the balance in American higher education is still overwhelmingly in favor of the study of the Western art canon. See also chapter 1, n. 7, this volume.

19. This impression is certainly borne out by a book like Allan Bloom's recent best-seller, *The Closing of the American Mind* (New York, 1987).

20. Such feelings have figured centrally in the wars over the literary canon that began to explode in American universities a few years after this essay was written.

21. See Nelson Goodman, *Languages of Art* (Indianapolis, 1968), pp. 186–92. See also chapter 9, n. 52, this volume.

22. Georg Lukács, "Narrate or Describe? A Preliminary Discussion of Naturalism and Formalism," *Writer and Critic*, ed. and trans. Arthur Kahn (London, 1970), pp. 110–12. See also chapter 2 in this volume, n. 105.

23. Stanley Sadie, *Mozart* (London, 1965), p. 67.

24. In this respect, too, the hard-line ideology of historical authenticity has come in for challenge in the past decade, as evidenced in Richard Taruskin's already classic formulation of the issue, "The Musicologist and the Performer," *Musicology in the 1980s*, ed. D. Kern Holoman and Richard Taruskin (New York, 1982), pp. 101–17.

25. Girolamo Frescobaldi, *Fiori musicali*, ed. Joseph Bonnet (Paris, 1922), p. xxxi. (This edition provides the original Italian preface plus a French translation and a poor English translation, which I have not used here. A fine German translation is provided by Pierre Pidoux at the end of the brief preface to his critical edition of *Fiore musicali*, which constitutes volume 5 of Frescobaldi's Orgel- und Klavierwerke [Kassel and Basel, 1953].)

26. Bonnet, ed., *Fiori musicali*, p. xxxi.

27. Ibid., p. xxxii.

28. In a letter to his father from Paris, dated July 9, 1778, Mozart wrote, "In order to satisfy [Le Gros] (and, as he maintains, some others) I have composed a fresh Andante — each is good in its own way — for each has a different character. But the last pleases me even more" See *Mozart's Letters*, ed. Eric Blom, trans. Emily Anderson (Baltimore, 1956), p. 116.

29. One is tempted to speculate that scholarship of intellectual depth was more characteristic in cultures without access to scientifically accurate editions; it may even be questioned whether the latest factual studies, which seem to supersede each other with remarkable rapidity, will ever generate work with the intellectual staying power of something like Romain Rolland's Nobel Prize–winning novel (credentials again!), *Jean-Christophe.*

30. The situation of orally transmitted music, or musical traditions that do not depend on scores, is not altogether different, at least in modern Western culture; in particular, jazz has managed to alter much music of a type that does not depend ultimately on notation for its identity, without destroying the recognizable identity of that music. (In other words, it has managed to fuse the preservative as well as the changing aspects of history; see n. 32, this chapter.) Over longer periods of time, unwritten traditions might well be subject to considerable physical alteration, though perhaps not so much in cultures where binding religious taboos, for example, constrict the framework in which change can take place.

On the other hand, notation itself provides no guarantee of identity once cultural continuity is lost and, with it, modes of deciphering. However different the buildings and statuary of ancient Greece may look now from their original appearance, they still convey a much clearer impression of meaning than do the remains of Greek notated music. But, of course, even if we were sure we could reconstruct that music with scientific accuracy, we could never regain the ability to hear it as it was once heard. In music as well as the visual arts, it is not just physical components, such as shapes or pitches, that have to be deciphered in order to find meaning. Perception and interpretation in both mediums also involve an indeterminate multitude of cultural associations and influences that shape the very act of perceiving. In both arts, finally, the very concept of an original identity must be deemed at best so highly problematical that one must question the wisdom of devoting most of the energies in a scholarly discipline to acts of restoring and preserving original identity. On painting see also next chapter, pp. 281 and 286.

31. This becomes much less of a problem, of course, if one grants in Derrida's manner that texts of any kind are always already translations of other texts (defined broadly). See Jacques Derrida, *Of Grammatology*, trans. Gayatri Chakravorty Spivak (Baltimore, 1976), translator's preface, p. lxxxvii.

32. It is worth recalling that in the decisive turn toward historical awareness that we associate with the nineteenth century can be found contradictory impulses toward notions of ongoing progress and toward an attitude of antiquarian disjunctness, whereby one looks back at a past from which one is now alienated and attempts to preserve it. On the philosophical complexities involved here see Carl Dahlhaus, *Foundations of Music History*, trans. J. B. Robinson (Cambridge, 1983), pp. 53–71.

Chapter 13. The Challenge of Contemporary Music

1. The shape of the following essay is governed by its title, which was assigned by Philip Alperson, the editor of the volume *What Is Music? An Introduction to the Philosophy of Music*, for which this essay, in a more tentative form, was written. Had I created the title myself, I might well have substituted the term "modern" for "contemporary." At any rate, it should be noted at the outset that I have treated the term "contemporary" throughout this essay as synonymous with "modern," that is, to designate an aesthetic that has been losing ground in the past two decades to an increasingly vital postcontemporary (i.e., postmodern) aesthetic. In addition, it should be noted that this essay was not intended as a comprehensive overview of Western art composition in the twentieth century, any more than it pretends to keep readers abreast of the music of postcontemporary composers, most of whom have been motivated by precisely the sorts of unease I describe in this chapter. Rather, this essay was designed as a philosophical analysis of the values behind the one tradition, Schoenberg's, that I believe, for reasons I will discuss here, has the best historical claim to the designation "contemporary music." To tie these values, above all, to an ideal of structural integrity is in no way to deny either Schoenberg's own widely acknowledged coloristic genius or his faith in the ability of the subconscious to produce formally sound inspirations. On the former, see my essay "Toward a Deconstruction of Structural Listening" (cited in this chapter, n. 24), p. 105, n. 49; on the latter, see, e.g., two essays by Schoenberg in his *Style and Idea* (ed. Leonard Stein [New York, 1975]): "Linear Counterpoint," p. 292, and "Composition with Twelve Tones (1)," p. 218. (All citations of Schoenberg's writings refer to this volume.) What matters is not the presence or absence of coloristic interest in contemporary works but the ultimate primacy given to structural integrity as a measure of aesthetic value.

The cornerstone of Alperson's volume was Francis Sparshott's essay, "Aesthetics of Music: Limits and Grounds" (Alperson, pp. 33–98); and the four quotations that head my own sections in the piece that follows are all taken from that essay by Sparshott. I list the pages here: Heading to "Introduction: The Historical Situation" is taken from Sparshott, p. 48; of "The Inability of Contemporary Music to Challenge Society Directly: The Composer," from Sparshott, p. 41; to the same section, "The Audience," from Sparshott, p. 85; and to "Contemporary Music: The Challenge of Its Historical Stituation," from Sparshott, p. 77. (Page references to Sparshott in the earlier version of this essay, over which I had no control, are often egregiously wrong.)

2. Relativism functions throughout this essay as a kind of nexus for general and individual principles. Once we decline to refer judgments to an absolute ground of value, we open our own general principles (scientific method, structural listening, even ideological neutrality, all discussed hereafter) to interpretation as functions of our own epistemologically unprivileged ideological foundation. And the more we deny our own ideological foundation, the more exclusively we are committed to assessing things on their own terms. Thus generality is dissolved into a radical relativism indistinguishable from radical individualism, and the dichotomy between generality and individuality, which both lie this side of metaphysics, seems in a fundamental sense false.

3. Sparshott, "Aesthetics of Music," p. 62 (also 45 and 60).

4. Kant himself could not secure the universal status of transcendental reason, any more than other self-styled "universal" Enlightenment structures, such as classical tonality, could prevent subsequent interpretations of themselves as culturally particular.

5. The historicizing tendency, which in effect treats the changing or contingent as necessary, helps account for the prominence of music, a temporal medium, in nineteenth-century European culture. Acceptance of a historical imperative is evident in both general and individualistic notions of progress — in the regularity with which scientific theses and political reforms supersede each other, and in the constant drive of modern artists to create "the new."

6. Indeed, advanced scientific research has often received so much outside funding as to approach financial autonomy within the American university.

7. See Martha Woodmansee, "The Interests in Disinterestedness: Karl Philipp Moritz and the Emergence of the Theory of Aesthetic Autonomy in Eighteenth-Century Germany," *Modern Language Quarterly*, 45 (1984), pp. 22–47.

8. See Edward A. Lippman, "Theory and Practice in Schumann's Aesthetics," *Journal of the American Musicological Society*, 17 (1964), pp. 310–45; and chapter 10 of this volume, n. 18.

9. See, e.g., Weber's piece (of 1817), "On the Opera 'Undine,'" *Source Readings in Music History*, ed. Oliver Strunk (New York, 1950), p. 805. For considerably earlier formulations, see the passage (from 1798) by Friedrich Schlegel, quoted here in chapter 9, n. 22, or even Goethe's description of writing (in 1774) as "the reproduction of the world around me by means of the internal world which takes hold of, combines, creates anew, kneads everything, and puts it down again in its own form, manner," quoted in Martha Woodmansee, "The Genius and the Copyright: Economic and Legal Conditions of the Emergence of the 'Author'" *Eighteenth-Century Studies*, 17 (Summer 1984), p. 347. See also Joseph Kerman, *Contemplating Music: Challenges to Musicology* (Cambridge, Mass., 1985), p. 65, on the growth of "organicism" and formalistic analysis (though not to the exclusion of metaphorical criticism) in the nineteenth century; and Arnold Schoenberg, "Constructed Music," p. 107.

10. See, e.g., Schoenberg's references to the technique of nonredundancy, in "New Music: My Music," pp. 102–4.

11. My thanks to the composer Alex Lubet (of the University of Minnesota), for

his help in clarifying this distinction. On the entire preceding line of argument, see also chapter 11, n. 30, this volume.

12. Though Kerman (p. 97) calls a work such as Milton Babbitt's *Philomel* (1964) "a classic of [its] genre [more accurately, medium]," he also readily acknowledges Stravinsky's status (p. 104) as "the last Grand Master of music."

13. Apart from Debussy, Berg, as Schoenberg's disciple, and Bartók, whose craft is particularly admired by the musically educated, would have the best chance of inclusion in such a course. Though Debussy himself would never be excluded from a survey of Western music since 1800, he is a transitional figure, and is often presented (as suggested by the common association of his work and Monet's) as a figure who predates modernism. In addition, of course, the particularly modern last works of 1915–17 (the twelve etudes for piano and the three sonatas: for cello and piano; for flute, viola, and harp; and for violin and piano) are not those for which he is popular. See Sparshott's notion of mutually exclusive audiences (p. 86), which evokes the image of parents with a mutually exclusive genetic stake in the same child.

14. See Schoenberg, "New Music, Outmoded Music," p. 124.

15. See, e.g., Schoenberg, "How I Became Lonely," p. 42, "Heart and Brain in Music," p. 54, and "My Public," pp. 96–99.

16. "In higher art, only that is worth being presented which has never before been presented. . . . *Art means New Art*," Schoenberg, "New Music, Outmoded Music," pp. 114–15 (italics his).

17. See Tom Wolfe, *The Painted Word* (New York, 1975); chapter 2 of this volume, pp. 30 and 34; and my essay "Toward a Deconstruction of Structural Listening," pp. 104–107 (cited in this chapter, n. 24).

18. Schoenberg, "New Music, Outmoded Music," pp. 122–23 (italics his), also 118 and 121; and "Composition with Twelve Tones (1)," p. 240. Stravinsky's rejection of "anarchic individualism" and deference to a "realm of necessity" are of course related. See Igor Stravinsky, *Poetics of Music* (New York, 1960), chapter 3, p. 67, and chapter 4, p. 76, in relation to Schoenberg, "Problems in Teaching Art," p. 365. The theorist William Benjamin's intriguing characterization of avant-garde music as "the first . . . which is not preceded by an unconscious theory" is different but leads to the similar conclusion that it "is hardly music at all" (see Kerman, p. 105).

19. A fine account of popular trends in relatively recent art music, starting with the unusually successful work of Philip Glass and Steve Reich, the neo-tonal school (including George Rochberg and David Del Tredici), and the so-called Downtown school, and working down through artistic rock, was provided in Gregory Sandow's lecture, "A New Era," given at the conference "Music and Society: The Politics of Composition, Performance and Reception," at the University of Minnesota, April 1985. In effect such music can be viewed as in the process of putting together what Thomas Kuhn might call a new paradigm for new music. See also chapter 12 of this volume, n. 11.

20. See, e.g., John Rockwell, "New Event Promotes Contemporary U.S. Music," *New York Times*, November 1, 1985, p. C 32, and this chapter, n. 49.

21. See, e.g., the apolitical stylistic descriptions of Penderecki's *Threnody: To the Victims of Hiroshima*, and the negative evaluation of Luigi Nono in Eric Salzman, *Twentieth-Century Music: An Introduction*, 2nd ed. (Englewood Cliffs, N.J., 1974), pp. 179–80. (The latter is softened in the 3rd ed. [1988] by the deletion of a key sentence, p. 187.)

22. During the 1970s I attended several meetings of the music department at the University of Chicago where a proposal of John Cage for an honorary degree, on the

basis of the importance of his ideas and influence, regularly disintegrated in an unease about the emperor's new clothes.

23. On time, see also Schoenberg, "New Music, Outmoded Music," p. 116.

24. See Schoenberg, "New Music, Outmoded Music," pp. 119 and 121, and T. W. Adorno, *Introduction to the Sociology of Music*, trans. E. B. Ashton (New York, 1976), pp. 4–5. My discussion here of structural listening is a generalized one, which makes no effort to conform entirely to Adorno's account. A more extended treatment of the notion, and of Adorno's theory, appears in my essay "Toward a Deconstruction of Structural Listening: A Critique of Schoenberg, Adorno, and Stravinsky," which grew out of the present essay and is published in *Explorations in Music, the Arts, and Ideas: Essays in Honor of Leonard B. Meyer*, ed. Eugene Narmour and Ruth A. Solie (New York, 1988), pp. 87–122 (and which will appear in the companion volume to the present one).

25. See, e.g., W. H. Wackenroder, "The Remarkable Musical Life of the Musician Joseph Berglinger," in Strunk, p. 760; Hector Berlioz, *A Critical Study of Beethoven's Nine Symphonies*, trans. Edwin Evans (London, 1958), p. 2; Schoenberg, "Criteria for the Evaluation of Music," p. 128; Adorno, *Introduction to the Sociology of Music*, pp. 4–6; and Robert Winter, "A Musicological Offering," *New York Review of Books*, 32 (July 18, 1985), p. 26.

26. This is not to deny Kerman's emphasis (e.g., p. 71) that *systematic* formal analysis, being mainly tonal, has tended to ignore early music, but to recall the degree to which even early music is regularly treated, and valued, by musical scholars as independent structure. The weakness of pretonal theory stems precisely from the resistance of the music in question to the concept of autonomy. See my essay "Toward a Deconstruction of Structural Listening," pp. 103–104.

27. See *The Critique of Judgment*, trans. James Creed Meredith (Oxford, 1952), section 45, pp. 166–67. A related idea turns up in Weber, p. 805, and even in Stravinsky, chapter 4, p. 78, where, however, the stated ideal must be measured against the requirements for perceiving "rightness" where general intelligibility can no longer be assumed. Detailed support for an absence of autonomy even in Beethoven's middle-period instrumental music can be found in Owen Jander's "Beethoven's 'Orpheus in Hades': the *Andante con moto* of the Fourth Piano Concerto," *19th Century Music*, 8 (Spring 1985), pp. 195–212.

28. For the view that values of sensuous abstraction continued in Renaissance music (where "accidentals" could still be construed as "accidents") see Carl Dahlhaus, "Tonsystem und Kontrapunkt um 1500," *Jahrbuch des staatlichen Instituts für Musikforschung (1969)*, (Berlin, 1970), p. 17. I am indebted to Peter Urquhart of Harvard University for calling my attention to this article.

29. Schoenberg's resistance to evaluations of twelve-tone music in terms of twelve-tone theory (see Kerman, p. 99) confirms rather than refutes his insistence on structural comprehension. My father recalls a fellow scholarship student at Harvard, around 1930, who would emerge sweating from his rare trips to Boston Symphony Orchestra concerts, explaining, "Listening is hard work." That student was Schoenberg's ideal audience. Contemporary music seems to emulate the distanced effect of music from earlier cultures, presumably to keep at bay "irrational" aspects of experience that it sees no way to address. See Susan McClary, "Afterword; The Politics of Silence and Sound," in Jacques Attali, *Noise: The Political Economy of Music*, trans. Brian Massumi (Minneapolis, 1985), p. 157.

30. See Kerman, p. 104, on the "impressionistic criticism" that has overtaken even the journal *Perspectives of New Music*. Though works such as Crumb's may well be characterized as postcontemporary, such categorizations do not in themselves (yet)

offer a solution to the problem of self-validation posed by the contemporary aesthetic (see p. 276 of this chapter).

31. Schoenberg, *Style and Idea*, pp. 377–82. Time is also involved in the demand by contemporary composers for numerous repeated hearings of their works, in order to break through the barrier of unfamiliarity caused by their avoidance of a common stylistic code.

32. Hilton Kramer, "What Abstract Art Achieved," *New York Times Magazine* (September 29, 1985), p. 90. Compare Babbitt's statement, as quoted by Kerman (p. 104) that "music 'will cease to evolve' if it is not taken into the academy, 'and in that important sense, will cease to live.'" Kerman's subsequent assertion (p. 105) that "the avant garde has extricated itself from the academy" makes sense more as a measure of the degree to which new music deviates from "contemporary music" than of the current economic status of the latter.

33. Sparshott's observation (p. 85) that "we isolate words for attention only when talk breaks down" is true enough from a perspective of structural comprehension but is perhaps not fully adequate to the selective manner in which the opaqueness of style is actually perceived. Of course, the ease with which my discussion here separates performance from composition points to another respect in which the individualistic aesthetic results in an isolated conception of musical structure, an issue that I examine more fully in chapter 12 of this volume. Those of us schooled traditionally in Western art music take this separation so for granted that we tend to forget that far from being necessary, it isn't even typical of music in other traditions (including many of our own popular ones).

34. Sparshott, "Aesthetics of Music," p. 87.

35. The success of Reich and Glass, among others, in filling concert halls and attracting the attention of popular journalists has certainly occurred despite, not thanks to, the contemporary musical tradition these composers reject (except perhaps in the sense that audiences are seeking alternatives to the contemporary tradition).

36. On musical architecture see Michael Forsyth, *Buildings for Music: The Architect, the Musican, and the Listener from the Seventeenth Century to the Present Day* (Cambridge, Mass., 1985).

37. To be sure, the balance shifted increasingly toward past repertory during the latter half of the nineteenth century. See William Weber, "Wagner, Wagnerism, and Musical Idealism," in *Wagnerism in European Culture and Politics*, ed. David C. Large and William Weber (Ithaca, 1984), especially pp. 38–40 and 48–50.

38. In part the greater alienation in the United States can perhaps be explained by a situation analyzed by David S. Josephson, of Brown University, in his penetrating response to Robert Cogan, at the annual conference of the American Musicological Society in Vancouver, 1985: the ongoing preoccupation of our academic musical elite with a past Germanic culture that has less of a stranglehold on Europe itself. No doubt this reflects our insecurities as adoptive parents; and the better situation of new music in Europe is no doubt helped also by the greater degree of political self-consciousness in European society.

39. Sparshott, p. 88.

40. A distinguishing aspect of "downtown" as opposed to "uptown" music has been the ability of the former to use such relatively informal environments as the club.

41. See Richard Dyer, "The BSO at the Crossroads," *Boston Globe*, (February 9, 1986), pp. 83, 85.

42. Charles Rosen's discussion of expressive possibility in a style, in *The Classical Style* (New York, 1972), p. 21, vigorously opposes lines of argument such as this. Arguing, in essence, that the same wide range of expressive values is available to any

style, Rosen admits that some expressive values involve more tension in a given style than others; he then counters, however, that "at the point that grace [of expression] begins to take on such importance, a style ceases to be strictly a system of expression or of communication." In effect this disclaimer dismisses as secondary the opaque elements that are needed to characterize styles from without (rather than from within, which is Rosen's interest), and to define the limits within which expression and communication take place. Could even the scatalogically obsessed Mozart have produced punk? (Of course, the "hit-and-run tactics" through which Rosen, and Kerman himself, have "scandalized" critics [Kerman, p. 152] indicate the degree to which these two are concerned with stylistic, as opposed to formalistic, analysis.)

43. From *TV Guide* (February 22–28, 1986, p. 18) comes the information, astounding from a "contemporary" viewpoint, that in the United States (though not in England), the success of a new pop recording often depends on the prior success of its video version. In terms of the electronic revolution, many experts in art music are now musically illiterate. (Did musical competence in the 1980s not require exposure to the *Gesamtkunst* of "Miami Vice"? Would Mozart necessarily have felt abused by the commercial success in the 1980s of the *Amadeus* video or by Falco's hit single, "Rock Me Amadeus"?)

44. See, e.g., John Rockwell's praise of the "minimalism and rigorous structuralism" of the album *Talking Heads: 77*, quoted in "David Byrne," *Current Biography* (June, 1985), p. 7; I am grateful to Nancy Newman, currently a student at the University of Minnesota, for calling this article to my attention.

45. See "David Byrne," p. 8, where Byrne says of his album *Remain in Light*, "It has . . . to do with a feeling of communication and forgetting oneself. . . . In our earlier music that might happen occasionally, but it still had more to do with Western music that's ego — and personality — centered." See also the distinction made in the *New York Times Book Review* of March 16, 1986 (p. 19) by Patricia Hampl (of the University of Minnesota), between "the personal voice" and " 'the self.'" The distance between contemporary art music and pop music can be gauged by the ease with which, say, Steve Van Zandt, in his promotions of *Sun City*, an album that attacks South African apartheid, distinguishes between "meaningless" rock and "good" rock. (The latter always has a social function; if nothing else, it lets you dance to it.)

46. One cannot help being aware, as we enter the 1990s, of heated controversies that have arisen over rock texts that to some seem racially, religiously, ethnically, or sexually offensive. In an article entitled "There's a New Sound in Pop Music: Bigotry" (in Section 2 of the Sunday *New York Times* [September 10, 1989], pp. 1 and 32), Jon Pareles singled out the rock band Guns-n-Roses, Andrew Dice Clay, and the rap group Public Enemy in this connection. For opposing views, see for instance the letter from Sean Penn, section 2 of the same newspaper (September 24, 1989, p. 3), or the exchange with Nat Hentoff in the *Village Voice* (April 10, 1990, p. 4). This divisiveness is disturbing to contemplate; it is also important to keep track of for what it tells us about the current state of American society.

47. A letter from Louis Torres to the *New York Times* (August 13, 1989), section 2, p. 3) illustrates the ongoing importance of this question among those "dedicated to traditional values in the arts" — an attitude now increasingly recognized as "conservative." Citing the authority of "observation and objective, logical analysis," Mr. Torres specifies "total creative control by [the] maker [of the work of art]" as one of the "essential characteristics common to the primary art forms — music, literature, painting and sculpture — throughout history." Arguing that *"the photographer does not himself select and shape every minute detail of the work* [italics his]," Mr. Torres denies photography (and thereby the works of the late, controversial Robert Mapplethorpe) the

status of "art." This position is very likely right, at least if we accept its implicit assumption of both "tradition" and "art" as exclusively modern Western categories. But the value judgment here could easily be turned on its head. To the extent that its reliance on modern technology limits its claim to autonomy, perhaps photography should be taken as a model for developing new, "postartistic" ideals of thoughtful expression.

48. No less a "contemporary" icon than Pierre Boulez now claims to have made this very transition. (See the interview in *Newsday*, March 2, 1986, part 2, p. 3; this claim has been received in some quarters with skepticism.) Even if Boulez's apparent shift merely perpetuates a cyclical exchange of formalistic and expressive values, which is an old story in the history of Western art music, it could be argued that this exchange itself reflects the degree to which both sets of values regularly become experienced as inhumane within the context of traditionally defined Western values. In a more genuinely humane culture, perhaps, this dichotomy, as an aspect of that between individual and general values, would be negated.

49. Why are the promotional events of contemporary music (see this chapter, n. 20) so characteristically for its own benefit? Reflecting on the evils of commercial investment, Robert Brustein has asked, "Why don't [the Broadway producers] go nonprofit . . . forming a profit-sharing cooperative? This way the big musical hit could help support the serious new play" (*Newsday*, "Ideas" section, March 16, 1986, p. 4). In music, at least, this question cuts both ways. Contemporary music is already nonprofit; by becoming cooperative as well, it could help counteract the evils of rugged individualism, typified by the competition among composers, in a framework of questionable fairness, for foundation grants. (Also it could be argued that commercial pressures exert a useful discipline on musical structure. See my article "Lortzing and the German Romantics: A Dialectical Assessment," *Musical Quarterly*, 62 [1976], especially pp. 259–64.)

50. From the standpoint of post-Enlightenment art music, society itself and the mediums it makes available are clearly connected. To appreciate fully the drive toward autonomy, one would want to examine closely the nature of this connection.

51. At "The Shaping of Contemporary Musical Taste," a conference at the University of Wisconsin, Milwaukee, April 3–5, 1986, Susan McClary noted a difference between communicating with a public and pandering to it. This distinction is assumed by thoughtful commercial artists, e.g., Sissy Spacek, who is quoted in *Newsday*, March 23, 1986, part 2, p. 5, as saying, "Essentially there's two ways of approaching films. One is to second-guess what the public wants. The other is to make movies that say something and have a positive effect on the world. . . . We use our work to advocate what we think is right. Political conscience in culture is not unimportant." Compare also the powerful year-end article by Robert Palmer, "Rock Flexed Its Social and Political Muscles," with John Rockwell's retrospective of classical music, which starts with the notion, "This was a year of reissues," a notion later qualified to be sure (both appear in the *New York Times*, December 29, 1985, section 2, pp. 23–24).

52. I would like to thank my copy editor Ann Klefstad for her particularly thoughtful contributions to this chapter.

Index

Compiled by Eileen Quam, Theresa Wolner, and the author

Rose Rosengard Subotnik is a musical scholar and cultural critic known for her work in critical and literary theory applied to music. From 1973 to 1980 she was a faculty member in the music department and a member of the Committee on the History of Culture at the University of Chicago, where she was awarded Guggenheim and American Council of Learned Society fellowships. She subsequently held visiting appointments in the graduate music programs at Boston University, the City University of New York Graduate Center, and the State University of New York at Stony Brook. In 1990 Subotnik was appointed associate professor of music at Brown University.